George Chapman

The Iliads of Homer, Prince of Poets

Volume I

George Chapman

The Iliads of Homer, Prince of Poets
Volume I

ISBN/EAN: 9783337085483

Printed in Europe, USA, Canada, Australia, Japan

Cover: Foto ©Thomas Meinert / pixelio.de

More available books at **www.hansebooks.com**

THE ILIADS OF HOMER,

PRINCE OF POETS,

NEVER BEFORE IN ANY LANGUAGE TRULY TRANSLATED,

WITH A COMMENT ON SOME OF HIS

CHIEF PLACES.

DONE ACCORDING TO THE GREEK
BY GEORGE CHAPMAN.

WITH INTRODUCTION AND NOTES,

BY THE

REV. RICHARD HOOPER, M.A.

VICAR OF UPTON AND ASTON UPTHORPE, BERKS.

VOLUME I.

THIRD EDITION.

LONDON:
JOHN RUSSELL SMITH.
1888.

TO

SAMUEL, LORD BISHOP OF OXFORD,

CHANCELLOR OF THE MOST NOBLE ORDER OF THE GARTER,

AND LORD HIGH ALMONER TO THE QUEEN,

THESE VOLUMES ARE DEDICATED

WITH EVERY SENTIMENT OF RESPECT,

BY HIS OBLIGED SERVANT,

THE EDITOR.

ADVERTISEMENT.

T is with sincere pleasure that the Editor has been informed that a third issue of his Edition of Chapman's Homer's Iliads is required. The steady and continued demand for this fine old book is very gratifying, and no slight proof of the hold that it has obtained on the public mind. In the present edition the sheets have been carefully read through, but as some had been printed off before they came under the editor's eye, he has thrown his Additional and Corrected Notes, and the very few typographical errors, into a page of *Addenda et Corrigenda*, which the reader is requested to peruse. The Introduction, corrected in a few places, remains as it stood in the last edition (1865), and the editor believes that, with that prefixed to the last edition of the Odyssey (1874), it contains the fullest account of Chapman and his works extant.

R. H.

UPTON, BERKS, *March* 7, 1888.

ADVERTISEMENT TO SECOND EDITION.

AVING been informed by my respected publisher that the former impression of these volumes has been entirely exhausted and long out of print, I have had much pleasure in acceding to his request to superintend a new edition. The text has been thoroughly revised by a collation with a fine copy of the first folio, and great care has been bestowed upon the punctuation. The Life of Chapman has, to a great extent, been re-written, though it is to be regretted that little additional information could be procured. Since the former publication much attention has been turned to the study of Homer, probably through the influence of the writings of Mr. Gladstone ; and some good versions of the Homeric Poems have been added to our literature. Among these the translations of the Iliad by Lord Derby and Mr. I. C. Wright, and one of the Odyssey, in the Spenserian stanza, by Mr. Philip Stanhope Worsley, have been deservedly commended. The noble version of George Chapman, however, has an independent value and interest. It is to be prized for its fine old language and the sweetness of its epithets, as much as its representation (however imperfect all such representations may be) of the original. The contemporary and friend of Shakespeare has left us a work worthy of the great age in which he lived ; and I hope I may not be accused of the undue partiality of an advocate, if I express my conviction that Chapman's Homer is (to use Mr. Godwin's words) " one of the greatest treasures the English language has to boast."

R. H.

Aston Upthorpe,
    March, 1865.

INTRODUCTION.

HE increasing interest in the sterling literature of the Elizabethan age is too obvious to need remark. The new era of criticism in the writings of Shakespeare has caused the dust which had accumulated upon the works of many of his less-known contemporaries to be shaken off, and the result has proved by no means disadvantageous to their reputation. "He, indeed, overlooks and commands the admiration of posterity, but he does it from *the table-land of the age in which he lived.* He towered above his fellows 'in shape and gesture proudly eminent,' but he was one of a race of giants, the tallest, the strongest, the most graceful and beautiful of them ; *but it was a common and a noble brood.*" * One branch, however, of this "giant family" has not hitherto met with that attention to which it is justly entitled ; a branch which contributed in no slight degree to enrich the language, and enlighten and enlarge the national mind—I mean the sturdy race of our old Translators. While Shakespeare and Spenser, Bacon, Sydney, Hooker, Ben Jonson, and a host of others, poets, philosophers, divines, and statesmen, "men whom Fame has eternised in her long and lasting scroll, and who, by their words and acts, were benefactors of their country and ornaments of human nature," were giving to the world the imperishable monuments

---

* Hazlitt's "Lectures on the Dramatic Literature of the Age of Elizabeth" p. 12.

of their genius, there was a hardly-to-be-less honoured race employed in culling from the rich and fascinating stores of the Greek and Latin Classics, in exploring the romantic poetry of Spain and Italy, and throwing open their treasures in noble and stately Translations. When James ascended the throne, himself no mean scholar, he found his people in possession of versions in their own language of most of the great writers of Classical Antiquity. And though it is true the rage for Translation had been so great that many of these were of mushroom growth, and have meritedly sunk into oblivion, yet there were others which were of too genuine worth to be merely ephemeral, which have stood the test of ages, and which, having done good service in their day, are now undeservedly laid aside, and sought after only by the scholar and the philologer, or, may be, the curious, yet to every true lover of his native language are they precious heir-looms of the genius and learning of a past and a glorious age.

It is not to be supposed that in the following remarks on some of these old Translations I specify all that could be enumerated, but I would wish to mention a few, which obtained no slight popularity in their time, and which seem to me still worth the attention of the lover of old literature. Virgil, as might be imagined, was an early favourite. The version by Thomas Phaier, first published in Queen Mary's reign, is no mean specimen of the art of Translation, and, though now supplanted by the great work of the "glorious John," contains much to admire. A late critic indeed has passed a very high eulogium upon it which may seem a little too laudatory, though I can add my sincere testimony to the worth of "Thomas Phaier, Doctour of Phisicke." Mr. Godwin describes it "as the most wonderful depository of living description and fervent feeling, that is to be found perhaps in all the circle of literature." *

Ovid, besides numerous translations of his other poems by various authors, was nobly "converted" in his Metamorphoses by Arthur Golding, a name of no faint lustre amongst our old Translators. In

* "Lives of Edward and John Philips," p. 247. (London, 4to. 1815.)

1567 Golding produced his charming work complete. Warton confesses that "his style is poetical, and spirited, and his versification clear, his manner ornamental and diffuse, yet with a sufficient observance of the original."* After such testimony it would seem hardly necessary to add an observation ; but I can assure the reader he would be much pleased by the smoothness and sweetness of diction in this fine version. Golding gave us several other translations ; and one in particular may be mentioned, namely Philip Mornay's Treatise "On the Truth of the Christian Religion," executed in conjunction with Sir Philip Sydney.

Sir Thomas North's Translation of Plutarch's Lives, 1579, though avowedly taken from the French of Amyot, has a claim to our veneration from the use that Shakespeare made of it. The popularity of this work may be estimated from the fact that it was a household book during the whole of the seventeenth century, and we have no less than six folio editions of it, viz., 1579, 1595, 1602, 1631, 1657, 1676. The edition of 1657 was published at the instance of the lately deceased Selden. I may be pardoned for giving Mr. Godwin's opinion of it. " I must confess that till this book fell into my hands, I had no genuine feeling of Plutarch's merits, or knowledge of what sort of writer he was. The philosopher of Cheronœa subjects himself in his biographical sketches to none of the rules of fine writing ; he has not digested the laws and ordonnance of composition, and the dignified and measured step of an historian ; but rambles just as his fancy suggests, and always tells you without scruple or remorse what comes next in his mind. How beautiful does all this show in the simplicity of the old English! How aptly does this dress correspond to the tone and manner of thinking in the author! While I read Plutarch in Sir Thomas North, methinks I see the grey-headed philosopher, full of information and anecdote, a veteran in reflection and experience, and smitten with the love of all that is most exalted in our nature, pouring out without restraint the collectious of his wisdom, as he reclines in his easy chair before a cheerful winter's blaze. How different does all this

* Warton's Hist. Engl. Poetry, vol. III. p. 332, ed. 1840.

appear in the translation of the Langhornes! All that was beautiful and graceful before becomes deformity in the finical and exact spruceness with which they have attired it." *

And ungrateful should I be if I passed over the labours of old Philemon Holland, that "Translator general," as Fuller styled him. His "Plinie's Natural Historie" has wiled away many a weary hour, and his "Livy" and "Plutarch's Morals" were noble efforts in their day. They contain a mine of wealth to the philologer. Pope's ill-natured sneer that
"here the groaning shelves Philemon bends"
would be vain now, his works have become so scarce, and are too precious to "bend the shelves" of the every-day collector. The student would do well to avail himself of every opportunity to secure them. Philemon Holland was no ordinary scholar.†

But, while attention was thus being turned to Classical lore, Foreign literature was not neglected. Edward Fairfax had given us his splendid version of Tasso. Ariosto, through Sir John Harington, had, upon the admission of Warton, "enriched our poetry by a com-

* Godwin, ut suprà, p. 245.
† Fuller, in his "*Worthies*," styles Philemon Holland "the Translator General of his age, so that those books alone of his turning into English will make a country gentleman a competent library for Historians, insomuch that one saith
<blockquote>Holland with translations doth so fill us
He will not let Suetonius be Tranquillus."</blockquote>
Poor Philemon seems to have been in much distress in his old age. (See a very interesting extract from various MSS. in Sir E. Brydges' "*Restituta*," vol. iii. p. 41.) The dates of his Translations are as follows: *Pliny*, fol. 1601, fol. 1634; *Plutarch's Morals*, fol. 1603, fol. 1657; *Livy*, fol. 1600, fol. 1659, fol. 1686; *Suetonius*, fol. 1606; *Ammianus Marcellinus*, fol. 1609; *Xenophon's Cyropædia*, fol. 1632; *Camden's Britannia*, fol. 1610, fol. 1637. Sir John Harington's *Ariosto* was published fol. 1591; fol. 1607; fol. 1634. Paynter's *Palace of Pleasure* was reprinted by Haslewood, 3 vols. 4to. 1813. Fenton's *Guicciardin* was published fol. 1579, fol. 1599, and fol. 1618. The two first editions, I think, are identical, the title being merely altered. The editions of Fairfax's *Tasso* I have met with are fol. 1600; fol. 1624; 8vo. 1687; 2 vols. 8vo. Dublin, 1726; 8vo. London, 1749; 8vo. 1817, 2 vols. by Knight, also in Knight's shilling volumes; and a most beautiful edition in the original orthography by Mr. Singer, 2 vols. small 8vo. 1817.

munication of new stores of fiction and imagination, both of the romantic and comic species, of Gothic machinery, and familiar manner."* In 1566-7 William Paynter displayed in his "Palace of Pleasure" the wealthy mine of Boccaccio, fertilizing the imagination of even Shakespeare himself. Geffray Fenton's "Historie of Guicciardin, containing the Warres of Italie," is a fine old book. Nor can we forget that Milton, in common with his age, is said to have been very partial to the translations from Du Bartas by that "famous philomusus" Joshua Sylvester. One work more, reader, and I have done—William Shelton's translation of "Don Quixote," 2 vols. 4to. 1612-20. Jarvis, it is true, thinks Shelton translated through the Italian, but, be this as it may, the version is most spirited, and, in my humble opinion, still the best in our language.

All, and each, of these grand old authors contain much, very much, for us to venerate and admire. In them the reader will find a vigour and a freshness, a grasp of the spirit of the originals, a stately flow of language, which we in vain look for in the more modern and finished Translations. In a word, it was essentially *the* age of Translation, and we might point triumphantly to the BIBLE, and ask, what period in all our literary annals could have produced such a version? A writer in the Edinburgh Review (vol. LVII. 112) observes: "The lovers of the English language owe the Church of England an obligation which they can never repay. Only let them think, what would have been our loss, if the translation of the Bible had been delayed to the present age!"

I will conclude by citing some very able remarks, which fully embody my own sentiments on this subject, and which contain pleasing testimony to the merits of GEORGE CHAPMAN.

"Translation," says Mr. Godwin, "ought to be considered in a very different light by scholars, and men to whom literature is their chosen occupation, than that in which it is regarded by persons to whom books are an amusement only. Translation is the parent, or more accurately speaking, the nurse of all modern languages, from whose fostering

* Warton, ut suprâ, p. 391.

breast they derive their soundness, the vigour, and the health, that renders them at once the delight and accomplished ministers of all by whom they are spoken and written. To Translation we are indebted for much of what is most excellent and important in our vernacular speech; and Translation, considered in this point of view, is a fundamental branch of true learning. Chaucer, Lydgate, Skelton, and Surrey, the fathers of our literature, were all eminent Translators; and it is to our version of the Bible that we are above all things indebted for the sober, majestic, and copious, flow of our English tongue. Translation, merely as Translation, would form no branch of reading to a scholar, merely in as far as he was a scholar; but, considered as the faithful repository of the history of a language, it is of inexpressible importance. Translation in itself is a dim and obscure medium, through which we become feebly acquainted with the merits of an original work. No man therefore would almost deign to look upon a Translation, except so far as he had no other way in which to obtain a knowledge of the original it pretends to represent.

"This character may be considered as applicable to all Translations at the time they are presented to the world. But an obsolete Translation is a very different thing. It is an object avoided by the fop and the fine lady; but it is precious to the man of taste, the man of feeling, and the philosopher. In the old English Homer, for example, I have some pleasure, inasmuch as I find Homer himself there; but I have also an inestimable pleasure added to this, while I remark, and feel in my inmost heart, the venerable and illustrious garb in which he is thus brought before me. This further pleasure I have which I could not find even in the original itself. The Translation of Homer, published by George Chapman in the reign of Queen Elizabeth and King James, is *one of the greatest treasures the English language has to boast*. This man had a deep and true feeling of what a poet is, when he appears, as Milton styles it, 'soaring in the high region of his fancies, with his garland and singing robes about him.' This is conspicuously shown in his Preface, Notes, and Dedication."*

* Ut suprà, p. 240.

Mr. Godwin proceeds to illustrate this by a comparison of passages from the Odyssey with Pope's version, in which the superiority of the elder poet is obvious. It will be unnecessary to pursue a similar course, for it is generally admitted at the present day, that, of all the versions of Homer in our language, that of Chapman approaches the nearest to the original in spirit and grandeur, and, from a most attentive perusal, I think faithfulness. Whether Homer has ever been *really* translated is a question which must be discussed elsewhere, but of the existing representations of him, there can be no doubt as to which the palm must be given. It may be pleasing to give a few testimonies of competent judges to the worth of this noble work. Dryden, in the Dedication to the third volume of his Miscellanies, says, "The Earl of Mulgrave and Mr. Waller, two of the best judges of our age, have assured me that they never could read over the translation of Chapman without incredible transport." Dryden himself translated the First Book of the Iliad, and Pope declares that, had he completed the work, he would not have ventured on his own translation. Pope, in a subsequent passage of his Preface, accuses Dryden of having "had too much regard to Chapman, whose words he sometimes copies, and has unhappily followed him in passages where he wanders from the original." This comes with an ill grace from Pope, for Dr. Johnson asserts that "with Chapman Pope had frequent consultations, and perhaps *never translated any passage till he had read his version; which indeed he has been sometimes suspected of using instead of the Greek.*" Pope has however done Chapman the justice to say that " he covers his defects by a daring fiery spirit that animates his translation; which is *something like what one might imagine Homer himself to have writ before he arrived to years of discretion.*" "He (Pope) might have added," says Mr. Hallam, "that Chapman's Translation, with all its defects, is often exceedingly Homeric; a praise which Pope himself *seldom attained.* Chapman deals abundantly in compound epithets, some of which have retained their place; his verse is rhymed, of fourteen syllables, which corresponds to the hexameter better than the decasyllable couplet; he is often uncouth, and often low, but the spirited and rapid flow of his metre makes him respectable to lovers of poetry."* In the Retrospective Review, vol. III. will be found an admirable article on the merits of Chapman, Pope and Cowper; and there are several interesting critiques on Sotheby's Homer in Blackwood's Magazine for 1830, 1832,† which do ample justice to Chapman. Coleridge, in sending a copy of Chapman's volume to Wordsworth (1807) says, "Chapman I have sent in order that you might read the Odyssey; the Iliad is fine, but less equal in the translation, as well as less interesting in itself. What is stupidly said of Shakespeare is really true and appropriate of Chapman: 'mighty faults counterpoised by mighty beauties.' Excepting his quaint epithets, which he affects to render literally from the Greek, a language above all others blest in the happy marriage of sweet words, and which in our language are mere printer's compound epithets—such as divine *joy-in-the-heart-of-man-infusing* wine (the undermarked is to be one word, because one sweet mellifluous word expresses it in Homer); excepting this it has no look, no air, of a translation. It is as truly an original poem as the Faery Queen;—it will give you small idea of Homer, though a far truer one than Pope's epigrams, or Cowper's cumbersome most anti-Homeric Miltonism. For Chapman writes and feels as a poet,—as Homer might have written had he lived in England in the reign of Queen Elizabeth. In short, it is an exquisite poem, in spite of its frequent and perverse quaintnesses and harshnesses, which are, however, amply repaid by almost unexampled sweetness and beauty of language, all over spirit and feeling." ‡ It is not improbable that Coleridge's attention had been called to Chapman by Charles Lamb, who writes to him in 1802, "I have just finished Chapman's Homer. Did you ever read it?—it has the most continuous power of interesting you all along, like a rapid original, of any; and in the uncommon excellence

* Literature of Europe, II. p. 130, ed. 1843.
† By Professor Wilson.
‡ Coleridge's Literary Remains by Henry Nelson Coleridge, 4 vols. 8vo. 1836, vol. I. pp. 259-60-61.

of the more finished parts goes beyond Fairfax or any of 'em. The metre is fourteen syllables, and capable of all sweetness and grandeur. Cowper's ponderous blank verse detains you every step with some heavy Miltonism ; Chapman gallops off with you his own free pace, &c."*

It would be unpardonable to omit Lamb's well-known criticism on Chapman in his "Specimens of English Dramatic Poets," first published in 1808. "The selections which I have made from this poet are sufficient to give an idea, of 'that full and heightened style' which Webster makes characteristic of Chapman. Of all the English play-writers, Chapman perhaps approaches nearest to Shakespeare in the descriptive and didactic, in passages which are less purely dramatic. Dramatic imitation was not his talent. He could not go out of himself, as Shakespeare could shift at pleasure, to inform and animate other existences ; but in himself he had an eye to perceive, and a soul to embrace, all forms. He would have made a great epic poet, if indeed he has not abundantly shown himself to be one ; for his Homer is not so properly a translation as the stories of Achilles and Ulysses re-written. The earnestness and passion which he has put into every part of these poems would be incredible to a reader of mere modern translations. His almost Greek zeal for the honour of his heroes is only paralleled by that fierce spirit of Hebrew bigotry with which Milton, as if personating one of the zealots of the old law, clothed himself when he sat down to paint the acts of Samson against the Uncircumcised. The great obstacle to Chapman's translations being read is their unconquerable quaintness. He pours out in the same breath the most just and natural, and the most violent and forced, expressions. He seems to grasp whatever words come first to hand during the impetus of inspiration, as if all other must be inadequate to the divine meaning. But passion (the all in all in poetry) is everywhere present, raising the low, dignifying the mean, and putting sense into the absurd. He makes his readers glow, weep, tremble, take any affection which he pleases, be

---

* The letters of Charles Lamb, by T. N. Talfourd, 2 vols. 8vo. 1837, vol. I. p. 236.

moved by words, or in spite of them be disgusted, and overcome their disgust. I have often thought that the vulgar misconception of Shakespeare as of a wild irregular genius, 'in whom great faults are compensated by great beauties,' would be true of Chapman."

In an article entitled "Remarks on Translation" in the Classical Museum (vol. I. p. 400) the writer, Mr. R. H. Horne, observes—"The name of George Chapman I mention with reverence and admiration; but his truly grand version of Homer must nevertheless be declared *no* translation. Chapman's version of Homer is a paraphrase by a kindred spirit; that of Pope is a paraphrase in his own* spirit. The works might be appropriately contradistinguished as 'Homer's Chapman,' and 'Pope's Homer.' By his in-door modern life, his drawing-room associates, his mechanical refinements and polished grace, his tasteful timidities and general misgivings, Pope was the natural opposite to Homer, and one of the very last men who should have meddled with his works; but Chapman, by his commanding energies, fulness of faith in his author's genius, and in his own inspired sympathies, his primitive power, and rough truthfulness of description, was the very man for the purpose, had he not been misled by the common notions of translation. He gives Homer's narrative as he feels it. Pope produced his own idea of Homer, and in his own (Pope's) peculiar words, with little reference to the words of the original: and this has been read to an immense extent; destroying the ears of the schoolboys and men, of at least two generations, for any sense of the varied harmonies of rhythm: Chapman produced in his own words, and often in his own images, a glorious adumbration of the effect of Homer upon the energies of his soul. When we consider the subtle influence of poetry upon the rising spirits of the age, it tempts me to hazard the speculation, that if Chapman's noble paraphrase had been read instead of Pope's enervating monotony, and as extensively, the present class of general readers would not only have been a more poetical class—as the fountain-head

---

* i. e. Pope's own.

from the rock is above the artificial cascade in a pleasure ground—but a finer order of human beings in respect of energy, love of nature at first-hand, and faith in their own impulses and aspirations." The reader, perhaps, will pardon one more extract, in which is an interesting tribute to what may be styled the practical effect of Chapman's work. Mr. Monckton Milnes, in his "Life and Letters of John Keats," (vol. I. p. 18. ed. 1848,) says, "Unable as he was to read the original Greek, Homer had as yet been to him a name of solemn significance and nothing more. His friend and literary counsellor, Mr. Clarke, happened to borrow Chapman's translation, and having invited Keats to read it with him one evening, they continued their study till daylight. He describes Keats' delight as intense, even to shouting aloud, as some passages of especial energy struck his imagination. It was fortunate that he was introduced to that heroic company through an interpretation which preserves so much of the ancient simplicity, and in a metre that, after all various attempts, including that of the hexameter, still appears the best adapted, from its pauses and its length, to represent in English, the Greek epic verse * * * The Sonnet, in which these his first impressions are concentrated, was left the following day on Mr. Clarke's table."

"ON FIRST LOOKING INTO CHAPMAN'S HOMER.

" Much have I travelled in the realms of gold,
  And many goodly states and kingdoms seen;
  Round many western islands have I been,
Which bards in fealty to Apollo hold.
Oft of one wide expanse had I been told
  That deep-brow'd Homer ruled as his demesne:
  Yet did I never breathe its pure serene
Till I heard Chapman speak out loud and bold:
Then felt I like some watcher of the skies
  When a new planet swims into his ken;
Or like stout Cortez, when with eagle eyes
  He stared at the Pacific—and all his men
Look'd at each other with a wild surmise—
  Silent, upon a peak in Darien."

INTRODUCTION.

The opinions of Coleridge, Lamb, and Mr. R. H. Horne, might lead the reader to infer that Chapman's noble work, of which they speak in such raptures, is in reality only a paraphrase. If however he will be at the pains to compare it with the original Greek, he will not fail to be struck with its closeness on the whole. He should remember the principles upon which Chapman translated, as expressed in his Preface :—
"It is the part of every knowing and judicial interpreter, not to follow the number and order of words, but the material things themselves, and sentences to weigh diligently ; and to clothe and adorn them with words and such a style and form of oration, as are most apt for the language into which they are converted." He tells us, in the noble poem "To the Reader,"

> " Custom hath made even th' ablest agents err
> In these translations ; all so much apply
> Their pains and cunnings word for word to render
> Their patient authors, when they may as well
> Make fish with fowl, camels with whales, engender,
> Or their tongue's speech in other mouths compell."

And again, though he "laughs to see"

> ———"the brake
> That those translators stick in, that affect
> Their word-for-word traductions,"

yet he as much abhors

> "More license from the words than may express
> Their full compression, and make clear the author ; "

and he says of the various translators of Homer in other languages,

> "They failed to search his deep and treasurous heart.
> The cause was, since they wanted the fit key
> Of Nature, in their down-right strength of Art
> With Poesy to open Poesy."

This is the real secret of the success and beauty of Chapman's work. He has perfectly identified himself with Homer, and from his search of that 'treasurous heart,' from his thorough knowledge of its depths, with the 'fit key' of true natural poesy, with his own innative Homeric genius, he has opened to us (to use his own words) "the mysteries revealed in Homer."

It may not be too much to say that perhaps no man ever felt the Homeric inspiration to the same extent as Chapman. We pardon him even for his digressions, for they are such as we feel Homer himself would have written. Chapman conceived that our language was adapted to rythmical poetry above all others, on account of its numerous monosyllables:

> ——— " I can prove it clear
> That no tongue hath the Muses' utterance heired
> For verse, and that sweet music to the ear
> Struck out of rhyme, so naturally as this.
> Our monosyllables so kindly fall,
> And meet oppos'd in rhyme as they did kiss.
> French and Italian most immetrical;
> Their many syllables in harsh collision
> Fall as they break their necks, their bastard rhymes
> Saluting as they justled in transition,
> And set our teeth on edge ; nor tunes, nor times
> Kept in their falls."

Warton accuses him of "labouring with the inconvenience of an awkward, inharmonious, and unheroic measure, imposed by custom, but disgustful to modern ears." The judgment, however, of the present day would reverse this decision, for it is confessed that the fourteen-syllable verse is peculiarly fitting for Homeric translation. Chapman had met with a similar objection in his own time, but he defends himself with the observation that

> ——— "this long poem asks this length of verse."

However in the translation of the Odyssey, the Hymns, and the Georgics of Hesiod, at a subsequent period, he has adopted the ordinary heroic (or decasyllable) measure, in which he displays equal vigour.

"One of the peculiarities of Chapman's versification," says Mr. Singer,* "is the interlacing of the verses, or the running of the lines

* Preface to Chapman's "Hymns of Homer" (Chiswick, 1818) p. xxi.

one into the other, so that the sense does not close with the couplet; this is what the French critics object to under the name of *enjambement des vers*, and is what made Ben Jonson say, 'that the translations of Homer and Virgil in long Alexandrines were but prose.' The practice, however, when not injudiciously excessive in its use, gives freedom and spirit to long compositions, while the strict observance of confining the sense to terminate with the couplet gives a stiff and formal air, and makes one rather seem to be reading a string of epigrams, than a poem. The following judicious reflections of an excellent old poet and critic, in which our author's custom is defended, will place this subject in a just point of view:

'I must confess that, to mine own ear, those continual cadences in couplets used in long continued poems are very tiresome and unpleasing, by reason that still methinks they run on with a sound of one nature, and a kind of certainty which stuffs the delight rather than entertains it. But yet, notwithstanding, I must not but of my own daintiness condemn this kind of writing, which peradventure to another may seem most delightful; and many worthy compositions we see to have passed with commendation in that kind. Besides methinks sometimes to beguile the ear with a running out and passing over the rhyme, as no bound to stay us in the line where the violence of the matter will break through, rather graceful than otherwise. Wherein I find my Homer-Lucan, as if he gloried to seem to have no bounds albeit he were confined within his measures, to be in my conceit most happy; for so thereby they who care not for verse or rhyme may pass over it without taking any notice thereof, and please themselves with a well-measured prose.'" * Lamb's charge of "*unconquerable* quaintness" in Chapman is too sweeping. He is undoubtedly quaint, and too fond of silly quibbling on words. He is often low, and uses forced expressions; but it should be borne in mind that he wrote with great rapidity, and paid little regard to correcting and polishing his work.

---

* Samuel Daniel's "Defence of Rhyme," 1602.

The reader must not expect to be pleased at once. Chapman, like most of the writers of his day, requires patience and study. It has been well said of him that he is "a rough nut externally, but contains a most sweet kernel."

ANTONY WOOD says that George Chapman was born in 1557, and conjectures that he might have been of a family seated at Stone Castle in Kent. But he is in error both as to the date and place of the poet's birth. That Chapman was born at, or in the neighbourhood of, Hitchin in Hertfordshire, and that he there translated at least the earlier portions of his Homer, we have the evidence of his own writings. In a small poem entitled, "*Euthymiæ Raptus, or the Teares of Peace*," 4to. 1609, he introduces himself in a reverie, when the Shade of Homer appears, and in reply to the Poet's enquiry—

> "What may I reckon thee,
> Whose heav'nly look showes not, nor voice sounds, man?
> 'I am,' sayd he, 'that spirit Elysian
> That *in thy native ayre, and on the Hill
> Next Hitchin's left hand*, did thy bosome fill
> With such a floode of soule that thou wert faine
> (With acclamations of her rapture then)
> To vent it to the echoes of the vale;
> When meditating of me, a sweet gale
> Brought me upon thee; and thou didst inherit
> My true sense (for the time then) in my spirit,
> And I invisible went prompting thee
> *To those fayre greenes where thou didst English me.*'"

His friend and contemporary, William Browne, in his "Britannia's Pastorals" (Book I. Song 5) also styles him

> "The learned shepherd of fair Hitching Hill."

INTRODUCTION.

The date of his birth we fix by inference in 1559, as round the portrait affixed to the title of the Complete Homer in the legend, "Georgius Chapmanus Homeri Metaphrastes Æta. LVII. M.DC.XVI." The Hitchin Registers unfortunately only commence with the year 1562, so we are unable to arrive at any facts relative to his parentage. There are, however, several entries relating to the families of John and Thomas Chapman, who were possibly the poet's brothers. In 1593, Aug. 5, was baptized George, the son of John Chapman; and from Easter 1603 to Easter 1605 the same John Chapman was one of the Churchwardens, and has signed the Parish Registers in a bold and scholarlike hand. Amongst the Additional MSS. in the British Museum (No. 16,273) is a "Survey of the King's timber and woods in Hertfordshire and Essex in 1608," and under the "Manēr de Hutchin" (Hitchin) is "*Upon the Copyhold of Thomas Chapman, in Longe Close 27 Saplings £4. In Beerton closes 260 Elmes £18, Fire wood £35.* This Thomas Chapman was probably a man of respectability and substance, for in the Harleian MSS. No. 781, p. 28, is a petition to Prince Charles from Thomas Chapman, in 1619, for the bailiwick of Hitchin, which he formerly held under the Exchequer Seal, but of which the Earl of Salisbury had deprived him. On November 30 of the same year the claim was referred to the Commissioners of the Revenue of the Prince of Wales. The relationship, however, to the poet is mere conjecture, as we have no positive proof of any facts connected with his family. We have carefully examined the various Heraldic visitations of Hertfordshire, and the County Histories, but have been unable to discover any traces of him. Nothing is known of his youth, or where he was educated.

"In 1574, or thereabouts," says Antony Wood,* "he, being well-grounded in school-learning, was sent to the university, but whether first to this of Oxon, or that of Cambridge, is to me unknown. Sure I

---

* The account of Chapman in Bliss's Edition of Antony Wood is in inverted commas, which would lead one to suppose that it was a communication; but it seems to be generally quoted as Wood's.

am that he spent some time in Oxon, where he was observed to be most excellent in the Latin and Greek tongues, but not in logic or philosophy, and therefore I presume that that was the reason why he took no degree here." Warton also says (from the information of Mr. Wise, late Radcliffe's Librarian, and Keeper of the Archives at Oxford) "that he passed two years at Trinity College, with a contempt of philosophy, but in a close attention to the Greek and Roman Classics." The present Keeper of the Archives,* however, has been unable to discover Chapman's name. It is probable from the date of his birth (1559) that he would have been matriculated before the year 1581, when Subscription to the Articles began. Before that date (Mr. Griffiths says) the Matriculation Register is very incomplete. Mr. Wise's communication to Warton seems merely a repetition of Wood's information with the addition of the name of the College (Trinity) of which Chapman is supposed to have been a member. But this point cannot be satisfactorily ascertained. The present learned President of Trinity College † writes, "I am sorry to discover that the records of our Admissions, at the period when Chapman would have entered, are either lost or destroyed; which is a great disappointment to me." We must be content then with Antony Wood's assurance "that he spent some time in Oxon." Researches as to his residence or admission at Cambridge would probably be equally fruitless, as he is not mentioned in that admirable and accurate work, Cooper's "*Athenæ Cantabrigienses.*"

Quitting the University without a degree, he afterwards settled, says Wood, in the metropolis, and associated with Shakespeare, Spenser, Marlowe, Daniel, and other celebrated persons of the day. Though he undoubtedly knew Marlowe, it is not very probable, as Mr. Dyce well observes, that they were very intimate, as their dispositions and characters were very dissimilar. He early acquired the patronage and friendship of Sir Thomas Walsingham, and his son, "whom Chapman loved from his birth." The date of Chapman's first acknowledged publication in 1594 is such a long interval from the time of his quitting

---

* Rev. John Griffiths.   † Rev. John Wilson, D.D.

Oxford in 1576 (or 1578) that Mr. Singer conjectured that he probably appeared as a writer anonymously,* although we have no clue to his earlier performances. But though, upon the authority of Wood, we have said he settled immediately in London, his time seems to have been occasionally spent at Hitchin, from his informing us that he there translated Homer. In 1594, however, he published two fine poems "*The Shadow of Night: containing two poetical Hymnes, devised by G. C. Gent,*" and dedicated to his "deare and most worthy friend Master Mathew Roydon." They have been reprinted by Mr. Singer in his edition of "Chapman's Hymns of Homer," (Chiswick, 1818). In the following year (1595) appeared "*Ovid's Banquet of Sence, a Coronet for his Mistresse Philosophie, and his amorous Zodiacke: with a translation of a Latine Copie (sc. of verses) written by a fryer, Anno Dom. 1400.*" 4to. This was also dedicated to Matthew Roydon, with Commendatory Verses by Richard Stapilton, Thomas Williams, and I. D. of the Middle Temple. It was reprinted in 1639, 12mo. without the dedication and verses. John Davis of Hereford has an epigram "To the right-well-deserving Mr. Matthew Roydon."

Chapman was now in London, and employed in writing for the stage. From an entry in "Henslowe's Diary," p. 64, we learn that his comedy of the "Blind Beggar of Alexandria" was first brought out and acted by the Lord Admiral's (the Earl of Nottingham's) servants, on the 12th of February, 1595. It seems to have been very successful, and to have attracted large houses, from the receipts being always considerable. It continued to be acted till April 1597,

---

* In a small 4to. tract of thirty-two leaves, published in 1596, entitled "*A relation of the Second Voyage to Guiana, perfourmed and written in the yeare 1596. By Lawrence Keymis, Gent.*" is an English poem in blank verse, "*De Guianâ Carmen Epicum,* by G. C." George Steevens, writing to Bishop Percy (Nicholl's "Literary Illustrations," vol. VII. p. 121) assigned this to Chapman, and it bears evidence of his style. It is interesting as an early specimen of blank verse. In the same volume is a short Latin poem, "*Ad Thomam Hariotum Matheseos et universæ philosophiæ peritissimum, by L. K.*" This was, doubtless, the M. Harriots to whom Chapman addressed a poem at the end of his translation of the "*Shield of Achilles,*" and who is mentioned in the Preface to the Iliad. Keymis's Tract was reprinted by Hakluyt.

when it was withdrawn, and published in the following year, 1598. It was revived in 1601. "There is a coincidence," says Mr. Payne Collier, "between a line in it and Marlowe's Paraphrase of Hero and Leander. Marlowe's line is correctly cited, with acknowledgment to the 'dead Shepherd,' by Shakespeare in 'As you like it,' Act. III. Sc. 5.

'Who ever lov'd that lov'd not at first sight?'

Which Chapman, near the close of his '*Blind Beggar of Alexandria,*' gives thus:

'None ever lov'd but at first sight they lov'd.'

The circumstance might have been passed over without notice, if Chapman's play and Marlowe's poem had not been printed in the same year, and if Chapman, at a subsequent date, had not finished the poem which Marlowe left incomplete. Marlowe's portion having been published in 1598, Chapman immediately continued the subject, and the six sestiads appeared together in 1600."* The coincidence of the date of the publications is all that is remarkable. Marlowe's poem, though only printed in 1598, was entered in the Stationers' Registers as early as September 28, 1593, and again in 1597. It had probably been handed about in MS. as was not infrequently the case. Chapman, perhaps, had seen the line, and adopted the idea. It is equally possible that Marlowe might have been present at the representation of Chapman's play, and transferred the sentiment to his own poem, though the evidence of priority would seem to be in his favour. An allusion in Chapman's subsequent portion of the poem has led to the inference that Marlowe had at some time or other expressed a wish that he should conclude it. The reader will find an able criticism on Chapman's plays in the fourth and fifth volume of the "*Retrospective Review.*"

The rapidity with which Chapman now issued his publications is astonishing. In this same year (1598) appeared his "*Seaven Bookes*

* Henslowe's Diary, p. 65 (Shakespeare Society).

of the *Iliades of Homere, Prince of Poetes*, &c., and the "*Shield of Achilles*" from Homer, both small 4tos. "*printed by John Windet, and are to be sold at the signe of the Crosse-Keyes neare Paules Wharffe.*" The "*Seaven Bookes of the Iliades*" are dedicated to Lord Essex, who is described as "the most honoured now living instance of the Achilleian virtues." They are not the first seven books continuously, but the first and second, and then the seventh to the eleventh inclusive. In explaining this circumstance, Chapman denies that Homer set the books together, but they were collected into an entire poem at a subsequent period. "In the next edition," he adds, "when they come out by the dozen, I will reserve the ancient and common received forme. In the meane time do me the encouragement to confer that which I have translated with the same in Homer, and according to the worth of that, let this edition passe: so shall you do me but lawfull favor, and make me take paines to give you this Emperor of all wisdome (for so Plato will allow him) in your owne language, which will more honor it (if my part bee worthily discharged) than anything else can be translated. In the meane time peruse the pamphlet of errors in the impression, and helpe to pointe the rest with your judgement; wherein, and in purchase of the whole seaven, if you be quicke and acceptive, you shall in the next edition have the life of Homer, a table, a prettie comment, true printing, the due praise of your mother tongue above all others for Poesie, and such demonstrative proofe of our English wits above beyond-sea Muses (if he would use them) that a proficient wit should be the better to heare it."

These books are written in the fourteen-syllable measure. The copy of them in the British Museum has the autograph, "*Sum Ben Jonsonii.*" "*The Shield of Achilles*," taken from the xviiith Book of the Iliad, was published later in the year. It is in the ordinary heroic measure of ten syllables, and is also dedicated to Lord Essex, "The most honored Earle Marshall." In the "Epistle Dedicatorie" is the following amusing invective against Scaliger, who seems to have been the object of Chapman's special aversion : "But thou soul-blind Scaliger, that never hadst anything but place, time, and terms, to paint thy proficiency in learning, nor ever writest anything of thine own impotent brain, but thy only impalsied diminution of Homer (which I may swear was the absolute inspiration of thine own ridiculous genius) never didst thou more palpably damn thy drossy spirit in all thy all-countries-exploded filcheries, which are so grossly illiterate that no man will vouchsafe their refutation, than in thy senseless reprehensions of Homer, whose spirit flew as much above thy grovelling capacity as Heaven moves above Barathrum." The Preface is "To the Understander," and Chapman commences, "You are not everybody: to you (as to one of my very few friends) I may be bold to utter my mind." He alludes to his already published "Seven Books." "My Epistle dedicatory before my Seven Books is accounted dark and too much laboured." He declares that it could only be dark "to ranke riders or readers, that have no more soules than burbolts." As for the labour—"I protest two mornings both ended it, and the Reader's Epistle." I regret that space prevents my giving more extracts from this interesting Preface, in which would be shown Chapman's thorough enthusiasm for Homer. He also alludes to the new words and epithets with which he has enriched our language from Homer. At the conclusion is a poetical address "To my admired and soule-loved friend, mayster of all essentiall and true knowledge, M. Harriots."

The publication of his Homer gained him great reputation. Meres, in his "*Wit's Treasury*," p. 156 (edit. Haslewood—Mere's first edit. was in 1598), speaks of Chapman's "inchoate Homer," for which he ranks him amongst the learned translators. As a proof that he was now in high fame, the same writer says: "As the Greeke tongue is made famous and eloquent by Homer, Hesiod, Euripides, Æschylus, Sophocles, Pindarus, Phocylides, and Aristophanes ; and the Latine tongue by Virgill, Ouid, Horace, Silius Italicus, Lucanus, Lucretius, Ausonius, and Claudianus; so the English tongue is mightilie enriched, and gorgeouslie inuested in rare ornaments, and resplendent abiliments by Sir Philip Sydney, Spenser, Daniel, Drayton, Warner, Shakespeare, Marlowe, and *Chapman*," (p. 150). In the next page he mentions Chapman as one of the best of our Tragedians, and, in the following, as a Comedian. This latter assertion is remarkable, as at this time Chapman had published but one drama. He had probably, therefore, written others which had been acted, though never published, and the authorship of which cannot now be determined. At this period are frequent entries in Henslowe's Diary relating to advances of money made to him. In p. 123 we have, "Lent unto Mr Chapmane, the 16 of Maye 1598, in earneste of a boocke for the companye xxxx^s Wittnes, Wm BIRDE." Again, "Lent unto Wm Birde, the 23 of Maye 1598, which he lent unto Mr Chappmann, upon his boocke, which he promised us: xx^s." "Lent unto the companey, the 10 of June 1598, to lend unto Mr Chapman x^s." And again, "Lent unto Robart Shawe and Edward Jube, the 15 of June 1598, to geve Mr Chapman, in earneste of his boocke called the *Wylle of a Woman* .. xx^s." It would seem, then, that this is the name of the "boocke" for the Company so often alluded to. Mr. Payne Collier, in a note on this passage, thinks that it was only the same play mentioned by Henslowe, in pp. 119-122, as "*A Woman will have her Wille*," and which is there given to Harton (William Haughton), and that Chapman may have added to it, or assisted him in it, as it would seem unlikely that two plays, so resembling in title, would have been produced at the same time. This may be true; but it is equally improbable that Chapman should have received such considerable and frequent sums for merely assisting in writing a play, which is, moreover, constantly styled his book. An entry is made on the 31st of September, 1598, of £3 to buy a "Boocke" of Mr. Chapman entitled "*The Fountain of New Fashions;*" and on the 12th of October he received xx^s. in full payment for the same play. On the 23rd* of the same

---

* Of this date also is the following memorandum in Henslowe, p. 191. "Be it knowen unto all men by thes presentes, that I George Chapman of London,

INTRODUCTION.   xxxi

month is an advance of £3 to Mr. Chapman on "his playe boocke and ij ectes of a tragedie of *bengemen's plotte.*" We have no farther information respecting this "tragedy of *Benjamin's Plot.*" In November, 1598, Henslowe records the expenses incurred for the production of "*The Fountain of New Fashions,*" and in December an advance of x^s. to Chapman. On the 4th and 8th of January 159$\frac{8}{9}$, Chapman received the respective sums of £3 for a tragedy, the name of which is not given. But though these plays were not printed,* in 1599 was published "*An Humorous Day's Mirth,*" a comedy, which had been frequently acted by the Lord Admiral's company. We are inclined to think that this is the play referred to by Henslowe under the entry of May 11, 1597, and elsewhere, where he says "*Rd at the Comodey of Umers.*" Malone was of opinion that this piece was Ben Jonson's "*Every Man in his Humour;*" but this is absurd, as Ben Jonson himself tells us (folio edit. 1616) that his comedy was first acted by the Lord Chamberlain's servants in 1598. See Collier's Life of Shakespeare, p. CLXV. Notwithstanding his labours for the stage, Chapman found time to continue and publish, in 1600, *Marlowe's Hero and Leander,* a poem of great beauty. We have seen that it is supposed Marlowe had at some time or other expressed a wish that Chapman should continue this work. From this fact is alleged the intimacy between Chapman and Marlowe; yet it proves nothing, whereas the extreme dissimilarity of their lives would tend to negative the supposition. Warton and others are in error in supposing it to be a transla-

gentleman, doe owe unto Mr Phillip Henslowe, of the parishe of St Saviours, gentleman, the some of x^{li} x^s of lawfull money of England. In witnesse whereof I have hereunto sett my hand, this xxiiij^{tb} of Octobr. 1598. GEO. CHAPMAN." The signature only is in the handwriting of Chapman.

* "*The Fountain of New Fashions,*" and "*The Will of a Woman,*" were in MS. in the late Mr. Heber's library. Where are they now? If the "*Will of a Woman*" could be discovered, it would settle the question as to Haughton's play, which was printed, in 1616, under the title, "*Englishmen for my Money, or a Woman will have her Will,*" and several times reprinted. Mr. Collier says it is an extremely good comedy. In the last old edition, 4to. 1631, the printer dropped the first part of the title, and reverted to the name it bears in Henslowe's Diary. It was not given to any author till the discovery of Henslowe's MS.

tion from the Greek. It is a story founded on Musæus. Chapman subsequently translated Musæus, as we shall see. Chapman divided the work into its present form of Sestyads, and published it in 1600 (4to.) without his name, which was first attached to the edition of 1606.*

The year 1605 was marked by the publication of "*Eastward Hoe*," which Chapman had written conjointly with Ben Jonson and Marston. This play had been acted by the Children of the Revels. "The play was well received," says Mr. Gifford, "as indeed it deserved to be, for it is exceedingly pleasant; but there was a passage in it reflecting on the Scotch, which gave offence to Sir James Murray, who represented it to the King in so strong a light that orders were given to arrest the authors." They do not seem to have been long in prison. "When they were first committed, a report had been propagated, Jonson says, that they should have their ears and noses cut, i. e. slit. This had reached his mother, and at an entertainment which he made on his deliverance, she drank to him, and showed him a paper which she designed, if the sentence had taken effect, to have mixed with his drink, and it was strong and lusty poison. To show that she was no churl, she designed to have first drunk it herself." Mr. Gifford, ever zealous for the honour of Jonson, says that he disclaimed to Drummond having anything to do with the offensive passage, but that "Chapman and Marston had written it amongst them;" having, however, had a share in the play, from a high sense of honour, he *voluntarily* accompanied his friends to prison. The 'play has an additional interest, as it is supposed to have suggested to Hogarth the plan of his set of prints of the "Idle and Industrious Apprentices." It was revived at Drury Lane in 1751. This alteration was published 12mo. n. d. with the additional title of "*The Prentices*," but it did not succeed. Mrs. Charlotte Lennox altered it; and it was once more revived at Drury

* Reprinted, 4to. 1609, 4to. 1613, 4to. 1629, 4to. 1637; in Sir Egerton Brydges' "Restituta," vol. II.; in Mr. Singer's "Select Early English Poets," Chiswick, 1821; in Mr. Bell's "Annotated Poets," 1856; and in Mr. Dyce's edition of Marlowe's works.

INTRODUCTION. xxxiii

Lane in 1775, with the title of "*Old City Manners,*" when it met with a more favourable reception. It will be found in Dodsley's Old Plays. It appears that Chapman underwent a second imprisonment with Jonson, shortly after their release, in consequence of supposed reflections upon some individual in a play of their joint composition. A letter was found by Dr. Birch amongst the Hatfield State Papers, inscribed "Ben Jonson to the Earl of Salisbury, praying his lordship's protection against some evil reports." It is dated 1605, and contains the following passage: "I am here, my most honoured Lord, unexamined and unheard, committed to a vile prison, and with me a gentleman (whose name may, perhaps, have come to your lordship) one Mr. George Chapman,* a learned and honest man." The whole letter is interesting, and will be found in the "Memoirs of Ben Jonson," prefixed to the one volume edition of Gifford's Jonson, 1838. It is gratifying to know that it met with instant success. In this year (1605) also was published "All Fools," a comedy, the plot of which is taken from Terence's "*Heautontimorumenos.*" It does not appear when this play was acted, but there are several curious entries in Henslowe's Diary, which all seem to refer to it. "Lent unto Thomas Downton, the 22 of Janewary 1598, to lend unto Mr Chapman, in earneste of a boocke called *the world rones a whelles*, the some of iij^{li}." "Lent unto Mr Chapman the 13 of febreary 1598, in p^t of payment of his boocke called the world ronnes on whelles, xx^s." Similar advances of xx^s and xxxx^s are made on the 2nd and 21st of June, 1599; and on the 2nd of July, 1599, is "Lent unto Thomas Downton to paye Mr Chapman in full paymente for his boocke called *the world rones on whelles*, and now *all foolles*, but *the foolle*, some of xxx^s." Mr. Payne Collier, in a note on this passage, thinks we have a notice of three separate works by Chapman, "*The World runs on Wheels,*" "*All Fools,*" and "*The Fool;*" yet he doubts "whether Henslowe does not mean that the title of '*All Fools*' was substituted for the '*World runs on*

* Chapman's name might have been known to Lord Salisbury not only from his literary fame, but from his connection with Hertfordshire.

VOL. I. c

Wheels.'" There seems little doubt on the subject, and all three names meant the same play. We may observe that in the same page Henslowe enters, "Lent unto Thomas Downton the 17th of Julye 1599 to lend unto Mr Chapman in earneste of a pastrall tragedie, the some of xxxx^s." What this *Pastoral Tragedy* was it is impossible to say, as we have no further notice of it. "*All Fools*," though not published till 1605, had evidently been completed, and probably acted in 1599. It is an excellent play; and a writer in the Edinburgh Review (April, 1841, vol. 73. p. 226) considers it Chapman's best—"a piece in which the situations are devised with an infinity of comic and histrionic effect." The Retrospective Review* says: "The characters in general are well sustained; the dialogue is spirited; and the incidents interesting and agreeable; added to which the versification is rich and musical, and many passages of considerable merit are scattered over it. The talents of Chapman nowhere appear to so great advantage." To one or two copies only was prefixed a sonnet to Sir Thomas Walsingham, in which Chapman says that "he was marked by age for aims of greater weight." As this sonnet, from its rarity, may be esteemed a literary curiosity, it is here inserted, through the kindness of my friend Mr. Payne Collier. It is printed verbatim.

TO MY LONG LOU'D AND HONOURABLE FRIEND,
SIR THOMAS WALSINGHAM, KNIGHT.

Should I expose to euery common eye,
   The least allow'd birth of my shaken braine;
And not entitle it perticulerly
   To your acceptance, I were wurse than vaine.
And though I am most loth to passe your sight
   with any such light marke of vanitie,
Being markt with Age for Aimes of greater weight,
   and drownd in darke Death-vshering melancholy,
Yet least by others stealth it be imprest,
   without my pasport, patcht with others wit,
Of two enforst ills I elect the least;
   and so desire your loue will censure it;
Though my old fortune keepe me still obscure,
   The light shall still bewray my ould loue sure.

* Vol. v. p. 316.

Mr. Collier* has also shewn that a very beautiful passage in the play is taken from an Italian Madrigal by Andrea Navagero, Venice, 1546. "*All Fools*" was reprinted in Dodsley's Collection, and in the "Ancient British Drama," Vol. II. 1810. In 1606, Chapman published two comedies, "*Monsieur D'Olive*," and "*The Gentleman Usher*," the former of which had been frequently acted with great success at the Blackfriars. It is one of his happier efforts; and has been reprinted in "Old Plays" vol. III. 1816. In 1607 appeared the first tragedy of "*Bussy d'Ambois.*" It had been frequently represented "at Paules." Though the most popular of Chapman's tragedies, it is on the whole but a poor performance. Dryden tells us, in the dedication to his "Spanish Fryer," he had resolved to burn a copy of it "annually to the memory of Jonson," as "a famous modern poet used to sacrifice every year a Statius to the manes of Virgil." It had pleased him however, at its representation, for he says, "I have sometimes wondered in the reading what was become of those glaring colours which amazed me in *Bussy d'Ambois* upon the theatre; but when I had taken up what I supposed a fallen star, I found I had been cozened with a jelly, &c." "*Bussy d'Ambois*" was reprinted in 4to. 1608, 1616, 1641, 1657; and was altered and revived by T. D'Urfey in 1691. It was also reprinted in "Old Plays," 1816. The following year (1608) produced "*The Conspiracie and Tragedie of Charles Duke of Byron, Marshall of France,*" acted in two plays, and dedicated to Sir Thomas Walsingham. These two plays, we are told, have not come down to us as they were originally written, in consequence of the remonstrance of the French Ambassador. (Collier's Shakespeare, vol. I. p. 218.) They are fine, and are styled by Mr. Collier "noble poems, full of fine thoughts, and rich in diversity and strength of expression." The Edinburgh Reviewer (*ut suprà*) calls the latter play "the finest tragic composition Chapman has left." "*Euthymiæ Raptus, or the Teares of Peace, with interlocutions,*" a small poem dedicated to Prince Henry, appeared in 1609, 4to. This work is chiefly interesting from the allu-

* Hist. of Dramatic Poetry, III. p. 257.

sion to Chapman's birth-place, and the spot where he translated Homer. In 1611 we have "*May Day*," a comedy, reprinted in "Old Plays;" and the "*Widow's Tears*," another comedy in 1612. This last play is very fine in parts, but the plot, taken from the story of the Ephesian matron in Petronius, is objectionable. But, while enumerating Chapman's dramatic efforts, we have omitted to mention that in 1609 appeared the long promised Twelve Books of the Iliad. Warton is in error in saying that *Fifteen Books* were printed in 1600 in a thin folio. Chapman had mentioned, in his Preface to the Seven Books of 1598, that his next issue should be of *Twelve Books;* and consequently appeared in this year (1609) a small thin folio, the title of which is "*Homer, Prince of Poets, translated according to the Greeke in Twelve Books of his Iliads, by George Chapman. At London, printed for Samuel Matcham.*" This work is printed in Italic type, and has (in a smaller size) the engraved title by William Hole, which was used in an enlarged form for the subsequent editions of the Complete Iliad, and the Whole Works, and a facsimile of which accompanies our present volumes. It contains the epistle Dedicatory to Prince Henry, the Poem to the Reader, and the Sonnet to Queen Anne. The version is the same as that of the edition of 1598, with the addition of the Third, Fourth, Fifth, Sixth, and Twelfth Books. The volume is closed with fourteen Sonnets. The date may be inferred from the following facts. In the Stationers' Register is the entry of the "Seven Bookes of Homer's Iliades, translated into English by George Chapman, to Samuel Matcham, by assignment from M[r] Windet, November 14, 1608." Now one of the Sonnets is addressed to the Earl of Salisbury, who is styled Lord Treasurer, which office was conferred on him on May 4, 1609. The volume, therefore, was published, probably, a little later in that year. Mr. Payne Collier possesses an interesting copy with Chapman's autograph. "*For Love to the true Love of Virtue in y[e] worthye Knighte, and his constant friende, S[r] Henrye Crofts: Geo. Chapman gives this as testimonie of his true inclination, wth this most affectionate inscription.*" The complete version of the Iliad appeared in 1611, and will be noticed hereafter. In 1612, Chapman published "*Petrarch's Seven Penitentiall Psalms, paraphrastically translated: with other philosophical poems, and a Hymne to Christ upon the Crosse,*" a small 12mo. dedicated to Sir Edward Philips, Master of the Rolls. This is a very rare volume, and the only copy I have seen (or even heard of) is in the Bodleian Library. From an examination of this little book, I find that I was misled in my information that Chapman speaks in it of his yet unfinished translation of Homer, which the Prince of Wales had commanded him to conclude. There is no mention whatever of his Homer.

In November 1612 died Henry Prince of Wales, and in him, to whom he had dedicated his "Iliad," Chapman lost his best patron. He deeply lamented the young prince, and published on the occasion "*An Epicede, or Funerall Song,*" 4to. 1614, dedicated to Mr. Henry Jones. It is a beautiful poem, and was reprinted at the Lee Priory Press, 4to. 1818. In the early part of 1613, he wrote the poetry for the masque performed at Whitehall by the Societies of Lincoln's Inn and the Middle Temple, in honour of the nuptials of the Princess Elizabeth and the Palsgrave. Inigo Jones designed the machinery. The magnificence displayed by these learned Societies may be estimated from the fact that, according to Dugdale, the expenses incurred amounted to the then enormous sum of £1086 8s. 11d. Ben Jonson told Drummond that, "next himself (i. e. Jonson) only Fletcher and Chapman could make a mask." Chapman published this mask (4to. 1614), and dedicated it to Sir Edward Philips, Master of the Rolls, from whose house the masquers proceeded to Whitehall. At the close of the volume is an Epithalamium. Mr. Payne Collier is in possession of a copy corrected by Chapman in his own handwriting. It has been reprinted in Nichols' Progresses of K. James I. In this year (1613) he printed his tragedy of "*Bussy d'Ambois his Revenge.*" In 1614 appeared "*Andromeda Liberata, or the Nuptials of Perseus and Andromeda,*" a poem with a long dedicatory epistle to Robert Carr, Earl of Somerset, and Frances his Countess. According to Wood, "this being not rightly understood, and carped at by many, came out soon after a pamphlet written in prose and poetry, entitled, '*A free and offenceless justification of a late published and most maliciously misinterpreted Poem, &c.* London 1614,' 4to. in two sheets, pen'd I presume by Chapman." We may readily suppose that a dedication to such persons would be cavilled at, but Chapman (as is generally the case in his Prefaces) had anticipated objections, and had therefore addressed one preface of this work to "the prejudicate and peremptory reader," to whom he says, "'twill be most ridiculous and pleasing, to sit in a corner, and spend your teeth to the stumps in mumbling an old sparrow till your lips bleed and your eyes water : when all the faults you can find are first in yourselves, 'tis no Herculean labour to cracke what you breede." According to Mr. Payne Collier, Somerset himself had conceived that "*Andromeda Liberata*" was a covert attack upon him, and from this notion Chapman was anxious to relieve himself. It does not appear when Carr became Chapman's patron, but in the early part of this year (1614) appeared the first Twelve Books of the Odyssey also dedicated to him. It is to be feared Chapman was suffering under the pressure of poverty at this period, for in this Dedication he says :—

> "Twelve labours of your Thespian Hercules
> I now present your Lordship ; *do but please*
> *To lend life means*, till th' other twelve receive
> Equal achievement."

Somerset's patronage of Chapman, whatever it may have been, met with no unworthy return : for the distressed poet of 1614, when the royal favourite was still basking in the declining sunshine of his career, did not forget him when that sun had set. On November 2, 1614, is an entry in the Stationers' Register to Nathaniel Butter of "Twenty-four Bookes of Homer's Odisses by George Chapman," and the complete translation appeared with the old dedication. Besides which, some years after, when the Earl was living in obscurity, the Hymns and Batrachomyomachia are inscribed to him in a noble strain, which reflects great credit on Chapman's goodness of heart, however we may lament the unworthiness of the subject of his panegyric. In this same year (1614) also appeared "*Eugenia; or True Nobilitie's Trance, For the memorable death of the thrice noble and religious William Lord Russel, &c. Divided into foure vigils of the nighte.*" 4to. pp. 44, not numbered. (See Brydges' "Restituta," vol. II. p. 57.)

In 1616 he published his *Translation of Musæus*. He informs us in the Preface that it is a different work to the continuation of Marlowe's poem. This extremely rare volume, not two inches long and scarcely one broad, is fully described by Dr. Bliss in vol. II. col. 9, of his admirable edition of Wood's "Athenæ Oxonienses." The only known copy is in the Bodleian. It is dedicated to his "Auncient poore frierde" Inigo Jones. I had the great gratification of reprinting it in the ifth volume of the present edition of Chapman's Translations. In 1616 he also published the Iliad and Odyssey collected into one volume, which will be noticed hereafter. "*The Georgics of Hesiod, transated elaborately out of the Greek*," appeared in a thin 4to. London, 1618. This volume is so rare that Warton was not aware of its existence. It is amusing to see how pertinaciously he refused to believe that it had been printed, although he discovered its entry in the Stationers' Registers (Hist. English Poetry, III. 360. ed. 1840). Elton, who, from his own noble version of Hesiod, was a competent judge, pronounces it "close, vigorous, and elegant." (Habington's "Casara," p. 155. ed. Elton, Bristol, 1812.) It has commendatory verses by Ben Jonson and Drayton, and is dedicated to Sir Francis Bacon, Lord Chancellor, who had been a student of Gray's Inn, which gave Chapman the opportunity of punning : "All judgments of this season (savouring anything the truth) preferring to the wisdom of all other nations these most wise, learned, and circularly-spoken Grecians; according to that of the poet

GRAIIS INGENIUM, GRAIIS DEDIT ORE ROTUNDO
MUSA LOQUI.

And why may not this Romane elogie of the Graians extend in praise-full intention (by waie of prophetick poesie) to *Graies-Inne* wits and orators?" From the extreme rarity of Chapman's Hesiod,* its price is usually great. It has been reprinted, however, in our fifth volume above mentioned, with a facsimile of the original title.

In 1619 was printed "*Two Wise Men, and all the rest Fooies,*" a comedy, or as the title styles it, "A Comical Moral, censuring the Follies of this Age." There is a peculiarity about this play, if it may be so called, which is remarkable. It is extended to *seven* acts, instead of five. "It is, however, on tradition only that this piece is ranked among Chapman's writings; it being published without any author's name, or even so much as a mention of the place where it was printed." (Biograph. Dramat.) In 1622 we have a small poem, "*Pro Vere Autumni Lachrymæ*" to the memory of Sir Horatio Vere. In 1629 appeared "*A justification of a strange actioi of Nero in burying with a solemne Funerall one of the cast hayres of his Mistress Poppæa; also a just reproofe of a Roman Smellfeast, being the fifth Satyre of Juvenall.*" The version of Juvenal is spirited, and will be found reprinted in our above-mentioned fifth volume. At what time he published "*The Crowne of all Homers Workes; Batraclomyomachia; or the Battaile of Frogs and Mise. Translated according to the originall by George Chapman. London. Printed by John Bill, his Maiesties Printer,*" cannot now be precisely determined. Mr. Singer (who printed an elegant edition of it in 1818, Chiswick) says it would seem to have been after 1624, by comparing it with other books by the same printer. The volume, a thin folio, very rare, containing also the Hymns of Homer, will be noticed hereafter. In 1631, Chapman printed "*Cæsar and Pompey, a Roman Tragedy, concerning their Warres. Out of whose events is evicted this Proposi-*

---

* There are two copies in the Bodleian Library; that in the Malone Collection being large, though somewhat stained. There is also a fair one in the General Library of the British Museum. That in the Grenville has been much injured (as has my own) by the binder cutting into the notes, which are in the margin.

tion: Only a just Man is a free Man." This play is dedicated to the Earl of Middlesex, and does not seem to have been intended for the stage.* This was the last of Chapman's works that appeared in his lifetime.

"At length," says old Anthony Wood, "this most eminent and reverend poet, having lived 77 years† in this vain and transitory world, made his last exit in the Parish of St. Giles' in the Fields, near London, on the twelfth day of May, in sixteen hundred and thirty four, and was buried in the yard on the south side of the Church of St. Giles. Soon after was a monument erected over his grave, built after the way of the old Romans, by the care and charge of his most beloved friend Inigo Jones; whereon is engraven, Georgius Chapmanus, poeta Homericus, Philosophus verus (etsi Christianus poeta) plusquam celebris, &c." Le Neve also gives us the inscription on the monument: "D.O.M. Here lyes George Chapman, a Christian Philosopher and Homericall Poett; he liv'd 77 yeeres, and died ye 12 of May 1634, for whose worth and memory to posterity, Inigo Jones Architect to the King, for antient friendshipp made this." Le Neve's information was from Peter Le Neve's (Norroy's) MSS. Mislead by a letter from "Myrtilla Giovestring" to Sylvanus Urban in 1737 (Gentleman's Magazine vol. VII.), and by the assertion of Sir Egerton Brydges, in the first edition I stated that this monument was destroyed with the old church. It is, however, still standing on the south side of the present church, and the inscription, which had been effaced by time, was recut under the direction of the rector (the Rev. J. Endell Tyler, ὁ μακαρίτης)

---

* In the Biograph. Dram. "Cæsar and Pompey" is said to have been published in 4to. 1607, and to have been acted at the Blackfriars. This is probably a mistake.

† Wood erroneously says Chapman was born in 1557. If the date of his death be true, he was only 75. The Rev. A. W. Thorold, the present Rector of St. Giles' in the Fields, informs me that there is no Register of the Burials in that Parish between the years 1610 and 1637, so here again we are baffled in verifying a fact by the loss of records, a fatality which has attended all my enquiries into Chapman's life.

and churchwardens some years since. The present inscription does not tally with that recorded by Wood and Le Neve, and if their account be true, contains a strange anachronism.*

> GEORGIVS CHAPMAN
> POETA
> MDCXX (sic)
> IGNATIVS JONES
> ARCHITECTVS REGIVS
> OB HONOREM
> BONARVM LITERARVM
> FAMILIARI
> SVO HOC MON.
> D. S. P. F. C.

The monument is a small upright stone, similar to many Roman monumental remains. Habington, who published his "Castara" in the year of Chapman's death, has the following lines (p. 155. ed. Elton):—

> "Tis true that Chapman's reverend ashes must
> Lye rudely mingled with the vulgar dust,
> 'Cause carefull heyers the wealthy only have,
> To build a glorious trouble o're the grave.
> Yet doe I not despaire some one may be
> So seriously devout to poesie,
> As to translate his reliques, and find roome
> In the warme church to build him up a tombe,
> Since Spenser hath a stone, &c."

Habington's pious wish, we are sure, will find an echo in many a breast. The great Translator of Homer deserves a record in the aisles of Westminster, as his respectable character forms a happy contrast to many less-deserving recipients of that honour.

After Chapman's death appeared, in 1639, "*The Tragedy of Chabot, Admiral of France*," written conjointly with Shirley. The reviewer of Mr. Dyce's edition of Shirley's works (Quarterly Review,

---

* In a late examination of the monument, I find that the stone slab, upon which the inscription is cut, is a late insertion, so probably the above is not a copy of the original inscription.

vol. XLIX. p. 29) says: "In the fine and eloquent tragedy of Chabot, the obscurity of Chapman's manner, the hardness of which his contemporaries call his 'full and heightened style,' is greatly increased by the incorrectness of the press.* This play, as bearing the name of Shirley in its title-page conjoined with that of Chapman, ought not to have been omitted; yet it is very difficult to assign any part of it to Shirley; even the comic scenes are more in Chapman's close and pregnant manner, than in the light and airy style of Shirley." In the same year (1639) was published "*The Ball,*" a comedy, by Chapman and Shirley. "*Revenge for Honour,*" a tragedy, by Chapman alone, was published in 1654, 1659, 4to.; and in the same year "*The Tragedy of Alphonsus, Emperor of Germany.*" Dr. Bliss mentions five plays in MS. which were in the library of the late Richard Heber, Esq., "*The Fountain of New Fashions,*" 1598; "*The Will of a Woman,*" 1598; "*The Fatal Love,*" a tragedy; "*Tragedy of a Yorkshire Gentleman;*" and "*The Second Maiden's Tragedy.*" This last was published as No. I. of "*The Old English Drama,*" London, 1825. From the same authority (and from Sir Egerton Brydges' "Restituta") we are informed that there are poems by Chapman in "*Poetical Essays on the Turtle and Phœnix,*" published, with others on the same subject, by Shakespeare, Jonson, and Marston, at the end of "*Love's Martyr, or Rosalind's Complaint,*" 4to. 1601; a volume of exquisite rarity.

Such are the few details of Chapman's long and laborious life, consisting, after all, of a mere catalogue of his works—and what do we know more of many of his great contemporaries? The editions of his Homer will be considered by themselves. From the writings of his contemporaries, and from the gossip of Antony Wood, as well as from incidental allusions in his own works, we are enabled to gather a few unconnected circumstances, which only make us desire to know more of him. As a dramatic writer, he has been frequently criticised, and

---

* This remark applies equally to the original editions of his Homer, Hesiod, and all his works.

cannot be placed in the foremost rank. But we should not forget he was one of the earliest purveyors for the public taste. His style, in his original works, is intensely crabbed and confused, yet "as a poetical imaginer and thinker, far too little attention has been paid to him." (Edinb. Rev. vol. LXXII. p. 226.) Even as a writer for the stage, he attained great popularity in his day. The writings of his contemporaries are full of allusions to him. He is much quoted in "*England's Parnassus,*" by R. Allott, 12mo. 1600. In Thomas Freeman's Epigrams (4to. 1616, Pt. 2nd, Epig. 87) is the following:—

"TO GEORGE CHAPMAN.

George, it is thy genius innated,
Thou pick'st not flowers from another's field,
Stol'n similes, or sentences translated,
Nor seekest but what thine owne soile doth yielde:
Let barren wits go borrow what to write,
'Tis bred and born with thee what thou inditest,
And our Comedians thou outstrippest quite,
And all the hearers more than all delightest,
With unaffected style and sweetest strain.
Thy inambitious pen keeps on her pace,
And cometh near'st the ancient comic vein.
Thou hast beguil'd us all of that sweet grace;
And were Thalia to be sold and bought,
No *Chapman* but thyself were to be sought."

The following verses too, cited by Mr. Singer from "*The Scourge of Folly, by John Davies of Hereford,*" supposed to be printed about the year 1611, contain pleasing testimony to the estimation in which he was held, and also evidence of his straitened circumstances; but, if the date of the book be correct, both his patrons could then have assisted him, as the death of Prince Henry did not occur till the close of the following year, and Somerset was then in the zenith of favour.

"TO MY HIGHLY VALUED MR. GEORGE CHAPMAN, FATHER OF OUR ENGLISH POETS.

"I know thee not, good George, but by thy pen,
For which I rank thee with the rarest men.
And in that rank I put thee in the front,
Especially of Poets of account,

INTRODUCTION.

>Who art the treasurer of that company,
>But in thy hand too little coin doth lie.
>For of all arts that now in London are,
>Poets get least in uttering their ware.
>But thou hast in thy head and heart and hand
>Treasures of art that treasures can command.
>Ah! would they could! then should thy wealth and wit
>Be equal; and a lofty fortune fit.
>But, George, thou wert accurst, and so was I,
>To be of that most blessed company.
>For if the most are blest that most are crost,
>Then Poets, I am sure, are blessed most.
>Yet we with rhyme and reason trim the times,
>Though they give little reason for our rhymes.
>The reason is (else error blinds my wits)
>They reason want to do what honour fits.
>But let them do as please them, we must do
>What Phœbus, sire of Art, moves Nature to."

It is to his Homer, however, we must look for his greatest reputation. Immediately on the publication of his "*Seven Books*," in 1598, were his praises resounded. In Fitz-Geffrey's "*Affaniæ*," Oxon, 1601, p. 88, are two Epigrams, "*Ad Homerum e Græciâ in Britanniam a Georgio Chapmanno traductum;*" and in "*The Passionate Poet; with a description of the Thracian Ismarus.*" By T. P. (Thomas Powell) we read—

>"Out on thee, foole! blind of thy impotence,
>Thou dost admire but in a popular sense,
>Esteeming more a Pasquil's harsher lines
>Than Iliad's worth, which Chapman's hand refines."

(See Brydges' "Restituta," vol. iii. p. 169). Bolton, in his "*Hypercritica*" (p. 246, ed. Haslewood), mentions Chapman's "first seaven bookes of Iliades" amongst good writers of English style; and again (p. 250) he says, "brave language are Chapman's Iliades, those I mean which are translated into tessara-decasyllabons, or lines of fourteen syllables." Ben Jonson, Drayton, William Browne, and others, contributed their testimonies; and Samuel Sheppard, in his "*Six Bookes of Epigrams*," London, 1651, 12mo., has one which we will transcribe :—

"ON MR. CHAPMAN'S INCOMPARABLE TRANSLATION OF HOMER'S WORKES.

What none before durst ever venture on
Unto our wonder is by Chapman done,
Who by his skill hath made Great Homer's song
To vaile its bonnet to our English tongue,
So that the learned well may question it
Whether in Greek or English Homer writ?
O happy Homer, such an able pen
To have for thy translator, happier then
Ovid * or Virgil,† who beyond their strength
Are stretch'd, each sentence neare a mile in length.
But our renowned Chapman, worthy praise,
And meriting the never-blasted bayes,
Hath render'd Homer in a genuine sence,
Yea, and hath added to his eloquence:
And in his comments his true sence doth show.
Telling Spondanus what he ought to know.
Eustathius, and all that on them take
Great Homer's misticke meaning plain to make,
Yeeld him more dark with farr-fetcht allegories,
Sometimes mistaking clean his learned stories :
As 'bout the flie Menelaus did inspire,
Juno's retreate, Achilles' strange desire ;
But he to his own sence doth him restore,
And comments on him better than before
Any could do, for which (with Homer) wee
Will yeeld all honour to his memory."

But it is needless to multiply quotations. Chapman's personal character stood very high. Antony Wood describes him as "a person of most reverend aspect, religious and temperate, qualities rarely meeting in a poet." Oldys in his MS. notes on Langbaine's Dramatic Poets (British Museum) says, "Indeed his head was a poetical Treasury, Magazine, or Chronicle, of whatsoever was memorable amongst the poets of his time, which made him latterly much resorted to by young gentlemen of good taste and education. But he was choice of his company, shy of loose, shallow, and sordid associates, and preserved in his own conduct the true dignity of Poetry, which he compared to the Flower of the Sun, that disdains to open its leaves to the eye of a smoking taper."

    * By Golding.   † By Phaier.

Wood thinks he had some small appointment in the household of King James, or his consort Queen Anne; but researches in the State Paper Office and other sources have failed to throw any light on this point. With all the respect and admiration that Chapman enjoyed from his contemporaries, it is clear, from many passages in his writings, that he could not escape the breath of envy. In the Preface to Homer we find the following: "But there is a certain envious windsucker, that hovers up and down, laboriously engrossing all the air with his luxurious ambition; and buzzing into every ear my detraction, affirming I turn Homer out of the Latin only, &c. I have stricken, single him as you can." It is generally supposed that this allusion is to Ben Jonson. Mr. Gifford of course zealously defends Jonson, and with great show of reason. It is certain that if Jonson and Chapman had quarrelled at this period (1611) they were subsequently on terms again in 1618, for Jonson wrote the following commendatory verses in the translation of "Hesiod," published in that year:—

> "If all the vulgar tongues, that speak this day,
> Were ask'd of thy discoveries, they must say
> To the Greek coast thine only knew the way.
>
> Such passage hast thou found, such returns made,
> As now of all men it is call'd thy trade,
> And who make thither else rob, or invade."

Jonson in his conversations with Drummond declared that "he *loved* Chapman!" It cannot however be denied that Jonson was generally reputed to be envious of his successful contemporaries, and there is a tradition that Chapman was one of those marked out for his special envy. That there had been a quarrel at some period between him and Chapman is evident from some lines by the latter cited by Mr. Gifford from a MS. in the Ashmole Collection, with the following title, "*An Invective against Ben Jonson by Mr. George Chapman.*"

> "Greate-learned wittie Ben, be pleased to light
> The world with that three-forked fire; nor fright
> All us, the sublearn'd, with Luciferus' boast
> That thou art most great, learn'd, of all the earth

> As being a thing betwixt a humane birth
> And an infernal; no humanitye
> Of the divine soule shewing man in thee, &c."

"Chapman," adds Mr. Gifford, "(whom I am unwilling to believe guilty of this malicious trash) died, I fear, poor and neglected." In another poem among the Ashmole Papers, inscribed "The Genius of the Stage deploring the death of Ben Jonson," after noticing the general sorrow, the writer says:—

> —— "Why do Apollo's sons
> Meet in such throngs, and whisper as they go?
> There are no more by sad affliction hurl'd,
> And friends' neglect, from this inconstant world!
> *Chapman* alone went so; he that's now gone
> Commands him tomb; he, scarce a grave or stone."

This does not, however, agree with the fact of Inigo Jones placing a monument "built after the way of the old Romans" over his friend. With the exception of the "envious windsucker" (whoever he may have been) it has been seen that Chapman was universally esteemed by his contemporaries, and he well deserved it, not only for the fame of his talents, but from the admirable character Wood and Langbaine have given of him, a character which seems borne out by Drayton, who speaks of him

> "As *reverend* Chapman, who hath brought to us
> Musæus, Homer, and Hesiodus."

I trust that this fact may give additional pleasure to the reader as he peruses "Old George's" fine Translations.

But I cannot conclude without citing a rather unexpected testimony to the fame of "mine ancient friend," praise which, I am sure, amply repays him for the envy of that "castrill, with too hot a liver and lust after his own glory, who, to devour all himself, discourageth all appetites to the fame of another." Mr. Ralph Waldo Emerson, the well-known American writer, during the past year* (1856) published a work

---

* This Introduction was originally written in 1857.

entitled "English Traits," in which the merits and failings of this our native country are freely discussed.

In p. 26, under the Chapter on "*Race*," I find the following—"How came such men as King Alfred and Roger Bacon, William of Wykeham, Walter Raleigh, Philip Sydney, Isaac Newton, William Shakespeare, GEORGE CHAPMAN, Francis Bacon, George Herbert, Henry Vane, to exist here?" Reader, little did I think to introduce Master Chapman to you in such company, but there he is walking arm in arm with Shakespeare and Bacon! Mr. Emerson asks of these great men "what food they ate, what nursing, school, and exercises they had, which resulted in this mother-wit, delicacy of thought, and robust wisdom?" Alas! poor George's "robust wisdom," as we have seen, was not produced by quantity or quality of food. Again, in p. 144, we have a criticism on English Poetry—"Pope and his school wrote poetry fit to put round frosted cake. What did Walter Scott write without stint?—a rhymed traveller's guide to Scotland. And the libraries of verses they print have this Birmingham character. How many volumes of well-bred metre we must jingle through before we can be filled, taught, renewed! We want the miraculous; the beauty which we can manufacture at no mill—can give no account of; the beauty of which Chaucer and CHAPMAN had the secret!" O! reverend Chapman, full well did thy prophetic spirit foresee this two-fold tribute of "brother Jonathan" when thou didst put on the title of "Homer's Odysseys,"

AT MIHI QUOD VIVO DETRAXERIT INVIDA TURBA,
POST OBITUM DUPLICI FŒNORE REDDET HONOS.

It only remains for us to give an account of Chapman's various Translations of Homer.

Though Chapman claims the merit of being the first who gave an original and complete version of Homer, he had been anticipated in the honour of introducing him to the English reader. In 1581 Ten Books of the Iliad were translated from the French metrical version of

INTRODUCTION.

M. Salel (1555) by A. H. or Arthur Hall, Esq. of Grantham, and a Member of Parliament, and printed by Ralph Newberie at London. It is in the fourteen-syllable metre; and, in the Dedication to Sir Thomas Cecil, Hall compliments the distinguished translators of the day, Phaier, Golding, and others. He mentions that he began the work about 1563, under the advice of Roger Ascham. It is a small 4to. in black letter, and exceedingly rare.

Chapman's first essay towards his version was in 1598, when he printed "*Seaven Bookes of the Iliades of Homere, &c.*" 4to. "*printed by John Windet, and are to be sold at the signe of the Cross Keyes neare Paules Wharffe.*" This volume has already been described above (p. xxviii). It rarely occurs for sale. Mr. Joseph Lilley, of New Street, Covent Garden, in his interesting catalogue of 1863, marks a copy, bound in olive morocco by C. Lewis, at £7 7s. "*Achilles' Shield, translated as the other Seven Bookes of Homer, out of his Eighteenth booke of Iliades. By George Chapman, Gent.*" 4to. 1598, also printed by Windet. This small and rare volume has also been described above. The version is in the ordinary ten-syllable metre. "*Homer, Prince of Poets, translated according to the Greeke in Twelve Books of his Iliads, by George Chapman. At London, printed for Samuel Matcham,*" folio. It has been shewn (p. xxxvi) that this small folio must have been published in 1609, as Windet transferred to Matcham the copyright of the Seven Books on November 14, 1608, and one of the Sonnets in the folio is addressed to Lord Treasurer Salisbury, which office was conferred on him May 4, 1609. It is a rare volume. Mr. Payne Collier's copy with Chapman's autograph has already been described.

The complete version of the Iliad appeared without date, "printed for Nathaniell Butter," but from an entry in the Stationers' Books, and internal evidence, it must have been published in 1611, or early in 1612. The entry in the Stationers' Registers is "*Nathl Butter, April 8, 1611. A booke called Homer's Iliades in Englishe, containing 24 Bookes.*" Chapman tells us, in the Commentary on the

First Book, that he had entirely rewritten the two first Books, but had left the viith, viiith, ixth, and xth untouched. I do not find much correction, except a few verbal alterations, in the others. He mentions that he had translated the last twelve in less than fifteen weeks, and considers these the best portion of his work. To this edition he added the Prose Preface to the Reader, and the Commentaries on various Books, to obviate the accusation that had been made against him that he did not translate direct from the original Greek, but through the medium of the Latin. These Commentaries do not tend to raise the estimate of his scholarship; yet I think it evident from his version that he really did understand and thoroughly feel the Greek. Three of the Sonnets (those to the Lady Arabella, who had fallen into disgrace in 1609, to the Lord Wotton, and to Lord Arundel) were withdrawn, and five newly added. The volume (though not mentioned in the title) was printed by Richard Field, and is upon a fine paper, with good clear type, and very antiquated orthography. This is the *first folio* so often mentioned in the following pages. The fine engraved title, by William Hole, was the same as that of the folio of 1609, on an enlarged scale.

The Twelve First Books of the Odyssey appeared in 1614, with a dedication to Carr, Earl of Somerset. It is a thin folio. In the Douce Collection is a copy with Chapman's autograph: "*For my righte worthie Knighte, my exceeding noble friende, Sir Henry Fanshawe. A pore Homericall new yeare's gift.*" At the end of the Twelfth Book is "Finis duodecimi libri Hom. Odyss. Opus novem dierum. Σὺν Θεῷ." I can hardly imagine that Chapman meant by this that he had translated the Twelve Books in *nine days;* which would be incredible, and as Coleridge observes (in a MS. note to his copy mentioned below) would "indeed be a nine days' wonder," but probably the poet meant that the last book was the work of nine days. Chapman, however, in the Douce copy has run his pen through the words. The remaining Twelve Books were finished in the same year, and published probably in 1615, as the entry in the Stationers'

Register is "*November* 2. 1614 *Twenty - four Bookes of Homer's Odisses by George Chapman to Nathaniell Butter.*" When the last twelve Books were printed they were united with the previous twelve, a blank page being inserted between them, and the pagination was continued to give the volume the appearance of being printed at one and the same time. There is an observable difference, however, which we have preserved in our edition; the conclusions of the first twelve books are in Latin, while those of the latter part of the volume are in English. I presume the complete volume of the Odyssey appeared in a separate form, although I have never met with a copy which was not united with the Iliad, to form "The Whole Works of Homer, &c."

The engraved title to the Odyssey, reproduced in our edition, is very rare. To some copies a printed title is given. Coleridge, in his letter to Wordsworth (*supra*, p. xvi.) thought Chapman's version of the Odyssey finer than his Iliad; but then it must be remembered he also generally preferred the Odyssey in the original. "He told us," says Mr. Payne Collier, "that he liked the Odyssey, as a mere story, better than the Iliad; the Odyssey was the oldest and the finest romance that has ever been written." * The same authority informs us that he preferred the ordinary ten-syllable heroic measure to the longer fourteen-syllable line, employed by Chapman in his translation of the Iliad, and wished that he had always used it, as "it would have been more readable, and might have saved us from Pope." "Chapman had failed," added Coleridge, "where he had not succeeded, by endeavouring to write English as Homer had written Greek; Chapman's was Greekified English,—it did not want vigour or variety, but smoothness and facility. Detached passages could not be improved; they were Homer writing English." The late Dr. Maginn, whose Homeric Ballads have caught the true spirit of the old bard, says: "I am sorry that Chapman, *whose version must be considered the most Homeric ever attempted in our language,* did not apply to the Odyssey

---

* Coleridge's "Seven Lectures on Shakespeare and Milton," by J. Payne Collier, Esq. p. xxxi.

INTRODUCTION. liii

the fourteen-syllable verse, which had succeeded so well in the Iliad. There appears to me greater opportunity for its flowing use in the more discursive poem; and Chapman had by no means the same command of the ten-syllable distich." There is some truth in this; and perhaps many readers will share in Dr. Maginn's disappointment. Chapman, however, probably yielded to the objections made against the length of his lines, to which he alludes in his Introductory Poem to the Iliad. But it is surely a mistake to say he had not command over the ordinary heroic couplet! He has certainly not the epigrammatic smoothness of Pope and his school, but his verse has great vigour and terseness. It should be borne in mind that his Odyssey is the first and only considerable specimen of a poem of this measure in the Elizabethan age, and as such claims our interest and attention. "It is like the heroic measure only in its rhyme and its number of syllables. In all other respects, in the hands of Chapman, it has the freedom of blank verse. And in reading it, as well as the Iliad, the reader must not depend for aid too much on the melody of the verse."* Again, let it be remembered that "Chapman did not perform his task, as Pope was in the habit of doing, by small portions at a time, which were, each in order, burnished up to the highest polish by unremitting care and labour; but drinking in deep draughts of his author at a time, he became over-informed with his subject, and then breathed his spirit forth again with the enthusiasm of an original creator."† And if this be true of the liberties he takes with his original in expanding and contracting the text as suited his vein, it is not less true of his versification. He paid little regard to the polishing of his work; nay, perhaps, too little. He poured forth his sentiments as the poetic phrenzy seized him, and consequently, if we be disappointed at not finding the rich melody of a Dryden, we cannot but be struck with his unwonted freshness and freedom. When once the ear has become habituated to the rhythm, there is a dramatic power about Chapman's Odyssey that has never been attained by any subsequent translator. It may be said that this was

* Retrospective Review, vol. iii. p. 184.   † Ibid. p. 173.

not required in a simple ballad-poem like the Odyssey; but it is surely far preferable to the diluted weakness passing under Pope's name, or Cowper's abrupt lines. Gilbert Wakefield has said that "the bee of Twickenham" sipped the honey from the flowers of Chapman's garden; but a close examination will show that this was merely another phrase for simple plagiarism. Pope was indebted to Chapman for more than he was willing to acknowledge. It must not be disguised, however, that in his version of the Odyssey, Chapman has too frequently wandered from his original, and not seldom curtailed passages.

In 1616 the Iliad and Odyssey were united in one volume. The Title-page by Hole, which had previously served for the edition of the Iliad, was altered to *The Whole Works of Homer,* &c. as accompanies this our edition. At the back of the title was affixed the fine portrait of Chapman, and another engraved plate (which was not worth reproducing) was added, "To the immortall memorye of Henrye Prince of Wales, &c." In some copies of "The Whole Works," the Iliad is found of a later impression. The paper is thin and poor, the type bleared and inelegant, and the orthography somewhat modernized; it is, moreover, disfigured by many misprints; judging from the general appearance of the volume, it is considerably later in date than 1616.* I have never yet met with a copy which was separate from the Odyssey. This Edition, if I may so term it, differs in some few places from the first complete Iliad. I have called it in the following pages the *second folio.* I hazard the conjecture that it may have been printed to bind up with the surplus copies of the Odyssey, as the Iliad had been in circulation for the five preceding years. Dr. Cooke Taylor printed from this copy, but whether he was aware that it differed from the first folio is uncertain; he simply says he had adopted the "*third Edition,*" in which were many valuable corrections." The two folios have been most accurately collated, and the chief variations noted by me, and the reader will judge of the

* A writer in the "Gentleman's Magazine," vol. lvii. p. 300, states, I know not upon what authority, that "Chapman's translation of Homer was likewise published 1620." He does not mention what portion of Homer; probably it was the folio of the Hymns.

INTRODUCTION.

value of this third impression. I must apologize for using the terms *first* and *second folios*, but could not well apply the word *Edition*, as I refer solely to the *complete* version, there having been two previous editions of portions of the Iliad. The folios may be easily distinguished, from their general appearance; and from the vignettes or headings to the books, those of Richard Field's (or the best copy) being cornucopiæ of flowers, &c. while the inferior impression has a sort of Gothic ornament. The Grenville copy, in the British Museum, is the *second folio*, while that in the General Library is of the first impression. The portrait of Chapman is usually affixed to the back of the title of the "Whole Works of Homer," &c. but this is not always the case. At first I suspected that the copies of Chapman's Homer were corrected as the press was kept standing (as is well known to have been the case with early-printed books) as there are several minute differences, and that the portrait was added to the later worked-off copies; on second consideration, however, I am of opinion that there was no new impression of either the Iliad or Odyssey in 1616 (the date of the portrait), but the editions of the Iliad, 1611, and the Odyssey, 1614-15, were bound up in one volume with a new and general title. The titles without the portrait are far rarer than those with it.

In the Heber Catalogue, part iv. lot 1445, was a copy of the Iliad. It had belonged to George Steevens, and was bought at Heber's sale by the late Mr. Rodd. Park, in a note to vol. iii. of Warton's History of English Poetry, p. 358 (ed. 1840), says that "Chapman's own copy of his translation of Homer, *corrected by him throughout for a future edition*, was purchased for five shillings from the shop of Edwards by Mr. Steevens, and at the sale of his books in 1800 was transferred to the invaluable library of Mr. Heber." This is, however, not quite correct; I have traced the volume, and it is now in the magnificent library of Robert Holford, Esq. M.P. of Dorchester House; it is a fine volume of the Iliad of 1611, in red morocco of the period. At the back of the title is in Chapman's autograph, "*In witness of his best love so borne to his best deserving friende M^r. Henrye Jones:*

George Chapman gives him theise fruites of his best labors, and desires love betwixt us as long-lived as Homer." The corrections are merely three or four in the Preface, which may be here specified. In page lxxxvi of this present edition, lines 6, 7, the words "*how could they differ far from*, and be combined with eternity" are pasted over, and "how could they *defie fire, iron*, and &c." substituted in a printed slip. In p. xc, line 13, " to cast any rubs or *plasters*," Chapman has run his pen through this word and substituted *plashes*. In the same page, in the last line, " and therefore may my poor self put up *with* motion," is corrected to "*without* motion." In book VIII, line 437,

" And all did *wilfully* expect the silver-throned morn."

George Steevens remarks that the 4to. of 1598 reads "*wishfully*," a variation which we have adopted. Thus we see upon what slight grounds Mr. Park asserted that it was "Chapman's own copy, *corrected by him throughout* for a future edition!" The volume has three additional Sonnets (see "Sonnets" at the end of vol. ii. of this edition). Though this is a fine volume, it is not unique; I was fortunate enough to purchase a similar copy (though not in morocco), with the same corrections in the Preface and the additional Sonnets, but without Chapman's presentation autograph. Mr. Aldis Wright informs me that there is a copy in the library of Trinity College, Cambridge, with the corrections in the Preface entirely in MS. (i.e. without the printed slip, "*defie fire, iron*," &c.) and with the three Sonnets. When this Introduction was originally written Pope's copy of the Iliad was in the possession of my friend, the late Rev. John Mitford ; it was a most interesting volume, having Pope's autograph, "Ex libris Alexandri Popei, Pret. 3s." and marked in the margins by him. It subsequently belonged to Bishop Warburton, who gave it to Thomas Warton. It was shown to me lately by Mr. Joseph Lilly, who marked it at the very moderate price of £16 16s. Mr. Lilly also showed me, marked at £15 15s. the identical copy of the Whole Works—Iliad, Odyssey, and Hymns,—which Coleridge sent to Wordsworth, and which I have mentioned in this Introduction; it was full of Coleridge's MS. Notes. Surely such precious volumes ought to be deposited in the British Museum, or in one of our University Libraries.

Having completed the Iliad and Odyssey, Chapman seems to have been determined to translate every possible or probable portion of Homer. Hence he published, "*The Crowne of all Homer's Workes, Batrachomyomachia; or, the Battaile of Frogs and Mise. His Hymnes and Epigrams. Translated according to the Originall, by George Chapman. London: Printed by John Bill, his Maiestie's Printer.*" * This very rare volume is a thin folio; it has an exquisitely engraved title, by William Pass, which is very spirited, and called forth Coleridge's admiration.† Of this folio a singularly large copy is in the Archiepiscopal Library at Lambeth; the finest I have seen.

Messrs. Boone of Bond Street, whose collection of fine books is as well known as the liberality with which they communicate information on them, have permitted me to transcribe a dedication, in Chapman's autograph, from a beautiful copy in their possession (since sold). It is as follows:—"*In love & honor of ye Righte virtuouse and worthie Gent: Mr Henry Reynolds, and to crowne all his deservings with eternall memorie, Geo. Chapman formes this Crowne conclusion of all the Homericall meritts wth his accomplisht Improvements; advising that if at first sighte he seeme darcke or too fierie, He will yet holde him fast (like Proteus) till he appere in his propper similitude, and he will then shewe himselfe*

*—vatem egregium, cui non sit publica vena,
Qui nihil expositum soleat deducere; nec qui
Communi feriat carmen triviale monctâ.*" ‡

Chapman has with his pen made an alteration in his portrait, as possessing too much beard; and in the Preface, in the passage "all for

---

* He considers it his destiny,—
    "The work that I was born to do is done."
† It is reproduced in our fifth volume.
‡ Juvenal, Sat. VII. 53.

lviii   *INTRODUCTION.*

devouring a mouse," he writes *drowning;* and in the final Poem (line 17) for

<blockquote>All is extuberance and *exertion* all,</blockquote>

he reads "and *tumor* all."

The date of the folio is probably about 1624. In the year 1818, my friend the late Mr. Singer published an elegant edition of these Hymns, &c. at Chiswick. It contained two fine original poems by Chapman (first printed 1594) entitled "*The Shadowe of Night: containing two poetical hymnes, devised by G. C. Gent.*" It formed one of Mr. Singer's series of "Select Early English Poets," and has long since been numbered amongst scarce books, as but a limited impression was given. The original edition of "*The Shadowe of Night*" is very rare.

After the lapse of more than two centuries appeared an edition of Chapman's Iliad in two volumes, 8vo. London, 1843. It was elegantly printed, adorned with the beautiful designs of Flaxman, and edited by Dr. William Cooke Taylor. The Preface, Prefatory Poems, and Sonnets were omitted. I have no wish to criticise this book, but will merely observe that the editor followed, as will be seen, an inferior copy, and has paid little or no regard to the punctuation, which is almost as confused as that of the original folios. The Life of Chapman is full of the most patent errors. Nevertheless Dr. Taylor deserves our sincere thanks for being the first to bring this noble work before the public since the days of the Author.

The leading features of the present edition are these. The text of the first folio of 1611 has been adopted, and the variations of the second folio, and Dr. Taylor's edition, duly noted. The lines have been numbered for facility of reference, the speeches placed between inverted commas, and the punctuation throughout the whole work most carefully amended. The original folios of Chapman's Homer are so falsely printed as frequently to render the sense absolutely unintelligible. In correcting the punctuation the Editor carefully read the text through with the original Greek, and chiefly in the old folio edition of Spondanus, as Chapman used that copy. The orthography has been modernized, but great care has been taken not to lose sight of the original forms, the landmarks as it were, of our language. Wherever a word appears in its more etymological form it is preserved, e.g. *renowm, nosthril;* but Chapman does not adhere to one rule, and he more frequently spells the words *renown, nostril*. A few explanatory notes have been given, but the chief aim has been to set before the reader as correct a text as possible. The Sonnets at the end of the second volume have been illustrated by brief biographical notices, and their number increased by the restoration of three from the small folio of 1609, and the insertion of three others from choice copies of the first folio of 1611.

The reader is requested to correct with a pen the "Addenda et Corrigenda," on the following page.

ADDENDA ET CORRIGENDA.

Introduction, page xxiv, line 2, r. *is the legend;* page xli, line 19, r. *Misled;* page lxix, line 5, insert comma after *attending;* page lxxxviii, line 22, *seu;* page xciii, last line, r. ἄριστον. Book I. 146, r. *Peleüs;* 261, r. *Theseüs;* 373, r. *Atreüs;* 411, destroy comma after *thrall;* 586, r. *ev'ry;* Commentary, page 23, line 6, destroy all commas after *opinion;* page 24, line 18, r. *round-coming.* II. 14, r. *pow'rs;* 43, r. *begun;* 422, *these* r. *those;* 423, r. *Peleüs;* 440, r. *ev'ry;* Commentary, page 56, last line, r. ἀπόδοσις. III. Argument, line 5, for *and* r. *with;* line 13, r. *for him still;* 81, for *and* r. *the;* page 64, line 60, destroy note; page 67, *Spiny.* This word is frequently used by Sandys in his Ovid, who seems to have read Chapman carefully; 127, r. *ev'ry;* 224, r. *ev'ry.* IV. 24, r. *Heav'n's;* 33, r. *chariot-horse;* line 85, add to note: Perhaps we should read *exhall* in a neuter sense, *i.e., a thousand sparks exhall from his brand;* 528, add note—

> "Like to a stepdame or a dowager,
> Long *withering out a young man's revenue.*"
> —SHAKESPEARE, *Midsummer-Night's Dream,* Act i. sc. 1.

533, r. *prease.* V. 307, r. *prease;* 361, r. *him;* 612, r. *lighten'd;* 793, *outray.* Substitute for note: The Old Anglo-Norman word used by Chaucer *outraye,* to fly out, display passion. See XXIII. 413. VI. 214, destroy *this;* 420, r. *advertis'd.* VII. 247, add note—

> "O murd'rous slumber!
> *Lay'st thou thy leaden mace* upon my boy,
> That plays thee music?"
> —SHAKESPEARE, *Julius Cæsar,* Act iv. sc. 3.

VIII. 136, for *hast* r. *hadst;* 319, r. *Eurystheüs.* IX. 495, r. *with.* X. 106, place " after *inur'd.* XI. 64, destroy this note, and substitute: *Opposed*—striving with one another, pitted against one another. The original is ἐναντίοι ἀλλήλοισιν, which the Scholiast explains ἐρίζοντες ἀλλήλοις. XI. 55, r. *pow'r;* 286, r. *thicken'd;* 299, r. *even debates;* 466, r. *Disperpled*=sprinkled. Od. x. 473. XIII. 5, r. *unras'd.* XII. 98, r. *Paris and* Alcathous. XIII. 619, destroy comma after Menestheus; Commentary, page 32, line 17, r. εὔστροφος. XXII. 341, note: *Whitleather, i.e.,* white leather; leather dressed with alum to give it toughness. XXIII. 538, note: George Sandys in a marginal note to his Ovid's Metamorphoses, Bk. V. p. 174 (ed. 1632), says a hurl-bat is "a weapon with plummets of lead hung at the end of a staff." Again in Bk. VIII. p. 272, is a similar note, where he says "whorl-bats, plummets of lead hung at the end staves: weapons used in their solemn games." XXIII. 581, *To the nail*—exactly, accurately. Like the *ad unguem* of Horace (Sat. I. v. 32), and the *in unguem* of Virgil (Georg. II. 277).

HOMER'S ILIADS.

The following versus are on an engraving of Two Corinthian Columns, on the dexter of which is ILIAS, and on the sinister ODYSSÆA. On a scroll connecting the columns are the words

MUSAR : HERCUL : COLUM :
NE USQUE.

The whole surmounted by the Prince of Wales's Plume and Motto.
This plate was added on the death of the Prince, and is found in most copies of the Iliad and Odyssey united. The design being inelegant, it was not thought worth re-engraving for this edition.

TO THE IMMORTAL MEMORY OF THE INCOMPARABLE
HEROE, HENRY, PRINCE OF WALES.

HY tomb, arms, statue, all things fit to fall
    At foot of Death, and worship funeral,
    Form hath bestow'd ; for form is nought too dear
    Thy solid virtues yet, eterniz'd here,
My blood and wasted spirits have only found
Commanded cost, and broke so rich a ground,
Not to inter, but make thee ever spring,
As arms, tombs, statues, ev'ry earthy thing,
Shall fade and vanish into fume before.
What lasts thrives least ; yet wealth of soul is poor,
And so 'tis kept. Not thy thrice-sacred will,
Sign'd with thy death, moves any to fulfill
Thy just bequests to me. Thou dead, then I
Live dead, for giving thee eternity.

Ad Famam.

To all times future this time's mark extend,
Homer no patron found, nor Chapman friend.
        Ignotus nimis omnibus,
        Sat notus moritur sibi.

TO THE HIGH BORN PRINCE OF MEN,

HENRY, THRICE ROYAL INHERITOR TO THE UNITED KINGDOMS OF GREAT BRITAIN, ETC.

SINCE perfect happiness, by Princes sought,
Is not with birth born, nor exchequers bought,
Nor follows in great trains, nor is possest
With any outward state, but makes him blest
That governs inward, and beholdeth there
All his affections stand about him bare,
That by his pow'r can send to Tower and death
All traitorous passions, marshalling beneath
His justice his mere will, and in his mind
Holds such a sceptre as can keep confin'd
His whole life's actions in the royal bounds
Of virtue and religion, and their grounds
Takes in to sow his honours, his delights,
And cómplete empire; you should learn these rights,
Great Prince of men, by princely precedents,
Which here, in all kinds, my true zeal presents
To furnish your youth's groundwork and first state,
And let you see one godlike man create

All sorts of worthiest men, to be contriv'd
In your worth only, giving him reviv'd   20
For whose life Alexander would have given
One of his kingdoms; who (as sent from heav'n,
And thinking well that so divine a creature
Would never more enrich the race of nature)
Kept as his crown his works, and thought them still   25
His angels, in all pow'r to rule his will;
And would affirm that Homer's poesy
Did more advance his Asian victory,
Than all his armies. O! 'tis wond'rous much,
Though nothing priz'd, that the right virtuous touch   30
Of a well written soul to virtue moves;
Nor have we souls to purpose, if their loves
Of fitting objects be not so inflam'd.
How much then were this kingdom's main soul maim'd,
To want this great inflamer of all pow'rs   35
That move in human souls! All realms but yours
Are honour'd with him, and hold blest that state
That have his works to read and contemplate:
In which humanity to her height is rais'd,
Which all the world, yet none enough, hath prais'd;   40
Seas, earth, and heav'n, he did in verse comprise,
Out-sung the Muses, and did equalize
Their king Apollo; being so far from cause
Of Princes' light thoughts, that their gravest laws
May find stuff to be fashion'd by his lines.   45
Through all the pomp of kingdoms still he shines,
And graceth all his gracers. Then let lie
Your lutes and viols, and more loftily
Make the heroics of your Homer sung,
To drums and trumpets set his angel's tongue,   50

[29] Coleridge styles the lines from this to 61 "sublime."

And, with the princely sport of hawks you use,
Behold the kingly flight of his high muse,
And see how, like the phœnix, she renews
Her age and starry feathers in your sun,
Thousands of years attending ev'ry one⁣   55
Blowing the holy fire, and throwing in
Their seasons, kingdoms, nations, that have been
Subverted in them ; laws, religions, all
Offer'd to change and greedy funeral ;
Yet still your Homer, lasting, living, reigning,   60
And proves how firm truth builds in poet's feigning.

  A prince's statue, or in marble carv'd,
Or steel, or gold, and shrin'd, to be preserv'd,
Aloft on pillars or pyramides,
Time into lowest ruins may depress ;   65
But drawn with all his virtues in learn'd verse,
Fame shall resound them on oblivion's hearse,
Till graves gasp with her blasts, and dead men rise.
No gold can follow where true Poesy flies.

  Then let not this divinity in earth,   70
Dear Prince, be slighted as she were the birth
Of idle fancy, since she works so high ;
Nor let her poor disposer, Learning, lie
Still bed-rid. Both which being in men defac'd,
In men with them is God's bright image ras'd ;   75
For as the Sun and Moon are figures giv'n
Of his refulgent Deity in heav'n,
So Learning, and, her light'ner, Poesy,
In earth present His fiery Majesty.
Nor are kings like Him, since their diadems   80
Thunder and lighten and project brave beams,
But since they His clear virtues emulate,
In truth and justice imaging His state,

In bounty and humanity since they shine,
Than which is nothing like Him more divine ; 85
Not fire, not light, the sun's admiréd course,
The rise nor set of stars, nor all their force
In us and all this cope beneath the sky,
Nor great existence, term'd His treasury ;
Since not for being greatest He is blest, 90
But being just, and in all virtues best.
   What sets His justice and His truth best forth,
Best Prince, then use best, which is Poesy's worth ;
For, as great princes, well inform'd and deck'd
With gracious virtue, give more sure effect 95
To her persuasions, pleasures, real worth,
Than all th' inferior subjects she sets forth ;
Since there she shines at full, hath birth, wealth, state,
Pow'r, fortune, honour, fit to elevate
Her heav'nly merits, and so fit they are, 100
Since she was made for them, and they for her ;
So Truth, with Poesy grac'd, is fairer far,
More proper, moving, chaste, and regular,
Than when she runs away with untruss'd Prose ;
Proportion, that doth orderly dispose 105
Her virtuous treasure, and is queen of graces ;
In Poesy decking her with choicest phrases,
Figures and numbers ; when loose Prose puts on
Plain letter-habits, makes her trot upon
Dull earthly business, she being mere divine ; 110
Holds her to homely cates and harsh hedge-wine,
That should drink Poesy's nectar ; ev'ry way
One made for other, as the sun and day,
Princes and virtues. And, as in a spring,
The pliant water, mov'd with anything 115

Let fall into it, puts her motion out
In perfect circles, that move round about
The gentle fountain, one another raising;
So Truth and Poesy work; so Poesy, blazing
All subjects fall'n in her exhaustless fount, 120
Works most exactly, makes a true account
Of all things to her high discharges giv'n,
Till all be circular and round as heav'n.
  And lastly, great Prince, mark and pardon me:—
As in a flourishing and ripe fruit-tree, 125
Nature hath made the bark to save the bole,
The bole the sap, the sap to deck the whole
With leaves and branches, they to bear and shield
The useful fruit, the fruit itself to yield
Guard to the kernel, and for that all those, 130
Since out of that again the whole tree grows;
So in our tree of man, whose nervy root
Springs in his top, from thence ev'n to his foot
There runs a mutual aid through all his parts,
All join'd in one to serve his queen of arts, 135
In which doth Poesy like the kernel lie
Obscur'd, though her Promethean faculty
Can create men, and make ev'n death to live,
For which she should live honour'd, kings should give
Comfort and help to her that she might still 140
Hold up their spirits in virtue, make the will
That governs in them to the pow'r conform'd,
The pow'r to justice, that the scandals, storm'd
Against the poor dame, clear'd by your fair grace,
Your grace may shine the clearer. Her low place, 145
Not showing her, the highest leaves obscure.
Who raise her raise themselves, and he sits sure

    [135] "*Queen of arts*—the soul."—CHAPMAN.

Whom her wing'd hand advanceth, since on it
Eternity doth, crowning virtue, sit.
All whose poor seed, like violets in their beds, 150
Now grow with bosom-hung and hidden heads;
For whom I must speak, though their fate convinces
Me worst of poets, to you best of princes.

> By the most humble and faithful implorer for all
> the graces to your highness eternized
> by your divine Homer.
> GEO. CHAPMAN.

AN ANAGRAM OF THE NAME OF OUR DREAD PRINCE,
MY MOST GRACIOUS AND SACRED MÆCENAS,
HENRYE PRINCE OF VVALES
OVR SVNN, HEYR, PEACE, LIFE.

BE to us, as thy great name doth import,
    Prince of the people, nor suppose it vain
That in this secret and prophetic sort
    Thy name and noblest title doth contain
So much right to us, and as great a good.
    Nature doth nothing vainly ; much less Art
Perfecting Nature. No spirit in our blood
    But in our soul's discourses bears a part ;
What nature gives at random in the one,
    In th' other order'd our divine part serves.
Thou art not HEYR then to our State alone,
    But SVNN, PEACE, LIFE ; and, what thy pow'r deserves
Of us and our good in thy utmost strife,
Shall make thee to thyself HEYR, SVNN, PEACE, LIFE.

TO THE SACRED FOUNTAIN OF PRINCES,
SOLE EMPRESS OF BEAUTY AND VIRTUE, ANNE, QUEEN OF ENGLAND, ETC.

WITH whatsoever honour we adorn
   Your royal issue, we must gratulate you,
   Imperial Sovereign; who of you is born
   Is you, one tree make both the bole and bow.
If it be honour then to join you both
   To such a pow'rful work as shall defend
Both from foul death and age's ugly moth,
   This is an honour that shall never end.
They know not virtue then, that know not what
   The virtue of defending virtue is;
It comprehends the guard of all your State,
   And joins your greatness to as great a bliss.
Shield virtue and advance her then, great Queen,
And make this book your glass to make it seen.

Your Majesty's in all subjection most
humbly consecrate,
GEO. CHAPMAN.

ANNE, daughter of FREDERICK II. of Denmark, Married King James Ist 20 Aug. 1590, and died 2 March, 1619.

TO THE READER.

LEST with foul hands you touch these holy rites,
  And with prejudicacies too profane,
Pass Homer in your other poets' slights,
  Wash here. In this porch to his num'rous fane,
Hear ancient oracles speak, and tell you whom
  You have to censure. First then Silius hear,
Who thrice was consul in renowned Rome,
  Whose verse, saith Martial, nothing shall out-wear.

SILIUS ITALICUS, LIB. XIII. 777.

HE, in Elysium having cast his eye
    Upon the figure of a youth, whose hair,
  With purple ribands braided curiously,
    Hung on his shoulders wond'rous bright and fair,
Said: 'Virgin, what is he whose heav'nly face   5
  Shines past all others, as the morn the night;
Whom many marvelling souls, from place to place,
  Pursue and haunt with sounds of such delight;
Whose count'nance (were't not in the Stygian shade)
  Would make me, questionless, believe he were   10
A very God?' The learned virgin made
  This answer: 'If thou shouldst believe it here,
Thou shouldst not err. He well deserv'd to be
  Esteem'd a God; nor held his so-much breast

A little presence of the Deity, 15
    His verse compris'd earth, seas, stars, souls at rest;
In song the Muses he did equalize,
    In honour Phœbus. He was only soul,
Saw all things spher'd in nature, without eyes,
    And rais'd your Troy up to the starry pole.' 20
Glad Scipio, viewing well this prince of ghosts,
    Said: 'O if Fates would give this poet leave
To sing the acts done by the Roman hosts,
    How much beyond would future times receive
The same facts made by any other known! 25
    O blest Æacides, to have the grace
That out of such a mouth thou shouldst be shown
    To wond'ring nations, as enrich'd the race
Of all times future with what he did know!
    Thy virtue with his verse shall ever grow.' 30

      Now hear an Angel sing our poet's fame,
      Whom fate, for his divine song, gave that name.

    ANGELUS POLITIANUS, IN NUTRICIA.*

More living than in old Demodocus,
    Fame glories to wax young in Homer's verse.
And as when bright Hyperion holds to us
    His golden torch, we see the stars disperse,
And ev'ry way fly heav'n, the pallid moon 35
    Ev'n almost vanishing before his sight;
So, with the dazzling beams of Homer's sun,
    All other ancient poets lose their light.
Whom when Apollo heard, out of his star,
    Singing the godlike acts of honour'd men, 40

---

* The lines begin,—
    ——"nam Demodoci vivacior ævo
    *   *   *   *   *   *
    Obstrepuit, prorsusque parem confessus Apollo est."

And equalling the actual rage of war,
   With only the divine strains of his pen,
He stood amaz'd and freely did confess
   Himself was equall'd in Mæonides.

> Next hear the grave and learned Pliny use
> His censure of our sacred poet's muse.
>   Plin. Nat. Hist. lib. 7. cap. 29.
> Turned into verse, that no prose may come near Homer.

Whom shall we choose the glory of all wits,   45
   Held through so many sorts of discipline
And such variety of works and spirits,
   But Grecian Homer, like whom none did shine
For form of work and matter? And because
   Our proud doom of him may stand justified   50
By noblest judgments, and receive applause
   In spite of envy and illiterate pride,
Great Macedon, amongst his matchless spoils
   Took from rich Persia, on his fortunes cast,
A casket finding, full of precious oils,   55
   Form'd all of gold, with wealthy stones enchas'd,
He took the oils out, and his nearest friends
   Ask'd in what better guard it might be us'd?
All giving their conceits to sev'ral ends,
   He answer'd: 'His affections rather choos'd   60
An use quite opposite to all their kinds,
   And Homer's books should with that guard be serv'd,
That the most precious work of all men's minds
   In the most precious place might be preserv'd.
The Fount of Wit* was Homer, Learning's Sire,†   65
   And gave antiquity her living fire.'

VOLUMES of like praise I could heap on this,
    Of men more ancient and more learn'd than these,

---

* Plin. Nat. Hist. XVII. 5.   † Idem, XXV. 3.

TO THE READER.

But since true virtue enough lovely is
    With her own beauties, all the suffrages   70
Of others I omit, and would more fain
    That Homer for himself should be belov'd,
Who ev'ry sort of love-worth did contain.
    Which how I have in my conversion prov'd
I must confess I hardly dare refer   75
    To reading judgments, since, so gen'rally,
Custom hath made ev'n th' ablest agents err
    In these translations; all so much apply
Their pains and cunnings word for word to render
    Their patient authors, when they may as well   80
Make fish with fowl, camels with whales, engender,
    Or their tongues' speech in other mouths compell.
For, ev'n as diff'rent a production
    Ask Greek and English, since as they in sounds
And letters shun one form and unison;   85
    So have their sense and elegancy bounds
In their distinguish'd natures, and require
    Only a judgment to make both consent
In sense and elocution; and aspire,
    As well to reach the spirit that was spent   90
In his example, as with art to pierce
    His grammar, and etymology of words.
But as great clerks can write no English verse,
    Because, alas, great clerks! English affords,
Say they, no height nor copy; a rude tongue,   95
    Since 'tis their native; but in Greek or Latin
Their writs are rare, for thence true Poesy sprung;
    Though them (truth knows) they have but skill to chat in,

---

77 "Of Translation, and the natural difference of Dialects necessarily to be observed in it."—CHAPMAN.
93 "Ironicè."—CHAPMAN.

TO THE READER. lxxix

Compar'd with that they might say in their own;
    Since thither th' other's full soul cannot make 100
The ample transmigration to be shown
    In nature-loving Poesy; so the brake
That those translators stick in, that affect
    Their word-for-word traductions (where they lose
The free grace of their natural dialect, 105
    And shame their authors with a forcéd gloss)
I laugh to see; and yet as much abhor
    More license from the words than may express
Their full compression, and make clear the author;
    From whose truth, if you think my feet digress, 110
Because I use needful periphrases,
    Read Valla, Hessus, that in Latin prose,
And verse, convert him; read the Messines
    That into Tuscan turns him; and the gloss
Grave Salel makes in French, as he translates; 115
    Which, for th' aforesaid reasons, all must do;
And see that my conversion much abates
    The license they take, and more shows him too,
Whose right not all those great learn'd men have done,
    In some main parts, that were his commentors. 120
But, as the illustration of the sun
    Should be attempted by the erring stars,
They fail'd to search his deep and treasurous heart;
    The cause was, since they wanted the fit key
Of Nature, in their downright strength of Art, 125
    With Poesy to open Poesy:
Which, in my poem of the mysteries
    Reveal'd in Homer, I will clearly prove;

---

107 "The necessary nearness of Translation to the example."—CHAPMAN.
125 "The power of Nature above Art in Poesy."—CHAPMAN.

Till whose near birth, suspend your calumnies,
　　And far-wide imputations of self-love.
'Tis further from me than the worst that reads,
　　Professing me the worst of all that write;
Yet what, in following one that bravely leads,
　　The worst may show, let this proof hold the light.
But grant it clear; yet hath detraction got
　　My blind side in the form my verse puts on;
Much like a dung-hill mastiff, that dares not
　　Assault the man he barks at, but the stone
He throws at him takes in his eager jaws,
　　And spoils his teeth because they cannot spoil.
The long verse hath by proof receiv'd applause
　　Beyond each other number; and the foil,
That squint-ey'd Envy takes, is censur'd plain;
　　For this long poem asks this length of verse,
Which I myself ingenuously maintain
　　Too long our shorter authors to rehearse.
And, for our tongue that still is so impair'd
　　By travelling linguists, I can prove it clear,
That no tongue hath the Muse's utt'rance heir'd
　　For verse, and that sweet music to the ear
Strook out of rhyme, so naturally as this;
　　Our monosyllables so kindly fall,
And meet oppos'd in rhyme as they did kiss;
　　French and Italian most immetrical,
Their many syllables in harsh collision
　　Fall as they break their necks; their bastard rhymes
Saluting as they justled in transition,
　　And set our teeth on edge; nor tunes, nor times
Kept in their falls; and, methinks, their long words
　　Shew in short verse as in a narrow place

---

[147] "Our English language above all others for Rhythmical Poesy."—CHAPMAN.

Two opposites should meet with two-hand swords
    Unwieldily, without or use or grace.
Thus having rid the rubs, and strow'd these flow'rs
    In our thrice-sacred Homer's English way,
What rests to make him yet more worthy yours?   165
    To cite more praise of him were mere delay
To your glad searches for what those men found
    That gave his praise, past all, so high a place;
Whose virtues were so many, and so crown'd
    By all consents divine, that, not to grace   170
Or add increase to them, the world doth need
    Another Homer, but ev'n to rehearse
And number them, they did so much exceed.
    Men thought him not a man; but that his verse
Some mere celestial nature did adorn;   175
    And all may well conclude it could not be,
That for the place where any man was born,
    So long and mortally could disagree
So many nations as for Homer striv'd,
    Unless his spur in them had been divine.   180
Then end their strife and love him, thus receiv'd,
    As born in England; see him over-shine
All other-country poets; and trust this,
    That whosesoever Muse dares use her wing
When his Muse flies, she will be truss'd by his,   185
    And show as if a bernacle should spring
Beneath an eagle. In none since was seen
    A soul so full of heav'n as earth's in him.
O! if our modern Poesy had been
    As lovely as the lady he did limn,   190
What barbarous worldling, grovelling after gain,
    Could use her lovely parts with such rude hate,

As now she suffers under ev'ry swain ?
    Since then 'tis nought but her abuse and Fate,
That thus impairs her, what is this to her   195
    As she is real, or in natural right ?
But since in true Religion men should err
    As much as Poesy, should the abuse excite
The like contempt of her divinity,
    And that her truth, and right saint-sacred merits,   200
In most lives breed but rev'rence formally,
    What wonder is't if Poesy inherits
Much less observance, being but agent for her,
    And singer of her laws, that others say ?
Forth then, ye moles, sons of the earth, abhor her,   205
    Keep still on in the dirty vulgar way,
Till dirt receive your souls, to which ye vow,
    And with your poison'd spirits bewitch our thrifts.
Ye cannot so despise us as we you ;
    Not one of you above his mole-hill lifts   210
His earthy mind, but, as a sort of beasts,
    Kept by their guardians, never care to hear
Their manly voices, but when in their fists
    They breathe wild whistles, and the beasts' rude ear
Hears their curs barking, then by heaps they fly   215
    Headlong together ; so men, beastly giv'n,
The manly soul's voice, sacred Poesy,
    Whose hymns the angels ever sing in heav'n,
Contemn and hear not ; but when brutish noises,
    For gain, lust, honour, in litigious prose   220
Are bellow'd out, and crack the barbarous voices
    Of Turkish stentors, O, ye lean to those,
Like itching horse to blocks or high may-poles ;
    And break nought but the wind of wealth, wealth, all

In all your documents; your asinine souls,
  Proud of their burthens, feel not how they gall.
But as an ass, that in a field of weeds
  Affects a thistle, and falls fiercely to it,
That pricks and galls him, yet he feeds, and bleeds,
  Forbears a while, and licks, but cannot woo it
To leave the sharpness; when, to wreak his smart,
  He beats it with his foot, then backward kicks,
Because the thistle gall'd his forward part;
  Nor leaves till all be eat, for all the pricks,
Then falls to others with as hot a strife,
  And in that honourable war doth waste
The tall heat of his stomach, and his life;
  So in this world of weeds you worldlings taste
Your most-lov'd dainties, with such war buy peace,
  Hunger for torment, virtue kick for vice,
Cares for your states do with your states increase,
  And though ye dream ye feast in Paradise,
Yet reason's daylight shews ye at your meat
  Asses at thistles, bleeding as ye eat.

THE PREFACE TO THE READER.

F all books extant in all kinds, Homer is the first and best. No one before his, Josephus affirms; nor before him, saith Velleius Paterculus, was there any whom he imitated, nor after him any that could imitate him. And that Poesy may be no cause of detraction from all the eminence we give him, Spondanus (preferring it to all arts and sciences) unanswerably argues and proves; for to the glory of God, and the singing of His glories, no man dares deny, man was chiefly made. And what art performs this chief end of man with so much excitation and expression as Poesy; Moses, David, Solomon, Job, Esay, Jeremy, &c. chiefly using that to the end abovesaid? And since the excellence of it cannot be obtained by the labour and art of man, as all easily confess it, it must needs be acknowledged a Divine infusion. To prove which in a word, this distich, in my estimation, serves something nearly:

> Great Poesy, blind Homer, makes all see
> Thee capable of all arts, none of thee.

For out of him, according to our most grave and judicial Plutarch, are all Arts deduced, confirmed, or illustrated. It is not therefore the world's vilifying of it that can make it vile; for so we might argue, and blaspheme the most incomparably sacred. It is not of the world indeed, but, like truth, hides itself from it. Nor is there any such reality of wisdom's truth in all human excellence, as in Poets' fictions. That most vulgar and foolish receipt of poetical licence being of all knowing men to be exploded, accepting it, as if Poets had a tale-telling privilege above others, no Artist being so strictly and inextricably confined to all the laws of learning, wisdom, and truth, as a Poet. For were not his fictions composed of the sinews and souls of all those, how could they defy fire, iron, and be combined with eternity? To all sciences therefore, I must still, with our learned and ingenious Spondanus, prefer it, as having a perpetual commerce with the Divine Majesty, embracing and illustrating all His most holy precepts, and enjoying continual discourse with His thrice perfect and most comfortable Spirit. And as the contemplative life is most worthily and divinely preferred by Plato to the active, as much as the head to the foot, the eye to the hand, reason to sense, the soul to the body, the end itself to all things directed to the end, quiet to motion, and eternity to time; so much prefer I divine Poesy to all worldly wisdom. To the only shadow of whose worth, yet, I entitle not the bold rhymes of every apish and impudent braggart, though he dares assume anything; such I turn over to the weaving of cobwebs, and shall but chatter on molehills (far under the hill of the Muses) when their fortunatest self-love and ambition hath advanced them highest. Poesy is the flower of the Sun, and disdains to open to the eye of a candle. So kings hide their treasures and counsels from the vulgar, *ne evilescant* (saith our Spond.). We have example sacred enough, that true Poesy's humility, poverty, and contempt, are badges of divinity, not vanity. Bray then, and bark against it, ye wolf-faced worldlings, that nothing but honours, riches, and magistracy, *nescio quos turgidè spiratis* (that I may use the words of our friend still) *qui solas leges Justinianas crepatis; paragraphum unum aut alterum, pluris quàm vos ipsos facitis*, &c. I (for my part) shall ever esteem it much more manly and sacred, in this harmless and pious study, to sit till I sink into my grave, than shine in your vainglorious bubbles and impieties; all your poor policies, wisdoms, and their trappings, at no more valuing than a musty nut. And much less I weigh the frontless detractions of some stupid ignorants, that, no more knowing me than their own beastly ends, and I ever (to my knowledge) blest from their sight, whisper behind me vilifyings of my translation, out of the French affirming them, when both in French, and all other languages but his own, our with-all-skill-enriched Poet is so poor and unpleasing that no man can discern from whence flowed his so generally given eminence and admiration. And therefore (by any reasonable creature's conference of my slight comment and conversion) it will easily appear how I shun them, and whether the original be my rule or not. In which he shall easily see, I understand the understandings of all other interpreters and commentors in places of his most depth, importance, and rapture. In whose exposition and illustration, if I abhor from the sense that others wrest and wrack out of him, let my best detractor examine how the Greek word warrants me. For my other fresh fry, let them fry in their foolish galls, nothing so much weighed as the barkings of puppies, or foisting hounds, too vile to think of our sacred Homer, or set their profane feet within their lives' length of his thresholds. If I fail in something, let my full performance in other some restore me ; haste spurring me on with other necessities. For as at my conclusion I protest, so here at my entrance, less than fifteen weeks was the time in which all the last twelve books were entirely new translated. No conference had with any one living in all the novelties I presume I have found. Only some one or two places I have showed to my worthy and most learned friend, M. Harriots, for his censure how much mine own weighed ; whose judgment and knowledge in all kinds, I know to be incomparable and bottomless, yea, to be admired as much, as his most blameless life, and the right sacred expense of his time, is to be honoured and reverenced. Which affirmation of his clear unmatchedness in all manner of learning I make in contempt of that nasty objection often thrust upon me,—that he that will judge must know more than he of whom he judgeth ; for so a man should know neither God nor himself. Another right learned, honest, and entirely loved friend of mine, M. Robert Hews, I must needs put into my confess'd conference touching

Homer, though very little more than that I had with M. Harriots. Which two, I protest, are all, and preferred to all. Nor charge I their authorities with any allowance of my general labour, but only of those one or two places, which for instances of my innovation, and how it showed to them, I imparted. If any tax me for too much periphrasis or circumlocution in some places, let them read Laurentius Valla, and Eobanus Hessus, who either use such shortness as cometh nothing home to Homer, or, where they shun that fault, are ten parts more paraphrastical than I. As for example, one place I will trouble you (if you please) to confer with the original, and one interpreter for all. It is in the end of the third book, and is Helen's speech to Venus fetching her to Paris from seeing his cowardly combat with Menelaus; part of which speech I will here cite :

> Οὕνεκα δὴ νῦν δῖον ᾽Αλέξανδρον Μενέλαος
> Νικήσας, &c.

For avoiding the common reader's trouble here, I must refer the more Greekish to the rest of the speech in Homer, whose translation *ad verbum* by Spondanus I will here cite, and then pray you to confer it with that which followeth of Valla.

> Quoniam verò nunc Alexandrum Menelaus
> Postquam vicit, vult odiosam me domum abducere,
> Propterea verò nunc dolum (ceu dolos) cogitans advenisti?
> Sede apud ipsum vadens, deorum abnega vias,
> Neque unquam tuis pedibus revertaris in cœlum,
> Sed semper circa eum ærumnas perfer, et ipsum serva
> Donec te vel uxorem faciat, vel hic servam, &c.

Valla thus :

> Quoniam victo Paride, Menelaus me miseram est reportaturus ad lares, ideo tu, ideo falsâ sub imagine venisti, ut me deciperes ob tuam nimiam in Paridem benevolentiam : eò dum illi ades, dum illi studes, dum pro illo satagis, dum illum observas atque custodis, deorum commercium reliquisti, nec ad eos reversura es amplius ; adeò (quantum suspicor) aut uxor ejus efficieris, aut ancilla, &c.

Wherein note if there be any such thing as most of this in Homer; yet only to express, as he thinks, Homer's conceit, for the more pleasure of the reader, he useth this overplus, *dum illi ades, dum illi studes, dum pro illo satagis, dum illum observas, atque custodis,' deorum commercium reliquisti.* Which (besides his superfluity) is utterly false. For where he saith *reliquisti deorum commercium*, Helen saith, Θεῶν δ' ἀπόειπε κελεύθους, *deorum autem abnega,* or *abnue, vias,* ἀπείπειν (*vel* ἀποείπειν as it is used poetically) signifying *denegare,* or *abnuere;* and Helen (in contempt of her too much observing men) bids her renounce heaven, and come live with Paris till he make her his wife or servant; sceptically or scornfully speaking it; which both Valla, Eobanus, and all other interpreters (but these *ad verbum*) have utterly missed. And this one example I thought necessary to insert here, to show my detractors that they have no reason to vilify my circumlocution sometimes, when their most approved Grecians, Homer's interpreters generally, hold him fit to be so converted. Yet how much I differ, and with what authority, let my impartial and judicial reader judge. Always conceiving how pedantical and absurd an affectation it is in the interpretation of any author (much more of Homer) to turn him word for word, when (according to Horace and other best lawgivers to translators) it is the part of every knowing and judicial interpreter, not to follow the number and order of words, but the material things themselves, and sentences to weigh diligently, and to clothe and adorn them with words, and such a style and form of oration, as are most apt for the language in which they are converted. If I have not turned him in any place falsely (as all other his interpreters have in many, and most of his chief places) if I have not left behind me any of his sentences, elegancy, height, intention, and invention, if in some few places (especially in my first edition, being done so long since, and following the common tract) I be something paraphrastical and faulty, is it justice in that poor fault (if they will needs have it so) to drown all the rest of my labour? But there is a certain envious windsucker,* that hovers up and down, laboriously engrossing all the air with his lux-

* *Windsucker*—the kestrel, or kite, hovering hawk; called also a *windhover.*

urious ambition, and buzzing into every ear my detraction, affirming I turn Homer out of the Latin only, &c. that sets all his associates, and the whole rabble of my maligners on their wings with him, to bear about my impair, and poison my reputation. One that, as he thinks, whatsoever he gives to others, he takes from himself; so whatsoever he takes from others, he adds to himself. One that in this kind of robbery doth like Mercury, that stole good and supplied it with counterfeit bad still. One like the two gluttons, Philoxenus and Gnatho, that would still empty their noses in the dishes they loved, that no man might eat but themselves. For so this castrill,* with too hot a liver, and lust after his own glory, and to devour all himself, discourageth all appetites to the fame of another. I have stricken, single him as you can. Nor note I this, to cast any rubs or plashes out of the particular way of mine own estimation with the world; for I resolve this with the wilfully obscure:

> Sine honore vivam, nulloque numero ero.
>
> *Without men's honours I will live, and make
> No number in the manless course they take.*

But, to discourage (if it might be) the general detraction of industrious and well-meaning virtue, I know I cannot too much diminish and deject myself; yet that passing little that I am, God only knows, to Whose ever-implored respect and comfort I only submit me. If any further edition of these my silly endeavours shall chance, I will mend what is amiss (God assisting me) and amplify my harsh Comment to Homer's far more right, and mine own earnest and ingenious love of him. Notwithstanding, I know, the curious and envious will never sit down satisfied. A man may go over and over, till he come over and over, and his pains be only his recompense, every man is so loaded with his particular head, and nothing in all respects perfect, but what is perceived by few. Homer himself hath met with my fortune, in many maligners; and therefore may my poor self put up without motion.

* *Castrill*—kestrel, or hovering hawk.

And so little I will respect malignity, and so much encourage myself with mine own known strength, and what I find within me of comfort and confirmance (examining myself throughout with a far more jealous and severe eye than my greatest enemy, imitating this :

. Judex ipse sui totum se explorat ad unguem, &c).

that after these Iliads, I will (God lending me life and any meanest means) with more labour than I have lost here, and all unchecked alacrity, dive through his Odysseys. Nor can I forget here (but with all hearty gratitude remember) my most ancient, learned, and right noble friend, M. Richard Stapilton, first most desertful mover in the frame of our Homer. For which (and much other most ingenious and utterly undeserved desert) God make me amply his requiter ; and be his honourable family's speedy and full restorer. In the mean space, I entreat my impartial and judicial Reader, that all things to the quick he will not pare, but humanely and nobly pardon defects, and, if he find anything perfect, receive it unenvied.

OF HOMER.

OF his country and time, the difference is so infinite amongst all writers, that there is no question, in my conjecture, of his antiquity beyond all. To which opinion, the nearest I will cite, Adam Cedrenus placeth him under David's and Solomon's rule; and the Destruction of Troy under Saul's. And of one age with Solomon, Michael Glycas Siculus affirmeth him. Aristotle (*in tertio de Poeticâ*) affirms he was born in the isle of Io, begot of a Genius, one of them that used to dance with the Muses, and a virgin of that isle compressed by that Genius, who being quick with child (for shame of the deed) came into a place called Ægina, and there was taken of thieves, and brought to Smyrna, to Mæon king of the Lydians, who for her beauty married her. After which, she walking near the flood Meletes, on that shore being overtaken with the throes of her delivery, she brought forth Homer, and instantly died. The infant was received by Mæon, and brought up as his own till his death, which was not long after. And, according to this, when the Lydians in Smyrna were afflicted by the Æolians, and thought fit to leave the city, the captains by a herald willing all to go out that would, and follow them, Homer, being a little child, said he would also ὁμηρεῖν (that is, *sequi*); and of that, for Melesigenes, which was his first name, he was called Homer. These Plutarch.

The varieties of other reports touching this I omit for length; and in place thereof think it not unfit to insert something of his praise and honour amongst the greatest of all ages; not that our most absolute of himself needs it, but that such authentical testimonies of his splendour and excellence may the better convince the malice of his maligners.

TO THE READER.

First, what kind of person Homer was, saith Spondanus, his statue teacheth, which Cedrenus describeth. The whole place we will describe that our relation may hold the better coherence, as Xylander converts it. "Then was the Octagonon at Constantinople consumed with fire; and the bath of Severus, that bore the name of Zeuxippus, in which there was much variety of spectacle, and splendour of arts; the works of all ages being conferred and preserved there, of marble, rocks, stones, and images of brass; to which this only wanted, that the souls of the persons they presented were not in them. Amongst these master-pieces and all-wit-exceeding workmanships stood Homer, as he was in his age, thoughtful and musing, his hands folded beneath his bosom, his beard untrimmed and hanging down, the hair of his head in like sort thin on both sides before, his face with age and cares of the world, as these imagine, wrinkled and austere, his nose proportioned to his other parts, his eyes fixed or turned up to his eyebrows, like one blind, as it is reported he was." (Not born blind, saith Vell. Paterculus, which he that imagines, saith he, is blind of all senses.) "Upon his under-coat he was attired with a loose robe, and at the base beneath his feet a brazen chain hung."* This was the statue of Homer, which in that conflagration perished. Another renowned statue of his, saith Lucian in his Encomion of Demosthenes, stood in the temple of Ptolemy, on the upper hand of his own statue. Cedrenus likewise remembereth a library in the palace of the king, at Constantinople, that contained a thousand a hundred and twenty books, amongst which there was the gut of a dragon of an hundred and twenty foot long, in which, in letters of gold, the Iliads and Odysseys of Homer were inscribed;† which miracle, in Basiliscus the Emperor's time, was consumed with fire.

For his respect amongst the most learned, Plato *in Ione* calleth him ἄρισον καὶ θειότατον τῶν ποιητῶν, *Poetarum omnium et prastantissimum*

---

* Georgii Cedreni Historiarum Compendium, vol. I. p. 369 (ed. Paris, 2 vols. fol. 1647).

† Cedrenus, ut suprà, p. 351.

et divinissimum; in *Phædone,* θεῖον ποιητήν, *divinum Poetam;* and in *Theætetus,* Socrates citing divers of the most wise and learned for confirmation of his there held opinion, as Protagoras, Heraclitus, Empedocles, Epicharmus, and Homer, who, saith Socrates, against such an army, being all led by such a captain as Homer, dares fight or resist, but he will be held ridiculous? This for Scaliger and all Homer's envious and ignorant detractors. Why therefore Plato in another place banisheth him with all other poets out of his Common-wealth, dealing with them like a Politician indeed, use men, and then cast them off, though Homer he thinks fit to send out crowned and anointed, I see not, since he maketh still such honourable mention of him, and with his verses, as with precious gems, everywhere enchaceth his writings. So Aristotle continually celebrateth him. Nay, even amongst the barbarous, not only Homer's name, but his poems have been recorded and reverenced. The Indians, saith Ælianus (Var. Hist. lib. XII. cap. 48.) in their own tongue had Homer's Poems translated and sung. Nor those Indians alone, but the kings of Persia. And amongst the Indians, of all the Greek poets, Homer being ever first in estimation; whensoever they used any divine duties according to the custom of their households and hospitalities, they invited ever Apollo and Homer. Lucian in his Encomion of Demosth. affirmeth all Poets celebrated Homer's birthday, and sacrificed to him the first fruits of their verses. So Thersagoras answereth Lucian, he used to do himself. Alex. Paphius, saith Eustathius, delivers Homer as born of Egyptian parents, Dmasagoras, being his father, and Æthra his mother, his nurse being a certain prophetess and the daughter of Oris, Isis' priest, from whose breasts, oftentimes, honey flowed in the mouth of the infant. After which, in the night, he uttered nine several notes or voices of fowls, viz. of a swallow, a peacock, a dove, a crow, a partridge, a redshank, a stare, a blackbird, and a nightingale; and, being a little boy, was found playing in his bed with nine doves. Sibylla being at a feast of his parents was taken with sudden fury, and sung verses whose beginning was Δμασαγόρα πολύνικε: *polynice,* signifying much victory, in which song also she called him μεγάκλεα, *great in glory*, and στεφανίτην, signifying *garland-seller*, and commanded him to build a temple to the Pegridarij, that is, to the Muses. Herodotus affirms that Phæmius, teaching a public school at Smyrna, was his master; and Dionysius in his 56th Oration saith, Socrates was Homer's scholar. In short, what he was, his works show most truly; to which, if you please, go on and examine him.

THE FIRST BOOK OF HOMER'S ILIADS.

ARGUMENT.

APOLLO's priest to th' Argive fleet doth bring
Gifts for his daughter, pris'ner to the king ;
For which her tender'd freedom he entreats ;
But, being dismiss'd with contumelious threats,
At Phœbus' hands, by vengeful pray'r, he seeks
To have a plague inflicted on the Greeks.
Which had ; Achilles doth a council cite,
Embold'ning Calchas, in the king's despite,
To tell the truth why they were punish'd so.
From hence their fierce and deadly strife did grow.
For wrong in which Æacides* so raves,
That goddess Thetis, from her throne of waves
Ascending heav'n, of Jove assistance won,
To plague the Greeks by absence of her son,
And make the general himself repent
To wrong so much his army's ornament.
This found by Juno, she with Jove contends ;
Till Vulcan, with heav'n's cup, the quarrel ends.

ANOTHER ARGUMENT.

Alpha the prayer of Chryses sings :
The army's plague : the strife of kings.

ACHILLES' baneful wrath resound, O Goddess, that impos'd
Infinite sorrows on the Greeks, and many brave souls los'd
From breasts heroic ; sent them far to that invisible cave
That no light comforts ; and their limbs to dogs and
    vultures gave :

---

* *Æacides*—Achilles, grandson of Æacus.   ³ *Invisible cave*—Hades.

To all which Jove's will gave effect; from whom first strife begun 5
Betwixt Atrides, king of men, and Thetis' godlike son.

What god gave Eris their command, and op'd that fighting vein?
Jove's and Latona's son: who fir'd against the king of men,
For contumély shown his priest, infectious sickness sent
To plague the army, and to death by troops the soldiers went. 10
Occasion'd thus: Chryses, the priest, came to the fleet to buy,
For presents of unvalu'd price, his daughter's liberty;
The golden sceptre and the crown of Phœbus in his hands
Proposing; and made suit to all, but most to the commands
Of both th' Atrides, who most rul'd. "Great Atreus' sons," said he,
"And all ye well-greav'd Greeks, the gods, whose habitations be 16
In heav'nly houses, grace your pow'rs with Priam's razéd town,
And grant ye happy conduct home! To win which wish'd renown
Of Jove, by honouring his son, far-shooting Phœbus, deign
For these fit presents to dissolve the ransomable chain 20
Of my lov'd daughter's servitude." The Greeks entirely gave
Glad acclamatións, for sign that their desires would have
The grave priest reverenc'd, and his gifts of so much price embrac'd.
The Gen'ral yet bore no such mind, but viciously disgrac'd
With violent terms the priest, and said:—"Dotard! avoid our fleet,
Where ling'ring be not found by me; nor thy returning feet 26
Let ever visit us again; lest nor thy godhead's crown,
Nor sceptre, save thee! Her thou seek'st I still will hold mine own,
Till age deflow'r her. In our court at Argos, far transferr'd
From her lov'd country, she shall ply her web, and see prepar'd 30

---

⁶ *Atrides*—patronymic of Agamemnon and Menelaus. *Thetis' son*—Achilles.
⁷ *Eris*—the goddess of strife, personification of strife.
⁸ *Jove's and Latona's son*—Apollo.
¹² *Unvalued*—invaluable, not to be valued. So Shakespeare—
   "Inestimable stones, unvalu'd jewels."—*Rich. III.* I. 4.
¹⁴ *Proposing*—holding before him.
³⁰ "*See my bed made*," it may be Englished. The word is ἀντιόωσαν, which signifies *contra stantem*, as *standing of one side opposite to another on the other side;* which yet others translate *capessentem et adornantem;* which, since it shows best to a reader, I follow.—CHAPMAN.

With all fit ornaments my bed. Incense me then no more,
But, if thou wilt be safe, be gone." This said, the sea-beat shore,
Obeying his high will, the priest trod off with haste and fear;
And, walking silent, till he left far off his enemies' ear,
Phœbus, fair hair'd Latona's son, he stirr'd up with a vow,   35
To this stern purpose: "Hear, thou God that bear'st the silver bow,
That Chrysa guard'st, rul'st Tenedos with strong hand, and the round
Of Cilla most divine dost walk! O Smintheüs! if crown'd
With thankful off'rings thy rich fane I ever saw, or fir'd
Fat thighs of oxen and of goats to thee, this grace desir'd   40
Vouchsafe to me: pains for my tears let these rude Greeks repay,
Forc'd with thy arrows." Thus he pray'd, and Phœbus heard him pray,
And, vex'd at heart, down from the tops of steep heav'n stoop'd; his
      bow,
And quiver cover'd round, his hands did on his shoulders throw;
And of the angry Deity the arrows as he mov'd   45
Rattled about him. Like the night he rang'd the host, and rov'd
(Apart the fleet set) terribly; with his hard-loosing hand
His silver bow twang'd; and his shafts did first the mules command,
And swift hounds; then the Greeks themselves his deadly arrows shot.
The fires of death went never out; nine days his shafts flew hot   50
About the army; and the tenth, Achilles called a court
Of all the Greeks; heav'n's white-arm'd Queen (who, ev'rywhere cut
      short,
Beholding her lov'd Greeks, by death) suggested it; and he
(All met in one) arose, and said: "Atrides, now I see
We must be wandering again, flight must be still our stay,   55
If flight can save us now, at once sickness and battle lay
Such strong hand on us. Let us ask some prophet, priest, or prove
Some dream-interpreter (for dreams are often sent from Jove)
Why Phœbus is so much incens'd; if unperform'd vows
He blames in us, or hecatombs; and if these knees he bows   60

[50] *Went*—the second folio omits this word.   [52] *White-arm'd queen*—Juno.

To death may yield his graves no more, but off'ring all supply
Of savours burnt from lambs and goats, avert his fervent eye,
And turn his temp'rate." Thus, he sat; and then stood up to them
Calchas, surnam'd Thestorides, of augurs the supreme;
He knew things present, past, to come, and rul'd the equipage   65
Of th' Argive fleet to Ilion, for his prophetic rage
Giv'n by Apollo; who, well-seen in th' ill they felt, propos'd
This to Achilles: "Jove's belov'd, would thy charge see disclos'd
The secret of Apollo's wrath? then cov'nant and take oath
To my discov'ry, that, with words and pow'rful actions both,   70
Thy strength will guard the truth in me; because I well conceive
That he whose empire governs all, whom all the Grecians give
Confirm'd obedience, will be mov'd; and then you know the state
Of him that moves him. When a king hath once mark'd for his hate
A man inferior, though that day his wrath seems to digest   75
Th' offence he takes, yet evermore he rakes up in his breast
Brands of quick anger, till revenge hath quench'd to his desire
The fire reservéd. Tell me, then, if, whatsoever ire
Suggests in hurt of me to him, thy valour will prevent?"

    Achilles answer'd: "All thou know'st speak, and be confident;   80
For by Apollo, Jove's belov'd, (to whom performing vows,
O Calchas, for the state of Greece, thy spirit prophetic shows
Skills that direct us) not a man of all these Grecians here,
I living, and enjoy'ng the light shot through this flow'ry sphere,
Shall touch thee with offensive hands; though Agamemnon be   85
The man in question, that doth boast the mightiest empery
Of all our army." Then took heart the prophet unreprov'd,
And said: "They are not unpaid vows, nor hecatombs, that mov'd

    66 *Rage*—i. e. power, a frequent use of the word,—the poetic inspiration.
    70 *Discovery*—declaration.
    86 *Empery*—sovereign authority;—
        "Ruling in large and ample *empery*
        O'er France, and all her almost kingly dukedoms."
                                      SHAKESPEARE. *Hen. V.* I. 2.
    87 *Unreproved*—irreproachable. See II. 785.

The God against us; his offence is for his priest impair'd
By Agamemnon, that refus'd the present he preferr'd, 90
And kept his daughter. This is cause why heav'n's Far-darter darts
These plagues amongst us; and this still will empty in our hearts
His deathful quiver, uncontain'd till to her lovéd sire
The black-eyed damsel be resign'd; no redemptory hire
Took for her freedom,—not a gift, but all the ransom quit, 95
And she convey'd, with sacrifice, till her enfranchis'd feet
Tread Chrysa under; then the God, so pleas'd, perhaps we may
Move to remission." Thus, he sate; and up, the great in sway,
Heroic Agamemnon rose, eagerly bearing all;
His mind's seat overcast with fumes; an anger general 100
Fill'd all his faculties; his eyes sparkled like kindling fire,
Which sternly cast upon the priest, thus vented he his ire:
"Prophet of ill! for never good came from thee towards me
Not to a word's worth; evermore thou took'st delight to be
Offensive in thy auguries, which thou continu'st still, 105
Now casting thy prophetic gall, and vouching all our ill,
Shot from Apollo, is impos'd since I refus'd the price
Of fair Chryseis' liberty; which would in no worth rise
To my rate of herself, which moves my vows to have her home,
Past Clytemnestra loving her, that grac'd my nuptial room 110
With her virginity and flow'r. Nor ask her merits less
For person, disposition, wit, and skill in housewif'ries.
And yet, for all this, she shall go, if more conducible
That course be than her holding here. I rather wish the weal
Of my lov'd army than the death. Provide yet instantly 115
Supply for her, that I alone of all our royalty

[93] *Uncontain'd*—not to be emptied, unrestrainable.
[95] *Quit*—paid. To quite, or quit, often used in this sense by Chapman.
[99] *Eagerly bearing all*—treating all angrily, *sourly* (from the French *aigre*).
"If thou think'st so, vex him with *eager* words."
SHAKESPEARE. 3 *Hen. VI.* II. 6.
[116] *Supply for her*—compensation for her loss.

Lose not my winnings. 'Tis not fit. Ye see all I lose mine
Forc'd by another, see as well some other may resign
His prise to me." To this replied the swift-foot, god-like, son
Of Thetis, thus: "King of us all, in all ambition 120
Most covetous of all that breathe, why should the great-soul'd Greeks
Supply thy lost prise out of theirs? Nor what thy av'rice seeks
Our common treasury can find; so little it doth guard
Of what our ras'd towns yielded us; of all which most is shar'd,
And giv'n our soldiers; which again to take into our hands 125
Were ignominious and base. Now then, since God commands,
Part with thy most-lov'd prise to him; not any one of us
Exacts it of thee, yet we all, all loss thou suffer'st thus,
Will treble, quadruple, in gain, when Jupiter bestows
The sack of well-wall'd Troy on us; which by his word he owes." 130

"Do not deceive yourself with wit," he answer'd, "god-like man,
Though your good name may colour it; 'tis not your swift foot can
Outrun me here; nor shall the gloss, set on it with the God,
Persuade me to my wrong. Wouldst thou maintain in sure abode
Thine own prise, and slight me of mine? Resolve this: if our friends,
As fits in equity my worth, will right me with amends, 135
So rest it; otherwise, myself will enter personally
On thy prise, that of Ithacus, or Ajax, for supply;
Let him on whom I enter rage. But come, we'll order these
Hereafter, and in other place. Now put to sacred seas 140
Our black sail; in it rowers put, in it fit sacrifice;
And to these I will make ascend my so much envied prise,

[119] *Prise*—booty, anything seized. I shall retain this orthography throughout, as more expressive of the original. Chapman uses *prize* elsewhere when meaning *value, price*. Thus, in the continuation of Marlowe's Musæus,—
"And five they hold in most especial *prize*,
Since 'tis the first odd number that doth rise
From the two foremost numbers' unity
That odd and even are."—*Sestyad V.*

[138] *Ithacus*—Ulysses.

[139] *Let him, &c.*—i. e. though he may rage.

Bright-cheek'd Chryseis. For condúct of all which, we must choose
A chief out of our counsellors. Thy service we must use,
Idomenëus; Ajax, thine; or thine, wise Ithacus; 145
Or thine, thou terriblest of men, thou son of Pelëus,
Which fittest were, that thou might'st see these holy acts perform'd
For which thy cunning zeal so pleads; and he, whose bow thus storm'd
For our offences, may be calm'd." Achilles, with a frown,
Thus answer'd: "O thou impudent! of no good but thine own 150
Ever respectful, but of that with all craft covetous,
With what heart can a man attempt a service dangerous,
Or at thy voice be spirited to fly upon a foe,
Thy mind thus wretched? For myself, I was not injur'd so
By any Trojan, that my pow'rs should bid them any blows; 155
In nothing bear they blame of me; Phthia, whose bosom flows
With corn and people, never felt impair of her increase
By their invasion; hills enow, and far-resounding seas,
Pour out their shades and deeps between; but thee, thou frontless man,
We follow, and thy triumphs make with bonfires of our bane; 160
Thine, and thy brother's, vengeance sought, thou dog's eyes, of this Troy
By our expos'd lives; whose deserts thou neither dost employ
With honour nor with care. And now, thou threat'st to force from me
The fruit of my sweat, which the Greeks gave all; and though it be,
Compar'd with thy part, then snatch'd up, nothing; nor ever is 165
At any sack'd town; but of fight, the fetcher in of this,
My hands have most share; in whose toils when I have emptied me
Of all my forces, my amends in liberality,
Though it be little, I accept, and turn pleas'd to my tent;
And yet that little thou esteem'st too great a continent 170
In thy incontinent avarice. For Phthia therefore now
My course is; since 'tis better far, than here t' endure that thou

¹⁵⁵ *Bid*—threaten, challenge.
¹⁶² The second folio has "*your* exposed lives;" evidently an error of the press.
¹⁶⁴ *The Greeks gave all*—i. e. all the Greeks gave. See 388.
¹⁷⁰ *Continent*—i. e. possession. *Continent incontinent*, a quibble of Chapman's.

Should'st still be ravishing my right, draw my whole treasure dry,
And add dishonour." He replied: "If thy heart serve thee, fly;
Stay not for my cause; others here will aid and honour me;   175
If not, yet Jove I know is sure; that counsellor is he
That I depend on. As for thee, of all our Jove-kept kings
Thou still art most my enemy; strifes, battles, bloody things,
Make thy blood-feasts still. But if strength, that these moods build
  upon,
Flow in thy nerves, God gave thee it; and so 'tis not thine own,   180
But in his hands still. What then lifts thy pride in this so high?
Home with thy fleet, and Myrmidons; use there their empery;
Command not here. I weigh thee not, nor mean to magnify
Thy rough-hewn rages, but, instead, I thus far threaten thee:
Since Phœbus needs will force from me Chryseis, she shall go;   185
My ships and friends shall waft her home; but I will imitate so
His pleasure, that mine own shall take, in person, from thy tent
Bright-cheek'd Briseis; and so tell thy strength how eminent
My pow'r is, being compar'd with thine; all other making fear
To vaunt equality with me, or in this proud kind bear   190
Their beards against me." Thetis' son at this stood vex'd, his heart
Bristled his bosom, and two ways drew his discursive part;
If, from his thigh his sharp sword drawn, he should make room about
Atrides' person, slaught'ring him, or sit his anger out,   195
And curb his spirit. While these thoughts striv'd in his blood and mind,
And he his sword drew, down from heav'n Athenia stoop'd, and shin'd
About his temples, being sent by th' ivory-wristed Queen,
Saturnia, who out of her heart had ever loving been,
And careful for the good of both. She stood behind, and took
Achilles by the yellow curls, and only gave her look   200

   [174] *Fly*—the second folio and Dr. Taylor, &c.
   [175] *Others*—the second folio, *other.*   [192] *Discursive part*—reasoning power.
   [196] *Athenia*—Minerva.   [198] *Saturnia*—Juno.
   [200] *Only gave her look to him appearance*—i. e. only made her likeness seen by him.

To him appearance ; not a man of all the rest could see.
He turning back his eye, amaze strook every faculty ;
Yet straight he knew her by her eyes, so terrible they were,
Sparkling with ardour, and thus spake : "Thou seed of Jupiter,
Why com'st thou ? To behold his pride, that boasts our empery ? 205
Then witness with it my revenge, and see that insolence die
That lives to wrong me." She replied : "I come from heav'n to see
Thy anger settled, if thy soul will use her sov'reignty,
In fit reflection. I am sent from Juno, whose affects
Stand heartily inclin'd to both. Come, give us both respects, 210
And cease contention ; draw no sword ; use words, and such as may
Be bitter to his pride, but just ; for, trust in what I say,
A time shall come, when, thrice the worth of that he forceth now,
He shall propose for recompense of these wrongs ; therefore throw
Reins on thy passions, and serve us." He answer'd : "Though my heart
Burn in just anger, yet my soul must conquer th' angry part, 216
And yield you conquest. Who subdues his earthly part for heav'n,
Heav'n to his pray'rs subdues his wish." This said, her charge was given
Fit honour ; in his silver hilt he held his able hand,
And forc'd his broad sword up ; and up to heav'n did re-ascend 220
Minerva, who, in Jove's high roof that bears the rough shield, took
Her place with other deities. She gone, again forsook
Patience his passion, and no more his silence could confine
His wrath, that this broad language gave : "Thou ever steep'd in wine,
Dog's face, with heart but of a hart, that nor in th' open eye 225
Of fight dar'st thrust into a prease, nor with our noblest lie
In secret ambush ! These works seem too full of death for thee ;
'Tis safer far in th' open host to dare an injury
To any crosser of thy lust. Thou subject-eating king !
Base spirits thou govern'st, or this wrong had been the last foul thing 230
Thou ever author'dst ; yet I vow, and by a great oath swear,
Ev'n by this sceptre, that, as this never again shall bear

²⁰⁹ *Affects*—affections, passions.   ²²⁶ *Prease*—press.
²³² "This simile Virgil directly translates."—CHAPMAN.

Green leaves or branches, nor increase with any growth his size,
Nor did since first it left the hills, and had his faculties
And ornaments bereft with iron; which now to other end   235
Judges of Greece bear, and their laws, receiv'd from Jove, defend;
(For which my oath to thee is great); so, whensoever need
Shall burn with thirst of me thy host, no pray'rs shall ever breed
Affection in me to their aid, though well-deservéd woes
Afflict thee for them, when to death man-slaught'ring Hector throws 240
Whole troops of them, and thou torment'st thy vex'd mind with conceit
Of thy rude rage now, and his wrong that most deserv'd the right
Of all thy army." Thus, he threw his sceptre 'gainst the ground,
With golden studs stuck, and took seat. Atrides' breast was drown'd
In rising choler. Up to both sweet-spoken Nestor stood,   245
The cunning Pylian orator, whose tongue pour'd forth a flood
Of more-than-honey-sweet discourse; two ages were increas'd
Of divers-languag'd men, all born in his time and deceas'd,
In sacred Pylos, where he reign'd amongst the third-ag'd men.
He, well-seen in the world, advis'd, and thus express'd it then :   250

"O Gods! Our Greek earth will be drown'd in just tears; rapeful Troy,
Her king, and all his sons, will make as just a mock, and joy,
Of these disjunctions; if of you, that all our host excel
In counsel and in skill of fight, they hear this. Come, repel
These young men's passions. Y' are not both, put both your years in one,
So old as I. I liv'd long since, and was companion   255
With men superior to you both, who yet would ever hear
My counsels with respect. My eyes yet never witness were,
Nor ever will be, of such men as then delighted them;
Pirithous, Exadius, and god-like Polypheme,   260
Cæneus, and Dryas prince of men, Ægean Theseüs,
A man like heav'n's immortals form'd; all, all most vigorous,

²⁴² The second folio has "*this* wrong."
²⁵⁵ The second folio has "put both *you* years." It will not be necessary to note all the manifest errors that disfigure this second edition.

Of all men that ev'n those days bred; most vig'rous men, and fought
With beasts most vig'rous, mountain beasts, (for men in strength were
    nought
Match'd with their forces) fought with them, and bravely fought them
    down   265
Yet ev'n with these men I convers'd, being call'd to the renown
Of their societies, by their suits, from Pylos far, to fight
In th' Apian kingdom; and I fought, to a degree of might
That help'd ev'n their mights, against such as no man now would dare
To meet in conflict; yet ev'n these my counsels still would hear,   270
And with obedience crown my words. Give you such palm to them;
'Tis better than to wreath your wraths. Atrides, give not stream
To all thy pow'r, nor force his prise, but yield her still his own,
As all men else do. Nor do thou encounter with thy crown,
Great son of Peleus, since no king that ever Jove allow'd   275
Grace of a sceptre equals him. Suppose thy nerves endow'd
With strength superior, and thy birth a very goddess gave,
Yet he of force is mightier, since what his own nerves have
Is amplified with just command of many other. King of men,
Command thou then thyself; and I with my pray'rs will obtain   280
Grace of Achilles to subdue his fury; whose parts are
Worth our intreaty, being chief check to all our ill in war."

  "All this, good father," said the king, "is comely and good right;
But this man breaks all such bounds; he affects, past all men, height;

---

  [268] *Apian*—both folios have *Asian*, but the original is ἐξ Ἀπίης γαίης, *i. e.* Peloponnesus. Chapman says "*the land of Apia*," in his first translation of XII. Books.

  [272] *To wreath your wraths*—to allow your wrath to triumph: an allusion to the wreaths worn by victors.—Dr. COOKE TAYLOR. The expression is not in the Greek. Though both folios read *wreath*, perhaps *wreak* revenge, might be the true word.

  [274] *Encounter with thy crown*—enter into dispute with thy sovereign.

  [279] *Amplified.*—The second folio (which Dr. Taylor follows) has "*amplied*." The metre would require that the word "*many*" should be omitted.

  [283] *Good right*—right good, very good.

  [284] *Affects height*—aims at superiority above all men.

All would in his pow'r hold, all make his subjects, give to all 285
His hot will for their temp'rate law ; all which he never shall
Persuade at my hands. If the gods have giv'n him the great style
Of ablest soldier, made they that his licence to revile
Men with vile language?" Thetis' son prevented him, and said:
  "Fearful and vile I might be thought, if the exactions laid 290
By all means on me I should bear. Others command to this,
Thou shalt not me ; or if thou dost, far my free spirit is
From serving thy command. Beside, this I affirm (afford
Impression of it in thy soul) I will not use my sword
On thee or any for a wench, unjustly though thou tak'st 295
The thing thou gav'st ; but all things else, that in my ship thou mak'st
Greedy survey of, do not touch without my leave ; or do,—
Add that act's wrong to this, that these may see that outrage too,—
And then comes my part ; then be sure, thy blood upon my lance
Shall flow in vengeance." These high terms these two at variance 300
Us'd to each other ; left their seats ; and after them arose
The whole court. To his tents and ships, with friends and soldiers,
    goes
Angry Achilles. Atreus' son the swift ship launch'd, and put
Within it twenty chosen row'rs, within it likewise shut
The hecatomb t' appease the God ; then caus'd to come aboard 305
Fair-cheek'd Chryseis ; for the chief, he in whom Pallas pour'd
Her store of counsels, Ithacus, aboard went last ; and then
The moist ways of the sea they sail'd. And now the king of men
Bade all the host to sacrifice. They sacrific'd, and cast
The offal of all to the deeps ; the angry God they grac'd 310
With perfect hecatombs ; some bulls, some goats, along the shore
Of the unfruitful sea, inflam'd. To heav'n the thick fumes bore

  [286] *Their temp'rate*—the second folio and Dr. Taylor, *a temp'rate*.
  [295] *Wench*—originally meant a young woman only, without the contemptuous familiarity now annexed to it.—NARES. See 2 Sam. xvii. 17. It is still used in a good sense as a provincialism.
  [312] *Inflam'd*—burnt, set in flames.

Enwrappéd savours. Thus, though all the politic king made shew
Respects to heav'n, yet he himself all that time did pursue
His own affections; the late jar, in which he thunder'd threats 315
Against Achilles, still he fed, and his affections' heats
Thus vented to Talthybius, and grave Eurybates,
Heralds, and ministers of trust, to all his messages.
 "Haste to Achilles' tent; where take Briseis' hand, and bring
Her beauties to us. If he fail to yield her, say your king 320
Will come himself, with multitudes that shall the horribler
Make both his presence, and your charge, that so he dares defer."
 This said, he sent them with a charge of hard condition.
They went unwillingly, and trod the fruitless sea's shore; soon
They reach'd the navy and the tents, in which the quarter lay 325
Of all the Myrmidons, and found the chief Chief in their sway
Set at his black bark in his tent. Nor was Achilles glad
To see their presence; nor themselves in any glory had
Their message, but with rev'rence stood, and fear'd th' offended king,
Ask'd not the dame, nor spake a word. He yet, well knowing the thing
That caus'd their coming, grac'd them thus: "Heralds, ye men that bear 331
The messages of men and gods, y' are welcome, come ye near.
I nothing blame you, but your king; 'tis he I know doth send
You for Briseis; she is his. Patroclus, honour'd friend,
Bring forth the damsel, and these men let lead her to their lord. 335
But, heralds, be you witnesses, before the most ador'd,
Before us mortals, and before your most ungentle king,
Of what I suffer, that, if war ever hereafter bring
My aid in question, to avert any severest bane
It brings on others, I am 'scus'd to keep mine aid in wane, 340
Since they mine honour. But your king, in tempting mischief, raves,
Nor sees at once by present things the future; how like waves
Ills follow ills; injustices being never so secure
In present times, but after-plagues ev'n then are seen as sure; 344

Which yet he sees not, and so soothes his present lust, which, check'd,
Would check plagues future ; and he might, in succouring right, protect
Such as fight for his right at fleet.   They still in safety fight,
That fight still justly."   This speech us'd, Patroclus did the rite
His friend commanded, and brought forth Briseis from her tent,
Gave her the heralds, and away to th' Achive ships they went.   350
She sad, and scarce for grief could go.   Her love all friends forsook,
And wept for anger.   To the shore of th' old sea he betook
Himself alone, and casting forth upon the purple sea
His wet eyes, and his hands to heav'n advancing, this sad plea
Made to his mother ; "Mother ! Since you brought me forth to breathe
So short a life, Olympius had good right to bequeath   356
My short life honour ; yet that right he doth in no degree,
But lets Atrides do me shame, and force that prise from me
That all the Greeks gave."   This with tears he utter'd, and she heard,
Set with her old sire in his deeps, and instantly appear'd   360
Up from the grey sea like a cloud, sate by his side, and said :
   "Why weeps my son ? What grieves thee ? Speak, conceal not what
         hath laid
Such hard hand on thee, let both know."   He, sighing like a storm,
Replied: "Thou dost know.   Why should I things known again inform ?
We march'd to Thebes, the sacred town of king Eëtion,   365
Sack'd it, and brought to fleet the spoil, which every valiant son
Of Greece indifferéntly shar'd.   Atrides had for share
Fair cheek'd Chryseis.   After which, his priest that shoots so far,
Chryses, the fair Chryseis' sire, arriv'd at th' Achive fleet,
With infinite ransom, to redeem the dear imprison'd feet   370
Of his fair daughter.   In his hands he held Apollo's crown,
And golden sceptre ; making suit to ev'ry Grecian son,
But most the sons of Atreus, the others' orderers,
Yet they least heard him ; all the rest receiv'd with rev'rend ears

<small>³⁵¹ *Her love*—Achilles.   ³⁵⁶ *Olympius*—Jupiter.
³⁶⁸ *His priest that shoots so far*—the priest of far-darting Apollo.</small>

The motion, both the priest and gifts gracing, and holding worth 375
His wish'd acceptance. Atreus' son yet (vex'd) commanded forth
With rude terms Phœbus' rev'rend priest; who, angry, made retreat,
And pray'd to Phœbus, in whose grace he standing passing great
Got his petitión. The God an ill shaft sent abroad
That tumbled down the Greeks in heaps. The host had no abode 380
That was not visited. We ask'd a prophet that well knew
The cause of all; and from his lips Apollo's prophecies flew,
Telling his anger. First myself exhorted to appease
The anger'd God; which Atreus' son did at the heart displease,
And up he stood, us'd threats, perform'd. The black-eyed Greeks sent home 385
Chryseis to her sire, and gave his God a hecatomb.
Then, for Briseis, to my tents Atrides' heralds came,
And took her that the Greeks gave all. If then thy pow'rs can frame
Wreak for thy son, afford it. Scale Olympus, and implore
Jove (if by either word, or fact, thou ever didst restore 390
Joy to his griev'd heart) now to help. I oft have heard thee vaunt,
In court of Peleus, that alone thy hand was conversant.
In rescue from a cruel spoil the black-cloud-gath'ring Jove,
Whom other Godheads would have bound (the Pow'r whose pace doth move
The round earth, heav'n's great Queen, and Pallas); to whose bands
Thou cam'st with rescue, bringing up him with the hundred hands 395
To great Olympus, whom the Gods call Briarëus, men
Ægæon, who his sire surpass'd, and was as strong again,'
And in that grace sat glad by Jove. Th' immortals stood dismay'd
At his ascensïon, and gave free passage to his aid. 400
Of all this tell Jove; kneel to him, embrace his knee, and pray,
If Troy's aid he will ever deign, that now their forces may

---

376 *His wish'd acceptance*—that which he wished to be accepted.
389 *Wreak*—revenge. A frequent word in Elizabethan writers.
393 *Spoil*—injury.
394 Neptune, Juno, Minerva.

Beat home the Greeks to fleet and sea; embruing their retreat
In slaughter; their pains pay'ng the wreak of their proud sov'reign's heat;
And that far-ruling king may know, from his poor soldier's harms 405
His own harm falls; his own and all in mine, his best in arms."

Her answer she pour'd out in tears: "O me, my son," said she,
"Why brought I up thy being at all, that brought thee forth to be
Sad subject of so hard a fate? O would to heav'n, that since
Thy fate is little, and not long, thou might'st without offence 410
And tears perform it! But to live, thrall to so stern a fate
As grants thee least life, and that least so most unfortunate,
Grieves me t' have giv'n thee any life. But what thou wishest now,
If Jove will grant, I'll up and ask; Olympus crown'd with snow
I'll climb; but sit thou fast at fleet, renounce all war, and feed 415
Thy heart with wrath, and hope of wreak; till which come, thou shalt need
A little patience. Jupiter went yesterday to feast
Amongst the blameless Æthiops, in th' ocean's deepen'd breast,
All Gods attending him; the twelfth, high heav'n again he sees,
And then his brass-pav'd court I'll scale, cling to his pow'rful knees, 420
And doubt not but to win thy wish." Thus, made she her remove,
And left wrath tyring on her son, for his enforcèd love.

Ulysses, with the hecatomb, arriv'd at Chrysa's shore;
And when amidst the hav'n's deep mouth, they came to use the oar,
They straight strook sail, then roll'd them up, and on the hatches
 threw; 425
The top-mast to the kelsine then, with halyards down they drew;
Then brought the ship to port with oars; then forkèd anchor cast;
And, 'gainst the violence of storm, for drifting made her fast.

All come ashore, they all expos'd the holy hecatomb
To angry Phœbus, and, with it, Chryseis welcom'd home; 430

---

[422] *Tyring*—a term in falconry; from *tirer* (French), to drag or pull. The hawk was said to tire on her prey, when it was thrown at her, and she began to pull at it and tear it. Hence, metaphorically, for *being engaged eagerly on any thing*. Shakespeare thus uses it; Cymb. III. 4, Tim. of Athens, III. 6.—NARES.

[422] *For his enforced love*—for Briseis forced from him.

Whom to her sire, wise Ithacus, that did at th' altar stand,
For honour led, and, spoken thus, resign'd her to his hand:
"Chryses, the mighty king of men, great Agamemnon, sends
Thy lov'd seed by my hands to thine; and to thy God commends
A hecatomb, which my charge is to sacrifice, and seek 435
Our much-sigh-mix'd woe his recure, invok'd by ev'ry Greek."
  Thus he resign'd her, and her sire receiv'd her highly joy'd.
About the well-built altar, then, they orderly employ'd
The sacred off'ring, wash'd their hands, took salt cakes; and the priest,
With hands held up to heav'n, thus pray'd: "O thou that all things seest,
Fautour of Chrysa, whose fair hand doth guardfully dispose 441
Celestial Cilla, governing in all pow'r Tenedos,
O hear thy priest, and as thy hand, in free grace to my pray'rs,
Shot fervent plague-shafts through the Greeks, now hearten their affairs
With health renew'd, and quite remove th' infection from their blood." 445
  He pray'd; and to his pray'rs again the God propitious stood.
All, after pray'r, cast on salt cakes, drew back, kill'd, flay'd the beeves,
Cut out and dubb'd with fat their thighs, fair dress'd with doubled leaves,
And on them all the sweetbreads prick'd. The priest, with small sere wood,
Did sacrifice, pour'd on red wine; by whom the young men stood, 450
And turn'd, in five ranks, spits; on which (the legs enough) they eat
The inwards; then in giggots cut the other fit for meat,
And put to fire; which roasted well they drew. The labour done,
They serv'd the feast in, that fed all to satisfaction.
  Desire of meat and wine thus quench'd, the youths crown'd cups of wine
Drunk off, and fill'd again to all. That day was held divine, 456

---

⁴³² *Spoken thus.*—The second folio has "*speaking thus.*"
⁴³⁶ *Recure*—cure. *His* refers to cure—*our woe's recure.*
⁴⁴¹ *Fautour*—(Lat.) aider, favourer.
⁴⁴³ *Dubb'd.*—From the French *dauber*. We use the word *dubbed on* now in the same sense. Halliwell, in his Archaic Dict., quotes "Morte Arthure, MS. Linc. f. 88;—"
  "His dyademe was droppede downe
    Dubbyde with stonys."
⁴⁵² *Giggots*—quarters; from French *gigot.*

And spent in pæans to the Sun, who heard with pleaséd ear;
When whose bright chariot stoop'd to sea, and twilight hid the clear,
All soundly on their cables slept, ev'n till the night was worn.
And when the lady of the light, the rosy-finger'd Morn,   460
Rose from the hills, all fresh arose, and to the camp retir'd.
Apollo with a fore-right wind their swelling bark inspir'd.
The top-mast hoisted, milk-white sails on his round breast they put,
The mizens strooted with the gale, the ship her course did cut
So swiftly that the parted waves against her ribs did roar;   465
Which, coming to the camp, they drew aloft the sandy shore,
Where, laid on stocks, each soldier kept his quarter as before.

 But Peleus' son, swift-foot Achilles, at his swift ships sate,
Burning in wrath, nor ever came to councils of estate
That make men honour'd, never trod the fierce embattled field,   470
But kept close, and his lov'd heart pin'd, what fight and cries could yield
Thirsting at all parts to the host. And now, since first he told
His wrongs to Thetis, twelve fair morns their ensigns did unfold,
And then the ever-living gods mounted Olympus, Jove
First in ascension. Thetis then, remember'd well to move   475
Achilles' motion, rose from sea, and, by the morn's first light,
The great heav'n and Olympus climb'd; where, in supremest height
Of all that many-headed hill, she saw the far-seen son
Of Saturn, set from all the rest, in his free seat alone.
Before whom, on her own knees fall'n, the knees of Jupiter   480
Her left hand held, her right his chin, and thus she did prefer
Her son's petition: "Father Jove! If ever I have stood
Aidful to thee in word or work, with this imploréd good

---

   464 *Strooted*—swelled out. Halliwell spells it *strout*, which he says is still in use.
   466 *Aloft*—high up on.
   471 "Eagerly desirous of what fight and cries could yield at all parts of the host. The Greek is more simple: 'He ardently desired shout and war.'"
Dr. Cooke Taylor.

   476 The second folio reads "*rose from the sea.*"

Requite my aid, renown my son, since in so short a race
(Past others) thou confin'st his life. An insolent disgrace 485
Is done him by the king of men ; he forc'd from him a prise
Won with his sword. But thou, O Jove, that art most strong, most wise,
Honour my son for my sake ; add strength to the Trojans' side
By his side's weakness in his want ; and see Troy amplified
In conquest, so much, and so long, till Greece may give again 490
The glory reft him, and the more illustrate the free reign
Of his wrong'd honour." Jove at this sate silent ; not a word
In long space pass'd him. Thetis still hung on his knee, implor'd
The second time his help, and said : "Grant, or deny my suit,
Be free in what thou dost ; I know, thou canst not sit thus mute 495
For fear of any ; speak, deny, that so I may be sure,
Of all heav'n's Goddesses 'tis I, that only must endure
Dishonour by thee." Jupiter, the great cloud-gath'rer, griev'd
With thought of what a world of griefs this suit ask'd, being achiev'd,
Swell'd, sigh'd, and answer'd : "Works of death thou urgest. O, at this
Juno will storm, and all my pow'rs inflame with contumelies. 501
Ever she wrangles, charging me in ear of all the Gods
That I am partial still, that I add the displeasing odds
Of my aid to the Ilians. Begone then, lest she see ;
Leave thy request to my care ; yet, that trust may hearten thee 505
With thy desire's grant, and my pow'r to give it act approve
How vain her strife is, to thy pray'r my eminent head shall move ;
Which is the great sign of my will with all th' immortal states ;
Irrevocable ; never fails ; never without the rates
Of all pow'rs else ; when my head bows, all heads bow with it still 510
As their first mover ; and gives pow'r to any work I will."
 He said ; and his black eyebrows bent ; above his deathless head
Th' ambrosian curls flow'd ; great heav'n shook : and both were sever'd,
Their counsels broken. To the depth of Neptune's kingdom div'd
Thetis from heav'n's height ; Jove arose ; and all the Gods receiv'd 515

⁵⁰⁹ *Rates*—ratifications.

(A rising from their thrones) their Sire, attending to his court.
None sate when he rose, none delay'd the furnishing his port
Till he came near; all met with him, and brought him to his throne.
  Nor sate great Juno ignorant, when she beheld alone
Old Nereus' silver-footed seed with Jove, that she had brought   520
Counsels to heav'n; and straight her tongue had teeth in it, that
    wrought
This sharp invective: "Who was that (thou craftiest counsellor
Of all the Gods) that so apart some secret did implore?
Ever, apart from me, thou lov'st to counsel and decree
Things of more close trust than thou think'st are fit t' impart to me.
Whatever thou determin'st, I must ever be denied   525
The knowledge of it by thy will." To her speech thus replied
The Father both of men and Gods: "Have never hope to know,
My whole intentions, though my wife; it fits not, nor would show
Well to thine own thoughts; but what fits thy woman's ear to hear,   530
Woman, nor man, nor God, shall know before it grace thine ear.
Yet what, apart from men and Gods, I please to know, forbear
T' examine, or inquire of that." She with the cow's fair eyes,
Respected Juno, this return'd: "Austere king of the skies,
What hast thou utter'd? When did I before this time inquire,   535
Or sift thy counsels? Passing close you are still. Your desire
Is serv'd with such care, that I fear you can scarce vouch the deed
That makes it public, being seduc'd by this old sea-god's seed,
That could so early use her knees, embracing thine. I doubt,
The late act of thy bowéd head was for the working out   540
Of some boon she ask'd; that her son thy partial hand would please
With plaguing others." "Wretch!" said he, "thy subtle jealousies

---

   517 *Furnishing his port*—assuming a proper deportment.
   520 *Nereus' silver-footed seed*—Thetis.
   533 *With the cow's fair eyes*—Chapman has retained the original meaning of the word βοῶπις, and, I think, rightly. Oxen have beautiful eyes irrespective of their magnitude. In Bk. VII. 10, he translates it *"that had her eyes so clear."*

Are still exploring; my designs can never 'scape thine eye,
Which yet thou never canst prevent. Thy curiosity
Makes thee less car'd for at my hands, and horrible the end 545
Shall make thy humour. If it be what thy suspects intend,
What then? 'Tis my free will it should; to which let way be giv'n
With silence. Curb your tongue in time; lest all the Gods in heav'n
Too few be and too weak to help thy punish'd insolence,
When my inaccessible hands shall fall on thee." The sense 550
Of this high threat'ning made her fear, and silent she sate down,
Humbling her great heart. All the Gods in court of Jove did frown
At this offence giv'n; amongst whom heav'n's famous artizan,
Ephaistus, in his mother's care, this comely speech began:
"Believe it, these words will breed wounds, beyond our pow'rs to bear,
If thus for mortals ye fall out. Ye make a tumult here 555
That spoils our banquet. Evermore worst matters put down best.
But, mother, though yourself be wise, yet let your son request
His wisdom audience. Give good terms to our lov'd father Jove,
For fear he take offence again, and our kind banquet prove 560
A wrathful battle. If he will, the heav'nly Light'ner can
Take you and toss you from your throne; his pow'r Olympian
Is so surpassing. Soften then with gentle speech his spleen,
And drink to him; I know his heart will quickly down again."
This said, arising from his throne, in his lov'd mother's hand 565
He put the double-handed cup, and said: "Come, do not stand
On these cross humours, suffer, bear, though your great bosom grieve,
And lest blows force you; all my aid not able to relieve
Your hard condition, though these eyes behold it, and this heart
Sorrow to think it. 'Tis a task too dang'rous to take part 570

[543] *Still exploring*—ever prying.   [554] *Ephaistus*—Vulcan.
[559] *Wisdom audience*—i. e. a hearing for his wisdom.
[566] *Double-handed*—so reads the second folio; in the first it was "*double-handled*." The δέπας ἀμφικύπελλον, however, was not a cup with two handles, but which was held in the middle with a cup at each end.

Against Olympius. I myself the proof of this still feel.
When other Gods would fain have help'd, he took me by the heel,
And hurl'd me out of heav'n. All day I was in falling down ;
At length in Lemnos I strook earth. The likewise-falling sun
And I, together, set ; my life almost set too ; yet there   575
The Sintii cheer'd and took me up." This did to laughter cheer
White-wristed Juno, who now took the cup of him, and smil'd.
The sweet peace-making draught went round, and lame Ephaistus fill'd
Nectar to all the other Gods. A laughter never left
Shook all the blessèd deities, to see the lame so deft   580
At that cup service. All that day, ev'n till the sun went down,
They banqueted, and had such cheer as did their wishes crown.
Nor had they music less divine ; Apollo there did touch
His most sweet harp, to which, with voice, the Muses pleas'd as much.
But when the sun's fair light was set, each Godhead to his house   585
Address'd for sleep, where every one, with art most curious,
By heav'n's great both-foot-halting God a sev'ral roof had built.
Ev'n he to sleep went, by whose hand heav'n is with lightning gilt,
High Jove, where he had us'd to rest when sweet sleep seiz'd his eyes ;
By him the golden-thron'd Queen slept, the Queen of deities.   590

⁵⁸⁰ *Deft*—dexterous, neat.
⁵⁸⁷ *Great both-foot-halting God*—Vulcan

COMMENTARIUS.

SINCE I dissent from all other translators, and interpreters, that ever assayed exposition of this miraculous poem, especially where the divine rapture is most exempt from capacity in grammarians merely, and grammatical critics, and where the inward sense or soul of the sacred muse is only within eye-shot of a poetical spirit's inspection (lest I be prejudiced with opinion, to dissent, of ignorance, or singularity) I am bound, by this brief comment, to show I understand how all other extants understand; my reasons why I reject them; and how I receive my author. In which labour, if, where all others find discords and dissonances, I prove him entirely harmonious and proportionate; if, where they often alter and fly his original, I at all parts stand fast, and observe it; if, where they mix their most pitiful castigations with his praises, I render him without touch, and beyond admiration, (though truth in her very nakedness sits in so deep a pit, that from Gades to Aurora, and Ganges, few eyes can sound her) I hope yet those few here will so discover and confirm her, that, the date being out of her darkness in this morning of our Homer, he shall now gird his temples with the sun, and be confessed (against his good friend) *nunquam dormitare*. But how all translators, censors, or interpreters, have slept, and been dead to his true understanding, I hope it will neither cast shadow of arrogance in me to affirm, nor of difficulty in you to believe, if you please to suspend censure, and diminution, till your impartial conference of their pains and mine be admitted. For induction and preparative to which patience, and persuasion, trouble yourselves but to know this. This never-enough-glorified poet (to vary and quicken his eternal poem) hath inspired his chief persons with different spirits, most ingenious and inimitable characters, which not understood, how are their speeches, being one by another as conveniently and necessarily known as the instrument by the sound? If a translator or interpreter of a ridiculous and cowardly-described person (being deceived in his character) so violates, and vitiates, the original, to make his speech grave, and him valiant; can the negligence and numbness of such an interpreter or translator be less than the sleep and death I am bold to sprinkle upon him? Or could I do less than affirm and enforce this, being so happily discovered? This, therefore (in his due place) approved and explained, let me hope my other assumpts will prove as conspicuous.

This first and second book I have wholly translated again; the seventh, eighth, ninth, and tenth, books deferring still imperfect, being all Englished so long since, and my late hand (overcome with labour) not yet rested enough to refine them. Nor are the wealthy veins of this holy ground so amply discovered in my first twelve labours as my last; not having competent time, nor my profit in his mysteries being so ample, as when driving through his thirteenth and last books, I drew the main depth, and saw the round coming off this silver bow of our Phœbus; the clear scope and contexture of his work; the full and most beautiful figures of his persons. To those last twelve, then, I must refer you, for all the chief worth of my clear discoveries; and in the mean space I entreat your acceptance of some few new touches in the first. Not perplexing you in first or last with anything handled in any other interpreter, further than I must conscionably make congression with such as have diminished, mangled, and maimed, my most worthily most tendered author.

3. 'Αΐδι προΐαψεν. αΐδης (being compounded *ex ἀ privativa*, and εἴδω, *video*) signifies *locus tenebricosus*, or, according to Virgil, *sine luce domus;* and therefore (different from others) I so convert it.

4. Κύνεσσιν, οἰωνοῖσί τε πᾶσι (Διὸς, &c.) is the vulgar reading, which I read κύνεσσιν οἰωνοῖσί τε (πᾶσι Διὸς δὲ τελείετο βουλὴ), because πᾶσι referred to κύνεσσιν, &c., is redundant and idle; to the miseries of the Greeks by Jove's counsel, grave, and sententious.

5. Ἐξ οὗ δὴ τὰ πρῶτα, &c., *ex quo quidem primum:* Ἐξ οὗ δὴ τὰ πρῶτα, &c., *ex quo.* Here our common readers would have *tempore* understood, because βουλή (to which they think the poet must otherwise have reference) is the feminine gender. But Homer understands Jove; as in Ταυ, verse 273, he expounds himself in these words: ἀλλά ποθι Ζεὺς, &c., which Pindarus Thebanus, in his epitome of these Iliads, rightly observes in these verses:—

> "Conficiebat enim summi sententia Regis,
> Ex quo contulerant discordi pectore pugnas
> Sceptriger Atrides, et bello clarus Achilles."

21. Ἐπευφήμησαν Ἀχαιοί, *comprobárunt Græci* all others turn it; but since ἐπευφημέω signifies properly, *fausta acclamatione do significationem approbationis,* I therefore accordingly convert it, because the other intimates a comprobation of all the Greeks by word, which was not so, but only by inarticulate acclamations or shouts.

37. Ἀμφιβέβηκας· ἀμφιβεβάω* signifies properly *circumambulo,* and only metaphoricè *protego,* or *tueor,* as it is always in this place translated; which suffers alteration with me, since our usual phrase of walking the round in towns of garrison, for the defence of it, fits so well the property of the original.

197. Πρὸ γὰρ ἧκε θεὰ λευκώλενος Ἥρη. *Præmiserat enim Dea alba ulnis Juno.* Why Juno should send Pallas is a thing not noted by any; I therefore answer, because Juno is Goddess of state. The allegory, therefore, in the prosopopœia both of Juno and Pallas, is, that Achilles, for respect to the state there present, the rather used that discretion and restraint of his anger. So in divers other places, when state is represented, Juno procures it; as in the eighteenth book, for the state of Patroclus's fetching off, Juno commands the sun to go down before his time, &c.

300. Ὣς φάτο δακρυχέων: *sic dixit lachrymans,* &c. These tears are called, by our commentators, unworthy, and fitter for children or women than such a hero as Achilles; and therefore Plato is cited in iii.

---

* Chapman meant ἀμφιβάω, the obsolete, or radical, form of ἀμφιβαίνω.

de Repub. where he saith, 'Ορθῶς ἄρα, &c. *Meritò igitur clarorum virorum ploratus è medio tolleremus,* &c. To answer which, and justify the fitness of tears generally (as they may be occasioned) in the greatest and most renowned men (omitting examples of Virgil's Æneas, Alexander the Great, &c.,) I oppose against Plato, only one precedent of great and most perfect humanity (to Whom infinitely above all other we must prostrate our imitations) that shed tears, viz., our All-perfect and Almighty Saviour, Who wept for Lazarus. This then, leaving the fitness of great men's tears, generally, utterly unanswerable, these particular tears of unvented anger in Achilles are in him most natural; tears being the highest effects of greatest and most fiery spirits, either when their abilities cannot perform to their wills, or that they are restrained of revenge, being injured; out of other considerations, as now the consideration of the state and gravity of the counsel and public good of the army-curbed Achilles. Who can deny that there are tears of manliness and magnanimity, as well as womanish and pusillanimous? So Diomed wept for curst heart, when Apollo struck his scourge from him, and hindered his horse-race, having been warned by Pallas before not to resist the deities; and so his great spirits being curbed of revenge for the wrong he received then. So when not-enough-vented anger was not to be expressed enough by that tear-starting affection in courageous and fierce men, our most accomplished expressor helps the illustration in a simile of his fervour, in most fervent-spirited fowls, resembling the wrathful fight of Sarpedon and Patroclus to two vultures fighting, and crying on a rock; which thus I have afterwards Englished, and here for example inserted:—

> "Down jump'd he from his chariot; down leap'd his foe as light;
> And as, on some far-seeing rock, a cast of vultures fight,
> Fly on each other, strike, and truss, part, meet, and then stick by,
> Tug both with crooked beaks and seres, cry, fight, and fight, and cry.
> So fiercely fought these angry kings, &c."

Wherein you see that crying in these eagerly-fought fowls (which is like tears in angry men) is so far from softness or faintness, that to the superlative of hardiness and courage it expresseth both. Nor must we be so gross to imagine that Homer made Achilles or Diomed blubber, or sob, &c., but, in the very point and sting of their unvented anger, shed a few violent and seething-over tears. What ass-like impudence is it then for any merely vain-glorious and self-loving puff, that everywhere may read these inimitable touches of our Homer's mastery, anywhere to oppose his arrogant and ignorant castigations when he should rather (with his much better understander Spondanus) submit where he oversees him faulty, and say thus; "Quia tu tamen hoc voluisti, sacrosanctæ tuæ authoritati per me nihil detrahetur."

THE END OF THE FIRST BOOK

THE SECOND BOOK OF HOMER'S ILIADS.

THE ARGUMENT.

JOVE calls a vision up from Somnus' den
To bid Atrides muster up his men.
The King, to Greeks dissembling his desire,
Persuades them to their country to retire.
By Pallas' will, Ulysses stays their flight;
And wise old Nestor heartens them to fight.
They take their meat; which done, to arms they go,
And march in good array against the foe.
So those of Troy; when Iris, from the sky,
Of Saturn's son performs the embassy.

ANOTHER ARGUMENT.

Beta the dream and synod cites;
And catalogues the naval knights.

HE other Gods, and knights at arms, all night slept;
    only Jove
Sweet slumber seiz'd not; he discours'd how best he
    might approve
His vow made for Achilles' grace, and make the Grecians find
His miss in much death. All ways cast, this counsel serv'd his mind
With most allowance; to dispatch a harmful Dream to greet
The king of men, and gave this charge: "Go to the Achive fleet,

---

[4] *Miss*—absence, or loss.
[5] *Allowance*—approbation.
    "A stirring dwarf we most *allowance* give
      Before a sleeping giant."
              SHAKESPEARE. *Troil. and Cres.* II. 3.

Pernicious Dream, and, being arriv'd in Agamemnon's tent,
Deliver truly all this charge. Command him to convent
His whole host arm'd before these tow'rs ; for now Troy's broad-way'd
    town
He shall take in ; the heav'n-hous'd Gods are now indiff'rent grown :
Juno's request hath won them ; Troy now under imminent ills   11
At all parts labours." This charge heard, the Vision straight fulfils ;
The ships reach'd, and Atrides' tent, in which he found him laid,
Divine sleep pour'd about his powers. He stood above his head
Like Nestor, grac'd of old men most, and this did intimate :   15
    " Sleeps the wise Atreus' tame-horse son ? A councillor of state
Must not the whole night spend in sleep, to whom the people are
For guard committed, and whose life stands bound to so much care.
Now hear me, then, Jove's messenger, who, though far off from thee,
Is near thee yet in ruth and care, and gives command by me   20
To arm thy whole host. Thy strong hand the broad-way'd town of
    Troy
Shall now take in ; no more the Gods dissentiously employ
Their high-hous'd powers ; Juno's suit hath won them all to her ;
And ill fates overhang these tow'rs, address'd by Jupiter.
Fix in thy mind this, nor forget to give it action, when   25
Sweet sleep shall leave thee." Thus, he fled ; and left the king of men
Repeating in discourse his dream, and dreaming still, awake,
Of pow'r, not ready yet for act. O fool, he thought to take
In that next day old Priam's town ; not knowing what affairs
Jove had in purpose, who prepar'd, by strong fight, sighs and cares   30
For Greeks and Trojans. The Dream gone, his voice still murmured
About the king's ears ; who sate up, put on him in his bed

[8] *Convent*—convene.   [10] *Take in*—conquer. Shakespeare.
                                              " Is it not strange, Canidius,
                               He could so quickly cut th' Ionian sea,
                               And *take in* Toryne ?"—*Anton. and Cleop.* III. 7.
[16] *Tame-horse*—tamer of horses.
[20] *Ruth*—pity, tender care. A word in use even in Milton's time.
[24] *Address'd*—prepared. A frequent word.

His silken inner weed, fair, new; and then in haste arose,
Cast on his ample mantle, tied to his soft feet fair shoes,
His silver-hilted sword he hung about his shoulders, took 35
His father's sceptre never stain'd, which then abroad he shook,
And went to fleet. And now great heav'n Goddess Aurora scal'd,
To Jove, and all Gods, bringing light; when Agamemnon call'd
His heralds, charging them aloud to call to instant court
The thick-hair'd Greeks. The heralds call'd; the Greeks made quick
    resort. 40
The Council chiefly he compos'd of old great-minded men,
At Nestor's ships, the Pylian king. All there assembled then,
Thus Atreus' son began the court: "Hear, friends: A Dream divine,
Amidst the calm night in my sleep, did through my shut eyes shine,
Within my fantasy. His form did passing naturally 45
Resemble Nestor; such attire, a stature just as high.
He stood above my head, and words thus fashion'd did relate:
'Sleeps the wise Atreus' tame-horse son? A councillor of state
Must not the whole night spend in sleep, to whom the people are
For guard committed, and whose life stands bound to so much care. 50
Now hear me then, Jove's messenger, who, though far off from thee,
Is near thee yet in love and care, and gives command by me
To arm thy whole host. Thy strong hand the broad-way'd town of Troy
Shall now take in; no more the God's dissentiously employ
Their high-hous'd pow'rs; Saturnia's suit hath won them all to her; 55
And ill fates over-hang these tow'rs, address'd by Jupiter.
Fix in thy mind this.' This express'd, he took wing and away,
And sweet sleep left me. Let us then by all our means assay
To arm our army; I will first (as far as fits our right)
Try their addictions, and command with full-sail'd ships our flight; 60

---

[33] *Weed*—dress. Now generally used for mourning, but formerly for any dress. Thus Spenser,

"A goodlie ladie, clad in hunter's *weed.*"—*F.Q.* II. iii. 21.

[60] *Addictions*—will, inclinations.

Which if they yield to, oppose you." He sate, and up arose
Nestor, of sandy Pylos king, who, willing to dispose
Their counsel to the public good, propos'd this to the state:
 "Princes and Councillors of Greece, if any should relate
This vision but the king himself, it might be held a tale, 65
And move the rather our retreat; but since our General
Affirms he saw it, hold it true, and all our best means make
To arm our army." This speech us'd, he first the Council brake;
The other sceptre-bearing States arose too, and obey'd
The people's Rector. Being abroad, the earth was overlaid 70
With flockers to them, that came forth, as when of frequent bees
Swarms rise out of a hollow rock, repairing the degrees
Of their egression endlessly, with ever rising new
From forth their sweet nest; as their store, still as it faded, grew,
And never would cease sending forth her clusters to the spring, 75
They still crowd out so; this flock here, that there, belabouring
The loaded flow'rs; so from the ships and tents the army's store
Troop'd to these princes and the court, along th' unmeasur'd shore;
Amongst whom, Jove's ambassadress, Fame, in her virtue shin'd,
Exciting greediness to hear. The rabble, thus inclin'd, 80
Hurried together; uproar seiz'd the high court; earth did groan
Beneath the settling multitude; tumult was there alone.
Thrice-three vocif'rous heralds rose, to check the rout, and get
Ear to their Jove-kept governors; and instantly was set
That huge confusion; ev'ry man set fast, the clamour ceas'd. 85
Then stood divine Atrides up, and in his hand compress'd
His sceptre, th' elaborate work of fi'ry Mulciber,
Who gave it to Saturnian Jove; Jove to his messenger;

---

⁶⁹ *States*—rulers, persons of authority.
⁷¹ *Frequent*—numerous.
⁷² *Repairing the degrees*—filling up the ranks.
⁷⁸ *Unmeasur'd*—immeasurable. Chapman commonly uses the past participle thus.
⁸⁵ *That huge confusion*—the second folio has "*the* huge confusion."

His messenger, Argicides, to Pelops, skill'd in horse;
Pelops to Atreus, chief of men; he, dying, gave it course 90
To prince Thyestes, rich in herds; Thyestes to the hand
Of Agamemnon render'd it, and with it the command
Of many isles, and Argos all. On this he leaning, said:
  "O friends, great sons of Danaus, servants of Mars, Jove laid
A heavy curse on me, to vow, and bind it with the bent 95
Of his high forehead; that, this Troy of all her people spent,
I should return; yet now to mock our hopes built on his vow,
And charge ingloriously my flight, when such an overthrow
Of brave friends I have authoréd. But to his mightiest will
We must submit us, that hath raz'd, and will be razing still, 100
Men's footsteps from so many towns; because his pow'r is most,
He will destroy most. But how vile such and so great an host
Will show to future times, that, match'd with lesser numbers far,
We fly, not putting on the crown of our so long-held war,
Of which there yet appears no end! Yet should our foes and we 105
Strike truce, and number both our pow'rs; Troy taking all that be
Her arm'd inhabitants, and we, in tens, should all sit down
At our truce banquet, ev'ry ten allow'd one of the town
To fill his feast-cup; many tens would their attendant want;
So much I must affirm our pow'r exceeds th' inhabitant. 110
But their auxiliáry bands, those brandishers of spears,
From many cities drawn, are they that are our hinderers,
Not suff'ring well-rais'd Troy to fall. Nine years are ended now,
Since Jove our conquest vow'd; and now, our vessels rotten grow,
Our tackling fails; our wives, young sons, sit in their doors and long
For our arrival; yet the work, that should have wreak'd our wrong, 115

[89] *Argicides*—the slayer of Argus, Mercury.
[90] *Gave it course*—gave it in turn.
[95] *Bent*—bend, nod. See Bk. I. 575-6.
[104] *Putting on the crown*—concluding.
[110] *Inhabitant*—inhabiters, viz. of Troy; the Trojans as distinguished from their allies.

And made us welcome, lies unwrought. Come then, as I bid, all
Obey, and fly to our lov'd home; for now, nor ever, shall
Our utmost take-in broad-way'd Troy." This said, the multitude
Was all for home; and all men else that what this would conclude 120
Had not discover'd. All the crowd was shov'd about the shore,
In sway, like rude and raging waves, rous'd with the fervent blore
Of th' east and south winds, when they break from Jove's clouds, and
    are borne
On rough backs of th' Icarian seas: or like a field of corn
High grown, that Zephyr's vehement gusts bring eas'ly underneath, 125
And make the stiff up-bristled ears do homage to his breath;
For ev'n so eas'ly, with the breath Atrides us'd, was sway'd
The violent multitude. To fleet with shouts, and disarray'd,
All rush'd; and, with a fog of dust, their rude feet dimm'd the day; 129
Each cried to other, 'Cleanse our ships, come, launch, aboard, away.'
The clamour of the runners home reach'd heav'n; and then, past fate,
The Greeks had left Troy, had not then the Goddess of estate
Thus spoke to Pallas: "O foul shame, thou untam'd seed of Jove,
Shall thus the sea's broad back be charg'd with these our friends' remove,
Thus leaving Argive Helen here, thus Priam grac'd, thus Troy, 135
In whose fields, far from their lov'd own, for Helen's sake, the joy
And life of so much Grecian birth is vanish'd? Take thy way
T' our brass-arm'd people, speak them fair, let not a man obey
The charge now giv'n, nor launch one ship." She said, and Pallas did
As she commanded; from the tops of heav'n's steep hill she slid, 140
And straight the Greeks' swift ships she reach'd; Ulysses (like to Jove
In gifts of counsel) she found out; who to that base remove
Stirr'd not a foot, nor touch'd a ship, but griev'd at heart to see
That fault in others. To him close the blue-eyed Deity
Made way, and said: "Thou wisest Greek, divine Laertes' son, 145
Thus fly ye homewards to your ships? Shall all thus headlong run?

      [122] *Fervent blore*—raging gale, blast.
      [132] *Goddess of estate*—chief Goddess, Juno.

Glory to Priam thus ye leave, glory to all his friends,
If thus ye leave her here, for whom so many violent ends
Have clos'd your Greek eyes, and so far from their so lovéd home.
Go to these people, use no stay, with fair terms overcome 150
Their foul endeavour, not a man a flying sa͜il let hoice."

    Thus spake she; and Ulysses knew 'twas Pallas by her voice,
Ran to the runners, cast from him his mantle, which his man
And herald, grave Eurybates, the Ithacensian
That follow'd him, took up. Himself to Agamemnon went, 155
His incorrupted sceptre took, his sceptre of descent,
And with it went about the fleet. What prince, or man of name,
He found flight-giv'n, he would restrain with words of gentlest blame:
    "Good sir, it fits not you to fly, or fare as one afraid,
You should not only stay yourself, but see the people staid. 160
You know not clearly, though you heard the king's words, yet his mind;
He only tries men's spirits now, and, whom his trials find
Apt to this course, he will chastise. Nor you, nor I, heard all
He spake in council; nor durst press too near our General,
Lest we incens'd him to our hurt. The anger of a king 165
Is mighty; he is kept of Jove, and from Jove likewise spring
His honours, which, out of the love of wise Jove, he enjoys."
Thus he the best sort us'd; the worst, whose spirits brake out in noise,
He cudgell'd with his sceptre, chid, and said: "Stay, wretch, be still,
And hear thy betters; thou art base, and both in pow'r and skill 170
Poor and unworthy, without name in council or in war.
We must not all be kings. The rule is most irregular,
Where many rule. One lord, one king, propose to thee; and he,
To whom wise Saturn's son hath giv'n both law and empery
To rule the public, is that king." Thus ruling, he restrain'd 175
The host from flight; and then again the Council was maintain'd
With such a concourse, that the shore rung with the tumult made;

[151] *Hoice*—hoise, hoist; thus printed for rhyme's sake.
[156] *Sceptre of descent*—which had descended to him from his father, see v. 36.

As when the far-resounding sea doth in its rage invade
His sandy confines, whose sides groan with his involvéd wave,
And make his own breast echo sighs. All sate, and audience gave. 180
Thersites only would speak all. A most disorder'd store
Of words he foolishly pour'd out, of which his mind held more
Than it could manage ; any thing, with which he could procure
Laughter, he never could contain. He should have yet been sure
To touch no kings ; t'oppose their states becomes not jesters' parts. 185
But he the filthiest fellow was of all that had deserts
In Troy's brave siege ; he was squint-ey'd, and lame of either foot ;
So crook-back'd, that he had no breast ; sharp-headed, where did shoot
(Here and there spers'd) thin mossy hair. He most of all envied
Ulysses and Æacides, whom still his spleen would chide. 190
Nor could the sacred King himself avoid his saucy vein ;
Against whom since he knew the Greeks did vehement hates sustain,
Being angry for Achilles' wrong, he cried out, railing thus :
   "Atrides, why complain'st thou now ? What would'st thou more
     of us ?
Thy tents are full of brass ; and dames, the choice of all, are thine, 195
With whom we must present thee first, when any towns resign
To our invasion. Want'st thou then, besides all this, more gold
From Troy's knights to redeem their sons, whom to be dearly sold
I or some other Greek must take ? Or would'st thou yet again
Force from some other lord his prise, to soothe the lusts that reign 200
In thy encroaching appetite ? It fits no prince to be
A prince of ill, and govern us, or lead our progeny
By rape to ruin. O base Greeks, deserving infamy,
And ills eternal ! Greekish girls, not Greeks, ye are ! Come, fly
Home with our ships ; leave this man here to perish with his preys, 205
And try if we help'd him or not ; he wrong'd a man that weighs
Far more than he himself in worth ; he forc'd from Thetis' son,
And keeps his prise still. Nor think I that mighty man hath won

    [205] *Preys*—booty. See Judges, ch. v. ver. 30.

The style of wrathful worthily'; he's soft, he's too remiss;
Or else, Atrides, his had been thy last of injuries." 210
    Thus he the people's Pastor chid; but straight stood up to him
Divine Ulysses, who, with looks exceeding grave and grim,
This bitter check gave: "Cease, vain fool, to vent thy railing vein
On kings thus, though it serve thee well; nor think thou canst restrain,
With that thy railing faculty, their wills in least degree; 215
For not a worse, of all this host, came with our King than thee,
To Troy's great siege; then do not take into that mouth of thine
The names of kings, much less revile the dignities that shine
In their supreme states, wresting thus this motion for our home,
To soothe thy cowardice; since ourselves yet know not what will come
Of these designments, if it be our good to stay, or go. 221
Nor is it that thou stand'st on; thou revil'st our Gen'ral so,
Only because he hath so much, not giv'n by such as thou
But our heroës. Therefore this thy rude vein makes me vow
(Which shall be curiously observ'd) if ever I shall hear 225
This madness from thy mouth again, let not Ulysses bear
This head, nor be the father call'd of young Telemachus,
If to thy nakedness I take and strip thee not, and thus
Whip thee to fleet from council; send, with sharp stripes, weeping
    hence
This glory thou affect'st to rail." This said, his insolence 230
He settled with his sceptre; strook his back and shoulders so
That bloody wales rose. He shrunk round; and from his eyes did flow
Moist tears, and, looking filthily, he sate, fear'd, smarted, dried
His blubber'd cheeks; and all the prease, though griev'd to be denied
Their wish'd retreat for home, yet laugh'd delightsomely, and spake
Either to other: "O ye Gods, how infinitely take 236

    [225] *Curiously*—scrupulously, carefully.
    [230] *This glory thou affect'st to rail*—the sense (somewhat complicated) seems: "*This glory to rail thou affectest,*" this vaunted railing power you make pretensions to.
    [234] *Prease*—press, crowd.

Ulysses' virtues in our good! Author of counsels, great
In ord'ring armies, how most well this act became his heat,
To beat from council this rude fool! I think his saucy spirit,
Hereafter, will not let his tongue abuse the sov'reign merit, 240
Exempt from such base tongues as his." Thus spake the people; then
The city-razer Ithacus stood up to speak again,
Holding his sceptre. Close to him gray-eyed Minerva stood,
And, like a herald, silence caus'd, that all the Achive brood
(From first to last) might hear and know the counsel; when, inclin'd
To all their good, Ulysses said: "Atrides, now I find 245
These men would render thee the shame of all men; nor would pay
Their own vows to thee, when they took their free and honour'd way
From Argos hither, that, till Troy were by their brave hands rac'd,
They would not turn home. Yet, like babes, and widows, now they
    haste 250
To that base refuge. 'Tis a spite to see men melted so
In womanish changes; though 'tis true, that if a man do go
Only a month to sea, and leave his wife far off, and he,
Tortur'd with winter's storms, and toss'd with a tumultuous sea,
Grows heavy, and would home. Us then, to whom the thrice-three year
Hath fill'd his revoluble orb since our arrival here, 256
I blame not to wish home much more; yet all this time to stay,
Out of our judgments, for our end; and now to take our way
Without it, were absurd and vile. Sustain then, friends; abide
The time set to our object; try if Calchas prophesied 260
True of the time or not. We know, ye all can witness well,
(Whom these late death-conferring fates have fail'd to send to hell)
That when in Aulis, all our fleet assembled with a freight
Of ills to Ilion and her friends, beneath the fair grown height
A platane bore, about a fount, whence crystal water flow'd, 265
And near our holy altar, we upon the Gods bestow'd

    249 *Rac'd*—razed.
    258 *Out of our judgments*—against our inclinations.

Accomplish'd hecatombs ; and there appear'd a huge portent,
A dragon with a bloody scale, horrid to sight, and sent
To light by great Olympius ; which, crawling from beneath
The altar, to the platane climb'd, and ruthless crash'd to death 270
A sparrow's young, in number eight, that in a top-bough lay
Hid under leaves ; the dam the ninth, that hover'd every way,
Mourning her lov'd birth, till at length, the serpent, watching her,
Her wing caught, and devour'd her too. This dragon, Jupiter,
That brought him forth, turn'd to a stone, and made a pow'rful mean
To stir our zeals up, that admir'd, when of a fact so clean 275
Of all ill as our sacrifice, so fearful an ostent
Should be the issue. Calchas, then, thus prophesied th' event
' Why are ye dumb-strook, fair-hair'd Greeks ? Wise Jove is he hath shown
This strange ostent to us. 'Twas late, and passing lately done, 280
But that grace it foregoes to us, for suff'ring all the state
Of his appearance (being so slow) nor time shall end, nor fate.
As these eight sparrows, and the dam (that made the ninth) were eat
By this stern serpent ; so nine years we are t' endure the heat
Of rav'nous war, and, in the tenth, take-in this broad-way'd town.' 285
Thus he interpreted this sign ; and all things have their crown
As he interpreted, till now. The rest, then, to succeed
Believe as certain. Stay we all, till, that most glorious deed
Of taking this rich town, our hands are honour'd with." This said,
The Greeks gave an unmeasur'd shout ; which back the ships repaid
With terrible echoes, in applause of that persuasion 291
Divine Ulysses us'd ; which yet held no comparison
With Nestor's next speech, which was this : " O shameful thing ! Ye talk
Like children all, that know not war. In what air's region walk
Our oaths, and cov'nants ? Now, I see the fit respects of men 295
Are vanish'd quite ; our right hands giv'n, our faiths, our counsels vain,

[281] *That grace it foregoes to us*—the favour it foretells to us.

Our sacrifice with wine, all fled in that profanéd flame
We made to bind all; for thus still we vain persuasions frame,
And strive to work our end with words, not joining stratagems
And hands together, though, thus long, the pow'r of our extremes 300
Hath urg'd us to them. Atreus' son, firm as at first hour stand!
Make good thy purpose; talk no more in councils, but command
In active field. Let two or three, that by themselves advise,
Faint in their crowning; they are such as are not truly wise;
They will for Argos, ere they know if that which Jove hath said 305
Be false or true. I tell them all, that high Jove bow'd his head,
As first we went aboard our fleet, for sign we should confer
These Trojans their due fate and death; almighty Jupiter
All that day darting forth his flames, in an unmeasur'd light,
On our right hand. Let therefore none once dream of coward flight,
Till (for his own) some wife of Troy he sleeps withal, the rape 311
Of Helen wreaking, and our sighs enforc'd for her escape.
If any yet dare dote on home, let his dishonour'd haste
His black and well-built bark but touch, that (as he first disgrac'd
His country's spirit) fate, and death, may first his spirit let go. 315
But be thou wise, king, do not trust thyself, but others. Know
I will not use an abject word. See all thy men array'd
In tribes and nations, that tribes tribes, nations may nations, aid.
Which doing, thou shalt know what chiefs, what soldiers, play the
    men,
And what the cowards; for they all will fight in sev'ral then, 320
Easy for note. And then shalt thou, if thou destroy'st not Troy,
Know if the prophecy's defect, or men thou dost employ

---

³⁰⁰ *Extremes*—necessities.
³⁰⁴ *Crowning*—fulfilment of purpose.
³⁰⁷ *Confer these Trojans*—confer on.
³¹² *Escape*—frequently used for transgression of female virtue, thus Shakespeare,—

    "Rome will despise her for this foul *escape*."—*Titus And.* IV. 2.
³²⁰ *In several*—severally, separately.

In their approv'd arts want in war, or lack of that brave heat
Fit for the vent'rous spirits of Greece, was cause to thy defeat."

 To this the king of men replied : " O father, all the sons
Of Greece thou conquer'st in the strife of consultations.
I would to Jove, Athenia, and Phœbus, I could make,
Of all, but ten such counsellors ; then instantly would shake
King Priam's city, by our hands laid hold on and laid waste.
But Jove hath order'd I should grieve, and to that end hath cast
My life into debates past end. Myself, and Thetis' son,
Like girls, in words fought for a girl, and I th' offence begun.
But if we ever talk as friends, Troy's thus deferréd fall
Shall never vex us more one hour. Come then, to victuals all,
That strong Mars all may bring to field. Each man his lance's steel
See sharpen'd well, his shield well lin'd, his horses meated well,
His chariot carefully made strong, that these affairs of death
We all day may hold fiercely out. No man must rest, or breath ;
The bosoms of our targeteers must all be steep'd in sweat ;
The lancer's arm must fall dissolv'd ; our chariot-horse with heat
Must seem to melt. But if I find one soldier take the chace,
Or stir from fight, or fight not still fix'd in his enemy's face,
Or hid a-ship-board, all the world, for force, nor price, shall save
His hated life, but fowls and dogs be his abhorréd grave."

 He said ; and such a murmur rose, as on a lofty shore
The waves make, when the south wind comes, and tumbles them before
Against a rock, grown near the strand which diversely beset
Is never free, but, here and there, with varied uproars beat.

 All rose then, rushing to the fleet, perfum'd their tents, and eat ;
Each off'ring to th' immortal gods, and praying to 'scape the heat
Of war and death. The king of men an ox of five years' spring
T' almighty Jove slew, call'd the peers ; first Nestor ; then the king
Idomenëus ; after them th' Ajaces ; and the son
Of Tydeus ; Ithacus the sixth, in counsel paragon

  ³⁴¹ *Take the chace*—take to flight.

To Jove himself. All these he bade; but at-a-martial-cry 355
Good Menelaus, since he saw his brother busily
Employ'd at that time, would not stand on invitation,
But of himself came. All about the off'ring overthrown
Stood round, took salt-cakes, and the king himself thus pray'd for all:
"O Jove, most great, most glorious, that, in that starry hall, 360
Sitt'st drawing dark clouds up to air, let not the sun go down,
Darkness supplying it, till my hands the palace and the town
Of Priam overthrow and burn; the arms on Hector's breast
Dividing, spoiling with my sword thousands, in interest
Of his bad quarrel, laid by him in dust, and eating earth." 365

He pray'd; Jove heard him not, but made more plentiful the birth
Of his sad toils, yet took his gifts. Pray'rs past, cakes on they threw;
The ox then, to the altar drawn, they kill'd, and from him drew
His hide, then cut him up, his thighs, in two hewn, dubb'd with fat,
Prick'd on the sweetbreads, and with wood, leaveless, and kindled at 370
Apposéd fire, they burn the thighs; which done, the inwards, slit,
They broil'd on coals and eat; the rest, in giggots cut, they spit,
Roast cunningly, draw, sit, and feast; nought lack'd to leave allay'd
Each temp'rate appetite; which serv'd, Nestor began and said:

"Atrides, most grac'd king of men, now no more words allow, 375
Nor more defer the deed Jove vows. Let heralds summon now
The brazen-coated Greeks, and us range ev'rywhere the host,
To stir a strong war quickly up." This speech no syllable lost;
The high-voic'd heralds instantly he charg'd to call to arms
The curl'd-head Greeks; they call'd; the Greeks straight answer'd
    their alarms. 380
The Jove-kept kings, about the king all gather'd, with their aid
Rang'd all in tribes and nations. With them the gray-eyed Maid

---

355 *At-a-martial-cry good*—Menelaus good at a shout; βοὴν ἀγαθὸς is the epithet of Menelaus.
364 *In interest of*—on account of, &c.
378 *This speech no syllable lost*—i. e. Agamemnon attended to every syllable of the speech.
382 *Gray-eyed Maid*—Minerva.

Great Ægis (Jove's bright shield) sustain'd, that can be never old,
Never corrupted, fring'd about with serpents forg'd of gold,
As many as suffic'd to make an hundred fringes, worth 385
An hundred oxen, ev'ry snake all sprawling, all set forth
With wondrous spirit. Through the host with this the Goddess ran,
In fury casting round her eyes, and furnish'd ev'ry man
With strength, exciting all to arms, and fight incessant. None
Now liked their lov'd homes like the wars. And as a fire upon 390
A huge wood, on the heights of hills, that far off hurls his light;
So the divine brass shin'd on these, thus thrusting on for fight,
Their splendour through the air reach'd heav'n. And as about the flood
Caïster, in an Asian mead, flocks of the airy brood,
Cranes, geese, or long-neck'd swans, here, there, proud of their pinions fly,
And in their falls lay out such throats, that with their spiritful cry 395
The meadow shrieks again; so here, these many-nation'd men
Flow'd over the Scamandrian field, from tents and ships; the din
Was dreadful that the feet of men and horse beat out of earth.
And in the flourishing mead they stood, thick as the odorous birth 400
Of flow'rs, or leaves bred in the spring; or thick as swarms of flies
Throng then to sheep-cotes, when each swarm his erring wing applies
To milk dew'd on the milk-maid's pails; all eagerly dispos'd
To give to ruin th' Ilians. And as in rude heaps clos'd,
Though huge goatherds are at their food, the goatherds eas'ly yet 405
Sort into sundry herds; so here the chiefs in battle set
Here tribes, here nations, ord'ring all. Amongst whom shin'd the king,
With eyes like lightning-loving Jove, his forehead answering,
In breast like Neptune, Mars in waist. And as a goodly bull
Most eminent of all a herd, most wrong, most masterful, 410
So Agamemnon, Jove that day made overheighten clear
That heav'n-bright army, and preferr'd to all th' heroës there.

    Now tell me, Muses, you that dwell in heav'nly roofs, (for you
Are Goddesses, are present here, are wise, and all things know,

    [396] *In their falls*—when they alight.

We only trust the voice of fame, know nothing,) who they were
That here were captains of the Greeks, commanding princes here.
The multitude exceed my song, though fitted to my choice
Ten tongues were, harden'd palates ten, a breast of brass, a voice
Infract and trump-like; that great work, unless the seed of Jove,
The deathless Muses, undertake, maintains a pitch above
All mortal pow'rs. The princes then, and navy that did bring
These so inenarrable troops, and all their soils, I sing.

THE CATALOGUE OF THE GRECIAN SHIPS AND CAPTAINS.

Peneleüs, and Leitus, all that Bœotia bred,
Arcesilaus, Clonius, and Prothoenor, led;
Th' inhabitants of Hyria, and stony Aulida,
Schœne, Scole, the hilly Eteon, and holy Thespia,
Of Græa, and great Mycalesse, that hath the ample plain,
Of Harma, and Ilesius, and all that did remain
In Eryth, and in Eleon, in Hylen, Peteona,
In fair Ocalea, and, the town well-builded, Medeona,
Copas, Eutresis, Thisbe, that for pigeons doth surpass,
Of Coroneia, Haliart, that hath such store of grass,
All those that in Platæa dwelt, that Glissa did possess,
And Hypothebs, whose well-built walls are rare and fellowless,
In rich Onchestus' famous wood, to wat'ry Neptune vow'd,
And Arne, where the vine-trees are with vig'rous bunches bow'd,
With them that dwelt in Midea, and Nissa most divine,
All those whom utmost Anthedon did wealthily confine.
From all these coasts, in general, full fifty sail were sent;
And six score strong Bœotian youths in every burthen went.
But those who in Aspledon dwelt, and Minian Orchomen,
God Mars's sons did lead (Ascalaphus and Ialmen)
Who in Azidon Actor's house did of Astyoche come;
The bashful maid, as she went up into the higher room,

The War-god secretly compress'd. In safe conduct of these, 445
Did thirty hollow-bottom'd barks divide the wavy seas.
 Brave Schedius and Epistrophus, the Phocian captains were,
(Naubolida-Iphitus' sons) all proof 'gainst any fear ;
With them the Cyparissians went, and bold Pythonians,
Men of religious Chrysa's soil, and fat Daulidians, 450
Panopœans, Anemores, and fierce Hyampolists ;
And those that dwell where Cephisus casts up his silken mists ;
The men that fair Lilœa held, near the Cephisian spring ;
All which did forty sable barks to that designment bring.
About th' entoil'd Phocensian fleet had these their sail assign'd ; 455
And near to the sinister wing the arm'd Bœotians shin'd.
 Ajax the less, Oïleus' son, the Locrians led to war ;
Not like to Ajax Telamon, but lesser man by far,
Little he was, and ever wore a breastplate made of linne,
But for the manage of his lance he gen'ral praise did win. 460
The dwellers of Caliarus, of Bessa, Opoën,
The youths of Cynus, Scarphis, and Augias, lovely men,
Of Tarphis, and of Thronius, near flood Boagrius' fall ;
Twice-twenty martial barks of these, less Ajax sail'd withal.
 Who near Eubœa's blessèd soil their habitations had, 465
Strength-breathing Abants, who their seats in sweet Eubœa made,
The Histiœans rich in grapes, the men of Chalcida,
The Cerinths bord'ring on the sea, of rich Eretria,
Of Dion's highly-seated town, Charistus, and of Styre,
All these the duke Alphenor led, a flame of Mars's fire, 470
Surnam'd Chalcodontiades, the mighty Abants' guide,
Swift men of foot, whose broad-set backs their trailing hair did hide,
Well-seen in fight, and soon could pierce with far extended darts
The breastplates of their enemies, and reach their dearest hearts.

 [459] *Breastplate made of linne*—made of flax ; λινοθώρηξ.
 [470] *Duke*—leader. The translators of the Bible retained this word in mentioning Esau's descendants, Gen. xxxvi.

Forty black men of war did sail in this Alphenor's charge. 475
   The soldiers that in Athens dwelt, a city builded large,
The people of Eristhius, whom Jove-sprung Pallas fed,
And plenteous-feeding Tellus brought out of her flow'ry bed;
Him Pallas placed in her rich fane, and, ev'ry ended year,
Of bulls and lambs th' Athenian youths please him with off'rings there;
Mighty Menestheus, Peteus' son, had their divided care; 481
For horsemen and for targeteers none could with him compare,
Nor put them into better place, to hurt or to defend;
But Nestor (for he elder was) with him did sole contend;
With him came fifty sable sail. And out of Salamine 485
Great Ajax brought twelve sail, that with th' Athenians did combine.
   Who did in fruitful Argos dwell, or strong Tiryntha keep,
Hermion, or in Asinen whose bosom is so deep,
Trœzena, Eïon, Epidaure where Bacchus crowns his head,
Ægina, and Maseta's soil, did follow Diomed, 490
And Sthenelus, the dear-lov'd son of famous Capaneus,
Together with Euryalus, heir of Mecistens,
The king of Talæonides; past whom in deeds of war,
The famous soldier Diomed of all was held by far.
Four score black ships did follow these. The men fair Mycene held,
The wealthy Corinth, Cleon that for beauteous site excell'd, 496
Aræthyrea's lovely seat, and in Ornia's plain,
And Sicyona, where at first did king Adrastus reign,
High-seated Gonoëssa's towers, and Hyperisius,
That dwelt in fruitful Pellenen, and in divine Ægius, 500
With all the sea-side borderers, and wide Helice's friends,
To Agamemnon ev'ry town her native birth commends,
In double-fifty sable barks. With him a world of men
Most strong and full of valour went, and he in triumph then

---

   [477] *Eristhius*—Erectheus in the original.
   [496] Dr. Taylor has printed "*sight*," whereas if he had consulted the original he would have seen that Chapman meant "*site*." (Ἐῢ κτιμένας τε Κλεωνάς.)

Put on his most resplendent arms, since he did overshine
The whole heroic host of Greece, in pow'r of that design.

   Who did in Lacedæmon's rule th' unmeasur'd concave hold,
High Pharis, Sparta, Messe's tow'rs, for doves so much extoll'd,
Bryseia's and Augia's grounds, strong Laa, Oetylon,
Amyclas, Helos' harbour-town, that Neptune beats upon,
All these did Menelaus lead (his brother, that in cries
Of war was famous). Sixty ships convey'd these enemies
To Troy in chief, because their king was chiefly injur'd there,
In Helen's rape, and did his best to make them buy it dear.

   Who dwelt in Pylos' sandy soil, and Arene the fair,
In Thryon, near Alpheus' flood, and Aepy full of air,
In Cyparisseus, Amphigen, and little Pteleon,
The town where all the Iliots dwelt, and famous Doreon,
Where all the Muses, opposite, in strife of poesy,
To ancient Thamyris of Thrace, did use him cruelly,
(He coming from Eurytus' court, the wise Œchalian king,)
Because he proudly durst affirm he could more sweetly sing
Than that Pierian race of Jove ; who, angry with his vaunt,
Bereft his eyesight, and his song, that did the ear enchant,
And of his skill to touch his harp disfurnishèd his hand.
All these in ninety hollow keels grave Nestor did command.

   The richly-blest inhabitants of the Arcadian land
Below Cyllene's mount (that by Epytus' tomb did stand)
Where dwelt the bold near-fighting men, who did in Phœneus live,
And Orchomen, where flocks of sheep the shepherds clust'ring drive,
In Ripé, and in Stratié, the fair Mantinean town,
And strong Enispe, that for height is ever weather-blown,
Tegea, and in Stymphalus, Parrhasia strongly wall'd,
All these Alcæus' son to field (king Agapenor) call'd ;
In sixty barks he brought them on, and ev'ry bark well-mann'd
With fierce Arcadians, skill'd to use the utmost of a band.

       [511] *His brother*—Agamemnon's.

King Agamemnon, on these men, did well-built ships bestow
To pass the gulfy purple sea, that did no sea rites know.
 They who in Hermin, Buphrasis, and Elis, did remain,
What Olen's cliffs, Alisius, and Myrsin did contain,   540
Were led to war by twice-two dukes (and each ten ships did bring,
Which many vent'rous Epians did serve for burthening,)
Beneath Amphimachus's charge, and valiant Thalpius,
(Son of Eurytus-Actor one, the other Cteatus,)
Diores Amaryncides the other did employ,   545
The fourth divine Polixenus (Agasthenes's joy).
 The king of fair Angeiades, who from Dulichius came,
And from Echinaus' sweet isles, which hold their holy frame
By ample Elis region, Meges Phylides led;
Whom duke Phyleus, Jove's belov'd, begat, and whilome fled   550
To large Dulichius, for the wrath that fir'd his father's breast.
Twice-twenty ships with ebon sails were in his charge address'd.
 The warlike men of Cephale, and those of Ithaca,
Woody Neritus, and the men of wet Crocylia,
Sharp Ægilipa, Samos' isle, Zacynthus sea inclos'd,   555
Epirus, and the men that hold the continent oppos'd,
All these did wise Ulysses lead, in counsel peer to Jove;
Twelve ships he brought, which in their course vermilion sterns did move.

[538] Agamemnon furnished ships for the Arcadians, as they were an inland people, and "*did no sea rites know.*"
[544] Dr. Taylor has printed this and the following line, thus:—
  (Son of Eurytus-Actor one, *the next of* Cteatus)
  Diores Amaryncides the *third ships* did employ.
This is not authorized by either of the folios. The first has—
  Son of Eurytus-Actor one; *the other* Cteatus;
  Diores Amarincides the *other* did employ.
The second folio in line 544, with its usual typographical inaccuracy, omits "*the other.*" The first folio is correct—one, son of Eurytus-Actor; the other, son of Cteatus-Actor. Cteatus and Eurytus were sons of Actor, and are mentioned in bk. XI. 622, 661. The Scholiast says Amphimachus was son of Cteatus, and Thalpius son of Eurytus. It is hardly necessary to remark that Chapman is wrong in the quantity of Eurytus, as in many proper names; but, perhaps, he thought this a poetical license.

Thoas, Andremon's well-spoke son, did guide th' Ætolians well,
Those that in Pleuron, Olenon, and strong Pylene dwell, 560
Great Chalcis, that by sea-side stands, and stony Calydon ;
(For now no more of Œneus' sons surviv'd ; they all were gone ;
No more his royal self did live, no more his noble son
The golden Meleager now, their glasses all were run)
All things were left to him in charge, th' Ætolians' chief he was, 565
And forty ships to Trojan wars the seas with him did pass.

The royal soldier Idomen did lead the Cretans stout,
The men of Gnossus, and the town Gortyna wall'd about,
Of Lictus, and Miletus' tow'rs, of white Lycastus' state,
Of Phæstus, and of Rhytius, the cities fortunate, 570
And all the rest inhabiting the hundred towns of Crete ;
Whom warlike Idomen did lead, co-partner in the fleet
With kill-man Merion. Eighty ships with them did Troy invade.

Tlepolemus Heraclides, right strong and bigly made,
Brought nine tall ships of war from Rhodes, which haughty Rhodians
    mann'd, 575
Who dwelt in three dissever'd parts of that most pleasant land,
Which Lyndus and Jalissus were, and bright Camirus, call'd.
Tlepolemus commanded these, in battle unappall'd ;
Whom fair Astyoche brought forth, by force of Hercules,
Led out of Ephyr with his hand, from river Selleës, 580
When many towns of princely youths he levell'd with the ground.
Tlepolem, in his father's house (for building much renown'd)
Brought up to headstrong state of youth, his mother's brother slew,
The flow'r of arms, Licymnius, that somewhat aged grew ;
Then straight he gather'd him a fleet, assembling bands of men, 585
And fled by sea, to shun the threats that were denouncéd then
By other sons and nephews of th' Alciden fortitude.
He in his exile came to Rhodes, driv'n in with tempests rude.

₅₈₇ *The Alciden fortitude*—a pleonasm for Hercules himself.

The Rhodians were distinct in tribes, and great with Jove did stand,
The King of men and Gods, who gave much treasure to their land. 590
    Nireüs out of Syma's hav'n three well-built barks did bring ;
Nireüs, fair Aglaia's son, and Charopes' the king ;
Nireüs was the fairest man that to fair Ilion came
Of all the Greeks, save Peleus' son, who pass'd for gen'ral frame ;
But weak this was, not fit for war, and therefore few did guide. 595
    Who did in Cassus, Nisyrus, and Crapathus, abide,
In Co, Eurypylus's town, and in Calydna's soils,
Phidippus and bold Antiphus did guide to Trojan toils,
(The sons of crownéd Thessalus, deriv'd from Hercules)
Who went with thirty hollow ships well-order'd to the seas. 600
    Now will I sing the sackful troops Pelasgian Argos held,
That in deep Alus, Alopé, and soft Trechina dwell'd,
In Phthia, and in Hellade where live the lovely dames,
The Myrmidons, Hellenians, and Achives, rob'd of fames ;
All which the great Æacides in fifty ships did lead. 605
For these forgat war's horrid voice, because they lack'd their head
That would have brought them bravely forth ; but now at fleet did lie
That wind-like user of his feet, fair Thetis' progeny,
Wroth for bright-cheek'd Briseis' loss, whom from Lyrnessus' spoils
(His own exploit) he brought away as trophy of his toils, 610
When that town was depopulate ; he sunk the Theban tow'rs ;
Myneta, and Epistrophus, he sent to Pluto's bow'rs,
Who came of king Evenus' race, great Helepiades ;
Yet now he idly lives enrag'd, but soon must leave his ease.
    Of those that dwelt in Phylace, and flow'ry Pyrason 615
The wood of Ceres, and the soil that sheep are fed upon
Iton, and Antron built by sea, and Pteleus full of grass,
Protesilaus, while he liv'd, the worthy captain was,
Whom now the sable earth detains ; his tear-torn-facéd spouse
He woful left in Phylace, and his half-finish'd house ; 620

    [594] *Pass'd*—surpassed.   [595] *This*—Nireus.

A fatal Dardan first his life, of all the Greeks, bereft,
As he was leaping from his ship; yet were his men unleft
Without a chief, for though they wish'd to have no other man
But good Protesilay their guide, Podarces yet began
To govern them, (Iphitis' son, the son of Phylacus) 625
Most rich in sheep, and brother to short-liv'd Protesilaus,
Of younger birth, less, and less strong, yet serv'd he to direct
The companies, that still did more their ancient duke affect.
Twice-twenty jetty sails with him the swelling stream did take.

But those that did in Pheres dwell, at the Bœbeian lake, 630
In Bœbe, and in Glaphyra, Iaolcus builded fair,
In thrice-six ships to Pergamus did through the seas repair,
With old Admetus' tender son, Eumelus, whom he bred
Of Alcest, Pelius' fairest child of all his female seed.

The soldiers that before the siege Methone's vales did hold, 635
Thaumacie, flow'ry Melibœ, and Olison the cold,
Duke Philoctetes governéd, in darts of finest sleight;
Sev'n vessels in his charge convey'd their honourable freight,
By fifty rowers in a bark, most expert in the bow;
But he in sacred Lemnos lay, brought miserably low 640
By torment of an ulcer grown with Hydra's poison'd blood,
Whose sting was such, Greece left him there in most impatient mood;
Yet thought they on him at his ship, and choos'd, to lead his men,
Medon, Oïleus' bastard son, brought forth to him by Rhen.

From Tricce, bleak Ithomen's cliffs, and hapless Oechaly, 645
(Eurytus' city, rul'd by him in wilful tyranny,)
In charge of Æsculapius' sons, physician highly prais'd,
Machaon, Podalirius, were thirty vessels rais'd.

Who near Hyperia's fountain dwelt, and in Ormenius,
The snowy tops of Titanus, and in Asterius, 650
Evemon's son, Eurypylus, did lead into the field;
Whose towns did forty black-sail'd ships to that encounter yield.

Who Gyrton, and Argissa, held, Orthen, and Elon's seat,
And chalky Oloössone, were led by Polypœte,
The issue of Pirithous, the son of Jupiter. 655
Him the Athenian Theseus' friend Hippodamy did bear,
When he the bristled savages did give Ramnusia,
And drove them out of Pelius, as far as Æthica.
He came not single, but with him Leonteus, Coron's son,
An arm of Mars, and Coron's life Cenëus' seed begun. 660
Twice-twenty ships attended these. Gunëus next did bring
From Cyphus twenty sail and two; the Enians following;
And fierce Peræbi, that about Dodone's frozen mould
Did plant their houses; and the men that did the meadows hold,
Which Titaresius decks with flow'rs, and his sweet current leads 665
Into the bright Peneïus, that hath the silver heads,
Yet with his admirable stream doth not his waves commix,
But glides aloft on it like oil; for 'tis the flood of Styx,
By which th' immortal Gods do swear. Teuthredon's honour'd birth,
Prothous, led the Magnets forth, who near the shady earth 670
Of Pelius, and Peneïon, dwelt; forty revengeful sail
Did follow him. These were the dukes and princes of avail
That came from Greece. But now the man, that overshin'd them all,
Sing, Muse; and their most famous steeds to my recital call,
That both th' Atrides followéd. Fair Pheretiades 675
The bravest mares did bring by much; Eumelius manag'd these,
Swift of their feet as birds of wings, both of one hair did shine,
Both of an age, both of a height, as measur'd by a line,
Whom silver-bow'd Apollo bred in the Pierian mead,
Both slick and dainty, yet were both in war of wondrous dread. 680
   Great Ajax Telamon for strength pass'd all the peers of war,
While vex'd Achilles was away; but he surpass'd him far.

[680] *Slick*—sleek, smooth.

The horse that bore that faultless man were likewise past compare;
Yet lay he at the crook'd-stern'd ships, and fury was his fare,
For Atreus' son's ungracious deed; his men yet pleas'd their hearts   685
With throwing of the holéd stone, with hurling of their darts,
And shooting fairly on the shore; their horse at chariots fed
On greatest parsley, and on sedge that in the fens is bred.
His princes' tents their chariots held, that richly cover'd were.
His princes, amorous of their chief, walk'd storming here and there   690
About the host, and scorn'd to fight; their breaths as they did pass
Before them flew, as if a fire fed on the trembling grass;
Earth under-groan'd their high-rais'd feet, as when offended Jove,
In Arime, Typhœius with rattling thunder drove
Beneath the earth; in Arime, men say, the grave is still,   695
Where thunder tomb'd Typhœius, and is a monstrous hill;
And as that thunder made earth groan, so groan'd it as they past,
They trod with such hard-set-down steps, and so exceeding fast.

 To Troy the rainbow-girded Dame right heavy news relates
From Jove, as all to council drew in Priam's palace-gates,   700
Resembling Priam's son in voice, Polites, swift of feet;
In trust whereof, as sentinel, to see when from the fleet
The Grecians sallied, he was set upon the lofty brow
Of aged Æsyetes' tomb; and this did Iris show:
"O Priam, thou art always pleas'd with indiscreet advice,   705
And fram'st thy life to times of peace, when such a war doth rise
As threats inevitable spoil. I never did behold
Such and so mighty troops of men, who trample on the mould
In number like Autumnus' leaves, or like the marine sand,
All ready round about the walls to use a ruining hand.   710

  ⁶⁸³ *Faultless man*—Achilles.
  ⁶⁸⁶ *Throwing of the holed stone*—in the Greek, playing at *quoits*.
  ⁶⁹⁰ *Amorous of their chief*—ardently desiring their chief, viz., to lead them to battle.
  ⁶⁹⁹ Iris.

Hector, I therefore charge thee most, this charge to undertake.
A multitude remain in Troy, will fight for Priam's sake,
Of other lands and languages; let ev'ry leader then
Bring forth well-arm'd into the field his sev'ral bands of men."
    Strong Hector knew a Deity gave charge to this assay,   715
Dismiss'd the council straight; like waves, clusters to arms do sway;
The ports are all wide open set; out rush'd the troops in swarms,
Both horse and foot; the city rung with sudden-cried alarms.
    A column stands without the town, that high his head doth raise,
A little distant, in a plain trod down with divers ways,   720
Which men do Batieia call, but the Immortals name
Myrine's famous sepulchre, the wondrous active dame.
Here were th' auxiliary bands, that came in Troy's defence,
Distinguish'd under sev'ral guides of special excellence.
    The duke of all the Trojan pow'r great helm-deck'd Hector was,   725
Which stood of many mighty men well-skill'd in darts of brass.
Æneas of commixéd seed (a Goddess with a man,
Anchises with the Queen of love) the troops Dardanian
Led to the field; his lovely sire in Ida's lower shade
Begat him of sweet Cyprides; he solely was not made   730
Chief leader of the Dardan pow'rs, Antenor's valiant sons,
Archilochus and Acamas, were join'd companions.
    Who in Zelia dwelt beneath the sacred foot of Ide,
That drank of black Æsepus' stream, and wealth made full of pride,
The Aphnii, Lycaon's son, whom Phœbus gave his bow,   735
Prince Pandarus did lead to field. Who Adrestinus owe,
Apesus' city, Pityæ, and mount Tereiës,
Adrestus and stout Amphius led; who did their sire displease,
(Merops Percosius, that excell'd all Troy in heav'nly skill
Of futures-searching prophecy) for, much against his will,   740
His sons were agents in those arms; whom since they disobey'd,
The fates, in letting slip their threads, their hasty valours stay'd.

        736 *Owe*—own.

 Who in Percotes, Practius, Arisba, did abide,
Who Sestus and Abydus bred, Hyrtacides did guide;
Prince Asius Hyrtacides, that, through great Selees' force,   745
Brought from Arisba to that fight the great and fiery horse.
 Pylæus, and Hippothous, the stout Pelasgians led,
Of them Larissa's fruitful soil before had nourishéd;
These were Pelasgian Pithus' sons, son of Teutamidas.
 The Thracian guides were Pirous, and valiant Acamas,   750
Of all that the impetuous flood of Hellespont enclos'd.
 Euphemus, the Ciconian troops, in his command dispos'd,
Who from Trœzenius-Ceades right nobly did descend.
 Pyræchmes did the Pæons rule, that crookéd bows do bend;
From Axius, out of Amydon, he had them in command,   755
From Axius, whose most beauteous stream still overflows the land.
 Pylæmen with the well-arm'd heart, the Paphlagonians led,
From Enes, where the race of mules fit for the plough is bred.
The men that broad Cytorus' bounds, and Sesamus, enfold,
About Parthenius' lofty flood, in houses much extoll'd,   760
From Cromna and Ægialus, the men that arms did bear,
And Erythinus situate high, Pylæmen's soldiers were.
 Epistrophus and Dius did the Halizonians guide,
Far-fetch'd from Alybe, where first the silver mines were tried.
 Chromis, and augur Ennomus, the Mysians did command,   765
Who could not with his auguries the strength of death withstand,
But suffer'd it beneath the stroke of great Æacides,
In Xanthus; where he made more souls dive to the Stygian seas.
 Phorcys, and fair Ascanius, the Phrygians brought to war,
Well train'd for battle, and were come out of Ascania far.   770
 With Methles, and with Antiphus, (Pylæmen's sons) did fight
The men of Meïon, whom the fen Gygæa brought to light,
And those Meionians that beneath the mountain Tmolus sprung.
 The rude unletter'd Caribæ, that barbarous were of tongue,

Did under Nastes' colours march, and young Amphimachus, 775
(Nomion's famous sons) to whom, the mountain Phthirorus
That with the famous wood is crown'd, Miletus, Mycales
That hath so many lofty marks for men that love the seas,
The crookéd arms Mæander bow'd with his so snaky flood,
Resign'd for conduct the choice youth of all their martial brood. 780
The fool Amphimachus, to field, brought gold to be his wrack,
Proud-girl-like that doth ever bear her dow'r upon her back;
Which wise Achilles mark'd, slew him, and took his gold in strife,
At Xanthus' flood; so little Death did fear his golden life.
   Sarpedon led the Lycians, and Glaucus unreprov'd, 785
From Lycia, and the gulfy flood of Xanthus far remov'd.

        [785] *Unreprov'd*—irreproachable.

COMMENTARIUS.

72.

'Hῦτε ἔθνεα, &c. *Sicut examina prodeunt apum frequentium*, &c. In this simile Virgil (using the like in imitation) is preferred to Homer; with what reason I pray you see. Their ends are different; Homer intending to express the infinite multitude of soldiers every where dispersing; Virgil, the diligence of builders. Virgil's simile is this: I. Æneid, 430.

> "Qualis apes æstate novâ per florea rura
> Exercet sub sole labor; cum gentis adultos
> Educunt fœtus; aut cum liquentia mella
> Stipant; et dulci distendunt nectare cellas;
> Aut onera accipiunt venientum; aut, agmine facto,
> Ignavum fucos pecus a præsepibus arcent:
> Fervet opus, redolentque thymo fragrantia mella."

Now compare this with Homer's, but in my translation; and judge if, to both their ends, there be any such betterness in Virgil's but that the reverence of the scholar, due to the master (even in these his maligners), might well have contained their lame censures of the poetical fury from these unmannerly and hateful comparisons. Especially, since Virgil hath nothing of his own, but only elocution; his invention, matter, and form, being all Homer's; which laid by a man, that which he addeth is only the work of a woman, to netify and polish. Nor do I, alas, but the foremost rank of the most ancient and best learned that ever were, come to the field for Homer, hiding all other poets under his ensign. Hate not me then, but them, to whom, before my book, I refer you. But much the rather I insist on the former simile; for the word ἰλαδὸν, *catervatim*, or *confertim*, which is noted by Spondanus to contain all the ἀπίδοσις, reddition, or application of the comparison, and is nothing so.

For though it be all the reddition Homer expresseth, yet he intends two special parts in the application more, which he leaves to his judicial reader's understanding, as he doth in all his other similes; since a man may pervially (or, as he passeth) discern all that is to be understood. And here, besides their throngs of soldiers expressed in the swarms of bees, he intimates the infinite number in those throngs or companies, issuing from fleet so ceaselessly that there appeared almost no end of their issue; and thirdly, the every where dispersing themselves. But Spondanus would excuse Homer for expressing no more of his application, with affirming it impossible that the thing compared, and the comparison, should answer in all parts; and therefore alleges the vulgar understanding of a simile, which is as gross as it is vulgar, that a similitude must *uno pede semper claudicare.* His reason for it is as absurd as the rest; which is this, *Si ea inter se omnino responderent, falleret illud axioma, nullum simile est idem;* as though the general application of the compared and the comparison would make them any thing more the same, or all one; more than the swarms of bees and the throng of soldiers are all one or the same; for answering most aptly. But that a simile must needs halt of one foot still showeth how lame vulgar tradition is, especially in her censure of poesy. For who at first sight will not conceive it absurd to make a simile, which serves to the illustration and ornament of a poem, lame of a foot, and idle? The incredible violence suffered by Homer in all the rest of his most inimitable similes, being expressed in his place, will abundantly prove the stupidity of this tradition, and how injuriously short his interpreters must needs come of him in his strait and deep places, when in his open and fair passages they halt and hang back so.

275. Τὸν μὲν ἀρίζηλον θῆκεν Θεὸς, &c., *hunc quidem clarum* (or *illustrem*) *fecit Deus,* as it is by all translated; wherein I note the strange abuse (as I apprehend it) of the word ἀρίζηλος, beginning here, and continuing wheresoever it is found in these Iliads. It is by the transition of ζ into δ in derivation, according to the Doric; for which cause our interpreters will needs have Homer intend ἀρίδηλος, which is *clarus*

or *illustris*, when he himself saith ἀρίζηλος, which is a compound of ἄρι, which is *valde*, and ζῆλος, and signifies, *quem valde æmulamur*, or *valde æmulandus*, according to Scapula. But because ζῆλος is most authentically expounded, *impetus mentis ad cultum divinum*, that exposition I follow in this place, and expound τὸν μὲν ἀρίζηλον θῆκεν Θεὸς, *hunc quidem magnum impulsum ad cultum divinum fecit Deus;* because he turned so suddenly and miraculously the dragon to a stone. To make it ἀρίδηλον, and say *clarum* or *illustrem fecit Deus qui ostendit*, or *ostenderat*, which follows in the verse, and saith thus much in our tongue, *God that showed this, made it clear*, is very little more than, *God that showed this, showed it.* One way it observes the word (betwixt which, and the other, you see what great difference) and is fair, full, grave; the other alters the original, and is ugly, empty, idle.

355. Αὐτόματος δὲ οἱ ἦλθε βοὴν ἀγαθὸς Μενέλαος, &c. *Spontaneus autem ei venit voce bonus Menelaus;* and some say *bello strenuus Menelaus*, which is far estranged from the mind of our Homer, βοὴ signifying *vociferatio*, or *clamor*, though some will have it *pugna*, ex consequenti, *because fights are often made with clamour*. But *in bello strenuus* (unless it be ironically taken) is here strained beyond sufferance, and is to be expounded *vociferatione bonus Menelaus;* which agreeth with that part of his character in the next book, that telleth his manner of utterance or voice, which is μαλά λιγέως, *valde stridulè*, or *arguto cum stridore*, λιγέως being commonly and most properly taken in the worse part, and signifieth *shrilly*, or *noisefully, squeaking;* howsoever in the vulgar conversion it is in that place most grossly abused. To the consideration whereof, being of much importance, I refer you in his place, and in the mean time show you, that, in this first and next verse, Homer (speaking sceptically) breaks open the fountain of his ridiculous humour following, never by any interpreter understood, or touched at, being yet the most ingenious conceited person that any man can show in any heroical poem, or in any comic poet. And that you may something perceive him before you read to him in his several places, I will, as I can in haste, give you him here together as Homer at all parts presents

him ; viz. simple, well-meaning, standing still affectedly on telling truth, small, and shrill voice, (not sweet, or eloquent, as some most against the hair would have him) short spoken, after his country the Laconical manner, yet speaking thick and fast, industrious in the field, and willing to be employed, and (being *mollis bellator* himself) set still to call to every hard service the hardiest ; even by the wit of Ajax played upon, about whom he would still be diligent, and what he wanted of the martial fury and faculty himself, that he would be bold to supply out of Ajax, Ajax and he, to any for blows ; Antilochus and he for wit ; (Antilochus old Nestor's son, a most ingenious, valiant, and excellently formed person); sometimes valiant, or daring (as what coward is not ?) sometimes falling upon sentence and good matter in his speeches (as what meanest capacity doth not ?). Nor useth our most inimitable imitator of nature this cross and deformed mixture of his parts, more to colour and avoid too broad a taxation of so eminent a person, than to follow the true life of nature, being often, or always, expressed so disparent in her creatures. And therefore the decorum that some poor critics have stood upon, to make fools always foolish, cowards at all times cowardly, &c., is far from the variant order of nature, whose principle being contrary, her productions must needs contain the like opposition.

But now to the first ; αὐτόματος δὲ οἱ ἦλθε, &c., *spontaneus autem ei venit*, &c., about which a passing great piece of work is picked out by our greatest philosophers, touching the unbidden coming of Menelaus to supper or council, which some commend, others condemn in him ; but the reason why he staid not the invitement, rendered immediately by Homer, none of them will understand, viz., "Ηδεε γὰρ κατὰ θυμὸν, &c., *sciebat enim in animo quantum frater laborabat;* of which verse his interpreters cry out for the expunction, only because it was never entered in their apprehension, which I more than admire (for the easiness of it) so freely offering itself to their entertainment, and yet using the hoof of Pegasus, only with a touch breaking open (as above said) the fountain of his humour. For thus I expound it (laying all again together, to make it plain enough for you); Agamemnon, inviting all the chief commanders to supper, left out his brother; but he, seeing how much his brother was troubled about the dream, and busied, would not stand upon invitement, but came of himself. And this being spoken *scopticè*, or by way of irrision, argueth what manner of man he made of him. *Ineptus enim* (as it is affirmed in Plutarch, 1. Symp. and second question) *fuit* Menelaus, *et locum dedit proverbio, qui ad consilium dandum accessisset non vocatus.* And to this place he had reference, because a council of war was to be held at this supper. And here, I say, Homer opened the vein of his simplicity, not so much in his going unbidden to supper, and council, as in the reason for it ironically rendered, that he knew his brother was busy, &c. And yet that addition, without which the very sense of our poet is not safe, our interpreters would have rased.

THE END OF THE SECOND BOOK.

THE THIRD BOOK OF HOMER'S ILIADS.

THE ARGUMENT.

PARIS, betwixt the hosts, to single fight,
Of all the Greeks, dares the most hardy knight.
King Menelaus doth accept his brave,*
Conditioning that he again should have
Fair Helena, and all she brought to Troy,
If he subdu'd ; else Paris should enjoy
Her, and her wealth, in peace. Conquest doth grant
Her dear wreath to the Grecian combatant ; †
But Venus to her champion's life doth yield
Safe rescue, and conveys him from the field
Into his chamber, and for Helen sends,
Whom much her lover's foul disgrace offends ;
Yet Venus still for him makes good her charms,
And ends the second combat in his arms.

ANOTHER ARGUMENT.

Gamma the single fight doth sing
'Twixt Paris and the Spartan king.

WHEN ev'ry least commander's will best soldiers had obey'd,
   And both the hosts were rang'd for fight, the Trojans would have fray'd
   The Greeks with noises, crying out, in coming rudely on ;
At all parts like the cranes that fill, with harsh confusion,

---

* *His brave*—bravado, boasting speech, or challenge. A very frequent word.
† *Her dear wreath*—the wreath, or victor's crown, the sign of conquest. Here put for Helen herself.

Of brutish clangés all the air, and in ridiculous war 5
(Eschewing the unsuffer'd storms, shot from the winter's star)
Visit the ocean, and confer the Pygmei soldiers' death.
The Greeks charg'd silent, and like men, bestow'd their thrifty breath
In strength of far-resounding blows, still entertaining care
Of either's rescue, when their strength did their engagements dare. 10
And as, upon a hill's steep tops, the south wind pours a cloud,
To shepherds thankless, but by thieves, that love the night, allow'd,
A darkness letting down, that blinds a stone's cast off men's eyes;
Such darkness from the Greeks' swift feet (made all of dust) did rise.
But, ere stern conflict mix'd both strengths, fair Paris stept before 15
The Trojan host; athwart his back a panther's hide he wore,
A crookéd bow, and sword, and shook two brazen-headed darts;
With which well-arm'd, his tongue provok'd the best of Grecian hearts
To stand with him in single fight. Whom when the man, wrong'd most
Of all the Greeks, so gloriously saw stalk before the host; 20
As when a lion is rejoic'd, (with hunger half forlorn,)
That finds some sweet prey, as a hart, whose grace lies in his horn,
Or sylvan goat, which he devours, though never so pursu'd
With dogs and men; so Sparta's king exulted, when he view'd
The fair-fac'd Paris so expos'd to his so thirsted wreak, 25
Whereof his good cause made him sure. The Grecian front did break,
And forth he rush'd, at all parts arm'd, leapt from his chariot,
And royally prepar'd for charge. Which seen, cold terror shot

---

⁵ *Clanges*—so both the folios. Dr. Taylor has printed *clangour*. I have retained the old reading, as Chapman probably meant it for the plural of *clange* or *clang*.

⁶ *Unsuffer'd*—insufferable.   ⁷ *Confer*—see Bk. 11. 307.

⁷ *Pygmei*—Pygmy, the battle of the Cranes and Pygmies.

¹² *Thankless*—not liked by, not grateful to.

¹² *Allow'd*—liked by, approved of.

"O heavens
If you do love old men, if your sweet sway
Allow obedience."—SHAKESPEARE. *Lear*, II. 4.

¹³ *That blinds a stone's cast off men's eyes*—that prevents one seeing beyond a stone's throw.

²⁰ *Gloriously*—boastingly.   ²⁵ *So thirsted wreak*—so desired revenge.

The heart of Paris, who retir'd as headlong from the king
As in him he had shunn'd his death. And as a hilly spring   30
Presents a serpent to a man, full underneath his feet,
Her blue neck, swoln with poison, rais'd, and her sting out, to greet
His heedless entry, suddenly his walk he altereth,
Starts back amaz'd, is shook with fear, and looks as pale as death;
So Menelaus Paris scar'd; so that divine-fac'd foe   35
Shrunk in his beauties. Which beheld by Hector, he let go
This bitter check at him: "Accurs'd, made but in beauty's scorn,
Impostor, woman's man! O heav'n, that thou hadst ne'er been born,
Or, being so manless, never liv'd to bear man's noblest state,
The nuptial honour! Which I wish, because it were a fate   40
Much better for thee than this shame. This spectacle doth make
A man a monster. Hark! how loud the Greeks laugh, who did take
Thy fair form for a continent of parts as fair. A rape
Thou mad'st of nature, like their queen. No soul, an empty shape,
Takes up thy being; yet how spite to ev'ry shade of good   45
Fills it with ill! for as thou art, thou couldst collect a brood
Of others like thee, and far hence fetch ill enough to us,
Ev'n to thy father; all these friends make those foes mock them thus
In thee, for whose ridiculous sake so seriously they lay
All Greece, and fate, upon their necks. O wretch! Not dare to stay
Weak Menelaus? But 'twas well; for in him thou hadst tried   51
What strength lost beauty can infuse, and with the more grief died
To feel thou robb'dst a worthier man, to wrong a soldier's right.
Your harp's sweet touch, curl'd locks, fine shape, and gifts so exquisite,
Giv'n thee by Venus, would have done your fine dames little good,   55
When blood and dust had ruffled them, and had as little stood
Thyself in stead; but what thy care of all these in thee flies
We should inflict on thee ourselves. Infectious cowardice

---

[30] *As in him*—as if in him.   [39] *Manless*—unmanly, cowardly. Bk. IX. 64.
[42] *Monster*—strange sight, prodigy; as we say, *a show*.
[47] Dr. Taylor, following the second folio, has incorrectly printed "*fetched*."
[53] *Robb'dst*—hadst robbed.

In thee hath terrified our host; for which thou well deserv'st
A coat of tombstone, not of steel in which, for form, thou serv'st." 60
　　To this thus Paris spake, (for form, that might inhabit heav'n)
"Hector, because thy sharp reproof is out of justice giv'n,
I take it well; but though thy heart, inur'd to these affrights,
Cuts through them as an axe through oak, that more us'd more excites
The workman's faculty, whose art can make the edge go far, 65
Yet I, less practis'd than thyself in these extremes of war,
May well be pardon'd, though less bold; in these your worth exceeds,
In others mine. Nor is my mind of less force to the deeds
Requir'd in war, because my form more flows in gifts of peace.
Reproach not, therefore, the kind gifts of golden Cyprides. 70
All heav'n's gifts have their worthy price; as little to be scorn'd
As to be won with strength, wealth, state; with which to be adorn'd,
Some men would change state, wealth, or strength. But, if your martial
　　　　heart
Wish me to make my challenge good, and hold it such a part
Of shame to give it over thus, cause all the rest to rest, 75
And, 'twixt both hosts, let Sparta's king and me perform our best
For Helen and the wealth she brought; and he that overcomes,
Or proves superior any way, in all your equal dooms,
Let him enjoy her utmost wealth, keep her, or take her home;
The rest strike leagues of endless date, and hearty friends become; 80
You dwelling safe in gleby Troy, and Greeks retire their force
T' Achaia, that breeds fairest dames, and Argos, fairest horse."
　　He said, and his amendsful words did Hector highly please,
Who rush'd betwixt the fighting hosts, and made the Trojans cease,
By holding up in midst his lance. The Grecians noted not 85
The signal he for parley used, but at him fiercely shot,
Hurl'd stones, and still were levelling darts. At last the king of men,
Great Agamemnon, cried aloud: "Argives! for shame, contain;

---

⁶⁰ *A coat of tombstone.*—The expression *to put on a coat of stone* was a Greek mode of speaking of those who were *stoned.* Similarly *to put on the earth* (γαῖαν ἐφέσσασθαι) was a term for *burial.*
⁷⁸ *Equal dooms*—just decisions, judgments.

Youths of Achaia, shoot no more; the fair-helm'd Hector shows
As he desir'd to treat with us." This said, all ceas'd from blows, 90
And Hector spake to both the hosts: "Trojans, and hardy Greeks,
Hear now what he that stirr'd these wars, for their cessation seeks.
He bids us all, and you, disarm, that he alone may fight
With Menelaus, for us all, for Helen and her right,
With all the dow'r she brought to Troy; and he that wins the day, 95
Or is, in all the art of arms, superior any way,
The queen, and all her sorts of wealth, let him at will enjoy;
The rest strike truce, and let love seal firm leagues 'twixt Greece and Troy."
 The Greek host wonder'd at this brave; silence flew ev'rywhere;
At last spake Sparta's warlike king: "Now also give me ear, 100
Whom grief gives most cause of reply. I now have hope to free
The Greeks and Trojans of all ills, they have sustain'd for me,
And Alexander, that was cause I stretch'd my spleen so far.
Of both then, which is nearest fate, let his death end the war;
The rest immediately retire, and greet all homes in peace. 105
Go then (to bless your champion, and give his pow'rs success)
Fetch for the Earth, and for the Sun (the Gods on whom ye call)
Two lambs, a black one and a white, a female and a male;
And we another, for ourselves, will fetch, and kill to Jove.
To sign which rites bring Priam's force, because we well approve 110
His sons perfidious, envious, and (out of practis'd bane
To faith, when she believes in them) Jove's high truce may profane.
All young men's hearts are still unstaid; but in those well-weigh'd'deeds
An old man will consent to pass things past, and what succeeds
He looks into, that he may know, how best to make his way 115
Through both the fortunes of a fact, and will the worst obey."
 This granted, a delightful hope, both Greeks and Trojans fed,
Of long'd-for rest from those long toils, their tedious war had bred.
Their horses then in rank they set, drawn from their chariots round,
Descend themselves, took off their arms, and plac'd them on the ground,

---

[103] *Alexander*—Paris.   [110] *Priam's force*—see Bk. II. 587.

Near one another; for the space 'twixt both the hosts was small.　121
Hector two heralds sent to Troy, that they from thence might call
King Priam, and to bring the lambs, to rate the truce they swore.
But Agamemnon to the fleet Talthybius sent before,
To fetch their lamb; who nothing slack'd the royal charge was giv'n.
　　Iris, the rain-bow, then came down, ambassadress from heav'n,　126
To white-arm'd Helen. She assum'd at every part the grace
Of Helen's last love's sister's shape, who had the highest place
In Helen's love, and had to name Laodice, most fair
Of all the daughters Priam had, and made the nuptial pair　130
With Helicaon, royal sprout of old Antenor's seed.
She found queen Helena at home, at work about a weed,
Wov'n for herself; it shin'd like fire, was rich, and full of size,
The work of both sides being alike; in which she did comprise
The many labours warlike Troy and brass-arm'd Greece endur'd　135
For her fair sake, by cruel Mars and his stern friends procur'd.
Iris came in in joyful haste, and said: "O come with me,
Lov'd nymph, and an admiréd sight of Greeks and Trojans see,
Who first on one another brought a war so full of tears,
Ev'n thirsty of contentious war. Now ev'ry man forbears,　140
And friendly by each other sits, each leaning on his shield,
Their long and shining lances pitch'd fast by them in the field.
Paris, and Sparta's king, alone must take up all the strife;
And he that conquers only call fair Helena his wife."
　　Thus spake the thousand-colour'd Dame, and to her mind commends
The joy to see her first espous'd, her native tow'rs, and friends;　146
Which stirr'd a sweet desire in her; to serve the which she hied,
Shadow'd her graces with white veils, and (though she took a pride
To set her thoughts at gaze, and see, in her clear beauty's flood,
What choice of glory swum to her yet tender womanhood)　150
Season'd with tears her joys to see more joys the more offence,
And that perfection could not flow from earthly excellence.

　　　¹²³ *Rate*—see Bk. I. 508.　　¹²⁸ *Helen's last love's sister*—Paris's sister.

Thus went she forth, and took with her her women most of name,
Æthra, Pittheus' lovely birth, and Clymene, whom fame
Hath for her fair eyes memoris'd. They reach'd the Scæan tow'rs,
Where Priam sat, to see the fight, with all his counsellors; 155
Panthous, Lampus, Clytius, and stout Hicetaon,
Thymœtes, wise Antenor, and profound Ucalegon;
All grave old men; and soldiérs they had been, but for age
Now left the wars; yet counsellors they were exceeding sage. 160
And as in well-grown woods, on trees, cold spiny grasshoppers
Sit chirping, and send voices out, that scarce can pierce our ears
For softness, and their weak faint sounds; so, talking on the tow'r,
These seniors of the people sat; who when they saw the pow'r
Of beauty, in the queen, ascend, ev'n those cold-spirited peers, 165
Those wise and almost wither'd men, found this heat in their years,
That they were forc'd (though whispéring) to say: "What man can blame
The Greeks and Trojans to endure, for so admir'd a dame,
So many mis'ries, and so long? In her sweet count'nance shine
Looks like the Goddesses. And yet (though never so divine) 170
Before we boast, unjustly still, of her enforcéd prise,
And justly suffer for her sake, with all our progenies,
Labour and ruin, let her go; the profit of our land
Must pass the beauty." Thus, though these could bear so fit a hand
On their affections, yet, when all their gravest powers were us'd, 175
They could not choose but welcome her, and rather they accus'd
The Gods than beauty; for thus spake the most-fam'd king of Troy:
"Come, lovéd daughter, sit by me, and take the worthy joy
Of thy first husband's sight, old friends, and princes near allied,
And name me some of these brave Greeks, so manly beautified. 180
Come, do not think I lay the wars, endur'd by us, on thee,
The Gods have sent them, and the tears in which they swum to me.

[161] *Spiny*—Nares says he never met with this word. *Thin, thorny-looking.* It is peculiarly expressive here.

Sit then, and name this goodly Greek, so tall, and broadly spread,
Who than the rest, that stand by him, is higher by the head;
The bravest man I ever saw, and most majestical, 185
His only presence makes me think him king amongst them all."

   The fairest of her sex replied: " Most rev'rend father-in-law,
Most lov'd, most fear'd, would some ill death had seiz'd me, when I saw
The first mean why I wrong'd you thus; that I had never lost
The sight of these my ancient friends, of him that lov'd me most, 190
Of my sole daughter, brothers both, with all those kindly mates,
Of one soil, one age, born with me, though under diff'rent fates!
But these boons envious stars deny; the memory of these
In sorrow pines those beauties now, that then did too much please;
Nor satisfy they your demand, to which I thus reply: 195
That's Agamemnon, Atreus' son, the great in empery;
A king, whom double royalty doth crown, being great and good,
And one that was my brother-in-law, when I contain'd my blood,
And was more worthy; if at all I might be said to be,
My being being lost so soon in all that honour'd me." 200

   The good old king admir'd, and said: " O Atreus' blessèd son,
Born unto joyful destinies, that hast the empire won
Of such a world of Grecian youths, as I discover here!
I once march'd into Phrygia, that many vines doth bear,
Where many Phrygians I beheld, well-skill'd in use of horse, 205
That of the two men, like two Gods, were the commanded force,
Otröus, and great Mygdonus, who on Sangarius' sands
Set down their tents, with whom myself, for my assistant bands,
Was number'd as a man in chief; the cause of war was then
Th' Amazon dames, that in their facts affected to be men. 210
In all there was a mighty pow'r, which yet did never rise
To equal these Achaian youths, that have the sable eyes."

      186 *Only presence*—his mere appearance.
      194 *Pines*—causes to waste.
      198 *Contained my blood*—restrained my passions.

Then (seeing Ulysses next) he said : " Lov'd daughter, what is he
That, lower than great Atreus' son, seems by the head to me,
Yet, in his shoulders and big breast, presents a broader show ?   215
His armour lies upon the earth ; he up and down doth go,
To see his soldiers keep their ranks, and ready have their arms,
If, in this truce, they should be tried by any false alarms.
Much like a well-grown bell-wether, or feltred ram, he shows,
That walks before a wealthy flock of fair white-fleecéd ewes."   220
    High Jove and Leda's fairest seed to Priam thus replies :
" This is the old Laertes' son, Ulysses, call'd the wise ;
Who, though unfruitful Ithaca was made his nursing seat,
Yet knows he every sort of sleight, and is in counsels great."
    The wise Antenor answer'd her : " 'Tis true, renowméd dame ;   225
For, some times past, wise Ithacus to Troy a legate came,
With Menelaus, for your cause ; to whom I gave receipt
As guests, and welcom'd to my house, with all the love I might.
I learn'd the wisdom of their souls, and humours of their blood ;
For when the Trojan council met, and these together stood,   230
By height of his broad shoulders had Atrides eminence,
Yet, set, Ulysses did exceed, and bred more reverence.
And when their counsels and their words they wove in one, the speech
Of Atreus' son was passing loud, small, fast, yet did not reach
To much, being naturally born Laconical ; nor would   235
His humour lie for anything, or was, like th' other, old ;
But when the prudent Ithacus did to his counsels rise,
He stood a little still, and fix'd upon the earth his eyes,
His sceptre moving neither way, but held it formally,
Like one that vainly doth affect. Of wrathful quality,   240
And frantic (rashly judging him) you would have said he was,
But when, out of his ample breast, he gave his great voice pass,
And words that flew about our ears, like drifts of winter's snow,

    219 *Feltred*—matted close together, like *felt ;* applied to the wool.
    229 *Blood*—disposition, a sense in which it is used by Shakespeare and others.

None thenceforth might contend with him, tho' nought admir'd for show."
    The third man, aged Priam mark'd, was Ajax Telamon, 245
Of whom he ask'd : " What lord is that, so large of limb and bone,
So rais'd in height, that to his breast I see there reacheth none ?"
    To him the Goddess of her sex, the large-veil'd Helen, said :
" That Lord is Ajax Telamon, a bulwark in their aid.
On th' other side stands Idomen, in Crete of most command, 250
And round about his royal sides his Cretan captains stand ;
Oft hath the warlike Spartan king giv'n hospitable due
To him within our Lacene court, and all his retinue.
And now the other Achive dukes I gen'rally discern ;
All which I know, and all their names could make thee quickly learn.
Two princes of the people yet, I nowhere can behold, 256
Castor, the skilful knight on horse, and Pollux, uncontroll'd
For all stand-fights, and force of hand ; both at a burthen bred ;
My natural brothers ; either here they have not followed
From lovely Sparta, or, arriv'd within the sea-born fleet, 260
In fear of infamy for me, in broad field shame to meet."
    Nor so ; for holy Tellus' womb inclos'd those worthy men
In Sparta, their belovéd soil. The voiceful heralds then
The firm agreement of the Gods through all the city ring ;
Two lambs, and spirit-refreshing wine (the fruit of earth) they bring,
Within a goat-skin bottle clos'd ; Idæus also brought 266
A massy glitt'ring bowl, and cups, that all of gold were wrought ;
Which bearing to the king, they cried : " Son of Laomedon
Rise, for the well-rode peers of Troy, and brass-arm'd Greeks, in one,
Send to thee to descend the field, that they firm vows may make ; 270
For Paris, and the Spartan king, must fight for Helen's sake,
With long arm'd lances ; and the man that proves victorious,
The woman, and the wealth she brought, shall follow to his house ;
The rest knit friendship, and firm leagues ; we safe in Troy shall dwell,
In Argos and Achaia they, that do in dames excel." 275

    [259] *Natural*—by the same father and mother.

He said; and Priam's aged joints with chilléd fear did shake,
Yet instantly he bade his men his chariot ready make.
Which soon they did, and he ascends. He takes the reins, and guide
Antenor calls; who instantly mounts to his royal side,
And, through the Scæan ports to field, the swift-foot horse they drive.
And when at them of Troy and Greece the aged lords arrive, 281
From horse, on Troy's well-feeding soil, 'twixt both the hosts they go.
When straight up-rose the king of men, up-rose Ulysses too,
The heralds in their richest coats repeat (as was the guise)
The true vows of the Gods (term'd theirs, since made before their eyes)
Then in a cup of gold they mix the wine that each side brings, 286
And next pour water on the hands of both the kings of kings.
Which done, Atrides drew his knife, that evermore he put
Within the large sheath of his sword; with which away he cut
The wool from both fronts of the lambs, which (as a rite in use 290
Of execration to their heads, that brake the plighted truce)
The heralds of both hosts did give the peers of both; and then,
With hands and voice advanc'd to heav'n, thus pray'd the king of men:
  "O Jove, that Ida dost protect, and hast the titles won
Most glorious, most invincible; and thou all-seeing Sun, 295
All-hearing, all-recomforting; Floods; Earth; and Pow'rs beneath,
That all the perjuries of men chastise ev'n after death!
Be witnesses, and see perform'd the hearty vows we make.—
If Alexander shall the life of Menelaus take,
He shall from henceforth Helena, with all her wealth, retain, 300
And we will to our household Gods, hoise sail, and home again.
If, by my honour'd brother's hand, be Alexander slain,
The Trojans then shall his forc'd queen, with all her wealth, restore,
And pay convenient fine to us, and ours for evermore.
If Priam and his sons deny to pay this, thus agreed, 305
When Alexander shall be slain; for that perfidious deed,
And for the fine, will I fight here, till dearly they repay,
By death and ruin, the amends, that falsehood keeps away."

This said, the throats of both the lambs cut with his royal knife,
He laid them panting on the earth, till, quite depriv'd of life, 310
The steel had robb'd them of their strength ; then golden cups they crown'd,
With wine out of a cistern drawn ; which pour'd upon the ground,
They fell upon their humble knees to all the Deities,
And thus pray'd one of both the hosts, that might do sacrifice :
"O Jupiter, most high, most great, and all the deathless Pow'rs !
Who first shall dare to violate the late sworn oaths of ours, 316
So let the bloods and brains of them, and all they shall produce,
Flow on the stain'd face of the earth, as now this sacred juice ;
And let their wives with bastardice brand all their future race."
Thus pray'd they ; but, with wish'd effects, their pray'rs Jove did not grace ;
When Priam said : "Lords of both hosts, I can no longer stay 321
To see my lov'd son try his life, and so must take my way
To wind-exposéd Ilion. Jove yet and heav'n's high States
Know only, which of these must now pay tribute to the Fates."
 Thus, putting in his coach the lambs, he mounts and reins his horse ;
Antenor to him ; and to Troy, both take their speedy course. 326
 Then Hector, Priam's martial son, stepp'd forth, and met the ground,
With wise Ulysses, where the blows of combat must resound ;
Which done, into a helm they put two lots, to let them know
Which of the combatants should first his brass-pil'd jav'lin throw ; 330
When all the people standing by, with hands held up to heav'n,
Pray'd Jove the conquest might not be by force or fortune giv'n,
But that the man, who was in right the author of most wrong,
Might feel his justice, and no more these tedious wars prolong,
But, sinking to the house of death, leave them (as long before) 335
Link'd fast in leagues of amity, that might dissolve no more.
 Then Hector shook the helm that held the equal dooms of chance,
Look'd back, and drew ; and Paris first had lot to hurl his lance.
The soldiers all sat down enrank'd, each by his arms and horse 339
That then lay down and cool'd their hoofs. And now th' allotted course

  ³²⁷ *Met*—meted, measured.   ³³⁰ *Brass-pil'd*—brass-pointed.

Bids fair-hair'd Helen's husband arm; who first makes fast his greaves
With silver buckles to his legs; then on his breast receives
The curets that Lycaon wore (his brother) but made fit
For his fair body; next his sword he took, and fasten'd it,
All damask'd, underneath his arm; his shield then grave and great 345
His shoulders wore; and on his head his glorious helm he set,
Topp'd with a plume of horse's hair, that horribly did dance,
And seem'd to threaten as he mov'd; at last he takes his lance,
Exceeding big, and full of weight, which he with ease could use.

In like sort, Sparta's warlike king himself with arms indues. 350
Thus arm'd at either army both, they both stood bravely in,
Possessing both hosts with amaze, they came so chin to chin,
And, with such horrible aspécts, each other did salute.

A fair large field was made for them; where wraths, for hugeness mute,
And mutual, made them mutually at either shake their darts 355
Before they threw. Then Paris first with his long jav'lin parts;
It smote Atrides' orby targe, but ran not through the brass,
For in it (arming well the shield) the head reflected was.

Then did the second combatant apply him to his spear,
Which ere he threw, he thus besought almighty Jupiter: 360

"O Jove! Vouchsafe me now revenge, and that my enemy,
For doing wrong so undeserv'd, may pay deservedly
The pains he forfeited; and let these hands inflict those pains,
By conqu'ring, ay, by conqu'ring dead, him on whom life complains;
That any now, or any one of all the brood of men 365
To live hereafter, may with fear from all offence abstain,
Much more from all such foul offence to him that was his host,
And entertain'd him as the man whom he affected most."

This said, he shook and threw his lance; which strook through Paris'
shield,

₃₄₃ *Curets*—cuirass. Sometimes spelt *curace*, *curat*, and *curiet*.
₃₄₅ *Damask'd*—inlaid.
₃₅₈ *Reflected*—turned back.

And, with the strength he gave to it, it made the curets yield, 370
His coat of mail, his breast, and all, and drove his entrails in,
In that low region where the guts in three small parts begin ;
Yet he, in bowing of his breast, prevented sable death.
This taint he follow'd with his sword, drawn from a silver sheath,
Which lifting high, he strook his helm full where his plume did stand,
On which it piecemeal brake, and fell from his unhappy hand. 375
At which he sighing stood, and star'd upon the ample sky,
And said : " O Jove, there is no God giv'n more illiberally
To those that serve thee than thyself, why have I pray'd in vain ?
I hop'd my hand should have reveng'd, the wrongs I still sustain, 380
On him that did them, and still dares their foul defence pursue ;
And now my lance hath miss'd his end, my sword in shivers flew,
And he 'scapes all." With this, again he rush'd upon his guest,
And caught him by the horse-hair plume, that dangled on his crest,
With thought to drag him to the Greeks ; which he had surely done,
And so, besides the victory, had wondrous glory won, 386
(Because the needle-painted lace, with which his helm was tied
Beneath his chin, and so about his dainty throat implied,
Had strangled him ;) but that, in time, the Cyprian seed of Jove
Did break the string, with which was lin'd that which the needle wove,
And was the tough thong of a steer ; and so the victor's palm 391
Was, for so full a man-at-arms, only an empty helm.
That then he swung about his head, and cast among his friends,
Who scrambled, and took 't up with shouts. Again then he intends
To force the life-blood of his foe, and ran on him amain, 395
With shaken jav'lin ; when the Queen, that lovers loves, again
Attended, and now ravish'd him from that encounter quite,
With ease, and wondrous suddenly ; for she, a Goddess, might.

[374] *Taint*—a term at tilting, when the blow or thrust, given by the lance, failed in its effect. Halliwell explains it "injuring a lance without breaking it ;" Gifford, "breaking a staff, but not in the most honourable manner." Chapman however frequently uses it to express simply a thrust with a spear.
[396] *When the Queen, &c.*—" This place Virgil imitateth."—CHAPMAN.

She hid him in a cloud of gold, and never made him known,
Till in his chamber, fresh and sweet, she gently set him down,   400
And went for Helen; whom she found in Scæa's utmost height,
To which whole swarms of city dames had climb'd to see the sight.

To give her errand good success, she took on her the shape
Of beldame Græa, who was brought by Helen, in her rape,
From Lacedæmon, and had trust in all her secrets still,   405
Being old, and had (of all her maids) the main bent of her will,
And spun for her her finest wool. Like her, Love's Empress came,
Pull'd Helen by the heav'nly veil, and softly said: "Madáme,
My lord calls for you, you must needs make all your kind haste home;
He's in your chamber, stays, and longs; sits by your bed; pray come,
'Tis richly made, and sweet; but he more sweet, and looks so clear,   411
So fresh, and movingly attir'd, that, seeing, you would swear
He came not from the dusty fight, but from a courtly dance,
Or would to dancing." This she made a charm for dalliance;
Whose virtue Helen felt, and knew, by her so radiant eyes,   415
White neck, and most enticing breasts, the deified disguise.

At which amaz'd, she answer'd her: "Unhappy Deity!
Why lov'st thou still in these deceits to wrap my phantasy?
Or whither yet, of all the towns giv'n to their lust beside,
In Phrygia, or Mæonia, com'st thou to be my guide,   420
If there (of divers-languag'd men) thou hast, as here in Troy,
Some other friend to be my shame; since here thy latest joy
By Menelaus now subdu'd, by him shall I be borne
Home to his court, and end my life in triumphs of his scorn?
And, to this end, would thy deceits my wanton life allure?   425
Hence, go thyself to Priam's son, and all the ways abjure
Of Gods, or godlike-minded dames, nor ever turn again
Thy earth-affecting feet to heav'n, but for his sake sustain
Toils here; guard, grace him endlessly, till he requite thy grace
By giving thee my place with him; or take his servant's place,   430

---

404 *Beldame*—formerly a term of respect for an old woman.

If, all dishonourable ways, your favours seek to serve
His never-pleas'd incontinence ; I better will deserve,
Than serve his dotage now.   What shame were it for me to feed
This lust in him ; all honour'd dames would hate me for the deed !
He leaves a woman's love so sham'd, and shows so base a mind,   435
To feel nor my shame nor his own ; griefs of a greater kind
Wound me than such as can admit such kind delights so soon."
  The Goddess, angry that, past shame, her mere will was not done,
Replied : "Incense me not, you wretch, lest, once incens'd, I leave
Thy curs'd life to as strange a hate, as yet it may receive   440
A love from me ; and lest I spread through both hosts such despite,
For those plagues they have felt for thee, that both abjure thee quite,
And setting thee in midst of both, turn all their wraths on thee,
And dart thee dead ; that such a death may wreak thy wrong of me."
  This strook the fair dame with such fear, it took her speech away,
And, shadow'd in her snowy veil, she durst not but obey ;   446
And yet, to shun the shame she fear'd, she vanish'd undescried
Of all the Trojan ladies there, for Venus was her guide.
  Arriv'd at home, her women both fell to their work in haste ;
When she, that was of all her sex the most divinely grac'd,   450
Ascended to a higher room, though much against her will,
Where lovely Alexander was, being led by Venus still.
The laughter-loving Dame discern'd her mov'd mind by her grace,
And, for her mirth' sake, set a stool, full before Paris' face,
Where she would needs have Helen sit ; who, though she durst not
  choose   455
But sit, yet look'd away for all the Goddess' pow'r could use,
And used her tongue too, and to chide whom Venus sooth'd so much,
And chid, too, in this bitter kind : "And was thy cowardice such,
So conquer'd, to be seen alive ?   O would to God, thy life
Had perish'd by his worthy hand, to whom I first was wife !   460
Before this, thou wouldst glorify thy valour and thy lance,
And, past my first love's, boast them far.   Go once more, and advance

Thy braves against his single pow'r; this foil might fall by chance.
Poor conquer'd man! 'Twas such a chance, as I would not advise
Thy valour should provoke again.   Shun him, thou most unwise,   465
Lest next, thy spirit sent to hell, thy body be his prise."

He answer'd : " Pray thee, woman, cease, to chide and grieve me thus.
Disgraces will not ever last. Look on their end. On us
Will other Gods, at other times, let fall the victor's wreath,
As on him Pallas put it now. Shall our love sink beneath   470
The hate of fortune? In love's fire, let all hates vanish. Come,
Love never so inflam'd my heart; no, not when, bringing home
Thy beauty's so delicious prise, on Cranaë's blest shore,
I long'd for, and enjoy'd thee first." With this he went before,
She after, to the odorous bed. While these to pleasure yield,   475
Perplex'd Atrides, savage-like, ran up and down the field,
And ev'ry thickest troop of Troy, and of their far-call'd aid,
Search'd for his foe, who could not be by any eye betray'd;
Nor out of friendship (out of doubt) did they conceal his sight,
All hated him so like their deaths, and ow'd him such despite.   480

At last thus spake the king of men : " Hear me, ye men of Troy,
Ye Dardans, and the rest, whose pow'rs you in their aids employ.
The conquest on my brother's part, ye all discern is clear,
Do you then Argive Helena, with all her treasure here,
Restore to us, and pay the mulct, that by your vows is due,   485
Yield us an honour'd recompense, and, all that should accrue
To our posterities, confirm; that when you render it,
Our acts may here be memoris'd." This all Greeks else thought fit.

COMMENTARIUS.

126.

Ἴρις δ' αὖθ' Ἑλένῃ, &c. *Iris autem Helene,* &c. Elegantly and most aptly (saith Spondanus) is Helen called by Homer to the spectacle of this single fight, as being the chief person in cause of all the action. The chief end of whose coming yet, enviously and most vainly, Scaliger's Criticus taxeth; which was her relation to Priam of the persons he noted there; jesting (with his French wit) at this Greek father, and fount, of all wit, for making Priam to seek now of their names and knowledges, when nine years together they had lien there before. A great piece of necessity to make him therefore know them before, when there was no such urgent occasion before to bring Priam to note them, nor so calm a convenience in their ordered and quiet distinction! But let this criticism in this be weighed with his other faults found in our master;—as, for making lightning in winter before snow or rain, which the most ignorant upland peasant could teach him out of his observations. For which yet his Criticus hath the project impudence to tax Homer; most falsely repeating his words too; saying *ubi ningit,* when he saith, τεύχων ἢ πολὺν ὄμβρον, &c., *parans,* or *struens, vel multum imbrem, immensamve grandinem, vel nivem:* preparing, or going about those moist impressions in the air, not in present act with them. From this, immediately and most rabidly, he ranges to Ulysses' reprehension, for killing the wooers with his bow, in the Odysses. Then to his late vomit again in the Iliads the very next word, and envieth Achilles' horse for speaking (because himself would have all the tongue) when, in Sacred Writ, Balaam's ass could have taught him the like hath been heard of. Yet now to the Odysses again with a breath, and challenges Ulysses' ship for suffering Neptune to turn it to a rock.

Here is strange laying out for a master so curiously methodical. Not with what Graces, with what Muses, we may ask, he was inspired, but with what Harpies, what Furies, putting the *putidum mendacium* upon Homer? *Putidus, ineptus, frigidus, puerilis* (being terms fitter for a scold or a bawd, than a man softened by learning) he belcheth against him whom all the world hath reverenced, and admired, as the fountain of all wit, wisdom, and learning. What touch is it to me, then, to bear spots of depravations, when my great master is thus muddily daubed with it? But whoever saw true learning, wisdom, or wit, vouchsafe mansion in any proud, vain-glorious, and braggartly spirit, when their chief act and end is to abandon and abhor it? Language, reading, habit of speaking, or writing in other learning, I grant in this reviler great and abundant; but, in this poesy, redundant I affirm him, and rammish. To conclude, I will use the same words of him, that he of Erasmus, (*in calce Epinomidos*), which are these (as I convert it):—"Great was his name, but had been futurely greater, would himself have been less; where now, bold with the greatness of his wit, he hath undertaken the more, with much less exactness; and so his confidence, set on by the renown of his name, hath driven him headlong, &c."

102. "Ὄπα λειριόεσσαν ἱεῖσι. *Vocem suavem emittunt*, saith the interpreter (intending the grasshoppers, to whom he compareth the old counsellors); but it is here to be expounded, *vocem teneram* not *suavem* (λειριόεις in this place signifying *tener*) for grasshoppers sing not sweetly, but harshly and faintly, wherein the weak and tender voice of the old counsellors is to admiration expressed. The simile Spondanus highly commends is most apt and expressive; but his application in one part doth abuse it, in the other right it, and that is, to make the old men resemble grasshoppers for their cold and bloodless spininess, Tython being for age turned to a grasshopper, but where they were grave and wise counsellors, to make them garrulous, as grasshoppers are stridulous; that application holdeth not in these old men, though some old men are so, these being Ἐσθλοὶ ἀγορηταὶ *boni, et periti, concionatores*; the word ἐσθλός signifying *frugi* also, which is temperate or full of all

moderation, and, so, far from intimating any touch of garrulity. Nor was the conceit of our poet by Spondanus or any other understood in this simile.

234. Ἐπιτροχάδην ἀγόρευε, *succincte concionabatur Menelaus;* he speaks succinctly, or compendiously, say his interpreters; which is utterly otherwise, in the voice ἐπιτροχάδην, signifying *velociter*, properly, *modo eorum qui currunt;* he spake fast or thick.

παῦρα μὲν, &c., few words yet, he used, ἀλλὰ μάλα λιγέως, *sed valde acutè*, they expound it, when it is *valde stridulè*, shrilly, smally, or aloud; λιγέως, (as I have noted before) being properly taken in the worse part; and accordingly expounded, maketh even with his simple character at all parts, his utterance being noiseful, small, or squeaking; an excellent pipe for a fool. Nor is the voice or manner of utterance in a man the least key that discovereth his wisdom or folly. And therefore worth the noting is that of Ulysses in the second book—that he knew Pallas by her voice.

ἐπεὶ οὐ πολύμυθος, *quoniam non garrulus*, or *loquax;* being born naturally Laconical; which agreeth not the less with his fast or thick speaking: for a man may have that kind of utterance, and yet few words.

235. Οὐ δ' ἀφαμαρτοεπὴς: *neque in verbis peccans*, say the commentors, as though a fool were perfectly spoken; when the word here hath another sense, and our Homer a far other meaning, the words being thus to be expounded: *neque mendax erat*, he would not lie by any means, for that affectedly he stands upon hereafter. But to make a fool *non peccans verbis*, will make a man nothing wonder at any peccancy or absurdity in men of mere language.

You see, then, to how extreme a difference and contrariety the word and sense lie subject, and that, without first finding the true figures of persons in this kind presented, it is impossible for the best linguist living to express an author truly, especially any Greek author, the language being so differently significant, which not judicially fitted with the exposition that the place (and coherence with other places) requireth, what a motley and confused man a translator may present! As now they do all of Menelaus, who, wheresoever he is called 'Ἀρηίφιλος, is there untruly translated *bellicosus*, but *cui Mars est charus*, because he might love the war, and yet be no good warrior, as many love many exercises at which they will never be good; and Homer gave it to him for another of his peculiar epithets, as a vain-glorious affectation in him, rather than a solid affection.

And here haste makes me give end to these new annotations, deferring the like in the next nine books for more breath and encouragement, since time (that hath ever oppressed me) will not otherwise let me come to the last twelve, in which the first free light of my author entered and emboldened me; where so many rich discoveries importune my poor expression, that I fear rather to betray them to the world than express them to their price. But howsoever envy and prejudice stand squirting their poison through the eyes of my readers, this shall appear to all competent apprehensions, I have followed the original with authentical expositions, according to the proper signification of the word in his place, though I differ therein utterly from others; I have rendered all things of importance with answerable life and height to my author, though with some periphrasis, without which no man can worthily translate any worthy poet. And since the translation itself, and my notes (being impartially conferred) amply approve this, I will still be confident in the worth of my pains, how idly and unworthily soever I be censured. And thus to the last twelve books (leaving other horrible errors in his other interpreters unmoved) with those free feet that entered me, I haste, sure of nothing but my labour.

THE END OF THE THIRD BOOK.

THE FOURTH BOOK OF HOMER'S ILIADS.

THE ARGUMENT.

THE Gods in council, at the last, decree
That famous Ilion shall expugnéd be;
And that their own continu'd faults may prove
The reasons that have so incenséd Jove,
Minerva seeks, with more offences done
Against the lately injur'd Atreus' son,
(A ground that clearest would make seen their sin)
To have the Lycian Pandarus begin.
He ('gainst the truce with sacred cov'nants bound)
Gives Menelaus a dishonour'd wound.
Machaon heals him. Agamemnon then
To mortal war incenseth all his men.
The battles join; and, in the heat of fight,
Cold death shuts many eyes in endless night.

ANOTHER ARGUMENT.

In Delta is the Gods' Assize;
The truce is broke; wars freshly rise.

ITHIN the fair-pav'd court of Jove, he and the Gods conferr'd
About the sad events of Troy; amongst whom minister'd
Bless'd Hebe nectar. As they sat, and did Troy's tow'rs
behold,
They drank, and pledg'd each other round in full-crown'd cups of gold.

The mirth at whose feast was begun by great Saturnides 5
In urging a begun dislike amongst the Goddesses,
But chiefly in his solemn queen, whose spleen he was dispos'd
To tempt yet further, knowing well what anger it inclos'd,
And how wives' angers should be us'd. On which, thus pleas'd, he play'd:
"Two Goddesses there are that still give Menelaus aid, 10
And one that Paris loves. The two that sit from us so far
(Which Argive Juno is, and She that rules in deeds of war,)
No doubt are pleas'd to see how well the late-seen fight did frame;
And yet, upon the adverse part, the laughter-loving Dame 14
Made her pow'r good too for her friend; for, though he were so near
The stroke of death in th' others' hopes, she took him from them clear.
The conquest yet is questionless the martial Spartan king's.
We must consult then what events shall crown these future things,
If wars and combats we shall still with even successes strike,
Or as impartial friendship plant on both parts. If ye like 20
The last, and that it will as well delight as merely please
Your happy deities, still let stand old Priam's town in peace,
And let the Lacedæmon king again his queen enjoy."
As Pallas and Heav'ns Queen sat close, complotting ill to Troy,
With silent murmurs they receiv'd this ill-lik'd choice from Jove; 25
'Gainst whom was Pallas much incens'd, because the Queen of Love
Could not, without his leave, relieve in that late point of death
The son of Priam, whom she loath'd; her wrath yet fought beneath
Her supreme wisdom, and was curb'd; but Juno needs must ease
Her great heart with her ready tongue, and said; "What words are these,
Austere, and too-much-Saturn's son? Why wouldst thou render still 31
My labours idle, and the sweat of my industrious will
Dishonour with so little pow'r? My chariot horse are tir'd
With posting to and fro for Greece, and bringing banes desir'd
To people-must'ring Priamus, and his perfidious sons; 35
Yet thou protect'st, and join'st with them whom each just Deity shuns.

Go on, but ever go resolv'd all other Gods have vow'd
To cross thy partial course for Troy, in all that makes it proud."
    At this, the cloud-compelling Jove a far-fetch'd sigh let fly,
And said : "Thou fury ! What offence of such impiety
Hath Priam or his sons done thee, that, with so high a hate,
Thou shouldst thus ceaselessly desire to raze and ruinate
So well a builded town as Troy ? I think, hadst thou the pow'r,
Thou wouldst the ports and far-stretch'd walls fly over, and devour
Old Priam and his issue quick, and make all Troy thy feast,
And then at length I hope thy wrath and tiréd spleen would rest ;
To which run on thy chariot, that nought be found in me
Of just cause to our future jars. In this yet strengthen thee,
And fix it in thy memory fast, that if I entertain
As peremptory a desire to level with the plain
A city where thy lovéd live, stand not betwixt my ire
And what it aims at, but give way, when thou hast thy desire ;
Which now I grant thee willingly, although against my will.
For not beneath the ample sun, and heav'n's star-bearing hill,
There is a town of earthly men so honour'd in my mind
As sacred Troy ; nor of earth's kings as Priam and his kind,
Who never let my altars lack rich feast of off'rings slain,
And their sweet savours ; for which grace I honour them again."
    Dread Juno, with the cow's fair eyes, replied : "Three towns there are
Of great and eminent respect, both in my love and care ;
Mycene, with the broad highways ; and Argos, rich in horse ;
And Sparta ; all which three destroy, when thou envi'st their force,
I will not aid them, nor malign thy free and sov'reign will,
For if I should be envious, and set against their ill,
I know my envy were in vain, since thou art mightier far.
But we must give each other leave, and wink at either's war.
I likewise must have pow'r to crown my works with wishéd end,
Because I am a Deity, and did from thence descend

    [37] *Resolved*—informed.

Whence thou thyself, and th' elder born ; wise Saturn was our sire ;
And thus there is a two-fold cause that pleads for my desire, 70
Being sister, and am call'd thy wife ; and more, since thy command
Rules all Gods else, I claim therein a like superior hand.
All wrath before then now remit, and mutually combine
In either's empire ; I, thy rule, and thou, illustrate, mine ;
So will the other Gods agree, and we shall all be strong. 75
And first (for this late plot) with speed let Pallas go among
The Trojans, and some one of them entice to break the truce
By off'ring in some treach'rous wound the honour'd Greeks abuse."

The Father both of men and Gods agreed, and Pallas sent,
With these wing'd words, to both the hosts : " Make all haste, and invent
Some mean by which the men of Troy, against the truce agreed, 81
May stir the glorious Greeks to arms with some inglorious deed."

Thus charg'd he her with haste that did, before, in haste abound,
Who cast herself from all the heights, with which steep heav'n is crown'd.
And as Jove, brandishing a star, which men a comet call, 85
Hurls out his curled hair abroad, that from his brand exhals
A thousand sparks, to fleets at sea, and ev'ry mighty host,
Of all presages and ill-haps a sign mistrusted most ;
So Pallas fell 'twixt both the camps, and suddenly was lost,
When through the breasts of all that saw, she strook a strong amaze 90
With viewing, in her whole descent, her bright and ominous blaze.
When straight one to another turn'd, and said : " Now thund'ring Jove
(Great Arbiter of peace and arms) will either stablish love
Amongst our nations, or renew such war as never was."

Thus either army did presage, when Pallas made her pass 95
Amongst the multitude of Troy ; who now put on the grace
Of brave Laodocus, the flow'r of old Antenor's race,

---

[85] *Which men a comet call*—so both the folios. Dr. Taylor has printed "*which man a comet calls.*" This certainly suits the rhyme, but I adhere to Chapman's text.

And sought for Lycian Pandarus, a man that, being bred
Out of a faithless family, she thought was fit to shed
The blood of any innocent, and break the cov'nant sworn; 100
He was Lycaon's son, whom Jove into a wolf did turn
For sacrificing of a child, and yet in arms renown'd
As one that was inculpable. Him Pallas standing found,
And round about him his strong troops that bore the shady shields;
He brought them from Æsepus' flood, let through the Lycian fields;
Whom standing near, she whisper'd thus: "Lycaon's warlike son, 105
Shall I despair at thy kind hands to have a favour done?
Nor dar'st thou let an arrow fly upon the Spartan king?
It would be such a grace to Troy, and such a glorious thing,
That ev'ry man would give his gift; but Alexander's hand 110
Would load thee with them, if he could discover from his stand
His foe's pride strook down with thy shaft, and he himself ascend
The flaming heap of funeral. Come, shoot him, princely friend;
But first invoke the God of Light, that in thy land was born,
And is in archers' art the best that ever sheaf hath worn, 115
To whom a hundred first-ew'd lambs vow thou in holy fire,
When safe to sacred Zelia's tow'rs thy zealous steps retire."
 With this the mad gift-greedy man Minerva did persuade,
Who instantly drew forth a bow, most admirably made
Of th' antler of a jumping goat bred in a steep up-land, 120
Which archer-like (as long before he took his hidden stand,
The evicke skipping from a rock) into the breast he smote,
And headlong fell'd him from his cliff. The forehead of the goat
Held out a wondrous goodly palm, that sixteen branches brought;

  ⁹⁸ *A man that being bred out of a faithless family.*—This description of Pandarus has been introduced into the text by Chapman from the commentators, as Dr. Taylor observes.
  ¹¹⁵ *Sheaf*—bundle of arrows.
  ¹²² *The evicke*—the old spelling of *ibex*. Dr. Taylor, not knowing the word, suggested that it meant *crict*, or doomed one!
  ¹²⁴ *Palm*—Nares says "the broad part of a deer's horns, when fully grown."

Of all which join'd, an useful bow a skilful bowyer wrought, 125
Which pick'd and polish'd, both the ends he hid with horns of gold.
And this bow, bent, he close laid down, and bad his soldiers hold
Their shields before him, lest the Greeks, discerning him, should rise
In tumults ere the Spartan king could be his arrow's prise.
Mean space, with all his care he choos'd, and from his quiver drew, 130
An arrow, feather'd best for flight, and yet that never flew,
Strong headed, and most apt to pierce ; then took he up his bow,
And nock'd his shaft, the ground whence all their future grief did grow.
When, praying to his God the Sun, that was in Lycia bred,
And king of archers, promising that he the blood would shed 135
Of full an hundred first-fall'n lambs, all offer'd to his name,
When to Zelia's sacred walls from rescu'd Troy he came,
He took his arrow by the nock, and to his bended breast
The oxy sinew close he drew, ev'n till the pile did rest
Upon the bosom of the bow ; and as that savage prise 140
His strength constrain'd into an orb, as if the wind did rise
The coming of it made a noise, the sinew-forgéd string
Did give a mighty twang, and forth the eager shaft did sing,
Affecting speediness of flight, amongst the Achive throng.
Nor were the blesséd Heav'nly Pow'rs unmindful of thy wrong, 145
O Menelaus, but, in chief, Jove's seed, the Pillager,
Stood close before, and slack'd the force the arrow did confer,
With as much care and little hurt, as doth a mother use,
And keep off from her babe, when sleep doth through his pow'rs diffuse
His golden humour, and th' assaults of rude and busy flies 150
She still checks with her careful hand ; for so the shaft she plies
That on the buttons made of gold, which made his girdle fast,

---

126 *Pick'd*—piked, pointed.
133 "Virgil useth these verses"—CHAPMAN.
138 *Nock*—the notch of the arrow, where it rests upon the string.
139 *Pile*—point, barb of the arrow.
140 *Prise*—here used for *grasp*.
146 *The Pillager*—the goddess Ageleia.

And where his curets double were, the fall of it she plac'd.
And thus much proof she put it to : the buckle made of gold ;
The belt it fast'ned, bravely wrought ; his curets' double fold ;   155
And last, the charmèd plate he wore, which help'd him more than all,
And, 'gainst all darts and shafts bestow'd, was to his life a wall ;
So, through all these, the upper skin the head did only raoe ;
Yet forth the blood flow'd, which did much his royal person grace,
And show'd upon his ivory skin, as doth a purple dye   160
Laid, by a dame of Caïra, or lovely Mœony,
On ivory, wrought in ornaments to deck the cheeks of horse ;
Which in her marriage room must lie ; whose beauties have such force
That they are wish'd of many knights, but are such precious things,
That they are kept for horse that draw the chariots of kings,   165
Which horse, so deck'd, the charioteer esteems a grace to him ;
Like these, in grace, the blood upon thy solid thighs did swim,
O Menelaus, down thy calves and ankles to the ground.
For nothing decks a soldier so, as doth an honour'd wound.
Yet, fearing he had far'd much worse, the hair stood up on end   170
On Agamemnon, when he saw so much black blood descend.
And stiff'ned with the like dismay was Menelaus too,
But seeing th' arrow's stale without, and that the head did go
No further than it might be seen, he call'd his spirits again ;
Which Agamemnon marking not, but thinking he was slain,   175
He grip'd his brother by the hand, and sigh'd as he would break,
Which sigh the whole host took from him, who thus at last did speak :

"O dearest brother, is't for this, that thy death must be wrought,
Wrought I this truce ? For this hast thou the single combat fought
For all the army of the Greeks ? For this hath Ilion sworn,   180

¹⁵⁸ *Race*—rase, slightly scratch. I have retained this orthography through-out, for the rhyme's sake.
¹⁷³ *Stale*—"*stele*, the stem or stalk of any thing. The stem or body of an arrow :—
 'A shaft hath three principle parts, the *stele*, the fethers, and the head.'
         Ascham's *Toxophilus*, p. 161."
         Nares's Gloss. in voc.

And trod all faith beneath their feet? Yet all this hath not worn
The right we challeng'd out of force; this cannot render vain
Our stricken right hands, sacred wine, nor all our off'rings slain;
For though Olympius be not quick in making good our ill,
He will be sure as he is slow, and sharplier prove his will. 185
Their own hands shall be ministers of those plagues they despise,
Which shall their wives and children reach, and all their progenies.
For both in mind and soul I know, that there shall come a day
When Ilion, Priam, all his pow'r, shall quite be worn away,
When heav'n-inhabiting Jove shall shake his fiery shield at all, 190
For this one mischief. This, I know, the world cannot recall.
But be all this, all my grief still for thee will be the same,
Dear brother. If thy life must here put out his royal flame,
I shall to sandy Argos turn with infamy my face;
And all the Greeks will call for home; old Priam and his race 195
Will flame in glory; Helena untouch'd be still their prey;
And thy bones in our enemies' earth our cursed fates shall lay;
Thy sepulchre be trodden down; the pride of Troy desire
Insulting on it, 'Thus, O thus, let Agamemnon's ire
In all his acts be expiate, as now he carries home 200
His idle army, empty ships, and leaves here overcome
Good Menelaus.' When this brave breaks in their hated breath,
Then let the broad earth swallow me, and take me quick to death."

"Nor shall this ever chance," said he, "and therefore be of cheer,
Lest all the army, led by you, your passions put in fear. 205
The arrow fell in no such place as death could enter at,
My girdle, curets doubled here, and my most trusted plate,
Objected all 'twixt me and death, the shaft scarce piercing one."
"Good brother," said the king, "I wish it were no further gone,
For then our best in med'cines skilled shall ope and search the wound,
Applying balms to ease thy pains, and soon restore thee sound." 211
This said, divine Talthybius he call'd, and bad him haste

[208] *Objected*—interposed.

Machaon (Æsculapius' son, who most of men was grac'd
With physic's sov'reign remedies) to come and lend his hand
To Menelaus, shot by one well-skill'd in the command   215
Of bow and arrows, one of Troy, or of the Lycian aid,
Who much hath glorified our foe, and us as much dismay'd.
    He heard, and hasted instantly, and cast his eyes about
The thickest squadrons of the Greeks, to find Machaon out.
He found him standing guarded well with well-arm'd men of Thrace;
With whom he quickly join'd, and said: "Man of Apollo's race,   221
Haste, for the king of men commands, to see a wound impress'd
In Menelaus, great in arms, by one instructed best
In th' art of archery, of Troy, or of the Lycian bands,
That them with much renown adorns, us with dishonour brands."   225
    Machaon much was mov'd with this, who with the herald flew
From troop to troop alongst the host; and soon they came in view
Of hurt Atrides, circled round with all the Grecian kings;
Who all gave way, and straight he draws the shaft, which forth he
    brings
Without the forks; the girdle then, plate, curets, off he plucks,   230
And views the wound; when first from it the clotter'd blood he sucks,
Then med'cines, wondrously compos'd, the skilful leech applied,
Which loving Chiron taught his sire, he from his sire had tried.
    While these were thus employ'd to ease the Atrean martialist,
The Trojans arm'd, and charg'd the Greeks; the Greeks arm and resist.
Then not asleep, nor maz'd with fear, nor shifting off the blows,   236
You could behold the king of men, but in full speed he goes
To set a glorious fight on foot; and he examples this,
With toiling, like the worst, on foot; who therefore did dismiss
His brass-arm'd chariot, and his steeds, with Ptolemëus' son,   240
Son of Piraides, their guide, the good Eurymedon;
"Yet," said the king, "attend with them, lest weariness should seize
My limbs, surcharg'd with ord'ring troops so thick and vast as these."
    Eurymedon then rein'd his horse, that trotted neighing by;

The king a footman, and so scours the squadrons orderly. 245
Those of his swiftly-mounted Greeks, that in their arms were fit,
Those he put on with cheerful words, and bad them not remit
The least spark of their forward spirits, because the Trojans durst
Take these abhorr'd advantages, but let them do their worst;
For they might be assur'd that Jove would patronise no lies, 250
And that who, with the breach of truce, would hurt their enemies,
With vultures should be torn themselves; that they should raze their town,
Their wives, and children at their breast, led vassals to their own.
But such as he beheld hang off from that increasing fight,
Such would he bitterly rebuke, and with disgrace excite: 255
"Base Argives, blush ye not to stand as made for butts to darts?
Why are ye thus discomfited, like hinds that have no hearts,
Who, wearied with a long-run field, are instantly emboss'd,
Stand still, and in their beastly breasts is all their courage lost?
And so stand you strook with amaze, nor dare to strike a stroke. 260
Would ye the foe should nearer yet your dastard spleens provoke,
Ev'n where on Neptune's foamy shore our navies lie in sight,
To see if Jove will hold your hands, and teach ye how to fight?"
Thus he, commanding, rang'd the host, and, passing many a band,
He came to the Cretensian troops, where all did arméd stand 265
About the martial Idomen; who bravely stood before
In vanguard of his troops, and match'd for strength a savage boar;
Meriones, his charioteer, the rearguard bringing on.
Which seen to Atreus' son, to him it was a sight alone,
And Idomen's confirméd mind with these kind words he seeks: 270
"O Idomen! I ever lov'd thy self past all the Greeks,
In war, or any work of peace, at table, ev'rywhere;
For when the best of Greece besides mix ever, at our cheer,
My good old ardent wine with small, and our inferior mates

---

[245] *The king a footman*—i. e. the king went on foot.
[258] *Emboss'd.*—A hunting term. "When the hart is foamy at the mouth, we say, that he is *embossed*."—TURBERVILLE *on Hunt.* p. 242. See NARES'S GLOSSARY.

THE FOURTH BOOK

Drink ev'n that mix'd wine measur'd too, thou drink'st, without those rates,
Our old wine neat, and evermore thy bowl stands full like mine,   276
To drink still when and what thou wilt. Then rouse that heart of thine,
And, whatsoever heretofore thou hast assum'd to be,
This day be greater."   To the king in this sort answer'd he :
"Atrides, what I ever seem'd, the same at ev'ry part   280
This day shall show me at the full, and I will fit thy heart.
But thou shouldst rather cheer the rest, and tell them they in right
Of all good war must offer blows, and should begin the fight,
(Since Troy first brake the holy truce) and not endure these braves,
To take wrong first, and then be dar'd to the revenge it craves ;   285
Assuring them that Troy in fate must have the worst at last,
Since first, and 'gainst a truce, they hurt, where they should have embrac'd."
This comfort and advice did fit Atrides' heart indeed
Who still through new-rais'd swarms of men held his laborious speed,
And came where both th' Ajaces stood ; whom like the last he found   290
Arm'd, casqu'd, and ready for the fight. Behind them, hid the ground
A cloud of foot, that seem'd to smoke. And as a goatherd spies,
On some hill's top, out of the sea, a rainy vapour rise,
Driv'n by the breath of Zephyrus, which, though far off he rest,
Comes on as black as pitch, and brings a tempest in his breast,   295
Whereat he frighted, drives his herds apace into a den ;
So dark'ning earth with darts and shields show'd these with all their men.
This sight with like joy fir'd the king, who thus let forth the flame
In crying out to both the dukes : "O you of equal name,
I must not cheer, nay, I disclaim all my command of you,   300
Yourselves command with such free minds, and make your soldiers show
As you nor I led, but themselves. O would our father Jove,
Minerva, and the God of Light, would all our bodies move
With such brave spirits as breathe in you, then Priam's lofty town
Should soon be taken by our hands, for ever overthrown !"   305

²⁷⁵ *Rates*—ratifications, agreements. Here perhaps, qualifications.
³⁰² *As you nor I led*—as if neither you nor I.

Then held he on to other troops, and Nestor next beheld,
The subtle Pylian orator, range up and down the field
Embattelling his men at arms, and stirring all to blows,
Points ev'ry legion out his chief, and ev'ry chief he shows
The forms and discipline of war, yet his commanders were   310
All éxpert, and renowméd men. Great Pelagon was there,
Alastor, manly Chromius, and Hæmon worth a throne,
And Bias that could armies lead. With these he first put on
His horse troops with their chariots; his foot (of which he choos'd
Many, the best and ablest men, and which he ever us'd   315
As rampire to his gen'ral pow'r) he in the rear dispos'd.
The slothful, and the least of spirit, he in the midst inclos'd,
That, such as wanted noble wills, base need might force to stand.
His horse troops, that the vanguard had, he strictly did command
To ride their horses temp'rately, to keep their ranks, and shun 320
Confusion, lest their horsemanship and courage made them run
(Too much presum'd on) much too far, and, charging so alone,
Engage themselves in th' enemy's strength, where many fight with one.
"Who his own chariot leaves to range, let him not freely go,
But straight unhorse him with a lance; for 'tis much better so. 325
And with this discipline," said he, "this form, these minds, this trust,
Our ancestors have walls and towns laid level with the dust."

Thus prompt, and long inur'd to arms, this old man did exhort;
And this Atrides likewise took in wondrous cheerful sort,
And said: "O father, would to heav'n, that as thy mind remains 330
In wonted vigour, so thy knees could undergo our pains!
But age, that all men overcomes, hath made his prise on thee;
Yet still I wish that some young man, grown old in mind, might be
Put in proportion with thy years, and thy mind, young in age,
Be fitly answer'd with his youth; that still where conflicts rage, 335
And young men us'd to thirst for fame, thy brave exampling hand
Might double our young Grecian spirits, and grace our whole command."

The old knight answer'd: "I myself could wish, O Atreus' son,

I were as young as when I slew brave Ereuthalion,
But Gods at all times give not all their gifts to mortal men.   340
If then I had the strength of youth, I miss'd the counsels then
That years now give me; and now years want that main strength of youth;
Yet still my mind retains her strength (as you now said the sooth)
And would be where that strength is us'd, affording counsel sage
To stir youth's minds up; 'tis the grace and office of our age;   345
Let younger sinews, men sprung up whole ages after me,
And such as have strength, use it, and as strong in honour be."

   The king, all this while comforted, arriv'd next where he found
Well-rode Menestheus (Peteus' son) stand still, inviron'd round
With his well-train'd Athenian troops; and next to him he spied   350
The wise Ulysses, deedless too, and all his bands beside
Of strong Cephalians; for as yet th' alarm had not been heard
In all their quarters, Greece and Troy were then so newly stirr'd,
And then first mov'd, as they conceiv'd; and they so look'd about
To see both hosts give proof of that they yet had cause to doubt.   355

   Atrides seeing them stand so still, and spend their eyes at gaze,
Began to chide: "And why," said he, "dissolv'd thus in amaze,
Thou son of Peteus, Jove-nurs'd king, and thou in wicked sleight
A cunning soldier, stand ye off? Expect ye that the fight
Should be by other men begun? 'Tis fit the foremost band   360
Should show you there; you first should front who first lifts up his hand.
First you can hear, when I invite the princes to a feast,
When first, most friendly, and at will, ye eat and drink the best,
Yet in the fight, most willingly, ten troops ye can behold
Take place before ye." Ithacus at this his brows did fold,   365
And said: "How hath thy violent tongue broke through thy set of teeth,
To say that we are slack in fight, and to the field of death
Look others should enforce our way, when we were busied then,

---

[343] *Sooth*—truth, a common word. Thus Shakespeare,—
    "He looks like *sooth :* he says he loves my daughter,
    I think so too."—*Wint. Tale*, IV. 3.

Ev'n when thou spak'st, against the foe to cheer and lead our men?
But thy eyes shall be witnesses, if it content thy will, 370
And that (as thou pretend'st) these cares do so affect thee still,
The father of Telemachus (whom I esteem so dear,
And to whom, as a legacy, I'll leave my deeds done here)
Ev'n with the foremost band of Troy hath his encounter dar'd,
And therefore are thy speeches vain, and had been better spar'd." 375
    He, smiling, since he saw him mov'd, recall'd his words, and said:
"Most generous Laertes' son, most wise of all our aid,
I neither do accuse thy worth, more than thyself may hold
Fit, (that inferiors think not much, being slack, to be controll'd)
Nor take I on me thy command; for well I know thy mind 380
Knows how sweet gentle counsels are, and that thou stand'st inclin'd,
As I myself, for all our good. On then; if now we spake
What hath displeas'd, another time we full amends will make;
And Gods grant that thy virtue here may prove so free and brave,
That my reproofs may still be vain, and thy deservings grave." 385
    Thus parted they; and forth he went, when he did leaning find,
Against his chariot, near his horse, him with the mighty mind,
Great Diomedes, Tydeus' son, and Sthenelus, the seed
Of Capaneius; whom the king seeing likewise out of deed,
Thus cried he out on Diomed: "O me! In what a fear 390
The wise great warrior, Tydeus' son, stands gazing ev'rywhere
For others to begin the fight! It was not Tydeus' use
To be so daunted, whom his spirit would evermore produce
Before the foremost of his friends in these affairs of fright,
As they report that have beheld him labour in a fight. 395
For me, I never knew the man, nor in his presence came,
But excellent, above the rest, he was in gen'ral fame;
And one renown'd exploit of his, I am assur'd, is true.
He came to the Mycenian court, without arms, and did sue,
At godlike Polynices' hands, to have some worthy aid 400
To their designs that 'gainst the walls of sacred Thebes were laid.

He was great Polynices' guest, and nobly entertain'd,
And of the kind Mycenian state what he requested gain'd,
In mere consent; but when they should the same in act approve,
By some sinister prodigies, held out to them by Jove,   405
They were discourag'd. Thence he went, and safely had his pass
Back to Asopus' flood, renowm'd for bulrushes and grass.
Yet, once more, their ambassador, the Grecian peers address
Lord Tydeus to Eteocles; to whom being giv'n access,
He found him feasting with a crew of Cadmeans in his hall;   410
Amongst whom, though an enemy, and only one to all;
To all yet he his challenge made at ev'ry martial feat,
And eas'ly foil'd all, since with him Minerva was so great.
The rank-rode Cadmeans, much incens'd with their so foul disgrace,
Lodg'd ambuscadoes for their foe, in some well-chosen place   415
By which he was to make return. Twice five-and-twenty men,
And two of them great captains too, the ambush did contain.
The names of those two men of rule were Mæon, Hæmon's son,
And Lycophontes, Keep-field call'd, the heir of Autophon,
By all men honour'd like the Gods; yet these and all their friends 420
Were sent to hell by Tydeus' hand, and had untimely ends.
He trusting to the aid of Gods, reveal'd by augury,
Obeying which, one chief he sav'd, and did his life apply
To be the heavy messenger of all the others' deaths;
And that sad message, with his life, to Mæon he bequeaths.   425
So brave a knight was Tydeüs: of whom a son is sprung,
Inferior far in martial deeds, though higher in his tongue."
 All this Tydides silent heard, aw'd by the rev'rend king;
Which stung hot Sthenelus with wrath, who thus put forth his sting:
 "Atrides, when thou know'st the truth, speak what thy knowledge is,

[408] The construction is, "Once more the Grecian peers address (send) Tydeus to Eteocles as their ambassador."

[419] *Keep-field.*—The original is μενεπτόλεμος, one who remains in the battle. Dr. Taylor observes, "This is one of the happiest of Chapman's translations of Homer's compound epithets."

And do not lie so; for I know, and I will brag in this, 431
That we are far more able men than both our fathers were.
We took the sev'n-fold ported Thebes, when yet we had not there
So great help as our fathers had; and fought beneath a wall,
Sacred to Mars, by help of Jove, and trusting to the fall 435
Of happy signs from other Gods, by whom we took the town
Untouch'd; our fathers perishing there by follies of their own;
And therefore never more compare our fathers' worth with ours."

    Tydides frown'd at this, and said: "Suppress thine anger's pow'rs,
Good friend, and hear why I refrain'd. Thou seest I am not mov'd
Against our gen'ral, since he did but what his place behov'd, 441
Admonishing all Greeks to fight; for, if Troy prove our prise,
The honour and the joy is his; if here our ruin lies,
The shame and grief for that as much is his in greatest kinds.
As he then his charge, weigh we ours; which is our dauntless
    minds." 445
Thus, from his chariot, amply arm'd, he jump'd down to the ground;
The armour of the angry king so horribly did sound,
It might have made his bravest foe let fear take down his braves.
And as when with the west-wind flaws, the sea thrusts up her waves,
One after other, thick and high, upon the groaning shores, 450
First in herself loud, but oppos'd with banks and rocks she roars,
And, all her back in bristles set, spits ev'ry way her foam;
So, after Diomed, instantly the field was overcome
With thick impressions of the Greeks; and all the noise that grew
(Ord'ring and cheering up their men) from only leaders flew. 455
The rest went silently away, you could not hear a voice,
Nor would have thought, in all their breasts, they had one in their
    choice,
Their silence uttering their awe of them that them controll'd,
Which made each man keep bright his arms, march, fight still where
    he should.

The Trojans (like a sort of ewes, penn'd in a rich man's fold,   460
Close at his door, till all be milk'd, and never baaing hold
Hearing the bleating of their lambs) did all their wide host fill
With shouts and clamours, nor observ'd one voice, one baaing still,
But show'd mix'd tongues from many a land of men call'd to their aid.
Rude Mars had th' ordering of their spirits ; of Greeks, the learned Maid.
But Terror follow'd both the hosts, and Flight, and furious Strife   466
The sister, and the mate, of Mars, that spoil of human life ;
And never is her rage at rest, at first she is but small,
Yet after, but a little fed, she grows so vast and tall
That, while her feet move here in earth, her forehead is in heav'n ;   470
And this was she that made ev'n then both hosts so deadly giv'n.
Through ev'ry troop she stalk'd, and stirr'd rough sighs up as she went ;
But when in one field both the foes her fury did content,
And both came under reach of darts, then darts and shields oppos'd
To darts and shields ; strength answer'd strength ; then swords and
    targets clos'd   475
With swords and targets ; both with pikes ; and then did tumult rise
Up to her height ; then conqu'rors' boasts mix'd with the conquer'd's cries ;
Earth flow'd with blood. And as from hills rain-waters headlong fall,
That all ways eat huge ruts, which, met in one bed, fill a vall
With such a confluence of streams, that on the mountain grounds   480
Far off, in frighted shepherds' ears, the bustling noise rebounds :
So grew their conflicts, and so show'd their scuffling to the ear,
With flight and clamour still commix'd, and all effects of fear.

    And first renown'd Antilochus slew (fighting, in the face
Of all Achaia's foremost bands, with an undaunted grace)   485

   460 *Sort*—set, or, as we say, *a lot* of pigs, sheep, &c.
        " Remember who you are to cope withall,
        A *sort* of vagabonds, rascals, and runaways."
                        SHAKESPEARE. *Rich. III.* v. 3.
   465 *The learned Maid*—Pallas.
   470 Chapman observes that Virgil has applied this description of Strife to Fame.
   479 *Vall*—ravine, valley.

Echepolus Thalysiades; he was an arméd man;
Whom on his hair-plum'd helmet's crest the dart first smote, then ran
Into his forehead, and there stuck; the steel pile making way
Quite through his skull; a hasty night shut up his latest day.
His fall was like a fight-rac'd tow'r; like which lying there dispread,
King Elephenor (who was son to Chalcodon, and led 491
The valiant Abants) covetous that he might first possess
His arms, laid hands upon his feet, and hal'd him from the press
Of darts and jav'lins hurl'd at him. The action of the king
When great-in-heart Agenor saw, he made his jav'lin sing 495
To th' others' labour; and along as he the trunk did wrest,
His side (at which he bore his shield) in bowing of his breast
Lay naked, and recciv'd the lance, that made him lose his hold
And life together; which, in hope of that he lost, he sold.
But for his sake the fight grew fierce, the Trojans and their foes 500
Like wolves on one another rush'd, and man for man it goes.

The next of name, that serv'd his fate, great Ajax Telamon
Preferr'd so sadly. He was heir to old Anthemion,
And deck'd with all the flow'r of youth; the fruit of which yet fled,
Before the honour'd nuptial torch could light him to his bed. 505
His name was Simoisius; for, some few years before,
His mother walking down the hill of Ida, by the shore
Of silver Simois, to see her parents' flocks, with them
She, feeling suddenly the pains of child-birth, by the stream
Of that bright river brought him forth; and so (of Simois) 510
They call'd him Simoisius. Sweet was that birth of his
To his kind parents, and his growth did all their care employ;
And yet those rites of piety, that should have been his joy
To pay their honour'd years again in as affectionate sort,
He could not graciously perform, his sweet life was so short, 515

---

[490] *Fight-raced*—razed in battle.
[499] An unworthy conceit of Chapman's, as Dr. Taylor observes, and unwarranted.

Cut off with mighty Ajax' lance; for, as his spirit put on,
He strook him at his breast's right pap, quite through his shoulder-
    bone,
And in the dust of earth he fell, that was the fruitful soil
Of his friends' hopes; but where he sow'd he buried all his toil.
And as a poplar shot aloft, set by a river side,   520
In moist edge of a mighty fen, his head in curls implied,
But all his body plain and smooth, to which a wheelwright puts
The sharp edge of his shining axe, and his soft timber cuts
From his innative root, in hope to hew out of his bole
The fell'ffs, or out-parts of a wheel, that compass in the whole,   525
To serve some goodly chariot; but, being big and sad,
And to be hal'd home through the bogs, the useful hope he had,
Sticks there, and there the goodly plant lies with'ring out his grace:
So lay, by Jove-bred Ajax' hand, Anthemion's forward race,
Nor could through that vast fen of toils be drawn to serve the ends   530
Intended by his body's pow'rs, nor cheer his aged friends.

   But now the gay-arm'd Antiphus, a son of Priam, threw
His lance at Ajax through the press; which went by him, and flew
On Leucus, wise Ulysses' friend; his groin it smote, as fain
He would have drawn into his spoil the carcass of the slain,   535
By which he fell, and that by him; it vex'd Ulysses' heart,
Who thrust into the face of fight, well-arm'd at ev'ry part,
Came close, and look'd about to find an object worth his lance;
Which when the Trojans saw him shake, and he so near advance,
All shrunk; he threw, and forth it shin'd, nor fell but where it fell'd;
His friend's grief gave it angry pow'r, and deadly way it held   541

---

⁵¹⁶ *As his spirit put on*—urged him forwards.

⁵²⁵ *Fell'ffs*—fellies of a wheel.

⁵²⁶ *Sad*—heavy. In the North the word is applied to bread, when the dough, from bad yeast, or not being well kneaded, does not rise properly. HALLIWELL, ARCHAIC AND PROVIN. DICT.

⁵³⁴ From line 516 to this, Chapman has unwarrantably amplified, and somewhat distorted the original.

⁵⁴⁰ *Nor fell but where it fell'd*—a silly quibble of Chapman's.

Upon Democoon, who was sprung of Priam's wanton force,
Came from Abydus, and was made the master of his horse.
Through both his temples strook the dart, the wood of one side shew'd,
The pile out of the other look'd, and so the earth he strew'd 545
With much sound of his weighty arms. Then back the foremost went;
Ev'n Hector yielded; then the Greeks gave worthy clamours vent,
Effecting then their first-dumb pow'rs; some drew the dead, and spoil'd
Some follow'd, that, in open flight, Troy might confess it foil'd.
Apollo, angry at the sight, from top of Ilion cried: 550
"Turn head, ye well-rode peers of Troy, feed not the Grecians' pride,
They are not charm'd against your points, of steel, nor iron, fram'd;
Nor fights the fair-hair'd Thetis' son, but sits at fleet inflam'd."
    So spake the dreadful God from Troy. The Greeks, Jove's noblest Seed
Encourag'd to keep on the chace; and, where fit spirit did need, 555
She gave it, marching in the midst. Then flew the fatal hour,
Back on Diores, in return of Ilion's sun-burn'd pow'r;
Diores Amaryncides, whose right leg's ankle-bone,
And both the sinews, with a sharp and handful-charging stone
Pirus Imbrasides did break, that led the Thracian bands 560
And came from Ænos; down he fell, and up he held his hands
To his lov'd friends; his spirit wing'd to fly out of his breast;
With which not satisfied, again Imbrasides address'd
His jav'lin at him, and so ripp'd his navel, that the wound,
As endlessly it shut his eyes, so, open'd, on the ground 565
It pour'd his entrails. As his foe went then suffic'd away,
Thoas Ætolius threw a dart, that did his pile convey,
Above his nipple, through his lungs; when, quitting his stern part,
He clos'd with him, and, from his breast first drawing out his dart,
His sword flew in, and by the midst it wip'd his belly out; 570
So took his life, but left his arms; his friends so flock'd about,

---

⁵⁵² *Of steel, nor iron, fram'd*—i. e. they (the Greeks) are not framed of steel or iron.
⁵⁵⁴ *Jove's noblest Seed*—Pallas.
⁵⁶⁸ *His stern part*—breast-bone; from the Greek στέρνον.

And thrust forth lances of such length before their slaughter'd king,
Which, though their foe were big and strong, and often brake the ring
Forg'd of their lances, yet (enforc'd) he left th' affected prise.
The Thracian and Epeian dukes, laid close with closéd eyes   575
By either other, drown'd in dust; and round about the plain,
All hid with slaughter'd carcases, yet still did hotly reign
The martial planet; whose effects had any eye beheld,
Free and unwounded (and were led by Pallas through the field,
To keep off jav'lins, and suggest the least fault could be found)   580
He could not reprehend the fight, so many strew'd the ground.

THE END OF THE FOURTH BOOK.

THE FIFTH BOOK OF HOMER'S ILIADS.

THE ARGUMENT.

KING Diomed (by Pallas' spirit inspir'd
With will and pow'r) is for his acts admir'd.
Mere men, and men deriv'd from Deities,
And Deities themselves, he terrifies.
Adds wounds to terrors. His inflaméd lance
Draws blood from Mars, and Venus. In a trance
He casts Æneas, with a weighty stone;
Apollo quickens him, and gets him gone.
Mars is recur'd by Pæon, but by Jove
Rebuk'd for authoring breach of human love.

ANOTHER ARGUMENT.

In Epsilon, Heav'n's blood is shed
By sacred rage of Diomed.

THEN Pallas breath'd in Tydeus' son; to render whom supreme
To all the Greeks, at all his parts, she cast a hotter beam
On his high mind, his body fill'd with much superior might,
And made his cómplete armour cast a far more cómplete light.
From his bright helm and shield did burn a most unwearied fire, 5
Like rich Autumnus' golden lamp, whose brightness men admire
Past all the other host of stars, when, with his cheerful face
Fresh wash'd in lofty Ocean waves, he doth the skies enchase.

⁶ "This simile likewise Virgil learns of him."—CHAPMAN. *Autumnus' golden lamp*—Sirius, or the Dog Star.

To let whose glory lose no sight, still Pallas made him turn
Where tumult most express'd his pow'r, and where the fight did burn.
    An honest and a wealthy man inhabited in Troy, 11
Dares, the priest of Mulciber, who two sons did enjoy,
Idæus, and bold Phegeüs, well-seen in ev'ry fight.
These (singled from their troops, and hors'd) assail'd Minerva's knight,
Who rang'd from fight to fight on foot. All hasting mutual charge, 15
And now drawn near, first Phegeus threw a jav'lin swift and large,
Whose head the king's left shoulder took, but did no harm at all;
Then rush'd he out a lance at him, that had no idle fall,
But in his breast stuck 'twixt the paps, and strook him from his horse.
Which stern sight when Idæus saw, distrustful of his force 20
To save his slaughter'd brother's spoil, it made him headlong leap
From his fair chariot, and leave all; yet had not 'scap'd the heap
Of heav'y fun'ral, if the God, great President of fire,
Had not in sudden clouds of smoke, and pity of his sire
To leave him utterly unheir'd, giv'n safe pass to his feet. 25
He gone, Tydides sent the horse and chariot to the fleet.
    The Trojans seeing Dares' sons, one slain, the other fled,
Were strook amaz'd. The blue-ey'd Maid (to grace her Diomed
In giving free way to his pow'r) made this so ruthful fact
A fit advantage to remove the War-god out of act, 30
Who rag'd so on the Ilion side. She grip'd his hand, and said:
"Mars, Mars, thou ruiner of men, that in the dust hast laid
So many cities, and with blood thy godhead dost distain,
Now shall we cease to show our breasts as passionate as men,
And leave the mixture of our hands, resigning Jove his right, 35
As Rector of the Gods, to give the glory of the fight
Where he affecteth, lest he force what we should freely yield?"
He held it fit, and went with her from the tumultuous field,
Who set him in an herby seat on broad Scamander's shore.
He gone, all Troy was gone with him, the Greeks drave all before, 40

And ev'ry leader slew a man ; but first the king of men
Deserv'd the honour of his name, and led the slaughter then,
And slew a leader, one more huge than any man he led,
Great Odius, duke of Halizons ; quite from his chariot s head
He strook him with a lance to earth, as first he flight address'd ; 45
It took his forward-turnéd back, and look'd out of his breast ;
His huge trunk sounded, and his arms did echo the resound.
   Idomenæus to the death did noble Phæstus wound,
The son of Meon-Borus, that from cloddy Terna came ;
Who, taking chariot, took his wound, and tumbled with the same 50
From his attempted seat : the lance through his right shoulder strook,
And horrid darkness strook through him ; the spoil his soldiers took.
   Atrides-Menelaus slew, as he before him fled,
Scamandrius, son of Strophius, that was a huntsman bred ;
A skilful huntsman, for his skill Diana's self did teach, 55
And made him able with his dart infallibly to reach
All sorts of subtlest savages, which many a woody hill
Bred for him, and he much preserv'd, and all to show his skill.
Yet not the dart-delighting Queen taught him to shun this dart,
Nor all his hitting so far off, the mast'ry of his art ; 60
His back receiv'd it, and he fell upon his breast withal ;
His body's ruin, and his arms, so sounded in his fall,
That his affrighted horse flew off, and left him, like his life.
   Meriones slew Phereclus, whom she that ne'er was wife,
Yet Goddess of good housewives, held in excellent respect 65
For knowing all the witty things that grace an architect,
And having pow'r to give it all the cunning use of hand.
Harmonides, his sire, built ships, and made him understand,
With all the practice it requir'd, the frame of all that skill.
He built all Alexander's ships, that author'd all the ill 70
Of all the Trojans and his own, because he did not know
The oracles advising Troy (for fear of overthrow)

   [65] *Goddess of housewives*—Minerva.

To meddle with no sea affair, but live by tilling land.
This man Meriones surpris'd, and drave his deadly hand
Through his right hip; the lance's head ran through the región   75
About the bladder, underneath th' in-muscles and the bone;
He, sighing, bow'd his knees to death, and sacrific'd to earth.

    Phylides stay'd Pedæus' flight, Antenor's bastard birth,
Whom virtuous Theano his wife, to please her husband, kept
As tenderly as those she lov'd. Phylides near him stept,   80
And in the fountain of the nerves did drench his fervent lance,
At his head's back-part; and so far the sharp head did advance,
It cleft the organ of his speech, and th' iron, cold as death,
He took betwixt his grinning teeth, and gave the air his breath.

    Eurypylus, the much renowm'd, and great Evemon's son,   85
Divine Hypsenor slew, begot by stout Dolopion,
And consecrate Scamander's priest; he had a God's regard
Amongst the people; his hard flight the Grecian follow'd hard,
Rush'd in so close, that with his sword he on his shoulder laid
A blow that his arm's brawn cut off; nor there his vigour stay'd,   90
But drave down, and from off his wrist it hew'd his holy hand
That gush'd out blood, and down it dropp'd upon the blushing sand;
Death, with his purple finger, shut, and violent fate, his eyes.

    Thus fought these, but distinguish'd well. Tydides so implies
His fury that you could not know whose side had interest   95
In his free labours, Greece or Troy; but as a flood, increas'd
By violent and sudden show'rs, let down from hills, like hills
Melted in fury, swells and foams, and so he overfills
His natural channel; that besides both hedge and bridge resigns
To his rough confluence, far spread; and lusty flourishing vines   100
Drown'd in his outrage; Tydeus' son so overran the field,
Strew'd such as flourish'd in his way, and made whole squadrons yield.

    When Pandarus, Lycaon's son, beheld his ruining hand,
With such resistless insolence, make lanes through ev'ry band,

    [81] *Fountain of the nerves*—nape of the neck.

He bent his gold-tipp'd bow of horn, and shot him rushing in,
At his right shoulder, where his arms were hollow; forth did spin
The blood, and down his curets ran; then Pandarus cried out:
"Rank-riding Trojans, now rush in. Now, now, I make no doubt
Our bravest foe is mark'd for death; he cannot long sustain
My violent shaft, if Jove's fair Son did worthily constrain
My foot from Lycia." Thus he brav'd, and yet his violent shaft
Strook short with all his violence, Tydides' life was saft;
Who yet withdrew himself behind his chariot and steeds,
And call'd to Sthenelus: "Come friend, my wounded shoulder needs
Thy hand to ease it of this shaft." He hasted from his seat
Before the coach, and drew the shaft; the purple wound did sweat,
And drown his shirt of mail in blood, and as it bled he pray'd:
"Hear me, of Jove-Ægiochus thou most unconquer'd Maid!
If ever in the cruel field thou hast assistful stood
Or to my father, or myself, now love, and do me good.
Give him into my lance's reach, that thus hath giv'n a wound
To him thou guard'st, preventing me, and brags that never more
I shall behold the cheerful sun." Thus did the king implore.
The Goddess heard, came near, and took the weariness of fight
From all his nerves and lineaments, and made them fresh and light,
And said: "Be bold, O Diomed, in ev'ry combat shine,
The great shield-shaker Tydeus' strength (that knight, that sire of thine)
By my infusion breathes in thee; and from thy knowing mind
I have remov'd those erring mists that made it lately blind,
That thou may'st diff'rence Gods from men, and therefore use thy skill
Against the tempting Deities, if any have a will
To try if thou presum'st of that, as thine, that flows from them,
And so assum'st above thy right. Where thou discern'st a beam
Of any other Heav'nly Pow'r than She that rules in love,
That calls thee to the change of blows, resist not, but remove;

¹¹² *Saft*—secured, saved. The past tense of the verb to *safe*, to secure, or make safe, used by Shakespeare.

THE FIFTH BOOK

But if that Goddess be so bold (since she first stirr'd this war)
Assault and mark her from the rest with some infámous scar."
   The blue-eyed Goddess vanishéd, and he was seen again
Amongst the foremost, who before though he were prompt and fain
To fight against the Trojans' pow'rs, now, on his spirits were call'd   140
With thrice the vigour; lion-like, that hath been lately gall'd
By some bold shepherd in a field, where his curl'd flocks were laid,
Who took him as he leap'd the fold, not slain yet, but appaid
With greater spirit, comes again, and then the shepherd hides,
(The rather for the desolate place) and in his cote abides,   145
His flocks left guardless; which, amaz'd, shake and shrink up in heaps;
He, ruthless, freely takes his prey, and out again he leaps;
So sprightly, fierce, victorious, the great heroë flew
Upon the Trojans, and, at once, he two commanders slew,
Hypenor and Astynous; in one his lance he fix'd   150
Full at the nipple of his breast; the other smote betwixt
The neck and shoulder with his sword, which was so well laid on
It swept his arm and shoulder off. These left, he rush'd upon
Abas and Polyëidus, of old Eurydamas
The hapless sons; who could by dreams tell what would come to pass,
Yet, when his sons set forth to Troy, the old man could not read   156
By their dreams what would chance to them, for both were stricken dead
By great Tydides. After these, he takes into his rage
Xanthus and Thoön, Phænops' sons, born to him in his age;
The good old man ev'n pin'd with years, and had not one son more
To heir his goods; yet Diomed took both, and left him store   161
Of tears and sorrows in their steads, since he could never see
His sons leave those hot wars alive; so this the end must be
Of all his labours; what he heap'd, to make his issue great,
Authority heir'd, and with her seed fill'd his forgotten seat.   165

   [165] *Authority heir'd*—The word that Chapman here translates *authority* is in the Greek χηρωσταί, and means those more remote relatives who succeeded by authority, or law, to the property when there had been a χήρωσις, or the family had lost its nearer heirs.

Then snatch'd he up two Priamists, that in one chariot stood,
Echemon, and fair Chromius. As feeding in a wood
Oxen or steers are, one of which a lion leaps upon,
Tears down, and wrings in two his neck; so, sternly, Tydeus' son
Threw from their chariot both these hopes of old Dardanides, 170
Then took their arms, and sent their horse to those that ride the seas.

Æneas, seeing the troops thus toss'd, brake through the heat of fight,
And all the whizzing of the darts, to find the Lycian knight,
Lycaon's son; whom having found, he thus bespake the peer;
"O Pandarus, where's now thy bow, thy deathful arrows where,
In which no one in all our host but gives the palm to thee, 175
Nor in the sun-lov'd Lycian greens, that breed our archery,
Lives any that exceeds thyself? Come, lift thy hands to Jove,
And send an arrow at this man, if but a man he prove,
That wins such god-like victories, and now affects our host 180
With so much sorrow, since so much of our best blood is lost
By his high valour. I have fear some God in him doth threat,
Incens'd for want of sacrifice; the wrath of God is great."

Lycaon's famous son replied: "Great counsellor of Troy,
This man, so excellent in arms, I think is Tydeus' joy; 185
I know him by his fi'ry shield, by his bright three-plum'd casque,
And by his horse; nor can I say, if or some God doth mask
In his appearance, or he be whom I nam'd Tydeus' son,
But without God the things he does for certain are not done.
Some great Immortal, that conveys his shoulders in a cloud, 190
Goes by and puts by ev'ry dart at his bold breast bestow'd,
Or lets it take with little hurt; for I myself let fly
A shaft that shot him through his arms, but had as good gone by,
Yet which I gloriously affirm'd had driv'n him down to hell.
Some God is angry, and with me; for far hence, where I dwell, 195
My horse and chariots idle stand, with which some other way
I might repair this shameful miss. Elev'n fair chariots stay

---

[171] *That ride the seas*—Greek "to the ships."

In old Lycaon's court, new made, new trimm'd to have been gone,
Curtain'd, and arrast under foot; two horse to ev'ry one,
That eat white barley and black oats, and do no good at all;   200
And these Lycaon (that well knew how these affairs would fall)
Charg'd, when I set down this design, I should command with here,
And gave me many lessons more, all which much better were
Than any I took forth myself. The reason I laid down
Was but the sparing of my horse, since in a siegéd town   205
I thought our horse-meat would be scant, when they were us'd to have
Their manger full; so I left them, and like a lackey slave
Am come to Ilion, confident in nothing but my bow
That nothing profits me. Two shafts I vainly did bestow
At two great princes, but of both my arrows neither slew,   210
Nor this, nor Atreus' younger son; a little blood I drew,
That serv'd but to incense them more. In an unhappy star
I therefore from my armoury have drawn those tools of war
That day, when, for great Hector's sake, to amiable Troy
I came to lead the Trojan bands. But if I ever joy,   215
In safe return, my country's sight, my wife's, my lofty tow'rs,
Let any stranger take this head, if to the fi'ry Pow'rs
This bow, these shafts, in pieces burst, by these hands be not thrown;
Idle companions that they are to me and my renown."

 Æneas said: "Use no such words; for, any other way   220
Than this, they shall not now be us'd. We first will both assay
This man with horse and chariot. Come then, ascend to me,
That thou mayst try our Trojan horse, how skill'd in field they be,
And in pursuing those that fly, or flying, being pursued,
How excellent they are of foot; and these, if Jove conclude   225
The 'scape of Tydeüs again, and grace him with our flight,
Shall serve to bring us safely off. Come, I'll be first shall fight,

---

216 Both the folios have "*wives*," but the true reading is "*wife's*," if we consult the Greek.

Take thou these fair reins and this scourge ; or, if thou wilt, fight thou,
And leave the horses' care to me." He answer'd : " I will now
Descend to fight, keep thou the reins, and guide thyself thy horse, 230
Who with their wonted manager will better wield the force
Of the impulsive chariot, if we be driv'n to fly,
Than with a stranger ; under whom they will be much more shy,
And, fearing my voice, wishing thine, grow resty, nor go on
To bear us off, but leave engag'd for mighty Tydeus' son 235
Themselves and us. Then be thy part thy one-hoof'd horses' guide,
I'll make the fight, and with a dart receive his utmost pride."
With this the gorgeous chariot both, thus prepar'd, ascend
And make full way at Diomed ; which noted by his friend,
" Mine own most-lovéd mind," said he, "two mighty men of war 240
I see come with a purpos'd charge ; one's he that hits so far
With bow and shaft, Lycaon's son ; the other fames the brood
Of great Anchises and the Queen that rules in amorous blood,
Æneas, excellent in arms. Come up, and use your steeds,
And look not war so in the face, lest that desire that feeds 245
Thy great mind be the bane of it." This did with anger sting
The blood of Diomed, to see his friend, that chid the king
Before the fight, and then preferr'd his ablesse and his mind
To all his ancestors in fight, now come so far behind ;
Whom thus he answer'd : " Urge no flight, you cannot please me so ;
Nor is it honest in my mind to fear a coming foe, 251
Or make a flight good, though with fight. My pow'rs are yet entire,
And scorn the help-tire of a horse. I will not blow the fire
Of their hot valours with my flight, but cast upon the blaze
This body borne upon my knees. I entertain amaze ? 255

[235] *Engag'd for.*—The second folio (which Dr. Taylor follows) omits "*for ;*" a typographical error.
[239] *Friend*—Sthenelus.
[248] *Ablesse*—The second folio reads "*ablenesse*," which Dr. Taylor has followed.
[255] *I entertain amaze ?*—Do you think I fear ?

Minerva will not see that shame. And since they have begun,
They shall not both elect their ends ; and he that 'scapes shall run,
Or stay and take the other's fate. And this I leave for thee ;—
If amply-wise Athenia give both their lives to me,
Rein our horse to their chariot hard, and have a special heed 260
To seize upon Æneas' steeds, that we may change their breed,
And make a Grecian race of them that have been long of Troy.
For these are bred of those brave beasts which, for the lovely boy
That waits now on the cup of Jove, Jove, that far-seeing God,
Gave Tros the king in recompense ; the best that ever trod 265
The sounding centre, underneath the morning and the sun.
Anchises stole the breed of them ; for, where their sires did run,
He closely put his mares to them, and never made it known
To him that heir'd them, who was then the king Laomedon.
Six horses had he of that race, of which himself kept four, 270
And gave the other two his son ; and these are they that scour
The field so bravely towards us, expert in charge and flight.
If these we have the pow'r to take, our prise is exquisite,
And our renown will far exceed." While these were talking thus,
The fir'd horse brought th' assailants near, and thus spake Pandarus :
 "Most suff'ring-minded Tydeus' son, that hast of war the art, 276
My shaft, that strook thee, slew thee not, I now will prove a dart."
This said, he shook, and then he threw, a lance, aloft and large,
That in Tydides' curets stuck, quite driving through his targe ;
Then bray'd he out so wild a voice that all the field might hear : 280
"Now have I reach'd thy root of life, and by thy death shall bear
Our praise's chief prise from the field." Tydides undismay'd
Replied : "Thou err'st, I am not touch'd ; but more charge will be laid
To both your lives before you part ; at least the life of one
Shall satiate the throat of Mars." This said, his lance was gone, 285
Minerva led it to his face, which at his eye ran in,
And, as he stoop'd, strook through his jaws, his tongue's root, and his
    chin.

Down from the chariot he fell, his gay arms shin'd and rung,
The swift horse trembled, and his soul for ever charm'd his tongue.
 Æneas with his shield, and lance, leapt swiftly to his friend,   290
Afraid the Greeks would force his trunk; and that he did defend,
Bold as a lion of his strength; he hid him with his shield,
Shook round his lance, and horribly did threaten all the field
With death, if any durst make in. Tydides rais'd a stone
With his one hand, of wondrous weight, and pour'd it mainly on   295
The hip of Anchisiades, wherein the joint doth move
The thigh ('tis call'd the huckle-bone) which all in sherds it drove,
Brake both the nerves, and with the edge cut all the flesh away.
It stagger'd him upon his knees, and made th' heroë stay
His strook-blind temples on his hand, his elbow on the earth;   300
And there this prince of men had died, if She that gave him birth,
(Kiss'd by Anchises on the green, where his fair oxen fed)
Jove's loving daughter, instantly had not about him spread
Her soft embraces, and convey'd within her heav'nly veil
(Us'd as a rampire 'gainst all darts that did so hot assail)   305
Her dear-lov'd issue from the field. Then Sthenelus in haste,
Rememb'ring what his friend advis'd, from forth the press made fast
His own horse to their chariot, and presently laid hand
Upon the lovely-coated horse Æneas did command.
Which bringing to the wond'ring Greeks, he did their guard command   310
To his belov'd Deipylus, who was his inward friend,
And, of his equals, one to whom he had most honour shown,
That he might see them safe at fleet; then stept he to his own
With which he cheerfully made in to Tydeus' mighty race.
He, mad with his great enemy's rape, was hot in desp'rate chace   315
Of her that made it, with his lance, arm'd less with steel than spite,
Well knowing her no Deity that had to do in fight,

  [315] *Rape*—here used for his being carried off by Venus.

Minerva his great patroness, nor, She that raceth towns,
Bellona, but a Goddess weak, and foe to men's renowns.
Her, through a world of fight pursu'd, at last he overtook, 320
And, thrusting up his ruthless lance, her heav'nly veil he strook
(That ev'n the Graces wrought themselves, at her divine command)
Quite through, and hurt the tender back of her delicious hand.
The rude point piercing through her palm, forth flow'd th' immortal blood;
Blood, such as flows in blessèd Gods, that eat no human food, 325
Nor drink of our inflaming wine, and therefore bloodless are,
And call'd Immortals; out she cried, and could no longer bear
Her lov'd son; whom she cast from her, and in a sable cloud
Phœbus, receiving, hid him close from all the Grecian crowd,
Lest some of them should find his death. Away flew Venus then, 330
And after her cried Diomed: "Away, thou spoil of men,
Though sprung from all-preserving Jove, these hot encounters leave.
Is't not enough that silly dames thy sorc'ries should deceive,
Unless thou thrust into the war, and rob a soldier's right?
I think a few of these assaults will make thee fear the fight, 335
Wherever thou shalt hear it nam'd." She, sighing, went her way
Extremely griev'd, and with her griefs her beauties did decay,
And black her ivory body grew. Then from a dewy mist
Brake swift-foot Iris to her aid, from all the darts that hiss'd
At her quick rapture; and to Mars they took their plaintive course, 340
And found him on the fight's left hand, by him his speedy horse,
And huge lance, lying in a fog. The Queen of all things fair
Her lovèd brother, on her knees, besought, with instant pray'r,
His golden-riband-bound-man'd horse to lend her up to heav'n,
For she was much griev'd with a wound a mortal man had giv'n, 345
Tydides, that 'gainst Jove himself durst now advance his arm.
  He granted, and his chariot (perplex'd with her late harm)
She mounted, and her waggoness was She that paints the air.
The horse she rein'd, and with a scourge importun'd their repair,

³⁴⁸ Iris.

That of themselves out-flew the wind, and quickly they ascend 350
Olympus, high seat of the Gods. Th' horse knew their journey's end,
Stood still, and from their chariot the windy-footed dame
Dissolv'd, and gave them heav'nly food ; and to Dione came
Her wounded daughter, bent her knees. She kindly bade her stand,
With sweet embraces help'd her up, strok'd her with her soft hand, 355
Call'd kindly by her name, and ask'd : "What God hath been so rude,
Sweet daughter, to chastise thee thus, as if thou wert pursu'd
Ev'n to the act of some light sin, and deprehended so?
For otherwise, each close escape is in the great let go."

  She answer'd : "Haughty Tydeus' son hath been so insolent, 360
Since, he whom most my heart esteems of all my lov'd descent,
I rescu'd from his bloody hand. Now battle is not giv'n
To any Trojans by the Greeks, but by the Greeks to heav'n."

  She answer'd : "Daughter, think not much, though much it grieve
  thee ; use
The patience, whereof many Gods examples may produce, 365
In many bitter ills receiv'd, as well that men sustain
By their inflictions as by men repaid to them again.
Mars suffer'd much more than thyself by Ephialtes' pow'r,
And Otus', Aloëus' sons ; who in a brazen tow'r,
And in inextricable chains, cast that war-greedy God, 370
Where twice-six months and one he liv'd, and there the period
Of his sad life perhaps had clos'd, if his kind stepdame's eye,
Fair Erebœa, had not seen ; who told it Mercury,
And he by stealth enfranchis'd him ; though he could scarce enjoy
The benefit of franchisement, the chains did so destroy 375
His vital forces with their weight. So Juno suffer'd more
When, with a three-fork'd arrow's head, Amphitryo's son did gore
Her right breast, past all hope of cure. Pluto sustain'd no less
By that self man, and by a shaft of equal bitterness

    [355] *Dione*—mother of Venus.

Shot through his shoulder at hell gates; and there, amongst the dead,
Were he not deathless, he had died; but up to heav'n he fled,   381
Extremely tortur'd, for recure, which instantly he won
At Pæon's hand, with sov'reign balm; and this did Jove's great son,
Unblest, great-high-deed-daring man, that car'd not doing ill,
That with his bow durst wound the Gods! But, by Minerva's will,   385
Thy wound the foolish Diomed was so profane to give;
Not knowing he that fights with Heav'n hath never long to live,
And for this deed, he never shall have child about his knee
To call him father, coming home. Besides, hear this from me,
Strength-trusting man, though thou be strong, and art in strength a
    tow'r,   390
Take heed a stronger meet thee not, and that a woman's pow'r
Contains not that superior strength, and lest that woman be
Adrastus' daughter, and thy wife, the wise Ægiale;
When, from this hour not far, she wakes, ev'n sighing with desire
To kindle our revenge on thee, with her enamouring fire,   395
In choosing her some fresh young friend, and so drown all thy fame,
Won here in war, in her court-piece, and in an opener shame."

    This said, with both her hands she cleans'd the tender back and palm
Of all the sacred blood they lost; and, never using balm,
The pain ceas'd, and the wound was cur'd of this kind Queen of love.
    Juno and Pallas, seeing this, assay'd to anger Jove,   401
And quit his late-made mirth with them, about the loving Dame,
With some sharp jest, in like sort, built upon her present shame.
Grey-ey'd Athenia began, and ask'd the Thunderer,
If, nothing moving him to wrath, she boldly might prefer,   405
What she conceiv'd, to his conceit; and, staying no reply,
She bade him view the Cyprian fruit he lov'd so tenderly,
Whom she thought hurt, and by this means;—intending to suborn
Some other lady of the Greeks (whom lovely veils adorn)

⁴⁰⁸ *Whom she thought hurt.*—Both the folios read "*though* hurt." Dr. Taylor prints "*thought*," which is perhaps the true reading.

To gratify some other friend of her much-lovéd Troy, 410
As she embrac'd and stirr'd her blood to the Venerean joy,
The golden clasp, those Grecian dames upon their girdles wear,
Took hold of her delicious hand, and hurt it, she had fear.

The Thund'rer smil'd, and call'd to him love's golden Arbitress,
And told her those rough works of war were not for her access; 415
She should be making marriages, embracings, kisses, charms,
Stern Mars and Pallas had the charge of those affairs in arms.

While these thus talk'd, Tydides' rage still thirsted to achieve
His prise upon Anchises' son, though well he did perceive
The Sun himself protected him; but his desires (inflam'd 420
With that great Trojan prince's blood, and arms so highly fam'd)
Not that great God did reverence. Thrice rush'd he rudely on,
And thrice, betwixt his darts and death, the Sun's bright target shone;
But when upon the fourth assault, much like a spirit, he flew,
The far-off-working Deity exceeding wrathful grew, 425
And ask'd him: "What! Not yield to gods? Thy equals learn to know.
The race of Gods is far above men creeping here below."

This drave him to some small retreat; he would not tempt more near
The wrath of him that strook so far; whose pow'r had now set clear
Æneas from the stormy field within the holy place 430
Of Pergamus, where, to the hope of his so sov'reign grace,
A goodly temple was advanc'd; in whose large inmost part
He left him, and to his supply inclin'd his mother's heart,
Latona, and the dart-pleas'd Queen; who cur'd, and made him strong.

The silver-bow'd fair God then threw in the tumultuous throng 435
An image, that in stature, look, and arms, he did create
Like Venus' son; for which the Greeks and Trojans made debate,
Laid loud strokes on their ox-hide shields, and bucklers eas'ly borne;
Which error Phœbus pleas'd to urge on Mars himself in scorn:

---

[434] *Dart-pleas'd Queen*—Diana.

"Mars, Mars," said he, "thou plague of men, smear'd with the
    dust and blood
Of humans, and their ruin'd walls, yet thinks thy Godhead good
To fright this fury from the field, who next will fight with Jove?
First in a bold approach he hurt, the moist palm of thy love,
And next, as if he did affect to have a Deity's pow'r,
He held out his assault on me." This said, the lofty tow'r
Of Pergamus he made his seat; and Mars did now excite
The Trojan forces, in the form of him that led to fight
The Thracian troops, swift Acamas. "O Priam's sons," said he,
"How long the slaughter of your men can ye sustain to see?
Ev'n till they brave you at your gates? Ye suffer beaten down
Æneas, great Anchises' son, whose prowess we renown
As much as Hector's; fetch him off from this contentious prease."

  With this, the strength and spirits of all his courage did increase;
And yet Sarpedon seconds him, with this particular taunt
Of noble Hector: "Hector, where is thy unthankful vaunt,
And that huge strength on which it built, that thou, and thy allies,
With all thy brothers (without aid of us or our supplies,
And troubling not a citizen) the city safe would hold?
In all which friends' and brothers' helps I see not, nor am told
Of any one of their exploits, but (all held in dismay
Of Diomed, like a sort of dogs, that at a lion bay,
And entertain no spirit to pinch) we, your assistants here,
Fight for the town as you help'd us; and I, an aiding peer,
No citizen, ev'n out of care, that doth become a man
For men and children's liberties, add all the aid I can;
Not out of my particular cause; far hence my profit grows,
For far hence Asian Lycia lies, where gulfy Xanthus flows,

---

⁴⁴³ *Thy love*—Venus.
⁴⁵¹ *Sort*—See Bk. IV. 460.
⁴⁶² *Pinch*—a term frequently used for dogs pressing on and seizing their game.
⁴⁶³ *As*—as if.

And where my lov'd wife, infant son, and treasure nothing scant,
I left behind me, which I see those men would have that want,
And therefore they that have would keep. Yet I, as I would lose   470
Their sure fruition, cheer my troops, and with their lives propose
Mine own life, both to gen'ral fight, and to particular cope
With this great soldier; though, I say, I entertain no hope
To have such gettings as the Greeks, nor fear to lose like Troy.
Yet thou, ev'n Hector, deedless stand'st, and car'st not to employ   475
Thy town-born friends, to bid them stand, to fight and save their wives,
Lest as a fowler casts his nets upon the silly lives
Of birds of all sorts, so the foe your walls and houses hales,
One with another, on all heads ; or such as 'scape their falls,
Be made the prey and prise of them (as willing overthrown)   480
That hope not for you with their force ; and so this brave-built town
Will prove a chaos. That deserves in thee so hot a care,
As should consume thy days and nights, to hearten and prepare
Th' assistant princes ; pray their minds to bear their far-brought toils ;
To give them worth with worthy fight ; in victories and foils   485
Still to be equal ; and thyself, exampling them in all,
Need no reproofs nor spurs. All this in thy free choice should fall."

 This stung great Hector's heart ; and yet, as ev'ry gen'rous mind
Should silent bear a just reproof, and show what good they find
In worthy counsels, by their ends put into present deeds,   490
Not stomach nor be vainly sham'd ; so Hector's spirit proceeds,
And from his chariot, wholly arm'd, he jump'd upon the sand,
On foot so toiling through the host, a dart in either hand,
And all hands turn'd against the Greeks. The Greeks despis'd their worst,
And, thick'ning their instructed pow'rs, expected all they durst.   495

 ⁴⁷¹ *Propose.*—Bk. I. 14.
 ⁴⁸¹ Both the folios read "*hope.*" Dr. Taylor has "*holp*"—help, which seems preferable.
  ⁴⁹¹ *Stomach*—be haughty, angry.
  ⁴⁹⁴ *All hands turn'd*—excited all the army. ⁴⁹⁵ *Expected*—awaited.

Then with the feet of horse and foot, the dust in clouds did rise.
And as, in sacred floors of barns, upon corn-winnow'rs flies
The chaff, driv'n with an opposite wind, when yellow Ceres dites,
Which all the diters' feet, legs, arms, their heads and shoulders whites;
So look'd the Grecians grey with dust, that strook the solid heav'n, 500
Rais'd from returning chariots, and troops together driv'n.
Each side stood to their labours firm. Fierce Mars flew through the air,
And gather'd darkness from the fight, and, with his best affair,
Obey'd the pleasure of the Sun, that wears the golden sword,
Who bade him raise the spirits of Troy, when Pallas ceas'd t' afford 505
Her helping office to the Greeks; and then his own hands wrought,
Which, from his fane's rich chancel, cur'd, the true Æneas brought,
And plac'd him by his peers in field; who did with joy admire
To see him both alive and safe, and all his pow'rs entire,
Yet stood not sifting how it chanc'd; another sort of task, 510
Then stirring th' idle sieve of news, did all their forces ask,
Inflam'd by Phœbus, harmful Mars, and Eris eag'rer far.
The Greeks had none to hearten them; their hearts rose with the war;
But chiefly Diomed, Ithacus, and both th' Ajaces us'd
Stirring examples and good words; their own fames had infus'd 515
Spirit enough into their bloods, to make them neither fear
The Trojans' force, nor Fate itself, but still expecting were,
When most was done, what would be more; their ground they still made good,
And in their silence, and set pow'rs, like fair still clouds, they stood,
With which Jove crowns the tops of hills, in any quiet day, 520
When Boreas and the ruder winds (that use to drive away
Air's dusky vapours, being loose, in many a whistling gale)
Are pleasingly bound up, and calm, and not a breath exhale;

[493] *Dites*—winnows. NARES quotes this passage for the word; but it is only another spelling for *dights*, prepares. See CHAPMAN's Hesiod, Georgics, bk. II. 343, and Days, 67, in vol. v. of this edition of his translations; where the word is also used for *winnowing*.   [503] *Affair*—action, endeavour.

So firmly stood the Greeks, nor fled for all the Ilion's aid.
 Atrides yet coasts through the troops, confirming men so staid : 525
"O friends," said he, "hold up your minds ; strength is but strength
 of will ;
Rev'rence each other's good in fight, and shame at things done ill.
Where soldiers show an honest shame, and love of honour lives,
That ranks men with the first in fight, death fewer liveries gives 529
Than life, or than where Fame's neglect makes cowards fight at length.
Flight neither doth the body grace, nor shows the mind hath strength."
He said, and swifty through the troops a mortal lance did send,
That reft a standard-bearer's life, renown'd Æneas' friend,
Deïcoön Pergasides, whom all the Trojans lov'd
As he were one of Priam's sons, his mind was so approv'd 535
In always fighting with the first. The lance his target took,
Which could not interrupt the blow, that through it clearly strook,
And in his belly's rim was sheath'd, beneath his girdle-stead.
He sounded falling, and his arms with him resounded, dead.
 Then fell two princes of the Greeks by great Æneas' ire, 540
Diocleus' sons (Orsilochus and Crethon), whose kind sire
In bravely-builded Phæra dwelt, rich, and of sacred blood.
He was descended lineally from great Alphæus' flood,
That broadly flows through Pylos' fields ; Alphæus did beget
Orsilochus, who in the rule of many men was set ; 545
And that Orsilochus begat the rich Diocleüs ;
Diocleus sire to Crethon was, and this Orsilochus.
Both these, arriv'd at man's estate, with both th' Atrides went,
To honour them in th' Ilion wars ; and both were one day sent,
To death as well as Troy, for death hid both in one black hour. 550
As two young lions (with their dam, sustain'd but to devour)

⁵²⁹ *Liveries*—deliveries.
⁵³⁰ The first folio has "*cow-herds.*" This has frequently been given as the derivation of the word "*coward.*"
⁵³⁸ *Girdle-stead.*—The composition *stead* is used to mark the place or position of anything, thus *homestead, noonsted ; Girdle-stead,* the place of the girdle.

Bred on the tops of some steep hill, and in the gloomy deep
Of an inaccessible wood, rush out, and prey on sheep,
Steers, oxen, and destroy men's stalls, so long that they come short,
And by the owner's steel are slain ; in such unhappy sort   555
Fell these beneath Æneas' pow'r. When Menelaus view'd
Like two tall fir-trees these two fall, their timeless falls he rued,
And to the first fight, where they lay, a vengeful force he took ;
His arms beat back the sun in flames, a dreadful lance he shook ;
Mars put the fury in his mind, that by Æneas' hands,   560
Who was to make the slaughter good, he might have strew'd the sands.
Antilochus, old Nestor's son, observing he was bent
To urge a combat of such odds, and knowing, the event
Being ill on his part, all their pains (alone sustain'd for him)
Err'd from their end, made after hard, and took them in the trim   565
Of an encounter. Both their hands and darts advanc'd, and shook,
And both pitch'd in full stand of charge ; when suddenly the look
Of Anchisiades took note of Nestor's valiant son,
In full charge too ; which, two to one, made Venus' issue shun
The hot adventure, though he were a soldier well-approv'd.   570
Then drew they off their slaughter'd friends ; who giv'n to their belov'd,
They turn'd where fight show'd deadliest hate ; and there mix'd with
       the dead
Pylæmen, that the targeteers of Paphlagonia led,
A man like Mars ; and with him fell good Mydon that did guide
His chariot, Atymnus' son. The prince Pylæmen died   575
By Menelaus ; Nestor's joy slew Mydon ; one before
The other in the chariot. Atrides' lance did gore
Pylæmen's shoulder, in the blade. Antilochus did force
A mighty stone up from the earth, and, as he turn'd his horse,
Strook Mydon's elbow in the midst ; the reins of ivory   580
Fell from his hands into the dust ; Antilochus let fly

⁵⁶⁵ "*Trim*—'order, or disposition.' Beaumont and Fletcher speak of 'the horrid *trims* of war.' "—Dr. Taylor.

His sword withal, and, rushing in, a blow so deadly laid
Upon his temples, that he groan'd, tumbled to earth, and stay'd
A mighty while preposterously (because the dust was deep)
Upon his neck and shoulders there, ev'n till his foe took keep   585
Of his pris'd horse, and made them stir; and then he prostrate fell.
His horse Antilochus took home. When Hector had heard tell,
Amongst the uproar, of their deaths, he laid out all his voice,
And ran upon the Greeks. Behind came many men of choice,
Before him march'd great Mars himself, match'd with his female mate,
The dread Bellona. She brought on, to fight for mutual fate,   591
A tumult that was wild and mad. He shook a horrid lance,
And now led Hector, and anon behind would make the chance.

This sight when great Tydides saw, his hair stood up on end;
And him, whom all the skill and pow'r of arms did late attend,   595
Now like a man in counsel poor, that, travelling, goes amiss,
And having pass'd a boundless plain, not knowing where he is,
Comes on the sudden where he sees a river rough, and raves
With his own billows ravishéd into the king of waves,
Murmurs with foam, and frights him back; so he, amaz'd, retir'd,   600
And thus would make good his amaze: "O friends, we all admir'd
Great Hector, as one of himself, well-darting, bold in war,
When some God guards him still from death, and makes him dare so far.
Now Mars himself, form'd like a man, is present in his rage,
And therefore, whatsoever cause importunes you to wage   605
War with these Trojans, never strive, but gently take your rod,
Lest in your bosoms, for a man, ye ever find a God."

As Greece retir'd, the pow'r of Troy did much more forward prease,
And Hector two brave men of war sent to the fields of peace;
Menesthes, and Anchialus; one chariot bare them both.   610
Their falls made Ajax Telamon ruthful of heart, and wroth,

---

[584] *Preposterously*—Chapman uses this word in a somewhat unusual way; pre-posterous, hind part foremost. Here, *on his head.*
[602] *One of himself*—peerless.
[606] *Take your rod*—submit.

Who light'ned out a lance that smote Amphius Selages,
That dwelt in Pæsos, rich in lands, and did huge goods possess,
But Fate, to Priam and his sons, conducted his supply.
The jav'lin on his girdle strook, and piercéd mortally 615
His belly's lower part ; he fell : his arms had looks so trim,
That Ajax needs would prove their spoil ; the Trojans pour'd on him
Whole storms of lances, large, and sharp, of which a number stuck
In his rough shield ; yet from the slain he did his jav'lin pluck,
But could not from his shoulders force the arms he did affect, 620
The Trojans with such drifts of darts the body did protect ;
And wisely Telamonius fear'd their valorous defence,
So many, and so strong of hand, stood in with such expense
Of deadly prowess ; who repell'd, though big, strong, bold, he were,
The famous Ajax, and their friend did from his rapture bear. 625
 Thus this place fill'd with strength of fight ; in th' army's other prease,
Tlepolemus, a tall big man, the son of Hercules,
A cruel destiny inspir'd, with strong desire to prove
Encounter with Sarpedon's strength, the son of cloudy Jove ;
Who, coming on to that stern end, had chosen him his foe. 630
Thus Jove's great nephew, and his son, 'gainst one another go.
Tlepolemus, to make his end more worth the will of fate,
Began as if he had her pow'r, and show'd the mortal state
Of too much confidence in man, with this superfluous brave :
"Sarpedon, what necessity or needless humour drave 635
Thy form to these wars, which in heart I know thou dost abhor,
A man not seen in deeds of arms, a Lycian counsellor ?
They lie that call thee son to Jove, since Jove bred none so late ;
The men of elder times were they, that his high pow'r begat,
Such men as had Herculean force. My father Hercules 640
Was Jove's true issue ; he was bold ; his deeds did well express

   614 *Conducted his supply*—led him to assist.
   623 *Expense*—profusion, giving forth.

They sprung out of a lion's heart. He whilome came to Troy,
(For horse that Jupiter gave Tros, for Ganymed, his boy)
With six ships only, and few men, and tore the city down,
Left all her broad ways desolate, and made the horse his own. 645
For thee, thy mind is ill dispos'd, thy body's pow'rs are poor,
And therefore are thy troops so weak ; the soldier evermore
Follows the temper of his chief ; and thou pull'st down a side.
But say thou art the son of Jove, and hast thy means supplied
With forces fitting his descent, the pow'rs that I compell   650
Shall throw thee hence, and make thy head run ope the gates of hell."

 Jove's Lycian issue answer'd him : " Tlepolemus, 'tis true
Thy father holy Ilion in that sort overthrew ;
Th' injustice of the king was cause, that, where thy father had
Us'd good deservings to his state, he quitted him with bad.   655
Hesione, the joy and grace of king Laomedon,
Thy father rescu'd from a whale, and gave to Telamon
In honour'd nuptials (Telamon, from whom your strongest Greek
Boasts to have issu'd) and this grace might well expect the like ;
Yet he gave taunts for thanks, and kept, against his oath, his horse,
And therefore both thy father's strength, and justice, might enforce   661
The wreak he took on Troy ; but this and thy cause differ far.
Sons seldom heir their fathers' worths. Thou canst not make his war.
What thou assum'st for him, is mine, to be on thee impos'd."

 With this, he threw an ashen dart ; and then Tlepolemus los'd   665
Another from his glorious hand. Both at one instant flew,
Both strook, both wounded. From his neck Sarpedon's jav'lin drew
The life blood of Tlepolemus ; full in the midst it fell ;
And what he threaten'd, th' other gave, that darkness, and that hell.
Sarpedon's left thigh took the lance ; it pierc'd the solid bone,   670
And with his raging head ran through ; but Jove preserv'd his son.
The dart yet vex'd him bitterly, which should have been pull'd out,
But none consider'd then so much, so thick came on the rout,

 ⁶⁴⁸ *Side*—your party.   ⁶⁵⁰ *Compell*—collect together, possess in myself.

And fill'd each hand so full of cause to ply his own defence ;
'Twas held enough, both fall'n, that both were nobly carried thence. 675
    Ulysses knew th' events of both, and took it much to heart
That his friend's enemy should 'scape ; and in a twofold part
His thoughts contended, if he should pursue Sarpedon's life,
Or take his friend's wreak on his men. Fate did conclude this
    strife,
By whom 'twas otherwise decreed than that Ulysses' steel 680
Should end Sarpedon. In this doubt Minerva took the wheel
From fickle Chance, and made his mind resolve to right his friend
With that blood he could surest draw. Then did Revenge extend
Her full pow'r on the multitude ; then did he never miss ;
Alastor, Halius, Chromius, Noemon, Prytanis, 685
Alcander, and a number more, he slew, and more had slain,
If Hector had not understood ; whose pow'r made in amain,
And strook fear through the Grecian troops, but to Sarpedon gave
Hope of full rescue, who thus cried : "O Hector ! Help and save
My body from the spoil of Greece, that to your lovéd town 690
My friends may see me borne, and then let earth possess her own
In this soil, for whose sake I left my country's ; for no day
Shall ever show me that again, nor to my wife display,
And young hope of my name, the joy of my much thirsted sight ;
All which I left for Troy, for them let Troy then do this right." 695
    To all this Hector gives no word, but greedily he strives
With all speed to repell the Greeks, and shed in floods their lives,
And left Sarpedon ; but what face soever he put on
Of following the common cause, he left this prince alone
For his particular grudge, because, so late, he was so plain 700
In his reproof before the host, and that did he retain ;
However, for example sake, he would not show it then,
And for his shame too, since 'twas just. But good Sarpedon's men
Ventur'd themselves, and forc'd him off, and set him underneath
The goodly beech of Jupiter, where now they did unsheath 705

The ashen lance; strong Pelagon, his friend, most lov'd, most true,
Enforc'd it from his maiméd thigh; with which his spirit flew,
And darkness over-flew his eyes; yet with a gentle gale,
That round about the dying prince cool Boreas did exhale,
He was reviv'd, recomforted, that else had griev'd and died. 710

All this time flight drave to the fleet the Argives, who applied
No weapon 'gainst the proud pursuit, nor ever turn'd a head,
They knew so well that Mars pursu'd, and dreadful Hector led.
Then who was first, who last, whose lives the iron Mars did seize,
And Priam's Hector? Helenus, surnam'd Œnopides; 715
Good Teuthras; and Orestes, skill'd in managing of horse;
Bold Œnomaus; and a man renown'd for martial force,
Trechus, the great Ætolian chief; Oresbius, that did wear
The gaudy mitre, studied wealth extremely, and dwelt near
Th' Atlantic lake Cephisides, in Hyla, by whose seat 720
The good men of Bœotia dwelt. This slaughter grew so great,
It flew to heav'n; Saturnia discern'd it, and cried out
To Pallas: "O unworthy sight! To see a field so fought,
And break our words to Sparta's king, that Ilion should be rac'd,
And he return reveng'd; when thus we see his Greeks disgrac'd, 725
And bear the harmful rage of Mars! Come, let us use our care,
That we dishonour not our pow'rs." Minerva was as yare
As she at the despite of Troy. Her golden-bridled steeds
Then Saturn's daughter brought abroad; and Hebe, she proceeds
T' address her chariot; instantly she gives it either wheel, 730
Beam'd with eight spokes of sounding brass; the axle-tree was steel;
The fell'ffs incorruptible gold, their upper bands of brass,
Their matter most unvalued, their work of wondrous grace;
The naves, in which the spokes were driv'n, were all with silver bound;
The chariot's seat two hoops of gold and silver strengthen'd round, 735

[727] *Yare*—quick, ready. Frequently used by Shakespeare; generally applied to sailors, sometimes not. "If you have occasion to use me for your own turn, you shall find me *yare*."—*Meas. for Meas.* IV. 2.
[730] i. e. she puts on both wheels.

Edg'd with a gold and silver fringe; the beam, that look'd before,
Was massy silver; on whose top, gears all of gold it wore,
And golden poitrils. Juno mounts, and her hot horses rein'd,
That thirsted for contentión, and still of peace complain'd.
    Minerva wrapt her in the robe, that curiously she wove,   740
With glorious colours, as she sate on th' azure floor of Jove,
And wore the arms that he puts on, bent to the tearful field.
About her broad-spread shoulders hung his huge and horrid shield,
Fring'd round with ever-fighting snakes; through it was drawn to life
The miseries and deaths of fight; in it frown'd bloody Strife,   745
In it shin'd sacred Fortitude, in it fell Púrsuit flew,
In it the monster Gorgon's head, in which held out to view
Were all the dire ostents of Jove; on her big head she plac'd
His four-plum'd glitt'ring casque of gold, so admirably vast
It would an hundred garrisons of soldiers comprehend.   750
Then to her shining chariot her vig'rous feet ascend;
And in her violent hand she takes his grave, huge, solid lance,
With which the conquests of her wrath she useth to advance,
And overturn whole fields of men, to show she was the Seed   754
Of him that thunders. Then heav'n's Queen, to urge her horses' speed,
Takes up the scourge, and forth they fly. The ample gates of heav'n
Rung, and flew open of themselves; the charge whereof is giv'n,
With all Olympus, and the sky, to the distinguish'd Hours,
That clear, or hide it all in clouds, or pour it down in show'rs.
This way their scourge-obeying horse made haste, and soon they won
The top of all the topful heav'ns, where agéd Saturn's son   761
Sat sever'd from the other Gods; then stay'd the white-arm'd Queen
Her steeds, and ask'd of Jove, if Mars did not incense his spleen
With his foul deeds, in ruining so many and so great
In the command and grace of Greece, and in so rude a heat?   765

    736 *The beam, &c.*—the pole.
    737 *Gears*—here for collars.
    738 *Poitrils*—breast-pieces, pectorals.
    758 *Distinguished*—varied, marked with distinctions.

At which, she said, Apollo laugh'd, and Venus, who still sue
To that mad God, for violence that never justice knew;
For whose impiety, she ask'd, if, with his wishéd love,
Herself might free the field of him? He bade her rather move
Athenia to the charge she sought, who us'd of old to be   770
The bane of Mars, and had as well the gift of spoil as he.

    This grace she slack'd not, but her horse scourg'd, that in nature flew
Betwixt the cope of stars and earth; and how far at a view
A man into the purple sea may from a hill descry,
So far a high-neighing horse of heav'n at ev'ry jump would fly.   775

    Arriv'd at Troy, where, broke in curls, the two floods mix their force,
Scamander and bright Simois, Saturnia stay'd her horse,
Took them from chariot, and a cloud of mighty depth diffus'd
About them; and the verdant banks of Simois produc'd
In nature what they eat in heav'n. Then both the Goddesses   780
March'd, like a pair of tim'rous doves, in hasting their access
To th' Argive succour. Being arriv'd, where both the most and best
Were heap'd together (showing all, like lions at a feast
Of new-slain carcasses, or boars, beyond encounter strong)
There found they Diomed; and there, 'midst all th' admiring throng,
Saturnia put on Stentor's shape, that had a brazen voice,   785
And spake as loud as fifty men; like whom she made a noise,
And chid the Argives: "O ye Greeks, in name and outward rite
But princes only, not in act, what scandal, what despite,

---

[775] "How far a heavenly horse took at one reach or stroke in galloping or running; wherein Homer's mind is far from being expressed in his interpreters, all taking it for how far Deities were borne from the earth, when instantly they came down to earth: τόσσον ἐπιθρώσκουσι, &c. *tantum uno saltu conficiunt, vel, tantum subsultim progrediuntur, deorum altizoni equi, &c. uno* being understood, and the horse's swiftness highly expressed. The sense, otherwise, is senseless and contradictory."—CHAPMAN.

[780] "'Αμβροσίην is the original word, which Scaliger taxeth very learnedly, asking how the horse came by it on those banks, when the text tells him Simois produced it; being willing to express by hyperbole the delicacy of that soil. If not, I hope the Deities could ever command it."—CHAPMAN.

Use ye to honour! All the time the great Æacides 790
Was conversant in arms, your foes durst not a foot address
Without their ports, so much they fear'd his lance that all controll'd,
And now they out-ray to your fleet." This did with shame make bold
The gen'ral spirit and pow'r of Greece; when, with particular note
Of their disgrace, Athenia made Tydeus' issue hot. 795
She found him at his chariot, refreshing of his wound
Inflicted by slain Pandarus; his sweat did so abound,
It much annoy'd him, underneath the broad belt of his shield;
With which, and tirèd with his toil, his soul could hardly yield
His body motion. With his hand he lifted up the belt, 800
And wip'd away that clotter'd blood the fervent wound did melt.
Minerva lean'd against his horse, and near their withers laid
Her sacred hand, then spake to him: "Believe me, Diomed,
Tydeus exampled not himself in thee his son; not great,
But yet he was a soldier; a man of so much heat, 805
That in his ambassy for Thebes, when I forbad his mind
To be too vent'rous, and when feasts his heart might have declin'd,
With which they welcom'd him, he made a challenge to the best,
And foil'd the best; I gave him aid, because the rust of rest,
That would have seiz'd another mind, he suffer'd not, but us'd 810
The trial I made like a man, and their soft feasts refus'd.
Yet, when I set thee on, thou faint'st; I guard thee, charge, exhort
That, I abetting thee, thou shouldst be to the Greeks a fort,
And a dismay to Ilion, yet thou obey'st in nought,
Afraid, or slothful, or else both; henceforth renounce all thought 815
That ever thou wert Tydeus' son." He answer'd her: "I know
Thou art Jove's daughter, and, for that, in all just duty owe
Thy speeches rev'rence, yet affirm ingenuously that fear
Doth neither hold me spiritless, nor sloth. I only bear
Thy charge in zealous memory, that I should never war 820
With any blessèd Deity, unless (exceeding far

₇₉₃ *Out-ray*—spread out in array; abbreviated from *array*.
₈₀₇ *Declin'd*—turned aside.

The limits of her rule) the Queen, that governs chamber sport,
Should press to field ; and her thy will enjoin'd my lance to hurt.
But, He whose pow'r hath right in arms, I knew in person here,
Besides the Cyprian Deity ; and therefore did forbear, 825
And here have gather'd in retreat these other Greeks you see,
With note and rev'rence of your charge." "My dearest mind," said she,
"What then was fit is chang'd. 'Tis true, Mars hath just rule in war,
But just war ; otherwise he raves, not fights. He's alter'd far.
He vow'd to Juno, and myself, that his aid should be us'd 830
Against the Trojans, whom it guards ; and therein he abus'd
His rule in arms, infring'd his word, and made his war unjust.
He is inconstant, impious, mad. Resolve then ; firmly trust
My aid of thee against his worst, or any Deity ; 834
Add scourge to thy free horse, charge home ; he fights perfidiously."
    This said ; as that brave king, her knight, with his horse-guiding friend,
Were set before the chariot, for sign he should descend,
That she might serve for waggoness, she pluck'd the wagg'ner back,
And up into his seat she mounts ; the beechen tree did crack
Beneath the burthen ; and good cause, it bore so huge a thing, 840
A Goddess so replete with pow'r, and such a puissant king.
    She snatch'd the scourge up and the reins, and shut her heav'nly look
In Hell's vast helm from Mars's eyes ; and full career she took
At him, who then had newly slain the mighty Periphas,
Renown'd son to Ochesius, and far the strongest was
Of all th' Ætolians ; to whose spoil the bloody God was run. 845
But when this man-plague saw th' approach of god-like Tydeus' son,
He let his mighty Periphas lie, and in full charge he ran
At Diomed ; and he at him. Both near ; the God began,
And, thirsty of his blood, he throws a brazen lance that bears 850
Full on the breast of Diomed, above the reins and gears ;

⁸³⁹ *Beechen tree*—axle.   ⁸⁴⁰ The second folio reads "*large*" for "*huge*."
⁸⁴² *Her look*—See Bk. i. 200.

But Pallas took it on her hand, and strook the eager lance
Beneath the chariot. Then the knight of Pallas doth advance,
And cast a jav'lin off at Mars, Minerva sent it on,
That, where his arming girdle girt, his belly graz'd upon, 855
Just at the rim, and ranch'd the flesh ; the lance again he got,
But left the wound, that stung him so, he laid out such a throat
As if nine or ten thousand men had bray'd out all their breaths
In one confusion, having felt as many sudden deaths.
The roar made both the hosts amaz'd. Up flew the God to heav'n ;
And with him was through all the air as black a tincture driv'n 861
To Diomed's eyes, as when the earth half-chok'd with smoking heat
Of gloomy clouds, that stifle men, and pitchy tempests threat,
Usher'd with horrid gusts of wind ; with such black vapours plum'd,
Mars flew t' Olympus, and broad heav'n, and there his place resum'd.
Sadly he went and sat by Jove, show'd his immortal blood, 866
That from a mortal-man-made wound pour'd such an impious flood,
And weeping pour'd out these complaints : " O Father, storm'st thou not
To see us take these wrongs from men ? Extreme griefs we have got
Ev'n by our own deep councils, held for gratifying them ; 870
And thou, our council's president, conclud'st in this extreme
Of fighting ever ; being rul'd by one that thou hast bred ;
One never well, but doing ill ; a girl so full of head
That, though all other Gods obey, her mad moods must command,
By thy indulgence, nor by word, nor any touch of hand, 875
Correcting her ; thy reason is, she is a spark of thee,
And therefore she may kindle rage in men 'gainst Gods, and she
May make men hurt Gods, and those Gods that are besides thy seed.
First in the palm 's hit Cyprides; then runs the impious deed
On my hurt person ; and, could life give way to death in me, 880
Or had my feet not fetch'd me off, heaps of mortality

[856] *Ranch'd*—wrenched, tore.   *He*—Diomede.
[875] *Nor by word.*—The second folio has incorrectly "*sword.*"
[879] *First in the Palm 's hit.*—Both the folios have " *First in the palms height Cyprydes ;* " and Dr. Taylor has thus printed, but the true meaning and reading must be obvious.

Had kept me consort." Jupiter, with a contracted brow,
Thus answer'd Mars: "Thou many minds, inconstant changeling thou,
Sit not complaining thus by me, whom most of all the Gods,
Inhabiting the starry hill, I hate; no periods 885
Being set to thy contentions, brawls, fights, and pitching fields;
Just of thy mother Juno's moods, stiff-neck'd, and never yields,
Though I correct her still, and chide, nor can forbear offence,
Though to her son; this wound I know tastes of her insolence;
But I will prove more natural; thou shalt be cur'd, because 890
Thou com'st of me, but hadst thou been so cross to sacred laws,
Being born to any other God, thou hadst been thrown from heav'n
Long since, as low as Tartarus, beneath the giants driv'n."

This said, he gave his wound in charge to Pæon, who applied
Such sov'reign med'cines, that as soon the pain was qualified, 895
And he recur'd; as nourishing milk, when runnet is put in,
Runs all in heaps of tough thick curd, though in his nature thin,
Ev'n so soon his wound's parted sides ran close in his recure;
For he, all deathless, could not long the parts of death endure.
Then Hebe bath'd, and put on him fresh garments, and he sate 900
Exulting by his sire again, in top of all his state.
So, having, from the spoils of men, made his desir'd remove,
Juno and Pallas re-ascend the starry court of Jove.

THE END OF THE FIFTH BOOK.

THE SIXTH BOOK OF HOMER'S ILIADS.

THE ARGUMENT.

THE Gods now leaving an indiff'rent * field,
The Greeks prevail, the slaughter'd Trojans yield.
Hector, by Helenus' advice, retires
In haste to Troy, and Hecuba desires
To pray Minerva to remove from fight
The son of Tydeus, her affected knight,
And vow to her, for favour of such price,
Twelve oxen should be slain in sacrifice.
In mean space Glaucus and Tydides meet;
And either other with remembrance greet
Of old love 'twixt their fathers, which inclines
Their hearts to friendship; who change arms for signs
Of a continu'd love for either's life.
Hector, in his return, meets with his wife,
And, taking in his arméd arms his son,
He prophesies the fall of Ilion.

ANOTHER ARGUMENT.

In Zeta, Hector prophesies;
Prays for his son; wills sacrifice.

THE stern fight freed of all the Gods, conquest with doubtful
    wings
Flew on their lances; ev'ry way the restless field she flings
Betwixt the floods of Simois and Xanthus, that confin'd
All their affairs at Ilion, and round about them shin'd.

* *Indifferent*—impartial.

The first that weigh'd down all the field, of one particular side, 5
Was Ajax, son of Telamon ; who, like a bulwark, plied
The Greeks' protection, and of Troy the knotty orders brake,
Held out a light to all the rest, and show'd them how to make
Way to their conquest.   He did wound the strongest man of Thrace,
The tallest and the biggest set, Eussorian Acamas ; 10
His lance fell on his casque's plum'd top, in stooping ; the fell head
Drave through his forehead to his jaws ; his eyes night shadow'd.
 Tydides slew Teuthranides Axylus, that did dwell
In fair Arisba's well-built tow'rs.   He had of wealth a well,
And yet was kind and bountiful ; he would a traveller pray 15
To be his guest, his friendly house stood in the broad highway,
In which he all sorts nobly us'd ; yet none of them would stand
'Twixt him and death, but both himself, and he that had command
Of his fair horse, Calesius, fell lifeless on the ground.
Euryalus, Opheltius and Dresus, dead did wound ; 20
Nor ended there his fi'ry course, which he again begins,
And ran to it successfully, upon a pair of twins,
Æsepus, and bold Pedasus, whom good Bucolion
(That first call'd father, though base-born, renown'd Laomedon)
On Nais Abarbaræa got, a nymph that, as she fed 25
Her curlèd flocks, Bucolion woo'd, and mix'd in love and bed.
Both these were spoil'd of arms and life, by Mecistiades.
 Then Polypœtes, for stern death, Astyalus did seize ;
Ulysses slew Percosius ; Teucer Aretaön ;
Antilochus (old Nestor's joy) Ablerus ; the great son 30
Of Atreüs, and king of men, Elatus, whose abode
He held at upper Pedasus, where Satnius' river flowed ;
The great heroë Leitus stay'd Phylacus in flight
From further life ; Eurypylus, Melanthius reft of light.
 The brother to the king of men, Adrestus took alive ; 35
Whose horse, affrighted with the flight, their driver now did drive

---

[35] *The brother*—Menelaus.

Amongst the low-grown tam'risk trees, and at an arm of one
The chariot in the draught-tree brake; the horse brake loose, and ron
The same way other flyers fled, contending all to town;
Himself close at the chariot wheel, upon his face was thrown, 40
And there lay flat, roll'd up in dust. Atrides inwards drave;
And, holding at his breast his lance, Adrestus sought to save
His head by losing of his feet, and trusting to his knees;
On which the same parts of the king he hugs, and offers fees
Of worthy value for his life, and thus pleads their receipt: 45
"Take me alive, O Atreus' son, and take a worthy weight
Of brass, elab'rate iron, and gold. A heap of precious things
Are in my father's riches hid, which, when your servant brings
News of my safety to his ears, he largely will divide
With your rare bounties." Atreus' son thought this the better side, 50
And meant to take it, being about to send him safe to fleet;
Which when, far off, his brother saw, he wing'd his royal feet,
And came in threat'ning, crying out: "O soft heart! What's the cause
Thou sparst these men thus? Have not they observ'd these gentle laws
Of mild humanity to thee, with mighty argument 55
Why thou shouldst deal thus; in thy house, and with all precedent
Of honour'd guest-rites, entertain'd? Not one of them shall fly
A bitter end for it from heav'n, and much less, dotingly,
'Scape our revengeful fingers; all, ev'n th' infant in the womb,
Shall taste of what they merited, and have no other tomb 60
Than razéd Ilion; nor their race have more fruit than the dust."
This just cause turn'd his brother's mind, who violently thrust
The pris'ner from him; in whose guts the king of men impress'd
His ashen lance, which (pitching down his foot upon the breast
Of him that upwards fell) he drew; then Nestor spake to all: 65
    "O friends, and household men of Mars, let not your pursuit fall,

  [39] The second folio reads,—
         "The same way *others* fled, contending all to town;"
omitting "*flyers*."
    [47] "This Virgil imitates."—CHAPMAN.   [55] *Argument*—example.

With those ye fell, for present spoil; nor, like the king of men,
Let any 'scape unfell'd; but on, dispatch them all, and then
Ye shall have time enough to spoil." This made so strong their chace,
That all the Trojans had been hous'd, and never turned a face, 70
Had not the Priamist Helenus, an augur most of name,
Will'd Hector and Æneas thus: "Hector! Anchises' fame!
Since on your shoulders, with good cause, the weighty burden lies
Of Troy and Lycia (being both of noblest faculties
For counsel, strength of hand, and apt to take chance at her best 75
In ev'ry turn she makes) stand fast, and suffer not the rest,
By any way search'd out for 'scape, to come within the ports,
Lest, fled into their wives' kind arms, they there be made the sports
Of the pursuing enemy. Exhort, and force your bands
To turn their faces; and, while we employ our ventur'd hands, 80
Though in a hard condition, to make the other stay,
Hector, go thou to Ilion, and our queen-mother pray
To take the richest robe she hath; the same that's chiefly dear
To her court fancy; with which gem, assembling more to her
Of Troy's chief matrons, let all go, for fear of all our fates, 85
To Pallas' temple, take the key, unlock the leavy gates,
Enter, and reach the highest tow'r, where her Palladium stands,
And on it put the precious veil with pure and rev'rend hands,
And vow to her, besides the gift, a sacrificing stroke
Of twelve fat heifers-of-a-year, that never felt the yoke, 90
(Most answ'ring to her maiden state) if she will pity us,
Our town, our wives, our youngest joys, and him, that plagues them thus,
Take from the conflict, Diomed, that fury in a fight,
That true son of great Tydeus, that cunning lord of flight,
Whom I esteem the strongest Greek; for we have never fled 95
Achilles, that is prince of men, and whom a Goddess bred,
Like him; his fury flies so high, and all men's wraths commands."
   Hector intends his brother's will, but first through all his bands

---

[86] *Leavy*—leafy, folding doors.
[99] *Intends*—attends to; a common use of the word in old writers.

He made quick way, encouraging; and all, to fear afraid,
All turn'd their heads, and made Greece turn. Slaughter stood still
       dismay'd   100
On their parts, for they thought some God, fall'n from the vault of
       stars,
Was rush'd into the Ilions' aid, they made such dreadful wars.
    Thus Hector, toiling in the waves, and thrusting back the flood
Of his ebb'd forces, thus takes leave : "So, so, now runs your blood
In his right current ; forwards now, Trojans, and far-call'd friends ! 105
Awhile hold out, till, for success to this your brave amends,
I haste to Ilion, and procure our counsellors and wives
To pray, and offer hecatombs, for their states in our lives."
    Then fair-helm'd Hector turn'd to Troy, and, as he trode the field,
The black bull's hide, that at his back he wore about his shield, 110
In the extreme circumference, was with his gait so rock'd,
That, being large, it both at once his neck and ankles knock'd.
    And now betwixt the hosts were met, Hippolochus' brave son,
Glaucus, who in his very look hope of some wonder won,
And little Tydeus' mighty heir; who seeing such a man   115
Offer the field, for usual blows, with wondrous words began :
    "What art thou, strong'st of mortal men, that putt'st so far before,
Whom these fights never show'd mine eyes? They have been
       evermore
Sons of unhappy parents born, that came within the length
Of this Minerva-guided lance, and durst close with the strength   120
That she inspires in me. If heav'n be thy divine abode,
And thou a Deity thus inform'd, no more with any God
Will I change lances. The strong son of Dryus did not live
Long after such a conflict dar'd, who godlessly did drive

    [102] *Ilions' aid.*—Chapman not infrequently uses Ilions for people of Ilion, or Troy. Probably a misprint for *Ilians.*
    [108] *Their states in our lives.*—This is a somewhat complicated expression. The meaning is probably, as Dr. Taylor says, "for their lives and properties which depend on our lives."

Nysæus' nurses through the hill made sacred to his name, 125
And called Nysseius; with a goad he punch'd each furious dame,
And made them ev'ry one cast down their green and leavy spears.
This th' homicide Lycurgus did; and those ungodly fears,
He put the froes in, seiz'd their God. Ev'n Bacchus he did drive
From his Nysseius; who was fain, with huge exclaims, to dive 130
Into the ocean. Thetis there in her bright bosom took
The flying Deity; who so fear'd Lycurgus' threats, he shook.
For which the freely-living Gods so highly were incens'd,
That Saturn's great Son strook him blind, and with his life dispens'd
But small time after; all because th' Immortals lov'd him not, 135
Nor lov'd him since he striv'd with them; and his end hath begot
Fear in my pow'rs to fight with heav'n. But, if the fruits of earth
Nourish thy body, and thy life be of our human birth,
Come near, that thou mayst soon arrive on that life-bounding shore,
To which I see thee hoise such sail." "Why dost thou so explore,"
Said Glaucus, "of what race I am, when like the race of leaves 141
The race of man is, that deserves no question; nor receives
My being any other breath? The wind in autumn strows
The earth with old leaves, then the spring the woods with new endows;
And so death scatters men on earth, so life puts out again 145
Man's leavy issue. But my race, if, like the course of men,
Thou seek'st in more particular terms, 'tis this, to many known:
In midst of Argos, nurse of horse, there stands a walléd town,
Ephyré, where the mansion-house of Sisyphus did stand,
Of Sisyphus-Æölides, most wise of all the land. 150
Glaucus was son to him, and he begat Bellerophon,
Whose body heav'n indu'd with strength, and put a beauty on,

---

[125] *Nysæus*—Bacchus.
[127] *Leavy spears*—the thyrsi, or wands, of the Bacchanals.
[129] "*Froes*—for frows, Dutch for women.
'Buxom as Bacchus' *froes*, revelling and dancing.'
BEAUM. AND FLETCHER."—NARES.
[134] *Him*—Lycurgus. [146] *Leavy*—leafy. [149] *Ephyré*—Corinth.

THE SIXTH BOOK

Exceeding lovely.   Prœtus yet his cause of love did hate,
And banish'd him the town ; he might ; he rul'd the Argive state.
The virtue of the one Jove plac'd beneath the other's pow'r, 155
His exile grew, since he denied to be the paramour
Of fair Anteia, Prœtus' wife, who felt a raging fire
Of secret love to him ; but he, whom wisdom did inspire
As well as prudence, (one of them advising him to shun
The danger of a princess' love, the other not to run 160
Within the danger of the Gods, the act being simply ill,)
Still entertaining thoughts divine, subdu'd the earthly still.
She, rul'd by neither of his wits, preferr'd her lust to both,
And, false to Prœtus, would seem true, with this abhorr'd untroth :
"Prœtus, or die thyself," said she, "or let Bellerophon die. 165
He urg'd dishonour to thy bed ; which since I did deny,
He thought his violence should grant, and sought thy shame by
　　force."
The king, incens'd with her report, resolv'd upon her course,
But doubted how it should be run ; he shunn'd his death direct,
(Holding a way so near not safe) and plotted the effect 170
By sending him with letters seal'd (that, open'd, touch his life)
To Rhëuns king of Lycia, and father to his wife.
He went ; and happily he went, the Gods walk'd all his way ;
And being arriv'd in Lycia, where Xanthus doth display

[153] "*His cause of love*—his personal beauty."—TAYLOR.
[156] *His exile grew*—the origin of his exile was, &c.
[171] "*Bellerophontis literœ. Ad. Eras.* This long speech many critics tax as untimely, being, as they take it, in the heat of fight ; Hier. Vidas, a late observer, being eagerest against Homer. Whose ignorance in this I cannot but note, and prove to you ; for, besides the authority and office of a poet, to vary and quicken his poem with these episodes, sometimes beyond the leisure of their actions, the critic notes not how far his forerunner prevents his worst as far ; and sets down his speech at the sudden and strange turning of the Trojan field, set on a little before by Hector ; and that so fiercely, it made an admiring stand among the Grecians, and therein gave fit time for these great captains to utter their admirations, the whole field in that part being to stand like their commanders. And then how full of decorum this gallant show and speech was to sound understandings, I leave only to such, and let our critics go cavil."—CHAPMAN.

The silver ensigns of his waves, the king of that broad land 175
Receiv'd him with a wondrous free and honourable hand.
Nine days he feasted him, and kill'd an ox in ev'ry day,
In thankful sacrifice to heav'n, for his fair guest; whose stay,
With rosy fingers, brought the world, the tenth well-welcom'd morn,
And then the king did move to see, the letters he had borne 180
From his lov'd son-in-law; which seen, he wrought thus their contents:
Chimæra, the invincible, he sent him to convince,
Sprung from no man, but mere divine; a lion's shape before,
Behind a dragon's, in the midst a goat's shagg'd form, she bore,
And flames of deadly fervency flew from her breath and eyes; 185
Yet her he slew; his confidence in sacred prodigies
Render'd him victor. Then he gave his second conquest way
Against the famous Solymi, when (he himself would say,
Reporting it) he enter'd on a passing vig'rous fight.
His third huge labour he approv'd against a woman's spite, 190
That fill'd a field of Amazons; he overcame them all.
Then set they on him sly Deceit, when Force had such a fall;
An ambush of the strongest men, that spacious Lycia bred,
Was lodg'd for him; whom he lodg'd sure, they never rais'd a head.
His deeds thus showing him deriv'd from some celestial race, 195
The king detain'd, and made amends, with doing him the grace
Of his fair daughter's princely gift; and with her, for a dow'r,
Gave half his kingdom; and to this, the Lycians on did pour
More than was giv'n to any king; a goodly planted field,
In some parts thick of groves and woods, the rest rich crops did yield.
This field the Lycians futurely (of future wand'rings there 201
And other errors of their prince, in the unhappy rear

 182 *Convince*—overcome.
185 The second folio reads,—
"And flames of fervency flew from her breath and eyes;" omitting (obviously erroneously) *deadly*.
201 "*This field the Lycians futurely, &c.*—Chapman has transposed the clauses of the history to accommodate the theory of some commentators who assert that 'the field of wandering' was the original demesne assigned to Bellerophon."
COOKE TAYLOR.

Of his sad life) the Errant call'd. The princess brought him forth
Three children (whose ends griev'd him more, the more they were of
    worth)
Isander; and Hippolochus; and fair Laodomy,   205
With whom, ev'n Jupiter himself left heav'n itself, to lie,
And had by her the man at arms, Sarpedon, call'd divine.
The Gods then left him, lest a man should in their glories shine,
And set against him; for his son, Isandrus, in a strife
Against the valiant Solymi, Mars reft of light and life;   210
Laodamïa, being envied of all the Goddesses,
The golden-bridle-handling Queen, the maiden Patroness,
Slew with an arrow; and for this he wander'd evermore
Alone through this his Aleian field, and fed upon the core
Of his sad bosom, flying all the loth'd consórts of men.   215
Yet had he one surviv'd to him, of those three childeren,
Hippolochus, the root of me; who sent me here with charge
That I should always bear me well, and my deserts enlarge
Beyond the vulgar, lest I sham'd my race, that far excell'd
All that Ephyra's famous tow'rs, or ample Lycia, held.   220
This is my stock, and this am I." This cheer'd Tydides' heart,
Who pitch'd his spear down, lean'd, and talk'd in this affectionate part:
   "Certés, in thy great ancestor, and in mine own, thou art
A guest of mine, right ancient. King Oeneus twenty days
Detain'd, with feasts, Bellerophon, whom all the world did praise.   225
Betwixt whom mutual gifts were giv'n. My grandsire gave to thine
A girdle of Phœnician work, impurpl'd wondrous fine.
Thine gave a two-neck'd jug of gold, which, though I use not here,
Yet still it is my gem at home. But, if our fathers were
Familiar, or each other knew, I know not, since my sire   230
Left me a child, at siege of Thebes, where he left his life's fire.
But let us prove our grandsires' sons, and be each other's guests.
To Lycia when I come, do thou receive thy friend with feasts;

₂₁₂ Diana.

Peloponnesus, with the like, shall thy wish'd presence greet.
Mean space, shun we each other here, though in the press we meet.
There are enow of Troy beside, and men enow renown'd, 235
To right my pow'rs, whomever heav'n shall let my lance confound.
So are there of the Greeks for thee; kill who thou canst. And now,
For sign of amity 'twixt us, and that all these may know
We glory in th' hospitious rites our grandsires did commend, 240
Change we our arms before them all." From horse then both descend,
Join hands, give faith, and take; and then did Jupiter elate
The mind of Glaucus, who, to show his rev'rence to the state
Of virtue in his grandsire's heart, and gratulate beside
The offer of so great a friend, exchang'd, in that good pride, 245
Curets of gold for those of brass, that did on Diomed shine,
One of a hundred oxen's price, the other but of nine.

By this, had Hector reach'd the ports of Scæa, and the tow'rs.
About him flock'd the wives of Troy, the children, paramours,
Inquiring how their husbands did, their fathers, brothers, loves. 250
He stood not then to answer them, but said: "It now behoves
Ye should all go t' implore the aid of heav'n, in a distress
Of great effect, and imminent." Then hasted he access
To Priam's goodly builded court, which round about was run
With walking porches, galleries, to keep off rain and sun. 255
Within, of one side, on a rew, of sundry-colour'd stones,
Fifty fair lodgings were built out, for Priam's fifty sons,
And for as fair sort of their wives; and, in the opposite view,
Twelve lodgings of like stone, like height, were likewise built arew,

---

[242] "Φρένας ἐξέλετο Ζεὺς, *Mentem ademit Jup.*, the text hath it; which only I alter of all Homer's original, since Plutarch against the Stoics excuses this supposed folly in Glaucus. Spondanus likewise encouraging my alterations, which I use for the loved and simple nobility of the free exchange in Glaucus, contrary to others that, for the supposed folly in Glaucus, turned his change into a proverb, χρύσεα χαλκείων, golden for brazen."— CHAPMAN.

[256] *Rew*—row.

Where, with their fair and virtuous wives, twelve princes, sons in law
To honourable Priam, lay. And here met Hecuba, 261
The loving mother, her great son ; and with her needs must be
The fairest of her female race, the bright Laodice.
The queen gript hard her Hector's hand, and said : "O worthiest son,
Why leav'st thou field ? Is't not because the cursed nation 265
Afflict our countrymen and friends ? They are their moans that move
Thy mind to come and lift thy hands, in his high tow'r, to Jove.
But stay a little, that myself may fetch our sweetest wine
To offer first to Jupiter, then that these joints of thine
May be refresh'd ; for, woe is me, how thou art toil'd and spent ! 270
Thou for our city's gen'ral state, thou for our friends far sent,
Must now the press of fight endure ; now solitude, to call
Upon the name of Jupiter ; thou only for us all.
But wine will something comfort thee ; for to a man dismay'd
With careful spirits, or too much with labour overlaid, 275
Wine brings much rescue, strength'ning much the body and the mind."
   The great helm-mover thus receiv'd the auth'ress of his kind :
"My royal mother, bring no wine ; lest rather it impair
Than help my strength, and make my mind forgetful of th' affair
Committed to it ; and (to pour it out in sacrifice) 280
I fear with unwash'd hands to serve the pure-liv'd Deities.
Nor is it lawful, thus imbru'd with blood and dust, to prove
The will of heav'n, or offer vows to cloud-compelling Jove.
I only come to use your pains (assembling other dames,
Matrons, and women honour'd most, with high and virtuous names) 285
With wine and odours, and a robe most ample, most of price,
And which is dearest in your love, to offer sacrifice
In Pallas' temple ; and to put the precious robe ye bear.
On her Palladium ; vowing all, twelve oxen-of-a-year,
Whose necks were never wrung with yoke, shall pay her grace their lives,
If she will pity our seig'd town ; pity ourselves, our wives ; 291

              275 *Careful*—anxious.

Pity our children; and remove, from sacred Ilion,
The dreadful soldier Diomed. And, when yourselves are gone
About this work, myself will go, to call into the field,
If he will hear me, Helen's love; whom would the earth would yield, 295
And headlong take into her gulf, ev'n quick before mine eyes;
For then my heart, I hope, would cast her load of miseries,
Borne for the plague he hath been born, and bred to the deface,
By great Olympius, of Troy, our sire, and all our race."
 This said, grave Hecuba went home, and sent her maids about, 300
To bid the matrons. She herself descended, and search'd out,
Within a place that breath'd perfumes, the richest robe she had;
Which lay with many rich ones more, most curiously made
By women of Sidonia; which Paris brought from thence,
Sailing the broad sea, when he made that voyage of offence, 305
In which he brought home Helena. That robe, transferr'd so far,
(That was the undermost) she took; it glitter'd like a star;
And with it went she to the fane, with many ladies more;
Amongst whom fair-cheek'd Theano unlock'd the folded door;
Chaste Theano, Antenor's wife, and of Cisseus' race, 310
Sister to Hecuba, both born to that great king of Thrace.
Her th' Ilions made Minerva's priest; and her they follow'd all
Up to the temple's highest tow'r, where on their knees they fall,
Lift up their hands, and fill the fane with ladies' piteous cries.
Then lovely Theano took the veil, and with it she implies 315
The great Palladium, praying thus: "Goddess of most renown
In all the heav'n of Goddesses, great Guardian of our town,
Rev'rend Minerva, break the lance of Diomed, cease his grace,
Give him to fall in shameful flight, headlong, and on his face,
Before our ports of Ilion, that instantly we may, 320
Twelve unyok'd oxen-of-a-year, in this thy temple slay,
To thy sole honour; take their bloods, and banish our offence;
Accept Troy's zeal, her wives, and save our infants' innocence."

[315] *Implies*—enfolds.

She pray'd, but Pallas would not grant. Mean space was Hector come
Where Alexander's lodgings were, that many a goodly room 325
Had built in them by architects, of Troy's most curious sort,
And were no lodgings, but a house; nor no house, but a court;
Or had all these contain'd in them; and all within a tow'r,
Next Hector's lodgings and the king's. The lov'd of heav'n's chief
      Pow'r,
Hector, here enter'd. In his hand a goodly lance he bore, 330
Ten cubits long; the brazen head went shining in before,
Help'd with a burnish'd ring of gold. He found his brother then
Amongst the women, yet prepar'd to go amongst the men,
For in their chamber he was set, trimming his arms, his shield,
His curets, and was trying how his crookéd bow would yield 335
To his straight arms. Amongst her maids was set the Argive Queen,
Commanding them in choicest works. When Hector's eye had seen
His brother thus accompanied, and that he could not bear
The very touching of his arms but where the women were,
And when the time so needed men, right cunningly he chid. 340
That he might do it bitterly, his cowardice he hid,
That simply made him so retir'd, beneath an anger, feign'd
In him by Hector, for the hate the citizens sustain'd
Against him, for the foil he took in their cause; and again,
For all their gen'ral foils in his. So Hector seems to plain 345
Of his wrath to them, for their hate, and not his cowardice;
As that were it that shelter'd him in his effeminacies,
And kept him, in that dang'rous time, from their fit aid in fight;
For which he chid thus: "Wretched man! So timeless is thy spite

---

[335] *Argive Queen*—Helen, formerly Argive queen.
[345] *Plain*—complain.
[346] "Hector dissembles the cowardice he finds in Paris; turning it, as if he chid him for his anger at the Trojans for hating him, being conquered by Menelaus, when it is for his effeminacy. Which is all paraphrastical in my translation."—CHAPMAN.
[349] *Timeless*—untimely.
    "Poison I see has been his *timeless* end."—*Romeo and Jul.* v. 5.

That 'tis not honest; and their hate is just, 'gainst which it bends. 350
War burns about the town for thee; for thee our slaughter'd friends
Besiege Troy with their carcasses, on whose heaps our high walls
Are overlook'd by enemies; the sad sounds of their falls
Without, are echo'd with the cries of wives and babes within;
And all for thee; and yet for them thy honour cannot win 355
Head of thine anger. Thou shouldst need no spirit to stir up thine,
But thine should set the rest on fire, and with a rage divine
Chastise impartially the best, that impiously forbears.
Come forth, lest thy fair tow'rs and Troy be burn'd about thine ears."
    Paris acknowledg'd, as before, all just that Hector spake, 360
Allowing justice, though it were for his injustice' sake;
And where his brother put a wrath upon him by his art,
He takes it, for his honour's sake, as sprung out of his heart,
And rather would have anger seem his fault than cowardice;
And thus he answer'd: "Since, with right, you join'd check with advice,
And I hear you, give equal ear: It is not any spleen 366
Against the town, as you conceive, that makes me so unseen,
But sorrow for it; which to ease, and by discourse digest
Within myself, I live so close; and yet, since men might wrest
My sad retreat, like you, my wife with her advice inclin'd 370
This my addression to the field; which was mine own free mind,
As well as th' instance of her words; for though the foil were mine,
Conquest brings forth her wreaths by turns. Stay then this haste of thine
But till I arm, and I am made a cónsort for thee straight;—
Or go, I'll overtake thy haste." Helen stood at receipt, 375

    366 Dr. Taylor has printed "care," but probably through an oversight.
    372 *Foil*—defeat; alluding to the fight with Menelaus.
    375 *Stood at receipt.*—Dr. Taylor has strangely misunderstood this passage, when he says "*stood as to cover her husband's confusion*," which was the very thing she did not wish to do. The meaning is simply "*stood at hand,*" "*stood by,* or *ready.*" The next line would seem to be, "and took up Hector's powerful arguments to enforce her own words, which left Paris no escape;" but it might mean, as Dr. Taylor says, "occupied Hector's attention" by her speech. The whole passage is an interpolation by Chapman.

And took up all great Hector's pow'rs, t' attend her heavy words,
By which had Paris no reply. This vent her grief affords:
"Brother (if I may call you so, that had been better born
A dog, than such a horrid dame, as all men curse and scorn,
A mischief-maker, a man-plague) O would to God, the day,   380
That first gave light to me, had been a whirlwind in my way,
And borne me to some desert hill, or hid me in the rage
Of earth's most far-resounding seas, ere I should thus engage
The dear lives of so many friends! Yet since the Gods have been
Helpless foreseers of my plagues, they might have likewise seen   385
That he they put in yoke with me, to bear out their award,
Had been a man of much more spirit, and, or had noblier dar'd
To shield mine honour with this deed, or with his mind had known
Much better the upbraids of men, that so he might have shown
(More like a man) some sense of grief for both my shame and his.   390
But he is senseless, nor conceives what any manhood is,
Nor now, nor ever after will; and therefore hangs, I fear,
A plague above him. But come near, good brother; rest you here,
Who, of the world of men, stands charg'd with most unrest for me,
(Vile wretch) and for my lover's wrong; on whom a destiny   395
So bitter is impos'd by Jove, that all succeeding times
Will put, to our unended shames, in all men's mouths our crimes."
    He answer'd: "Helen, do not seek to make me sit with thee;
I must not stay, though well I know thy honour'd love of me.
My mind calls forth to aid our friends, in whom my absence breeds   400
Longings to see me; for whose sakes, importune thou to deeds
This man by all means, that your care may make his own make hast,
And meet me in the open town, that all may see at last
He minds his lover. I myself will now go home, and see
My household, my dear wife, and son, that little hope of me;   405
For, sister, 'tis without my skill, if I shall evermore
Return, and see them, or to earth, her right in me, restore.

    385 *Helpless*—unaiding.
    406 *Without my skill*—beyond my knowledge, more than I know.

The Gods may stoop me by the Greeks." This said, he went to see
The virtuous princess, his true wife, white-arm'd Andromache.
She, with her infant son and maid, was climb'd the tow'r, about 410
The sight of him that sought for her, weeping and crying out.
Hector, not finding her at home, was going forth ; retir'd ;
Stood in the gate ; her woman call'd, and curiously inquir'd
Where she was gone ; bad tell him true, if she were gone to see
His sisters, or his brothers' wives ; or whether she should be 415
At temple with the other dames, t' implore Minerva's ruth.

Her woman answer'd : Since he ask'd, and urg'd so much the truth,
The truth was she was neither gone, to see his brothers' wives,
His sisters, nor t' implore the ruth of Pallas on their lives ;
But she (advertis'd of the bane Troy suffer'd, and how vast 420
Conquest had made herself for Greece) like one distraught, made hast
To ample Ilion with her son, and nurse, and all the way
Mourn'd, and dissolv'd in tears for him. Then Hector made no stay,
But trod her path, and through the streets, magnificently built,
All the great city pass'd, and came where, seeing how blood was spilt,
Andromache might see him come : who made as he would pass 425
The ports without saluting her, not knowing where she was.
She, with his sight, made breathless haste, to meet him ; she, whose grace
Brought him withal so great a dow'r ; she that of all the race
Of king Aëtion only liv'd ; Aëtion, whose house stood 430
Beneath the mountain Placius, environ'd with the wood
Of Theban Hypoplace, being court to the Cilician land.
She ran to Hector, and with her, tender of heart and hand,
Her son, borne in his nurse's arms ; when, like a heav'nly sign,
Compact of many golden stars, the princely child did shine, 435
Whom Hector call'd Scamandrius, but whom the town did name
Astyanax, because his sire did only prop the same.
Hector, though grief bereft his speech, yet smil'd upon his joy.
Andromache cried out, mix'd hands, and to the strength of Troy

[408] *Stoop me by the Greeks*—cause me to succumb to the Greeks.

Thus wept forth her affection : " O noblest in desire ! 440
Thy mind, inflam'd with others' good, will set thyself on fire.
Nor pitiest thou thy son, nor wife, who must thy widow be,
If now thou issue ; all the field will only run on thee.
Better my shoulders underwent the earth, than thy decease ;
For then would earth bear joys no more ; then comes the black increase
Of griefs (like Greeks on Ilion). Alas ! What one survives 445
To be my refuge ? One black day bereft sev'n brothers' lives,
By stern Achilles ; by his hand my father breath'd his last,
His high-wall'd rich Cilician Thebes sack'd by him, and laid wast ;
The royal body yet he left unspoil'd ; religion charm'd 450
That act of spoil ; and all in fire he burn'd him cómplete arm'd ;
Built over him a royal tomb ; and to the monument
He left of him, th' Oreades (that are the high descent
Of Ægis-bearing Jupiter) another of their own
Did add to it, and set it round with elms ; by which is shown, 455
In theirs, the barrenness of death ; yet might it serve beside
To shelter the sad monument from all the ruffinous pride
Of storms and tempests, us'd to hurt things of that noble kind.
The short life yet my mother liv'd he sav'd, and serv'd his mind
With all the riches of the realm ; which not enough esteem'd, 460
He kept her pris'ner ; whom small time, but much more wealth, redeem'd,
And she, in sylvan Hypoplace, Cilicia rul'd again,
But soon was over-rul'd by death ; Diana's chaste disdain
Gave her a lance, and took her life. Yet, all these gone from me,
Thou amply render'st all ; thy life makes still my father be, 465
My mother, brothers ; and besides thou art my husband too,
Most lov'd, most worthy. Pity then, dear love, and do not go,
For thou gone, all these go again ; pity our common joy,
Lest, of a father's patronage, the bulwark of all Troy,

⁴⁴⁹ " Thebes, a most rich city of Cilicia."—CHAPMAN.
⁴⁵⁷ The second folio (which Dr. Taylor follows) reads " *said* monument ; " an evident typographical error.

Thou leav'st him a poor widow's charge. Stay, stay then, in this tow'r,
And call up to the wild fig-tree all thy retiréd pow'r; 471
For there the wall is easiest scal'd, and fittest for surprise,
And there, th' Ajaces, Idomen, th' Atrides, Diomed, thrice
Have both survey'd and made attempt; I know not if induc'd
By some wise augury, or the fact was naturally infus'd 475
Into their wits, or courages." To this, great Hector said:
"Be well assur'd, wife, all these things in my kind cares are weigh'd.
But what a shame, and fear, it is to think how Troy would scorn
(Both in her husbands, and her wives, whom long-train'd gowns adorn)
That I should cowardly fly off! The spirit I first did breath 480
Did never teach me that; much less, since the contempt of death
Was settled in me, and my mind knew what a worthy was,
Whose office is to lead in fight, and give no danger pass
Without improvement. In this fire must Hector's trial shine;
Here must his country, father, friends, be, in him, made divine. 485
And such a stormy day shall come (in mind and soul I know)
When sacred Troy shall shed her tow'rs, for tears of overthrow;
When Priam, all his birth and pow'r, shall in those tears be drown'd.
But neither Troy's posterity so much my soul doth wound,
Priam, nor Hecuba herself, nor all my brothers' woes, 490
(Who though so many, and so good, must all be food for foes)
As thy sad state; when some rude Greek shall lead thee weeping hence,
These free days clouded, and a night of captive violence
Loading thy temples, out of which thine eyes must never see,
But spin the Greek wives' webs of task, and their fetch-water be 495
To Argos, from Messeides, or clear Hyperia's spring;
Which howsoever thou abhorr'st, Fate's such a shrewish thing
She will be mistress; whose curs'd hands, when they shall crush out cries
From thy oppressions (being beheld by other enemies)

493 *Free days*—The second folio has "*three* days;" a misprint.
496 "The names of two fountains: of which one in Thessaly, the other near Argos, or, according to others, in Peloponnesus or Lacedæmon."—CHAPMAN.
497 *Shrewish*—cursed, malicious.

Thus they will nourish thy extremes: 'This dame was Hector's wife,
A man that, at the wars of Troy, did breathe the worthiest life   501
Of all their army.' This again will rub thy fruitful wounds,
To miss the man that to thy bands could give such narrow bounds.
But that day shall not wound mine eyes; the solid heap of night
Shall interpose, and stop mine ears against thy plaints, and plight."

 This said, he reach'd to take his son; who, of his arms afraid,   506
And then the horse-hair plume, with which he was so overlaid,
Nodded so horribly, he cling'd back to his nurse, and cried.
Laughter affected his great sire, who doff'd, and laid aside
His fearful helm, that on the earth cast round about it light;   510
Then took and kiss'd his loving son, and (balancing his weight
In dancing him) these loving vows to living Jove he us'd,
And all the other bench of Gods: "O you that have infus'd
Soul to this infant, now set down this blessing on his star;—
Let his renown be clear as mine; equal his strength in war;   515
And make his reign so strong in Troy, that years to come may yield
His facts this fame, when, rich in spoils, he leaves the conquer'd field
Sown with his slaughters: 'These high deeds exceed his father's
   worth.'
And let this echo'd praise supply the comforts to come forth
Of his kind mother with my life." This said, th' heroic sire   520
Gave him his mother; whose fair eyes fresh streams of love's salt fire
Billow'd on her soft cheeks, to hear the last of Hector's speech,
In which his vows compris'd the sum of all he did beseech
In her wish'd comfort. So she took into her od'rous breast
Her husband's gift; who, mov'd to see her heart so much oppress'd,
He dried her tears, and thus desir'd: "Afflict me not, dear wife,   526
With these vain griefs. He doth not live, that can disjoin my life
And this firm bosom, but my fate; and fate, whose wings can fly?
Noble, ignoble, fate controls. Once born, the best must die.

 [503] *To miss the man, &c.*—To miss him who could soon put an end or stop to your slavery.

Go home, and set thy housewif'ry on these extremes of thought; 530
And drive war from them with thy maids; keep them from doing nought.
These will be nothing; leave the cares of war to men, and me
In whom, of all the Ilion race, they take their high'st degree."

On went his helm; his princess home, half cold with kindly fears;
When ev'ry fear turn'd back her looks, and ev'ry look shed tears. 535
Foe-slaught'ring Hector's house soon reach'd, her many women there
Wept all to see her: in his life great Hector's fun'rals were;
Never look'd any eye of theirs to see their lord safe home,
'Scap'd from the gripes and pow'rs of Greece. And now was Paris come
From his high tow'rs; who made no stay, when once he had put on 540
His richest armour, but flew forth; the flints he trod upon
Sparkled with lustre of his arms; his long-ebb'd spirits now flow'd
The higher for their lower ebb. And as a fair steed, proud
With full-giv'n mangers, long tied up, and now, his head-stall broke,
He breaks from stable, runs the field, and with an ample stroke 545
Measures the centre, neighs, and lifts aloft his wanton head,
About his shoulders shakes his crest, and where he hath been fed,
Or in some calm flood wash'd, or, stung with his high plight, he flies
Amongst his females, strength put forth, his beauty beautifies,
And, like life's mirror, bears his gait; so Paris from the tow'r 550
Of lofty Pergamus came forth; he show'd a sun-like pow'r
In carriage of his goodly parts, address'd now to the strife;
And found his noble brother near the place he left his wife.
Him thus respected he salutes: "Right worthy, I have fear
That your so serious haste to field, my stay hath made forbear, 555
And that I come not as you wish." He answer'd: "Honour'd man,
Be confident, for not myself, nor any others, can
Reprove in thee the work of fight, at least, not any such
As is an equal judge of things; for thou hast strength as much

---

[543] "His simile, high and expressive; which Virgil almost word for word hath translated, Æn. XI. (v. 492)."—CHAPMAN.

As serves to execute a mind very important, but 600
Thy strength too readily flies off, enough will is not put
To thy ability. My heart is in my mind's strife sad,
When Troy (out of her much distress, she and her friends have had
By thy procurement) doth deprave thy noblesse in mine ears.
But come, hereafter we shall calm these hard conceits of theirs, 605
When, from their ports the foe expuls'd, high Jove to them hath giv'n
Wish'd peace, and us free sacrifice to all the Powers of heav'n."

⁶⁰⁰ *Important*—full of anxiety, restless.
⁶⁰⁴ *Noblesse.*—The second folio has "*noblenesse,*" which Dr. Taylor adopts; but the earlier reading is manifestly the true one. So *ablesse*, Bk. v. 248.

THE END OF THE SIXTH BOOK.

THE SEVENTH BOOK OF HOMER'S ILIADS.*

THE ARGUMENT.

HECTOR, by Helenus' advice, doth seek
Advent'rous combat on the boldest Greek.
Nine Greeks stand up, acceptants ev'ry one,
But lot selects strong Ajax Telamon.
Both, with high honour, stand th' important fight,
Till heralds part them by approached night.
Lastly, they grave the dead. The Greeks erect
A mighty wall, their navy to protect ;
Which angers Neptune. Jove, by hapless signs,
In depth of night, succeeding woes divines.

ANOTHER ARGUMENT.

In Eta, Priam's strongest son
Combats with Ajax Telamon.

HIS said, brave Hector through the ports, with Troy's
    bane-bringing knight,
Made issue to th' insatiate field, resolv'd to fervent fight.
And as the Weather-wielder sends to seamen prosp'rous
    gales,
When with their sallow polish'd oars, long lifted from their falls,

---

* "These next four books have not my last hand ; and because the rest (for a time) will be sufficient to employ your censures, suspend them of these. Spare not the other."—CHAPMAN.

Their wearied arms, dissolv'd with toil, can scarce strike one stroke more ;
Like those sweet winds appear'd these lords, to Trojans tir'd before. 6
Then fell they to the works of death. By Paris' valour fell
King Arëithous' hapless son, that did in Arna dwell,
Menesthius, whose renownéd sire a club did ever bear,
And of Phylomedusa gat, that had her eyes so clear, 10
This slaughter'd issue. Hector's dart strook Eionëus dead ;
Beneath his good steel casque it pierc'd, above his gorget-stead.
Glaucus, Hippolochus's son, that led the Lycian crew,
Iphinous-Dexiades with sudden jav'lin slew,
As he was mounting to his horse ; his shoulders took the spear, 15
And ere he sate, in tumbling down, his pow'rs dissolvéd were.
 When grey-ey'd Pallas had perceiv'd the Greeks so fall in fight,
From high Olympus' top she stoop'd, and did on Ilion light.
Apollo, to encounter her, to Pergamus did fly,
From whence he, looking to the field, wish'd Trojans' victory. 20
At Jove's broad beech these Godheads met ; and first Jove's son objects :
"Why, burning in contention thus, do thy extreme affects
Conduct thee from our peaceful hill? Is it to oversway
The doubtful victory of fight, and give the Greeks the day ?
Thou never pitiest perishing Troy. Yet now let me persuade, 25
That this day no more mortal wounds may either side invade.
Hereafter, till the end of Troy, they shall apply the fight,
Since your immortal wills resolve to overturn it quite."
 Pallas replied : "It likes me well ; for this came I from heav'n ;
But to make either armies cease, what order shall be giv'n ?" 30
He said : "We will direct the spirit, that burns in Hector's breast,
To challenge any Greek to wounds, with single pow'rs impress'd ;
Which Greeks, admiring, will accept, and make some one stand out
So stout a challenge to receive, with a defence as stout."
It is confirm'd ; and Helenus (king Priam's lovéd seed) 35
By augury discern'd th' event that these two pow'rs decreed,

[12] *Gorget-stead.*—See Bk. v. 538.   [22] *Affects.*—See Bk. I. 209.

And greeting Hector ask'd him this: "Wilt thou be once advis'd?
I am thy brother, and thy life with mine is ev'nly prized.
Command the rest of Troy and Greece, to cease this public fight,
And, what Greek bears the greatest mind, to single strokes excite.   40
I promise thee that yet thy soul shall not descend to fates;
So heard I thy survival cast, by the celestial States."
Hector with glad allowance gave his brother's counsel ear,
And, fronting both the hosts, advanc'd just in the midst his spear.
The Trojans instantly surcease; the Greeks Atrides stay'd.   45
The God that bears the silver bow, and war's triumphant Maid,
On Jove's beech like two vultures sat, pleas'd to behold both parts
Flow in to hear, so sternly arm'd with huge shields, helms, and
    darts.
And such fresh horror as you see, driv'n through the wrinkled waves
By rising Zephyr, under whom the sea grows black, and raves;   50
Such did the hasty gath'ring troops of both hosts make to hear;
Whose tumult settled, 'twixt them both, thus spake the challenger:
  "Hear, Trojans, and ye well-arm'd Greeks, what my strong mind,
    diffus'd
Through all my spirits, commands me speak: Saturnius hath not us'd
His promis'd favour for our truce, but, studying both our ills,   55
Will never cease, till Mars, by you, his rav'nous stomach fills
With ruin'd Troy, or we consume your mighty sea-borne fleet.
Since then the gen'ral peers of Greece in reach of one voice meet,
Amongst you all, whose breast includes the most impulsive mind,
Let him stand forth as combatant, by all the rest design'd.   60
Before whom thus I call high Jove, to witness of our strife:—
If he with home-thrust iron can reach th' exposure of my life,
Spoiling my arms, let him at will convey them to his tent,
But let my body be return'd, that Troy's two-sex'd descent
May waste it in the fun'ral pile. If I can slaughter him,   65
Apollo honouring me so much, I'll spoil his conquer'd limb,

    [49] *Horror*—in the classical sense of any thing that bristles up.

And bear his arms to Ilion, where in Apollo's shrine
I'll hang them, as my trophies due; his body I'll resign
To be disposèd by his friends in flamy funerals,
And honour'd with erected tomb, where Hellespontus falls   70
Into Ægæum, and doth reach ev'n to your naval road,
That, when our beings in the earth shall hide their period,
Survivors, sailing the black sea, may thus his name renew:
'This is his monument, whose blood long since did fates imbrue,
Whom, passing far in fortitude, illustrate Hector slew.'   75
This shall posterity report, and my fame never die."

  This said, dumb silence seiz'd them all; they shamèd to deny,
And fear'd to undertake. At last did Menelaus speak,
Check'd their remissness, and so sigh'd, as if his heart would break:
"Ah me! But only threat'ning Greeks, not worthy Grecian names!   80
This more and more, not to be borne, makes grow our huge defames,
If Hector's honourable proof be entertain'd by none.
But you are earth and water all, which, symboliz'd in one,
Have fram'd your faint unfi'ry spirits; ye sit without your hearts,
Grossly inglorious; but myself will use acceptive darts,   85
And arm against him, though you think I arm 'gainst too much
  odds;
But conquest's garlands hang aloft, amongst th' immortal Gods."

  He arm'd, and gladly would have fought; but, Menelaus, then,
By Hector's far more strength, thy soul had fled th' abodes of men,
Had not the kings of Greece stood up, and thy attempt restrain'd;   90
And ev'n the king of men himself, that in such compass reign'd,
Who took him by the bold right hand, and sternly pluck'd him back:
"Mad brother, 'tis no work for thee, thou seek'st thy wilful wrack!
Contain, though it despite thee much, nor for this strife engage
Thy person with a man more strong, and whom all fear t' enrage;   95

---

  ⁷⁵ *Illustrate.*—The second folio (followed by Dr. Taylor) has "*illustrious.*"
See Bk. VIII. 252.
  ⁸⁰ "*O verè Phrygiæ, neque enim Phryges;* saith his imitator."—CHAPMAN.

Yea whom Æacides himself, in men-renowning war,
Makes doubt t' encounter, whose huge strength surpasseth thine by
    far.
Sit thou then by thy regiment; some other Greek will rise
(Though he be dreadless, and no war will his desires suffice,
That makes this challenge to our strength) our valours to avow;   100
To whom, if he can 'scape with life, he will be glad to bow."
    This drew his brother from his will, who yielded, knowing it true,
And his glad soldiers took his arms; when Nestor did pursue
The same reproof he set on foot, and thus supplied his turn:
" What huge indignity is this! How will our country mourn!   105
Old Peleus that good king will weep, that worthy counsellor,
That trumpet of the Myrmidons, who much did ask me for
All men of name that went to Troy; with joy he did inquire
Their valour and their towardness, and I made him admire;
But, that ye all fear Hector now, if his grave ears shall hear,   110
How will he lift his hands to heav'n, and pray that death may bear
His grievéd soul into the deep! O would to heav'n's great King,
Minerva, and the God of light, that now my youthful spring
Did flourish in my willing veins, as when at Phæa's tow'rs,
About the streams of Jardanus, my gather'd Pylean pow'rs,   115
And dart-employ'd Arcadians, fought, near raging Celadon!
Amongst whom, first of all stood forth great Ereuthalion,
Who th' arms of Arëithoüs wore, brave Arëithoüs,
And, since he still fought with a club, surnam'd Clavigerus,
All men, and fair-girt ladies both, for honour call'd him so.   120
He fought not with a keep-off spear, or with a far-shot bow,
But, with a massy club of iron, he broke through arméd bands.
And yet Lycurgus was his death, but not with force of hands;
With sleight (encount'ring in a lane, where his club wanted sway)
He thrust him through his spacious waist; who fell, and upwards lay,

    [112] " O si præteritos referat mihi Jupiter annos
        Qualis eram, &c."—CHAPMAN.

In death not bowing his face to earth ; his arms he did despoil,   126
Which iron Mars bestow'd on him ; and those, in Mars's toil,
Lycurgus ever after wore ; but when he agéd grew,
Enforc'd to keep his peaceful house, their use he did renew
On mighty Ereuthalion's limbs, his soldier, lovéd well ;   130
And with these arms he challeng'd all, that did in arms excel ;
All shook, and stood dismay'd, none durst his adverse champion make.
Yet this same forward mind of mine, of choice, would undertake
To fight with all his confidence ; though youngest enemy
Of all the army we conduct, yet I fought with him, I,   135
Minerva made me so renown'd, and that most tall strong peer
I slew ; his big bulk lay on earth, extended here and there,
As it were covetous to spread the centre ev'rywhere.
O that my youth were now as fresh, and all my pow'rs as sound;
Soon should bold Hector be impugn'd ! Yet you that most are crown'd
With fortitude of all our host, ev'n you methinks are slow,   141
Not free, and set on fire with lust, t' encounter such a foe."

With this, nine royal princes rose. Atrides for the first ;
Then Diomed ; th' Ajaces then, that did th' encounter thirst ;
King Idomen and his consórts ; Mars-like Meriones ;   145
Evemon's son, Eurypylus : and Andrœmonides,
Whom all the Grecians Thoas call'd, sprung of Andræmon's blood ;
And wise Ulysses ; ev'ry one, propos'd for combat, stood.

Again Gerenius Nestor spake : "Let lots be drawn by all ;
His hand shall help the well-arm'd Greeks, on whom the lot doth
    fall,   150
And to his wish shall he be help'd, if he escape with life
The harmful danger-breathing fit of his advent'rous strife."

Each mark'd his lot, and cast it in to Agamemnon's casque.
The soldiers pray'd, held up their hands, and this of Jove did ask,
With eyes advanc'd to heav'n : "O Jove, so lead the herald's hand,
That Ajax, or great Tydeus' son, may our wish'd champion stand,   156
Or else the king himself that rules the rich Mycenian land."

This said, old Nestor mix'd the lots. The foremost lot survey'd
With Ajax Telamon was sign'd, as all the soldiers pray'd;
One of the heralds drew it forth, who brought and show'd it round, 160
Beginning at the right hand first, to all the most renown'd.
None knowing it, ev'ry man denied; but when he forth did pass
To him which mark'd and cast it in, which famous Ajax was,
He stretch'd his hand, and into it the herald put the lot,
Who, viewing it, th' inscription knew; the duke denied not, 165
But joyfully acknowledg'd it, and threw it at his feet,
And said: O friends, the lot is mine, which to my soul is sweet;
For now I hope my fame shall rise, in noble Hector's fall.
But, whilst I arm myself, do you on great Saturnius call,
But silently, or to yourselves, that not a Trojan hear; 170
Or openly, if you think good, since none alive we fear.
None with a will, if I will not, can my bold pow'rs affright,
At least for plain fierce swing of strength, or want of skill in fight;
For I will well prove that my birth, and breed, in Salamine
Was not all consecrate to meat, or mere effects of wine." 175
    This said, the well-giv'n soldiers pray'd; up went to heav'n their eyne:
"O Jove, that Ida dost protect, most happy, most divine,
Send victory to Ajax' side; fame; grace his goodly limb;
Or (if thy love bless Hector's life, and thou hast care of him,)
Bestow on both like pow'r, like fame." This said, in bright arms shone
The good strong Ajax; who, when all his war attire was on, 181
March'd like the hugely-figur'd Mars, when angry Jupiter
With strength, on people proud of strength, sends him forth to infer
Wreakful contention, and comes on with presence full of fear;
So th' Achive rampire, Telamon, did 'twixt the hosts appear; 185
Smil'd; yet of terrible aspéct; on earth, with ample pace,
He boldly stalk'd, and shook aloft his dart with deadly grace.
It did the Grecians good to see; but heartquakes shook the joints
Of all the Trojans. Hector's self felt thoughts, with horrid points,

Tempt his bold bosom ; but he now must make no counterflight, 190
Nor, with his honour, now refuse, that had provok'd the fight.
Ajax came near ; and, like a tow'r, his shield his bosom barr'd,
The right side brass, and sev'n ox-hides within it quilted hard ;
Old Tychius, the best currier, that did in Hyla dwell,
Did frame it for exceeding proof, and wrought it wondrous well. 195
With this stood he to Hector close, and with this brave began :
"Now, Hector, thou shalt clearly know, thus meeting man to man,
What other leaders arm our host, besides great Thetis' son,
Who with his hardy lion's heart hath armies overrun ;
But he lies at our crook'd-stern'd fleet, a rival with our king 200
In height of spirit ; yet to Troy he many knights did bring,
Coequal with Æacides, all able to sustain
All thy bold challenge can import. Begin then, words are vain."
    The helm-grac'd Hector answer'd him : "Renownéd Telamon,
Prince of the soldiers came from Greece, assay not me, like one 205
Young and immartial, with great words, as to an Amazon dame ;
I have the habit of all fights, and know the bloody frame
Of ev'ry slaughter ; I well know the ready right hand charge,
I know the left, and ev'ry sway of my secureful targe ;
I triumph in the cruelty of fixéd combat fight, 210
And manage horse to all designs ; I think then with good right
I may be confident as far as this my challenge goes,
Without being taxéd with a vaunt, borne out with empty shows.
But, being a soldier so renown'd, I will not work on thee
With least advantage of that skill I know doth strengthen me, 215
And so, with privity of sleight, win that for which I strive,
But at thy best, ev'n open strength, if my endeavours thrive."
    Thus sent he his long jav'lin forth. It strook his foe's huge
        shield
Near to the upper skirt of brass, which was the eighth it held. 219

    [193] " Hinc illud : Dominus clypei septemplicis Ajax."—CHAPMAN.
    [201] *He*—viz. Agamemnon.

Six folds th' untaméd dart strook through, and in the sev'nth tough hide
The point was check'd. Then Ajax threw; his angry lance did glide
Quite through his bright orbicular targe, his curace, shirt of mail,
And did his manly stomach's mouth with dang'rous taint assail;
But, in the bowing of himself, black death too short did strike.
Then both, to pluck their jav'lins forth, encounter'd, lion-like,   225
Whose bloody violence is increas'd by that raw food they eat,
Or boars whose strength wild nourishment doth make so wondrous great.
Again Priamides did wound in midst his shield of brass,
Yet pierc'd not through the upper plate, the head reflected was.
But Ajax, following his lance, smote through his target quite,   230
And stay'd bold Hector rushing in; the lance held way outright,
And hurt his neck; out gush'd the blood. Yet Hector ceas'd not so,
But in his strong hand took a flint, as he did backwards go,
Black, sharp, and big, laid in the field; the sev'nfold targe it smit
Full on the boss, and round about the brass did ring with it.   235
But Ajax a far greater stone lift up, and (wreathing round,
With all his body laid to it) he sent it forth to wound,
And gave unmeasur'd force to it; the round stone broke within
His rundled target; his lov'd knees to languish did begin;
And he lean'd, stretch'd out on his shield; but Phœbus rais'd him
    straight.   240
Then had they laid on wounds with swords, in use of closer fight,
Unless the heralds (messengers of Gods and godlike men)
The one of Troy, the other Greece, had held betwixt them then
Imperial sceptres; when the one, Idæus, grave and wise,
Said to them: "Now no more, my sons; the Sov'reign of the skies
Doth love you both; both soldiers are, all witness with good right;   246
But now night lays her mace on earth; 'tis good t' obey the night."
   "Idæus," Telamon replied, "to Hector speak, not me;
He that call'd all our Achive peers to station-fight, 'twas he;

---

[223] *Stomach's mouth*—pit of the stomach.
[244] *When the one.*—The second folio reads "*then the one,*" &c. and so Dr. Taylor.

If he first cease, I gladly yield." Great Hector then began : 250
"Ajax, since Jove, to thy big form, made thee so strong a man,
And gave thee skill to use thy strength, so much, that for thy spear
Thou art most excellent of Greece, now let us fight forbear.
Hereafter we shall war again, till Jove our herald be, 254
And grace with conquest which he will. Heav'n yields to night, and we.
Go thou and comfort all thy fleet, all friends and men of thine,
As I in Troy my favourers, who in the fane divine
Have offer'd orisons for me ; and come, let us impart
Some ensigns of our strife, to show each other's suppled heart, 259
That men of Troy and Greece may say, Thus their high quarrel ends.
Those that, encount'ring, were such foes, are now, being sep'rate, friends."
He gave a sword, whose handle was with silver studs through driv'n,
Scabbard and all, with hangers rich. By Telamon was giv'n
A fair well-glosséd purple waist. Thus Hector went to Troy,
And after him a multitude, fill'd with his safety's joy, 265
Despairing he could ever 'scape the puissant fortitude
And unimpeachéd Ajax' hands. The Greeks like joy renew'd
For their reputed victory, and brought him to the king ;
Who to the great Saturnides preferr'd an offering,
An ox that fed on five fair springs ; they flay'd and quarter'd him, 270
And then, in pieces cut, on spits they roasted ev'ry limb ;
Which neatly dress'd, they drew it off. Work done, they fell to feast ;
All had enough ; but Telamon, the king fed past the rest
With good large pieces of the chine. Thus thirst and hunger stay'd,
Nestor, whose counsels late were best, vows new, and first he said : 275
'Atrides, and my other lords, a sort of Greeks are dead,
Whose black blood, near Scamander's stream, inhuman Mars hath shed ;
Their souls to hell descended are. It fits thee then, our king,
To make our soldiers cease from war ; and, by the day's first spring,

₂₆₂ "Hector gives Ajax a sword ; Ajax, Hector a girdle. Both which gifts were afterwards cause of both their deaths."—CHAPMAN.
₂₇₀ "Virgil imit."—CHAPMAN.
₂₇₀ "*Springs*—springs-seasons, years ; i. e. was five years old.
₂₇₆ *Sort.*—See Bk. IV. 460.

Let us ourselves, assembled all, the bodies bear to fire, 280
With mules and oxen near our fleet, that, when we home retire,
Each man may carry to the sons, of fathers slaughter'd here,
Their honour'd bones. One tomb for all, for ever, let us rear,
Circling the pile without the field ; at which we will erect
Walls, and a rav'lin, that may safe our fleet and us protect. 285
And in them let us fashion gates, solid, and barr'd about,
Through which our horse, and chariots, may well get in and out.
Without all, let us dig a dike, so deep it may avail
Our forces 'gainst the charge of horse, and foot, that come t' assail.
And thus th' attempts, that I see swell, in Troy's proud heart, shall fail."

The kings do his advice approve. So Troy doth court convent 291
At Priam's gate, in th' Ilion tow'r, fearful and turbulent.
Amongst all, wise Antenor spake : " Trojans, and Dardan friends,
And peers assistants, give good ear to what my care commends
To your consents, for all our good. Resolve, let us restore 295
The Argive Helen, with her wealth, to him she had before.
We now defend but broken faiths. If, therefore, ye refuse,
No good event can I expect of all the wars we use."

He ceas'd ; and Alexander spake, husband to th' Argive queen:
" Antenor, to mine ears thy words harsh and ungracious been. 300
Thou canst use better if thou wilt : but, if these truly fit
Thy serious thoughts, the Gods with age have reft thy graver wit.
To warlike Trojans I will speak : I clearly do deny
To yield my wife, but all her wealth I'll render willingly,
Whatever I from Argos brought, and vow to make it more, 305
Which I have ready in my house, if peace I may restore."

Priam, surnam'd Dardanides, godlike, in counsels grave,
In his son's favour well-advis'd, this resolution gave :
" My royal friends of ev'ry state, there is sufficient done,
For this late council we have call'd, in th' offer of my son. 310
Now then let all take needful food, then let the watch be set,
And ev'ry court of guard held strong ; so, when the morn doth wet

The high-rais'd battlements of Troy, Idæus shall be sent
To th' Argive fleet, and Atreus' sons, t' unfold my son's intent,
From whose fact our contention springs ; and, if they will, obtain   315
Respite from heat of fight, till fire consume our soldiers slain ;
And after, our most fatal war let us importune still,
Till Jove the conquest have dispos'd to his unconquer'd will."
    All heard, and did obey the king ; and, in their quarters, all,
That were to set the watch that night, did to their suppers fall.   320
Idæus in the morning went, and th' Achive peers did find
In council at Atrides' ship ; his audience was assign'd ;
And, in the midst of all the kings, the vocal herald said :
    "Atrides ! My renownéd king, and other kings, his aid,
Propose by me, in their commands, the offers Paris makes,   325
From whose joy all our woes proceed. He princely undertakes
That all the wealth he brought from Greece (would he had died before !)
He will, with other added wealth, for your amends restore ;
But famous Menelaus' wife he still means to enjoy,
Though he be urg'd the contrary, by all the peers of Troy.   330
And this besides I have in charge, that, if it please you all,
They wish both sides may cease from war, that rites of funeral
May on their bodies be perform'd, that in the fields lie slain ;
And after, to the will of Fate, renew the fight again."
    All silence held at first ; at last Tydides made reply :   335
"Let no man take the wealth, or dame ; for now a child's weak eye
May see the imminent black end of Priam's empery."
    This sentence, quick and briefly giv'n, the Greeks did all admire.
Then said the king : " Herald, thou hear'st in him the voice entire
Of all our peers, to answer thee, for that of Priam's son.   340
But, for our burning of the dead, by all means I am won
To satisfy thy king therein, without the slend'rest gain
Made of their spoiléd carcasses ; but freely, being slain,
They shall be all consum'd with fire. To witness which I cite
High thund'ring Jove, that is the king of Juno's bed's delight."   345

With this, he held his sceptre up, to all the sky-thron'd Pow'rs;
And grave Idæus did return to sacred Ilion's tow'rs,
Where Ilians, and Dardanians, did still their counsels ply,
Expecting his return. He came, and told his legacy.
All, whirlwind-like, assembled then, some bodies to transport,   350
Some to hew trees. On th' other part, the Argives did exhort
Their soldiers to the same affairs. Then did the new fir'd sun
Smite the broad fields, ascending heav'n, and th' ocean smooth did run ;
When Greece and Troy mix'd in such peace, you scarce could either know.
Then wash'd they off their blood and dust, and did warm tears bestow
Upon the slaughter'd, and in cars convey'd them from the field.   356
Priam commanded none should mourn, but in still silence yield
Their honour'd carcasses to fire, and only grieve in heart.
All burn'd ; to Troy Troy's friends retire, to fleet the Grecian part.
Yet doubtful night obscur'd the earth, the day did not appear,   360
When round about the fun'ral pile, the Grecians gather'd were.
The pile they circled with a tomb, and by it rais'd a wall,
High tow'rs, to guard the fleet and them ; and in the midst of all
They built strong gates, through which the horse and chariots passage had ;
Without the rampire a broad dike, long and profound, they made,   365
On which they pallisadoes pitch'd ; and thus the Grecians wrought.
Their huge works in so little time were to perfection brought,
That all Gods, by the Lightner set, the frame thereof admir'd ;
'Mongst whom the Earthquake-making God, this of their king inquir'd :
"Father of Gods, will any man, of all earth's grassy sphere,   370
Ask any of the Gods' consents to any actions there,
If thou wilt see the shag-hair'd Greeks, with headstrong labours frame
So huge a work, and not to us due off'rings first enflame ?
As far as white Aurora's dews are sprinkled through the air,
Fame will renown the hands of Greece, for this divine affair ;   375
Men will forget the sacred work, the Sun and I did raise
For king Laomedon (bright Troy) and this will bear the praise."

[349] *Legacy*—embassy ; from legate. See Bk. ix. 220.   [369] Neptune.

Jove was extremely mov'd with him, and said : "What words are these,
Thou mighty Shaker of the earth, thou Lord of all the seas?
Some other God, of far less pow'r, might hold conceits, dismay'd 380
With this rare Grecian stratagem, and thou rest well apaid ;
For it will glorify thy name, as far as light extends ;
Since, when these Greeks shall see again their native soil and friends,
The bulwark batter'd, thou mayst quite devour it with thy waves,
And cover, with thy fruitless sands, this fatal shore of graves ; 385
That, what their fi'ry industries have so divinely wrought
In raising it, in razing it thy pow'r will prove it nought."
    Thus spake the Gods among themselves. Set was the fervent sun ;
And now the great work of the Greeks was absolutely done.
Then slew they oxen in their tents, and strength with food reviv'd, 390
When out of Lemnos a great fleet of od'rous wine arrived,
Sent by Eunëus, Jason's son, born of Hypsipyle.
The fleet contain'd a thousand tun, which must transported be
To Atreus' sons, as he gave charge, whose merchandise it was.
The Greeks bought wine for shining steel, and some for sounding brass,
Some for ox-hides, for oxen some, and some for prisoners. 396
A sumptuous banquet was prepar'd ; and all that night the peers
And fair-hair'd Greeks consum'd in feast. So Trojans, and their aid.
And all the night Jove thunder'd loud ; pale fear all thoughts dismay'd.
While they were gluttonous in earth, Jove wrought their banes in heav'n.
They pour'd full cups upon the ground, and were to off'rings driv'n 401
Instead of quaffings ; and to drink, none durst attempt, before
In solemn sacrifice they did almighty Jove adore.
Then to their rests they all repair'd ; bold zeal their fear bereav'd ;
And sudden sleep's refreshing gift, securely they receiv'd. 405

    [381] "The fortification that in the twelfth book is razed."—CHAPMAN.
    [398] So *Trojans*—in like manner.

THE END OF THE SEVENTH BOOK.

THE EIGHTH BOOK OF HOMER'S ILIADS.

THE ARGUMENT.

When Jove to all the Gods had giv'n command,
That none to either host should helpful stand,
To Ida he descends ; and sees from thence
Juno and Pallas haste the Greeks' defence ;
Whose purpose, his command, by Iris given,
Doth intervent. Then came the silent even,
When Hector charg'd fires should consume the night,
Lest Greeks in darkness took suspected flight.

ANOTHER ARGUMENT.

In Theta, Gods a Council have.
Troy's conquest. Glorious Hector's brave.

THE cheerful Lady of the light, deck'd in her saffron robe,
 Dispers'd her beams through ev'ry part of this enflow'red globe,
 When thund'ring Jove a Court of Gods assembled by his will,
In top of all the topful heights, that crown th' Olympian hill.
He spake, and all the Gods gave ear : "Hear how I stand inclin'd,
That God nor Goddess may attempt t' infringe my sov'reign mind,   6
But all give suffrage that with speed I may these discords end.
What God soever I shall find endeavour to defend
Or Troy or Greece, with wounds to heav'n he, sham'd, shall reascend ;

Or, taking with him his offence, I'll cast him down as deep
As Tartarus, the brood of night, where Barathrum doth steep
Torment in his profoundest sinks, where is the floor of brass,
And gates of iron; the place, for depth, as far doth hell surpass,
As heav'n, for height, exceeds the earth; then shall he know from thence
How much my pow'r, past all the Gods, hath sov'reign eminence.
Endanger it the whiles and see. Let down our golden chain,
And at it let all Deities their utmost strengths constrain,
To draw me to the earth from heav'n; you never shall prevail,
Though, with your most contention, ye dare my state assail.
But when my will shall be dispos'd, to draw you all to me,
Ev'n with the earth itself, and seas, ye shall enforced be;
Then will I to Olympus' top our virtuous engine bind,
And by it ev'rything shall hang, by my command inclin'd.
So much I am supreme to Gods, to men supreme as much."
The Gods sat silent, and admir'd, his dreadful speech was such.

 At last his blue-ey'd daughter spake: "O great Saturnides!
O father, O heav'n's highest king, well know we the excess
Of thy great pow'r, compar'd with all; yet the bold Greeks' estate
We needs must mourn, since they must fall beneath so hard a fate;
For, if thy grave command enjoin, we will abstain from fight.
But to afford them such advice, as may relieve their plight,
We will, with thy consent, be bold; that all may not sustain
The fearful burthen of thy wrath, and with their shames be slain."
He smil'd, and said: "Be confident, thou art belov'd of me;
I speak not this with serious thoughts, but will be kind to thee."

 This said, his brass-hoof'd wingéd horse he did to chariot bind,
Whose crests were fring'd with manes of gold; and golden garments shin'd
On his rich shoulders; in his hand he took a golden scourge,
Divinely fashion'd, and with blows their willing speed did urge

---

[11] "Virgil maketh this likewise his place, adding,
 Bis patet in præceps tantum, tenditque sub umbras, &c."—CHAPMAN.

Mid way betwixt the earth and heav'n. To Ida then he came, 40
Abounding in delicious springs, and nurse of beasts untame,
Where, on the mountain Gargarus, men did a fane erect
To his high name, and altars sweet ; and there his horse he check'd,
Dissolv'd them from his chariot, and in a cloud of jet
He cover'd them, and on the top took his triumphant seat, 45
Beholding Priam's famous town, and all the fleet of Greece.
The Greeks took breakfast speedily, and arm'd at ev'ry piece.
So Trojans ; who though fewer far, yet all to fight took arms,
Dire need enforc'd them to avert their wives' and children's harms.
All gates flew open ; all the host did issue, foot and horse, 50
In mighty tumult ; straight one place adjoin'd each adverse force.
Then shields with shields met, darts with darts, strength against strength
    oppos'd ;
The boss-pik'd targets were thrust on, and thunder'd as they clos'd
In mighty tumult ; groan for groan, and breath for breath did breathe,
Of men then slain, and to be slain ; earth flow'd with fruits of death.
While the fair morning's beauty held, and day increas'd in height, 56
Their jav'lins mutually made death transport an equal freight,
But when the hot meridian point, bright Phœbus did ascend,
Then Jove his golden balances did equally extend,
And, of long-rest-conferring death, put in two bitter fates 60
For Troy and Greece ; he held the midst ; the day of final dates
Fell on the Greeks ; the Greeks' hard lot sunk to the flow'ry ground,
The Trojans' leapt as high as heav'n. Then did the claps resound
Of his fierce thunder ; lightning leapt amongst each Grecian troop ;
The sight amaz'd them ; pallid fear made boldest stomachs stoop. 65
Then Idomen durst not abide, Atrides went his way,
And both th' Ajaces ; Nestor yet, against his will did stay,
That grave protector of the Greeks, for Paris with a dart
Enrag'd one of his chariot horse ; he smote the upper part
Of all his skull, ev'n where the hair, that made his foretop, sprung. 70
The hurt was deadly, and the pain so sore the courser stung,

(Pierc'd to the brain) he stamp'd and plung'd. One on another bears,
Entangled round about the beam ; then Nestor cut the gears
With his new-drawn authentic sword. Meanwhile the fi'ry horse
Of Hector brake into the press, with their bold ruler's force ;   75
Then good old Nestor had been slain, had Diomed not espy'd,
Who to Ulysses, as he fled, importunately cried :
"Thou that in counsels dost abound, O Laertiades,
Why fly'st thou ? Why thus, coward-like, shunn'st thou the honour'd
   prease ?
Take heed thy back take not a dart. Stay, let us both intend   80
To drive this cruel enemy, from our dear agéd friend."
He spake, but wary Ithacus would find no patient ear,
But fled forthright, ev'n to the fleet. Yet, though he single were,
Brave Diomed mix'd amongst the fight, and stood before the steeds
Of old Neleides, whose estate thus kingly he areeds :   85
  "O father, with these youths in fight, thou art unequal plac'd,
Thy willing sinews are unknit, grave age pursues thee fast,
And thy unruly horse are slow ; my chariot therefore use,
And try how ready Trojan horse, can fly him that pursues,
Pursue the flier, and ev'ry way perform the varied fight ;   90
I forc'd them from Anchises' son, well-skill'd in cause of flight.
Then let my squire lead hence thy horse ; mine thou shalt guard, whilst I,
By thee advanc'd, assay the fight, that Hector's self may try
If my lance dote with the defects, that fail best minds in age,
Or finds the palsy in my hands, that doth thy life engage."   95
  This noble Nestor did accept, and Diomed's two friends,
Eurymedon that valour loves, and Sthenelus, ascends
Old Nestor's coach. Of Diomed's horse Nestor the charge sustains,
And Tydeus' son took place of fight. Neleides held the reins,
And scourg'd the horse, who swiftly ran direct in Hector's face ;   100
Whom fierce Tydides bravely charg'd, but, he turn'd from the chace,

⁷⁴ *Authentic*—i.e., his own.   ⁸⁰ *Intend*—apply ourselves.
⁸⁵ *Areeds*—counsels, advises.   ⁸⁹ See Bk. v. 308.
⁹⁵ *Thy life.*—The second folio has "*my.*"

His jav'lin Eniopeus smit, mighty Thebæus' son,
And was great Hector's charioteer; it through his breast did run,
Near to his pap; he fell to earth, back flew his frighted horse,
His strength and soul were both dissolv'd. Hector had deep remorse
Of his mishap, yet left he him, and for another sought; 106
Nor long his steeds did want a guide, for straight good fortune brought
Bold Archeptolemus, whose life did from Iphitis spring;
He made him take the reins and mount. Then souls were set on wing;
Then high exploits were undergone; then Trojans in their walls 110
Had been infolded like meek lambs, had Jove wink'd at their falls,
Who hurl'd his horrid thunder forth, and made pale lightnings fly
Into the earth, before the horse that Nestor did apply.
A dreadful flash burnt through the air, that savour'd sulphur-like,
Which down before the chariot the dazzled horse did strike. 115
The fair reins fell from Nestor's hand, who did in fear entreat
Renown'd Tydides into flight to turn his fury's heat:
"For know'st thou not," said he, "our aid is not supplied from Jove?
This day he will give fame to Troy, which when it fits his love
We shall enjoy. Let no man tempt his unresisted will, 120
Though he exceed in gifts of strength; for he exceeds him still."

"Father," replied the king, "'tis true; but both my heart and soul
Are most extremely griev'd to think how Hector will control
My valour with his vaunts in Troy, that I was terror-sick 124
With his approach; which when he boasts, let earth devour me quick."

"Ah! warlike Tydeus' son," said he, "what needless words are
    these?
Though Hector should report thee faint, and amorous of thy case,
The Trojans, nor the Trojan wives, would never give him trust,
Whose youthful husbands thy free hand hath smother'd so in dust."
This said, he turn'd his one-hoof'd horse to flight, and troop did take,
When Hector and his men, with shouts, did greedy pursuit make, 131

    [130] *Troop did take*—to take troop is a frequent expression for taking shelter amidst the troops, running back.

And pour'd on darts that made air sigh.   Then Hector did exclaim :
"O Tydeus' son, the kings of Greece do most renown thy name
With highest place, feasts, and full cups ; who now will do the shame ;
Thou shalt be like a woman us'd, and they will say : 'Depart,   135
Immartial minion, since to stand Hector thou hast no heart.'
Nor canst thou scale our turrets' tops, nor lead the wives to fleet
Of valiant men, that wife-like fear'st my adverse charge to meet."
    This two ways mov'd him,—still to fly, or turn his horse and fight.
Thrice thrust he forward to assault, and ev'ry time the fright.   140
Of Jove's fell thunder drave him back, which he propos'd for sign
(To show the change of victory) Trojans should victors shine.
Then Hector comforted his men : "All my advent'rous friends,
Be men, and, of your famous strength, think of the honour'd ends.
I know benevolent Jupiter, did by his beck profess   145
Conquest and high renown to me, and to the Greeks distress.
O fools, to raise such silly forts, not worth the least account,
Nor able to resist our force !   With ease our horse may mount,
Quite over all their hollow dike.   But, when their fleet I reach,
Let Memory to all the world a famous bonfire teach,   150
For I will all their ships inflame, with whose infestive smoke,
Fear-shrunk, and hidden near their keels, the conquer'd Greeks shall
      choke."
    Then cherish'd he his famous horse : "O Xanthus, now," said he,
"And thou Podargus, Æthon too, and Lampus, dear to me,
Make me some worthy recompense, for so much choice of meat,   155
Giv'n you by fair Andromache ; bread of the purest wheat,
And with it, for your drink, mix'd wine, to make ye wishéd cheer,
Still serving you before myself, her husband young and dear.
Pursue, and use your swiftest speed, that we may take for prise
The shield of old Neleides, which Fame lifts to the skies,   160
Ev'n to the handles telling it to be of massy gold.
And from the shoulders let us take, of Diomed the bold,

---

[136] The second folio has a strange misprint in "*immortal*" for "*immartial*."

The royal curace Vulcan wrought, with art so exquisite.
These if we make our sacred spoil, I doubt not, but this night,
Ev'n to their navy to enforce the Greeks' unturnéd flight."   165
This Juno took in high disdain, and made Olympus shake
As she but stirr'd within her throne, and thus to Neptune spake :
"O Neptune, what a spite is this ! Thou God so huge in pow'r,
Afflicts it not thy honour'd heart, to see rude spoil devour
These Greeks that have in Helice, and Aege, offer'd thee   170
So many and such wealthy gifts? Let them the victors be.
If we, that are the aids of Greece, would beat home these of Troy,
And hinder broad-ey'd Jove's proud will, it would abate his joy."
He, angry, told her she was rash, and he would not be one,   174
Of all the rest, should strive with Jove, whose pow'r was match'd by none.
Whiles they conferr'd thus, all the space the trench contain'd before
(From that part of the fort that flank'd the navy-anchoring shore)
Was fill'd with horse and targeteers, who there for refuge came,
By Mars-swift Hector's pow'r engag'd ; Jove gave his strength the fame ;
And he with spoilful fire had burn'd the fleet, if Juno's grace   180
Had not inspir'd the king himself, to run from place to place,
And stir up ev'ry soldier's pow'r, to some illustrious deed.
First visiting their leaders' tents, his ample purple weed
He wore, to show all who he was, and did his station take
At wise Ulysses' sable barks, that did the battle make   185
Of all the fleet ; from whence his speech might with more ease be driv'n
To Ajax' and Achilles' ships, to whose chief charge were giv'n
The vantguard and the rearguard both, both for their force of hand,
And trusty bosoms. There arriv'd, thus urg'd he to withstand
Th' insulting Trojans : "O what shame, ye empty-hearted lords,   190
Is this to your admiréd forms ! Where are your glorious words,
In Lemnos vaunting you the best of all the Grecian host ?
'We are the strongest men,' ye said, 'we will command the most,

---

[171] The second folio and Dr. Taylor read, "*So many and so wealthy gifts.*"

Eating most flesh of high-horn'd beeves, and drinking cups full crown'd,
And ev'ry man a hundred foes, two hundred, will confound ;   195
Now all our strength, dar'd to our worst, one Hector cannot tame,'
Who presently with horrid fire, will all our fleet inflame.
O Father Jove, hath ever yet thy most unsuffer'd hand
Afflicted, with such spoil of souls, the king of any land,
And taken so much fame from him ? when I did never fail,   200
(Since under most unhappy stars, this fleet was under sail)
Thy glorious altars, I protest, but, above all the Gods,
Have burnt fat thighs of beeves to thee, and pray'd to raze th' abodes
Of rape-defending Ilions. Yet grant, almighty Jove,
One favour ;—that we may at least with life from hence remove,   205
Not under such inglorious hands, the hands of death employ ;
And, where Troy should be stoop'd by Greece, let Greece fall under Troy."

To this ev'n weeping king did Jove remorseful audience give,
And shook great heav'n to him, for sign his men and he should live.
Then quickly cast he off his hawk, the eagle prince of air,   210
That perfects his unspotted vows ; who seiz'd in her repair
A sucking hind calf, which she truss'd in her enforcive seres,
And by Jove's altar let it fall, amongst th' amazéd peers,
Where the religious Achive kings, with sacrifice did please
The author of all oracles, divine Saturnides.   215
Now, when they knew the bird of Jove, they turn'd courageous head.
When none, though many kings put on, could make his vaunt, he led
Tydides to renew'd assault, or issu'd first the dike,
Or first did fight ; but, far the first, stone dead his lance did strike

²⁰⁸ *Remorseful*—compassionate,—
                O Eglamour, thou art a gentleman,
                (Think not I flatter, for I swear I do not)
                Valiant, wise, *remorseful*.
                            SHAKESPEARE. *Two Gent. Ver.* IV. 3.
See infra, line 409.
  ²¹² *Seres*—talons.
  ²¹⁷ *Put on*—attempted, came forward. *Make his vaunt*—make good his boast. Dr. Taylor says, " gain the vantage, come first to fight."
  ²¹⁸ *Tydides.*—He led Tydides, i. e. Tydides he led. An unusual construction.

Arm'd Agelaus, by descent surnam'd Phradmonides; 220
He turn'd his ready horse to flight, and Diomed's lance did seize
His back betwixt his shoulder-blades, and look'd out at his breast;
He fell, and his arms rang his fall. Th' Atrides next address'd
Themselves to fight; th' Ajaces next, with vehement strength endued;
Idomeneüs and his friend, stout Merion, next pursued; 225
And after these Eurypylus, Evemon's honour'd race;
The ninth, with backward-wreathéd bow, had little Teucer place,
He still fought under Ajax' shield, who sometimes held it by,
And then he look'd his object out, and let his arrow fly,
And, whomsoever in the press he wounded, him he slew, 230
Then under Ajax' sev'n-fold shield, he presently withdrew.
He far'd like an unhappy child, that doth to mother run
For succour, when he knows full well, he some shrewd turn hath done.
What Trojans then were to their deaths, by Teucer's shafts, impress'd?
Hapless Orsilochus was first, Ormenus, Ophelest, 235
Dætor, and hardy Chromius, and Lycophon divine,
And Amopaon that did spring from Polyæmon's line,
And Menalippus; all, on heaps, he tumbled to the ground.
The king rejoic'd to see his shafts the Phrygian ranks confound,
Who straight came near, and spake to him: "O Teucer, lovely man,
Strike still so sure, and be a grace to ev'ry Grecian, 241
And to thy father Telamon, who took thee kindly home
(Although not by his wife his son) and gave thee foster room,
Ev'n from thy childhood; then to him, though far from hence remov'd,
Make good fame reach; and to thyself, I vow what shall be prov'd: 245
If he that dreadful Ægis bears, and Pallas, grant to me
Th' expugnance of well-builded Troy, I first will honour thee
Next to myself with some rich gift, and put it in thy hand:
A three-foot vessel, that, for grace, in sacred fanes doth stand;
Or two horse and a chariot; or else a lovely dame 250
That may ascend on bed with thee, and amplify thy name."

Teucer right nobly answer'd him : "Why, most illustrate king,
I being thus forward of myself, dost thou adjoin a sting?
Without which, all the pow'r I have, I cease not to employ,
For, from the place where we repuls'd the Trojans towards Troy, 255
I all the purple field have strew'd, with one or other slain.
Eight shafts I shot, with long steel heads, of which not one in vain,
All were in youthful bodies fix'd, well-skill'd in war's constraint ;
Yet this wild dog, with all my aim, I have no pow'r to taint."
This said, another arrow forth, from his stiff string he sent, 260
At Hector, whom he long'd to wound ; but still amiss it went.
His shaft smit fair Gorgythion, of Priam's princely race,
Who in Æpina was brought forth, a famous town in Thrace,
By Castianira, that, for form, was like celestial breed ;
And, as a crimson poppy flow'r, surchargéd with his seed, 265
And vernal humours falling thick, declines his heavy brow,
So, of one side, his helmet's weight his fainting head did bow.
Yet Teucer would another shaft at Hector's life dispose,
So fain he such a mark would hit, but still beside it goes ;
Apollo did avert the shaft ; but Hector's charioteer, 270
Bold Archeptolemus, he smit, as he was rushing near
To make the fight ; to earth he fell, his swift horse back did fly,
And there were both his strength and soul exil'd eternally.
Huge grief, for Hector's slaughter'd friend, pinch'd-in his mighty mind,
Yet was he forc'd to leave him there, and his void place resign'd 275
To his sad brother, that was by, Cebriones ; whose ear
Receiving Hector's charge, he straight the weighty reins did bear ;
And Hector from his shining coach, with horrid voice, leap'd on,
To wreak his friend on Teucer's hand ; and up he took a stone,
With which he at the archer ran ; who from his quiver drew 280
A sharp-pil'd shaft, and nock'd it sure ; but in great Hector flew

²⁵² *Illustrate.*—The second folio, which Dr. Taylor follows, has "*illustrious.*"
²⁵³ *Adjoin a sting*—add an impulse.
²⁵⁹ *Taint*—See Bk. III. 374.

With such fell speed, that, in his draught, he his right shoulder strook
Where, 'twixt his neck and breast, the joint his native closure took.
The wound was wondrous full of death, his string in sunder flees,
His numméd hand fell strengthless down, and he upon his knees.   285
Ajax neglected not to aid his brother thus depress'd,
But came and saft him with his shield ; and two more friends, address'd
To be his aid, took him to fleet, Mecisteus, Echius' son,
And gay Alastor. Teucer sigh'd, for all his service done.
 Then did Olympius, with fresh strength, the Trojan pow'rs revive,
Who, to their trenches once again, the troubled Greeks did drive.   291
Hector brought terror with his strength, and ever fought before.
As when some highly-stomach'd hound, that hunts a sylvan boar,
Or kingly lion, loves the haunch, and pincheth oft behind,
Bold of his feet, and still observes the game to turn inclin'd,   295
Not utterly dissolv'd in flight ; so Hector did pursue,
And whosoever was the last, he ever did subdue.
They fled, but, when they had their dike, and palisadoes, pass'd,
(A number of them put to sword) at ships they stay'd at last.
Then mutual exhortations flew, then, all with hands and eyes   300
Advanc'd to all the Gods, their plagues wrung from them open cries.
Hector, with his four rich-man'd horse, assaulting always rode,
The eyes of Gorgon burnt in him, and war's vermilion God.
The Goddess that all Goddesses, for snowy arms, out-shin'd,
Thus spake to Pallas, to the Greeks with gracious ruth inclin'd :   305
 "O Pallas, what a grief is this ! Is all our succour past
To these our perishing Grecian friends ? At least withheld at last,
Ev'n now, when one man's violence must make them perish all,
In satisfaction of a fate so full of funeral ?
Hector Priamides now raves, no more to be endur'd,   310
That hath already on the Greeks so many harms inur'd."
 The azure Goddess answer'd her : "This man had surely found
His fortitude and life dissolv'd, ev'n on his father's ground,

²⁸² *In his draught*—as he (Teucer) was drawing his bow.   ³⁰⁴ Juno.

By Grecian valour, if my sire, infested with ill moods,
Did not so dote on these of Troy, too jealous of their bloods,   315
And ever an unjust repulse stands to my willing pow'rs,
Little rememb'ring what I did, in all the desp'rate hours
Of his affected Hercules ; I ever rescu'd him,
In labours of Eurystheüs, untouch'd in life or limb,
When he, heav'n knows, with drownéd eyes look'd up for help to heav'n,
Which ever, at command of Jove, was by my suppliance giv'n.   321
But had my wisdom reach'd so far, to know of this event,
When to the solid-ported depths of hell his son was sent,
To hale out hateful Pluto's dog from darksome Erebus,
He had not 'scap'd the streams of Styx, so deep and dangerous.   325
Yet Jove hates me, and shows his love in doing Thetis' will,
That kiss'd his knees, and strok'd his chin, pray'd, and importun'd still,
That he would honour with his aid her city-razing son,
Displeas'd Achilles ; and for him our friends are thus undone.
But time shall come again, when he, to do his friends some aid,   330
Will call me his Glaucopides, his sweet and blue-eyed Maid.
Then harness thou thy horse for me, that his bright palace gates
I soon may enter, arming me, to order these debates ;
And I will try if Priam's son will still maintain his cheer,
When in the crimson paths of war, I dreadfully appear ;   335
For some proud Trojans shall be sure to nourish dogs and fowls,
And pave the shore with fat and flesh, depriv'd of lives and souls."

    Juno prepar'd her horse, whose manes ribands of gold enlac'd.
Pallas her party-colour'd robe on her bright shoulders cast,
Divinely wrought with her own hands, in th' entry of her sire.   340
Then put she on her ample breast her under-arming tire,
And on it her celestial arms. The chariot straight she takes,
With her huge heavy violent lance, with which she slaughter makes

    ³¹⁸ *Affected*—beloved.
    ³²¹ *Suppliance*—supply, assistance.

Of armies fatal to her wrath. Saturnia whipp'd her horse,
And heav'n-gates, guarded by the Hours, op'd by their proper force.
Through which they flew. Whom when Jove saw (set near th' Idalian
    springs) 346
Highly displeas'd, he Iris call'd, that hath the golden wings,
And said : "Fly, Iris, turn them back, let them not come at me,
Our meetings, sev'rally dispos'd, will nothing gracious be.
Beneath their o'erthrown chariot I'll shiver their proud steeds, 350
Hurl down themselves, their waggon break, and, for their stubborn deeds,
In ten whole years they shall not heal the wounds I will impress
With horrid thunder ; that my maid may know when to address
Arms 'gainst her father. For my wife, she doth not so offend,
'Tis but her use to interrupt whatever I intend." 355
Iris, with this, left Ida's hills, and up t' Olympus flew,
Met near heav'n-gates the Goddesses, and thus their haste withdrew :
  "What course intend you ? Why are you wrapp'd with your fancies'
    storm ?
Jove likes not ye should aid the Greeks, but threats, and will perform,
To crush in pieces your swift horse beneath their glorious yokes, 360
Hurl down yourselves, your chariot break, and, those impoison'd strokes
His wounding thunder shall imprint in your celestial parts,
In ten full springs ye shall not cure ; that She that tames proud hearts
(Thyself, Minerva) may be taught to know for what, and when,
Thou dost against thy father fight ; for sometimes childeren 365
May with discretion plant themselves against their fathers' wills,
But not, where humours only rule, in works beyond their skills.
For Juno, she offends him not, nor vexeth him so much,
For 'tis her use to cross his will, her impudence is such,
The habit of offence in this she only doth contract, 370
And so grieves or incenseth less, though ne'er the less her fact.

       344 *Fatal*—decreed by fate. See Bk. IX. 241.
       349 *Severally*—separately, oppositely.
       369 "Facilè facit quod semper facit."—CHAPMAN.

But thou most griev'st him, doggéd dame, whom he rebukes in time,
Lest silence should pervert thy will, and pride too highly climb
In thy bold bosom, desp'rate girl, if seriously thou dare
Lift thy unwieldy lance 'gainst Jove, as thy pretences are." 375
  She left them, and Saturnia said : "Ah me! Thou seed of Jove,
By my advice we will no more unfit contention move
With Jupiter, for mortal men ; of whom, let this man die,
And that man live, whoever he pursues with destiny ;
And let him, plotting all events, dispose of either host, 380
As he thinks fittest for them both, and may become us most."
  Thus turn'd she back, and to the Hours her rich-man'd horse resign'd,
Who them t' immortal mangers bound ; the chariot they inclin'd
Beneath the crystal walls of heav'n ; and they in golden thrones
Consorted other Deities, replete with passións. 385
Jove, in his bright-wheel'd chariot, his fi'ry horse now beats
Up to Olympus, and aspir'd the Gods' eternal seats.
Great Neptune loos'd his horse, his car upon the altar plac'd,
And heav'nly-linen coverings did round about it cast.
The Far-seer us'd his throne of gold. The vast Olympus shook 390
Beneath his feet. His wife, and maid, apart their places took,
Nor any word afforded him. He knew their thoughts, and said :
" Why do you thus torment yourselves ? You need not sit dismay'd
With the long labours you have us'd in your victorious fight,
Destroying Trojans, 'gainst whose lives you heap such high despite. 395
Ye should have held your glorious course ; for, be assur'd, as far
As all my pow'rs, by all means urg'd, could have sustain'd the war,
Not all the host of Deities should have retir'd my hand
From vow'd inflictions on the Greeks, much less you two withstand.
But you, before you saw the fight, much less the slaughter there, 400
Had all your goodly lineaments possess'd with shaking fear,
And never had your chariot borne their charge to heav'n again,
But thunder should have smit you both, had you one Trojan slain."

Both Goddesses let fall their chins upon their ivory breasts,
Set next to Jove, contriving still afflicted Troy's unrests. 405
Pallas for anger could not speak ; Saturnia, contrary,
Could not for anger hold her peace, but made this bold reply :
"Not-to-be-suff'red Jupiter, what need'st thou still enforce
Thy matchless pow'r ? We know it well ; but we must yield remorse
To them that yield us sacrifice. Nor need'st thou thus deride 410
Our kind obedience, nor our griefs, but bear our pow'rs applied
To just protection of the Greeks, that anger tomb not all
In Troy's foul gulf of perjury, and let them stand should fall."
"Grieve not," said Jove, "at all done yet ; for, if thy fair eyes please
This next red morning they shall see the great Saturnides 415
Bring more destruction to the Greeks ; and Hector shall not cease,
Till he have rouséd from the fleet swift-foot Æacides,
In that day, when before their ships, for his Patroclus slain,
The Greeks in great distress shall fight ; for so the Fates ordain.
I weigh not thy displeaséd spleen, though to th' extremest bounds 420
Of earth and seas it carry thee, where endless night confounds
Japet, and my dejected Sire, who sit so far beneath,
They never see the flying sun, nor hear the winds that breath,
Near to profoundest Tartarus. Nor, thither if thou went,
Would I take pity of thy moods, since none more impudent." 42
To this she nothing did reply. And now Sol's glorious light
Fell to the sea, and to the land drew up the drowsy night.
The Trojans griev'd at Phœbus' fall, which all the Greeks desir'd,
And sable night, so often wish'd, to earth's firm throne aspir'd.
Hector (intending to consult) near to the gulfy flood, 430
Far from the fleet, led to a place, pure and exempt from blood,
The Trojans' forces. From their horse all lighted, and did hear
Th' oration Jove-lov'd Hector made ; who held a goodly spear,
Elev'n full cubits long, the head was brass, and did reflect
A wanton light before him still, it round about was deck'd 435

⁴⁰⁹ *Remorse.*—See supra, line 208.
⁴²² Iapetus, and Chronos. *Dejected*—cast down from heaven.

With strong hoops of new-burnish'd gold. On this he lean'd, and said:
"Hear me, my worthy friends of Troy, and you our honour'd aid.
A little since, I had conceit we should have made retreat,
By light of the inflaméd fleet, with all the Greeks' escheat,
But darkness hath prevented us, and saft, with special grace, 410
These Achives and their shore-hal'd fleet. Let us then render place
To sacred Night, our suppers dress, and from our chariot free
Our fair-man'd horse, and meat them well. Then let there convoy'd be,
From forth the city presently, oxen and well-fed sheep,
Sweet wine, and bread ; and fell much wood, that all night we may keep 415
Plenty of fires, ev'n till the light bring forth the lovely morn,
And let their brightness glaze the skies, that night may not suborn
The Greeks' escape, if they for flight the sea's broad back would take ;
At least they may not part with ease, but, as retreat they make,
Each man may bear a wound with him, to cure when he comes home,
Made with a shaft or sharp'ned spear ; and others fear to come, 451
With charge of lamentable war, 'gainst soldiers bred in Troy.
Then let our heralds through the town their offices employ
To warn the youth, yet short of war, and time-white fathers, past,
That in our god-built tow'rs they see strong courts of guard be plac'd,
About the walls ; and let out dames, yet flourishing in years, 456
That, having beauties to keep pure, are most inclin'd to fears
(Since darkness in distressful times more dreadful is than light)
Make lofty fires in ev'ry house ; and thus, the dang'rous night,
Held with strong watch, if th' enemy have ambuscadoes laid 460
Near to our walls (and therefore seem in flight the more dismay'd,
Intending a surprise, while we are all without the town)
They ev'ry way shall be impugn'd, to ev'ry man's renown.
Perform all this, brave Trojan friends. What now I have to say
Is all express'd ; the cheerful morn shall other things display. 465
It is my glory (putting trust in Jove, and other Gods)
That I shall now expulse these dogs Fates sent to our abodes,

Who bring ostents of destiny, and black their threat'ning fleet.
But this night let us hold strong guards ; to-morrow we will meet
(With fierce-made war) before their ships, and I'll make known to all
If strong Tydides from their ships can drive me to their wall, 471
Or I can pierce him with my sword, and force his bloody spoil.
The wishéd morn shall show his pow'r, if he can shun his foil
I running on him with my lance. I think, when day ascends,
He shall lie wounded with the first, and by him many friends. 475
O that I were as sure to live immortal, and sustain
No frailties with increasing years, but evermore remain
Ador'd like Pallas, or the Sun, as all doubts die in me
That heav'n's next light shall be the last the Greeks shall ever see !"

   This speech all Trojans did applaud ; who from their traces los'd 480
Their sweating horse, which sev'rally with headstalls they repos'd,
And fast'ned by their chariots ; when others brought from town
Fat sheep and oxen, instantly, bread, wine, and hewéd down
Huge store of wood. The winds transferr'd into the friendly sky
Their supper's savour ; to the which they sat delightfully, 485
And spent all night in open field ; fires round about them shin'd.
As when about the silver moon, when air is free from wind,
And stars shine clear, to whose sweet beams, high prospects, and the brows
Of all steep hills and pinnacles, thrust up themselves for shows,
And ev'n the lowly valleys joy to glitter in their sight, 490
When the unmeasur'd firmament bursts to disclose her light,
And all the signs in heav'n are seen, that glad the shepherd's heart ;
So many fires disclos'd their beams, made by the Trojan part,
Before the face of Ilion, and her bright turrets show'd.
A thousand courts of guard kept fires, and ev'ry guard allow'd 495
Fifty stout men, by whom their horse ate oats and hard white corn,
And all did wishfully expect the silver-thronéd morn.

  [468] i. e. their fleet is black. The original is simply "*who bring fates upon their black ships.*"
  [497] *Wishfully.*—Both folios have *wilfully*, but Stevens remarks that in the 4to. of 1598, it is *wishfully*, which is evidently the true reading.

THE NINTH BOOK OF HOMER'S ILIADS.

THE ARGUMENT.

To Agamemnon, urging hopeless flight,
Stand Diomed, and Nestor, opposite.
By Nestor's counsel, legates are dismiss'd
To Thetis' son; who still denies t' assist.

ANOTHER ARGUMENT.

Iota sings the Ambassy,
And great Achilles' stern reply.

O held the Trojans sleepless guard; the Greeks to flight were giv'n,
The feeble consort of cold fear, strangely infus'd from heav'n;
Grief, not to be endur'd, did wound all Greeks of greatest worth.
And as two lateral-sited winds, the west wind and the north,
Meet at the Thracian sea's black breast, join in a sudden blore, 5
Tumble together the dark waves, and pour upon the shore
A mighty deal of froth and weed, with which men manure ground;
So Jove and Troy did drive the Greeks, and all their minds confound.

⁷ *With which men manure ground.*—This piece of agricultural information is an addition of Chapman's.

But Agamemnon most of all was tortur'd at his heart,
Who to the voiceful heralds went, and bade them cite, apart,
Each Grecian leader sev'rally, not openly proclaim.
In which he labour'd with the first ; and all together came.
They sadly sate. The king arose, and pour'd out tears as fast
As from a lofty rock a spring doth his black waters cast,
And, deeply sighing, thus bespake the Achives : " O my friends,
Princes, and leaders of the Greeks, heav'n's adverse King extends
His wrath, with too much detriment, to my so just design,
Since he hath often promis'd me, and bound it with the sign
Of his bent forehead, that this Troy our vengeful hands should race,
And safe return ; yet, now engag'd, he plagues us with disgrace,
When all our trust to him hath drawn so much blood from our friends.
My glory, nor my brother's wreak, were the proposéd ends,
For which he drew you to these toils, but your whole countries' shame,
Which had been huge to bear the rape of so divine a dame,
Made in despite of our revenge. And yet not that had mov'd
Our pow'rs to these designs, if Jove had not our drifts approv'd ;
Which since we see he did for blood, 'tis desp'rate fight in us
To strive with him ; then let us fly ; 'tis flight he urgeth thus."
   Long time still silence held them all ; at last did Diomed rise :
" Atrides, I am first must cross thy indiscreet advice,
As may become me, being a king, in this our martial court.
Be not displeas'd then ; for thyself didst broadly misreport
In open field my fortitude, and call'd me faint and weak,
Yet I was silent, knowing the time, loth any rites to break
That appertain'd thy public rule, yet all the Greeks knew well,
Of ev'ry age, thou didst me wrong. As thou then didst refell
My valour first of all the host, as of a man dismay'd ;
So now, with fit occasion giv'n, I first blame thee afraid.

   [30] " Diomed takes fit time to answer his wrong done by Agamemnon in the fourth book."—CHAPMAN.

Inconstant Saturn's son hath giv'n inconstant spirits to thee,
And, with a sceptre over all, an eminent degree ; 40
But with a sceptre's sov'reign grace, the chief pow'r, fortitude,
(To bridle thee) he thought not best thy breast should be endu'd.
Unhappy king, think'st thou the Greeks are such a silly sort,
And so excessive impotent, as thy weak words import ?
If thy mind move thee to be gone, the way is open, go ; 45
Mycenian ships enow ride near, that brought thee to this woe ;
The rest of Greece will stay, nor stir till Troy be overcome
With full eversion ; or if not, but (doters of their home)
Will put on wings to fly with thee. Myself and Sthenelus
Will fight till (trusting favouring Jove) we bring home Troy with us."

 This all applauded, and admir'd the spirit of Diomed ; 51
When Nestor, rising from the rest, his speech thus seconded :
" Tydides, thou art, questionless, our strongest Greek in war,
And gravest in thy counsels too, of all that equal are
In place with thee, and stand on strength ; nor is there any one 55
Can blame, or contradict thy speech ; and yet thou hast not gone
So far, but we must further go. Thou'rt young, and well mightst be
My youngest son, though still I yield thy words had high degree
Of wisdom in them to our king, since well they did become
Their right in question, and refute inglorious going home. 60
But I (well-known thy senior far) will speak, and handle all
Yet to propose, which none shall check ; no, not our general.
A hater of society, unjust, and wild, is he
That loves intestine war, being stuff'd with manless cruelty.
And therefore in persuading peace, and home-flight, we the less 65
May blame our gen'ral, as one loth to wrap in more distress

[58] *Yield*—acknowledge. *Had*—thus the first folio ; the second reads "*hath*,"
and Dr. Taylor "*have*."
 [62] *Propose*—so the first folio ; the second reads "*purpose*," which Dr. Taylor
has adopted, and explained in a note as meaning "*propose*."
 [64] *Manless*—opposite to *manful*, cowardly, inhuman. Bk. III. 39.

His lovéd soldiers. But because they bravely are resolv'd
To cast lives after toils, before they part in shame involv'd,
Provide we for our honour'd stay ; obey black night, and fall
Now to our suppers ; then appoint our guards without the wall, 70
And in the bottom of the dike ; which guards I wish may stand
Of our brave youth. And, Atreus' son, since thou art in command
Before our other kings, be first in thy command's effect.
It well becomes thee ; since 'tis both what all thy peers expect,
And in the royal right of things is no impair to thee. 75
Nor shall it stand with less than right, that they invited be
To supper by thee ; all thy tents are amply stor'd with wine,
Brought daily in Greek ships from Thrace ; and to this grace of thine
All necessaries thou hast fit, and store of men to wait ;
And, many meeting there, thou may'st hear ev'ry man's conceit, 80
And take the best. It much concerns all Greeks to use advice
Of gravest nature, since so near our ships our enemies
Have lighted such a sort of fires, with which what man is joy'd ?
Look, how all bear themselves this night ; so live, or be destroy'd."

    All heard, and follow'd his advice. There was appointed then 85
Sev'n captains of the watch, who forth did march with all their men.
The first was famous Thrasymed, adviceful Nestor's son ;
Ascalaphus ; and Ialmen ; and mighty Merion ;
Alphareus ; and Deipyrus ; and lovely Lycomed,
Old Creon's joy. These sev'n bold lords an hundred soldiers led, 90
In ev'ry sever'd company, and ev'ry man his pike,
Some placéd on the rampire's top, and some amidst the dike.
All fires made, and their suppers took. Atrides to his tent
Invited all the peers of Greece, and food sufficient
Appos'd before them, and the peers appos'd their hands to it. 95
Hunger and thirst being quickly quench'd, to counsel still they sit.
And first spake Nestor, who they thought of late advis'd so well,
A father grave, and rightly wise, who thus his tale did tell :

"Most high Atrides, since in thee I have intent to end,
From thee will I begin my speech, to whom Jove doth commend
The empire of so many men, and puts into thy hand
A sceptre, and establish'd laws, that thou mayst well command,
And counsel all men under thee. It therefore doth behove
Thyself to speak most, since of all thy speeches most will move;
And yet to hear, as well as speak; and then perform as well
A free just counsel; in thee still must stick what others tell.
For me, what in my judgment stands the most convenient
I will advise, and am assur'd advice more competent
Shall not be giv'n; the gen'ral proof, that hath before been made
Of what I speak, confirms me still, and now may well persuade,
Because I could not then, yet ought, when thou, most royal king,
Ev'n from the tent, Achilles' love didst violently bring,
Against my counsel, urging thee by all means to relent;
But you, obeying your high mind, would venture the event,
Dishonouring our ablest Greek, a man th' Immortals grace.
Again yet let's deliberate, to make him now embrace
Affection to our gen'ral good, and bring his force to field;
Both which kind words and pleasing gifts must make his virtues yield."
"O father," answeréd the king, "my wrongs thou tell'st me right.
Mine own offence mine own tongue grants. One man must stand in fight
For our whole army; him I wrong'd; him Jove loves from his heart,
He shows it in thus honouring him; who, living thus apart,
Proves us but number, for his want makes all our weakness seen.
Yet after my confess'd offence, soothing my hum'rous spleen,
I'll sweeten his affects again with presents infinite,
Which, to approve my firm intent, I'll openly recite:
Sev'n sacred tripods free from fire; ten talents of fine gold;
Twenty bright cauldrons; twelve young horse, well-shap'd, and well-controll'd,

[123] *Proves us but number*—numerous only, not powerful or valiant.

And victors too, for they have won the prize at many a race,
That man should not be poor that had but what their wingéd pace 130
Hath added to my treasury, nor feel sweet gold's defect.
Sev'n Lesbian ladies he shall have, that were the most select,
And in their needles rarely skill'd, whom, when he took the town
Of famous Lesbos, I did choose ; who won the chief renown
For beauty from their whole fair sex ; amongst whom I'll resign 135
Fair Brisis, and I deeply swear (for any fact of mine
That may discourage her receipt) she is untouch'd, and rests
As he resign'd her. To these gifts (if Jove to our requests
Vouchsafe performance, and afford the work, for which we wait,
Of winning Troy) with brass and gold he shall his navy freight ; 140
And, ent'ring when we be at spoil, that princely hand of his
Shall choose him twenty Trojan dames, excepting Tyndaris,
The fairest Pergamus enfolds ; and, if we make retreat
To Argos, call'd of all the world the Navel, or chief seat,
He shall become my son-in-law, and I will honour him 145
Ev'n as Orestes, my sole son, that doth in honours swim.
Three daughters in my well-built court unmarried are, and fair ;
Laodice, Chrysothemis that hath the golden hair,
And Iphianassa ; of all three the worthiest let him take
All-jointureless to Peleus' court ; I will her jointure make, 150
And that so great as never yet did any maid prefer.
Sev'n cities right magnificent, I will bestow on her ;
Enope, and Cardamyle, Hira for herbs renown'd,
The fair Æpea, Pedasus that doth with grapes abound,
Anthæa girded with green meads, Phera surnam'd Divine ; 155
All whose bright turrets on the seas, in sandy Pylos, shine.
Th' inhabitants in flocks and herds are wondrous confluent,
Who like a God will honour him, and him with gifts present,

¹⁴² *Tyndaris*—Helen.
¹⁵⁰ *Jointureless*—i. e. without the portion it was usual to pay the father on marrying his daughter.
¹⁵⁷ *Confluent*—affluent.

And to his throne will cóntribute what tribute he will rate.
All this I gladly will perform, to pacify his hate. 160
Let him be mild and tractable; 'tis for the God of ghosts
To be unrul'd, implacable, and seek the blood of hosts,
Whom therefore men do much abhor; then let him yield to me,
I am his greater, being a king, and more in years than he."

"Brave king," said Nestor, "these rich gifts must make him needs relent, 165
Choose then fit legates instantly to greet him at his tent.
But stay; admit my choice of them, and let them straight be gone.
Jove-lovéd Phœnix shall be chief, then Ajax Telamon,
And prince Ulysses; and on them let these two heralds wait,
Grave Odius and Eurybates. Come, lords, take water straight, 170
Make pure your hands, and with sweet words appease Achilles' mind,
Which we will pray the king of Gods may gently make inclin'd."

All lik'd his speech; and on their hands the heralds water shed,
The youths crown'd cups of sacred wine to all distributed.
But having sacrific'd, and drunk to ev'ry man's content, 175
With many notes by Nestor giv'n, the legates forward went.
With courtship in fit gestures us'd he did prepare them well,
But most Ulysses, for his grace did not so much excell.
Such rites beseem ambassadors; and Nestor urgéd these,
That their most honours might reflect enrag'd Æacides. 180
They went along the shore, and pray'd the God, that earth doth bind
In brackish chains, they might not fail, but bow his mighty mind.

The quarter of the Myrmidons they reach'd, and found him set
Delighted with his solemn harp, which curiously was fret
With works conceited, through the verge; the bawdrick that embrac'd
His lofty neck was silver twist; this, when his hand laid waste 186

---

[177] *With courtship in fit gestures us'd*—Chapman has well preserved the meaning of the original δενδίλλων.

[178] *For his grace did not so much excell.*—This is quite contrary to Homer's meaning. He simply says Nestor addressed each chief, but principally Ulysses. The reason doubtless being because he had most confidence in him.

[180] *Reflect*—turn back.

Aëtion's city, he did choose as his especial prise,
And, loving sacred music well, made it his exercise.
To it he sung the glorious deeds of great heroës dead,
And his true mind, that practice fail'd, sweet contemplation fed.   190
With him alone, and opposite, all silent sat his friend,
Attentive, and beholding him, who now his song did end.
Th' ambassadors did forwards press, renown'd Ulysses led,
And stood in view. Their sudden sight his admiration bred,
Who with his harp and all arose ; so did Menœtius' son   195
When he beheld them. Their receipt Achilles thus begun :
  "Health to my lords ! Right welcome men, assure yourselves you be,
Though some necessity, I know, doth make you visit me,
Incens'd with just cause 'gainst the Greeks." This said, a sev'ral seat
With purple cushions he set forth, and did their ease intreat,   200
And said : "Now, friend, our greatest bowl, with wine unmix'd and
          neat,
Appose these lords, and of the depth let ev'ry man make proof,
These are my best esteeméd friends, and underneath my roof."
  Patroclus did his dear friend's will ; and he that did desire
To cheer the lords, come faint from fight, set on a blazing fire   205
A great brass pot, and into it a chine of mutton put,
And fat goat's flesh. Automedon held, while he pieces cut,
To roast and boil, right cunningly ; then of a well-fed swine
A huge fat shoulder he cuts out, and spits it wondrous fine.
His good friend made a goodly fire ; of which the force once past,   210
He laid the spit low, near the coals, to make it brown at last,
Then sprinkled it with sacred salt, and took it from the racks.
This roasted and on dresser set, his friend Patroclus takes
Bread in fair baskets ; which set on, Achilles brought the meat,
And to divinest Ithacus took his opposéd seat   215
Upon the bench. Then did he will his friend to sacrifice,
Who cast sweet incense in the fire to all the Deities.

204 *He*—Achilles.

THE NINTH BOOK

Thus fell they to their ready food. Hunger and thirst allay'd,
Ajax to Phœnix made a sign, as if too long they stay'd
Before they told their legacy. Ulysses saw him wink, 220
And, filling the great bowl with wine, did to Achilles drink:
  "Health to Achilles! But our plights stand not in need of meat,
Who late supp'd at Atrides' tent, though for thy love we eat
Of many things, whereof a part would make a cómplete feast.
Nor can we joy in these kind rites, that have our hearts oppress'd, 225
O prince, with fear of utter spoil. 'Tis made a question now,
If we can save our fleet or not, unless thyself endow
Thy pow'rs with wonted fortitude. Now Troy and her consórts,
Bold of thy want, have pitch'd their tents close to our fleet and forts,
And made a firmament of fires; and now no more, they say, 230
Will they be prison'd in their walls, but force their violent way
Ev'n to our ships; and Jove himself hath with his lightnings show'd
Their bold adventures happy signs; and Hector grows so proud
Of his huge strength, borne out by Jove, that fearfully he raves,
Presuming neither men nor Gods can interrupt his braves. 235
Wild rage invades him, and he prays that soon the sacred Morn
Would light his fury; boasting then our streamers shall be torn,
And all our naval ornaments fall by his conqu'ring stroke,
Our ships shall burn, and we ourselves lie stifled in the smoke.
And I am seriously afraid, Heav'n will perform his threats, 240
And that 'tis fatal to us all, far from our native seats,
To perish in victorious Troy. But rise, though it be late,
Deliver the afflicted Greeks from Troy's tumultuous hate;
It will hereafter be thy grief, when no strength can suffice
To remedy th' effected threats of our calamities. 245
Consider these affairs in time, while thou mayst use thy pow'r.
And have the grace to turn from Greece fate's unrecover'd hour.

²²⁰ *Legacy*—embassy. Bk. VII. 348.
²⁴¹ *Fatal*—fated. Bk. VIII. 344.
²⁴⁷ *Unrecover'd*—irrecoverable.

O friend, thou know'st thy royal sire forewarn'd what should be done,
That day he sent thee from his court to honour Atreus' son:
'My son,' said he, 'the victory let Jove and Pallas use 250
At their high pleasures, but do thou no honour'd means refuse
That may advance her. In fit bounds contain thy mighty mind,
Nor let the knowledge of thy strength be factiously inclin'd,
Contriving mischiefs. Be to fame and gen'ral good profess'd.
The more will all sorts honour thee. Benignity is best.' 255
Thus charg'd thy sire, which thou forgett'st. Yet now those thoughts
    appease,
That torture thy great spirit with wrath; which if thou wilt surcease,
The king will merit it with gifts; and, if thou wilt give ear,
I'll tell how much he offers thee yet thou sitt'st angry here:
Sev'n tripods that no fire must touch; twice-ten pans, fit for flame; 260
Ten talents of fine gold; twelve horse that ever overcame,
And brought huge prises from the field, with swiftness of their feet,
That man should bear no poor account, nor want gold's quick'ning sweet,
That had but what he won with them; sev'n worthiest Lesbian dames,
Renown'd for skill in housewif'ry, and bear the sov'reign fames 265
For beauty from their gen'ral sex, which, at thy overthrow
Of well-built Lesbos, he did choose; and these he will bestow,
And with these her he took from thee, whom, by his state, since then,
He swears he touch'd not, as fair dames use to be touch'd by men.
All these are ready for thee now. And, if at length we take, 270
By helps of Gods, this wealthy town, thy ships shall burthen make
Of gold and brass at thy desires, when we the spoil divide;
And twenty beauteous Trojan dames thou shalt select beside,
Next Helen, the most beautiful; and, when return'd we be
To Argos, be his son-in-law, for he will honour thee 275
Like his Orestes, his sole son, maintain'd in height of bliss.
Three daughters beautify his court, the fair Chrysothemis,

    253 *Merit*—reward. An unusual application of the word.
    259 *Yet*—while.

Laodice, and Iphianesse ; of all the fairest take
To Peleus' thy grave father's court, and never jointure make ;
He will the jointure make himself, so great, as never sire   280
Gave to his daughter's nuptials. Sev'n cities left entire ;
Cardamyle, and Enope, and Hira full of flow'rs,
Anthæa for sweet meadows prais'd, and Phera deck'd with tow'rs,
The bright Epea, Pedasus that doth God Bacchus please ;
All, on the sandy Pylos' soil, are seated near the seas ;   285
Th' inhabitants in droves and flocks exceeding wealthy be,
Who, like a God, with worthy gifts will gladly honour thee,
And tribute of especial rate to thy high sceptre pay.
All this he freely will perform, thy anger to allay.
But if thy hate to him be more than his gifts may repress,   290
Yet pity all the other Greeks, in such extreme distress,
Who with religion honour thee ; and to their desp'rate ill
Thou shalt triumphant glory bring ; and Hector thou may'st kill,
When pride makes him encounter thee, fill'd with a baneful sprite,
Who vaunts our whole fleet brought not one, equal to him in fight."   295

   Swift-foot Æacides replied : " Divine Laertes' son,
'Tis requisite I should be short, and show what place hath won
Thy serious speech, affirming nought but what you shall approve
Establish'd in my settled heart, that in the rest I move
No murmur nor exceptión ; for, like hell mouth I loath,   300
Who holds not in his words and thoughts one indistinguish'd troth.
What fits the freeness of my mind, my speech shall make display'd.
Nor Atreus' son, nor all the Greeks, shall win me to their aid,
Their suit is wretchedly enforc'd, to free their own despairs,
And my life never shall be hir'd with thankless desp'rate pray'rs ;   305
For never had I benefit, that ever foil'd the foe ;
Ev'n share hath he that keeps his tent, and he to field doth go,
With equal honour cowards die, and men most valiant,
The much performer, and the man that can of nothing vaunt.

No overplus I ever found, when, with my mind's most strife 310
To do them good, to dang'rous fight I have expos'd my life.
But ev'n as to unfeather'd birds the careful dam brings meat,
Which when she hath bestow'd, herself hath nothing left to eat;
So, when my broken sleeps have drawn the nights t' extremest length,
And ended many bloody days with still-employéd strength, 315
To guard their weakness, and preserve their wives' contents infract,
I have been robb'd before their eyes. Twelve cities I have sack'd
Assail'd by sea, elev'n by land, while this siege held at Troy;
And of all these, what was most dear, and most might crown the joy
Of Agamemnon, he enjoy'd, who here behind remain'd; 320
Which when he took, a few he gave, and many things retain'd,
Other to optimates and kings he gave, who hold them fast,
Yet mine he forceth; only I sit with my loss disgrac'd.
But so he gain a lovely dame, to be his bed's delight,
It is enough; for what cause else do Greeks and Trojans fight? 325
Why brought he hither such an host? Was it not for a dame?
For fair-hair'd Helen? And doth love alone the hearts inflame
Of the Atrides to their wives, of all the men that move?
Ev'ry discreet and honest mind cares for his private love,
As much as they; as I myself lov'd Brisis as my life, 330
Although my captive, and had will to take her for my wife.
Whom since he forc'd, preventing me, in vain he shall prolong
Hopes to appease me that know well the deepness of my wrong.
But, good Ulysses, with thyself, and all you other kings,
Let him take stomach to repel Troy's fi'ry threatenings. 335
Much hath he done without my help, built him a goodly fort,
Cut a dike by it, pitch'd with pales, broad and of deep import;
And cannot all these helps repress this kill-man Hector's fright?
When I was arm'd among the Greeks, he would not offer fight
Without the shadow of his walls; but to the Scæan ports, 340
Or to the holy beech of Jove, come back'd with his consorts;

Where once he stood my charge alone, and hardly made retreat,
And to make new proof of our pow'rs, the doubt is not so great.
To-morrow then, with sacrifice perform'd t' imperial Jove
And all the Gods, I'll launch my fleet, and all my men remove ;   345
Which (if thou wilt use so thy sight, or think'st it worth respect)
In forehead of the morn, thine eyes shall see, with sails erect
Amidst the fishy Hellespont, help'd with laborious oars.
And, if the Sea-god send free sail, the fruitful Phthian shores
Within three days we shall attain, where I have store of prise   350
Left, when with prejudice I came to these indignities.
There have I gold as well as here, and store of ruddy brass,
Dames slender, elegantly girt, and steel as bright as glass.
These will I take as I retire, as shares I firmly save,
Though Agamemnon be so base to take the gifts he gave.   355
Tell him all this, and openly, I on your honours charge,
That others may take shame to hear his lusts command so large,
And, if there yet remain a man he hopeth to deceive
(Being dyed in endless impudence) that man may learn to leave
His trust and empire.   But alas, though, like a wolf he be,   360
Shameless and rude, he durst not take my prise, and look on me.
I never will partake his works, nor counsels, as before,
He once deceiv'd and injur'd me, and he shall never more
Tye my affections with his words.   Enough is the increase
Of one success in his deceits ; which let him joy in peace,   365
And bear it to a wretched end.   Wise Jove hath reft his brain
To bring him plagues, and these his gifts I, as my foes, disdain.
Ev'n in the numbness of calm death I will revengeful be,
Though ten or twenty times so much he would bestow on me,
All he hath here, or any where, or Orchomen contains,   370
To which men bring their wealth for strength, or all the store remains
In circuit of Egyptian Thebes, where much hid treasure lies,
Whose walls contain an hundred ports, of so admir'd a size

        [351] *Prejudice*—loss to myself.

Two hundred soldiers may a-front with horse and chariots pass.
Nor, would he amplify all this like sand, or dust, or grass,
Should he reclaim me, till this wreak pay'd me for all the pains
That with his contumely burn'd, like poison, in my veins.
Nor shall his daughter be my wife, although she might contend
With golden Venus for her form, or if she did transcend
Blue-ey'd Minerva for her works; let him a Greek select
Fit for her, and a greater king. For if the Gods protect
My safety to my father's court, he shall choose me a wife.
Many fair Achive princesses of unimpeachéd life
In Helle and in Phthia live, whose sires do cities hold,
Of whom I can have whom I will. And, more an hundred fold
My true mind in my country likes to take a lawful wife
Than in another nation; and there delight my life
With those goods that my father got, much rather than die here.
Not all the wealth of well-built Troy, possess'd when peace was there,
All that Apollo's marble fane in stony Pythos holds,
I value equal with the life that my free breast enfolds.
Sheep, oxen, tripods, crest-deck'd horse, though lost, may come again,
But when the white guard of our teeth no longer can contain
Our human soul, away it flies, and, once gone, never more
To her frail mansion any man can her lost pow'rs restore.
And therefore since my mother-queen, fam'd for her silver feet,
Told me two fates about my death in my direction meet:
The one, that, if I here remain t' assist our victory,
My safe return shall never live, my fame shall never die;
If my return obtain success, much of my fame decays,
But death shall linger his approach, and I live many days.
This being reveal'd, 'twere foolish pride, t' abridge my life for praise.
Then with myself, I will advise, others to hoise their sail,
For, 'gainst the height of Ilion, you never shall prevail,

---

[394] *Once gone*—the second folio erroneously reads "*once again.*"

Jove with his hand protecteth it, and makes the soldiers bold. 405
This tell the kings in ev'ry part, for so grave legates should,
That they may better counsels use, to save their fleet and friends
By their own valours; since this course, drown'd in my anger, ends.
Phœnix may in my tent repose, and in the morn steer course
For Phthia, if he think it good; if not, I'll use no force." 410

All wonder'd at his stern reply; and Phœnix, full of fears
His words would be more weak than just, supplied their wants with tears.

"If thy return incline thee thus, Peleus' renownéd joy,
And thou wilt let our ships be burn'd with harmful fire of Troy,
Since thou art angry, O my son, how shall I after be 415
Alone in these extremes of death, relinquishéd by thee?
I, whom thy royal father sent as ord'rer of thy force,
When to Atrides from his court he left thee for this course,
Yet young, and when in skill of arms thou didst not so abound,
Nor hadst the habit of discourse, that makes men so renown'd. 420
In all which I was set by him, t' instruct thee as my son,
That thou might'st speak, when speech was fit, and do, when deeds were
Not sit as dumb, for want of words, idle, for skill to move. [done,
I would not then be left by thee, dear son, begot in love,
No, not if God would promise me, to raze the prints of time 425
Carv'd in my bosom and my brows, and grace me with the prime
Of manly youth, as when at first I left sweet Helle's shore
Deck'd with fair dames, and fled the grudge my angry father bore;
Who was the fair Amyntor call'd, surnam'd Ormenides,
And for a fair-hair'd harlot's sake, that his affects could please, 430
Contemn'd my mother, his true wife, who ceaseless urgéd me
To use his harlot Clytia, and still would clasp my knee
To do her will, that so my sire might turn his love to hate
Of that lewd dame, converting it to comfort her estate.

⁴⁰⁶ Both folios have "*king;*" but it is evident from the context, and a reference to the original, that the plural is the true reading.
⁴⁰⁸ The second folio reads, "*since this course drown'd in my eager ends.*"

At last I was content to prove to do my mother good, 435
And reconcile my father's love ; who straight suspicious stood,
Pursuing me with many a curse, and to the Furies pray'd
No dame might love, nor bring me seed. The Deities obey'd
That govern hell ; infernal Jove, and stern Persephone.
Then durst I in no longer date with my stern father be. 440
Yet did my friends, and near allies, inclose me with desires
Not to depart ; kill'd sheep, boars, beeves ; roast them at solemn fires ;
And from my father's tuns we drunk exceeding store of wine.
Nine nights they guarded me by turns, their fires did ceaseless shine,
One in the porch of his strong hall, and in the portal one, 445
Before my chamber ; but when day beneath the tenth night shone,
I brake my chamber's thick-fram'd doors, and through the hall's guard pass'd,
Unseen of any man or maid. Through Greece then, rich and vast,
I fled to Phthia, nurse of sheep, and came to Peleus' court ;
Who entertain'd me heartily, and in as gracious sort 450
As any sire his only son, born when his strength is spent,
And bless'd with great possessions to leave to his descent.
He made me rich, and to my charge did much command commend.
I dwelt in th' utmost region rich Phthia doth extend,
And govern'd the Dolopians, and made thee what thou art, 455
O thou that like the Gods art fram'd. Since, dearest to my heart,
I us'd thee so, thou lov'dst none else ; nor anywhere wouldst eat,
Till I had crown'd my knee with thee, and carv'd thee tend'rest meat,
And giv'n thee wine so much, for love, that, in thy infancy
(Which still discretion must protect, and a continual eye) 460
My bosom lovingly sustain'd the wine thine could not bear.
Then, now my strength needs thine as much, be mine to thee as dear,
Much have I suffer'd for thy love, much labour'd, wishéd much,
Thinking, since I must have no heir (the Gods' decrees are such)

---

[439] *Infernal Jove*—Pluto.
[439] *Persephone*—the Greek form ; thus the first folio. The second has " *Proserpine.*"

I would adopt thyself my heir. To thee my heart did give 465
What any sire could give his son. In thee I hop'd to live.
O mitigate thy mighty spirits. It fits not one that moves
The hearts of all, to live unmov'd, and succour hates for loves.
The Gods themselves are flexible; whose virtues, honours, pow'rs,
Are more than thine, yet they will bend their breasts as we bend ours.
Perfumes, benign devotions, savours of off'rings burn'd, 471
And holy rites, the engines are with which their hearts are turn'd,
By men that pray to them, whose faith their sins have falsified.
For Pray'rs are daughters of great Jove, lame, wrinkled, ruddy-ey'd,
And ever following Injury, who, strong and sound of feet, 475
Flies through the world, afflicting men. Believing Prayers yet,
To all that love that Seed of Jove, the certain blessing get
To have Jove hear, and help them too; but if he shall refuse,
And stand inflexible to them, they fly to Jove, and use
Their pow'rs against him, that the wrongs he doth to them may fall
On his own head, and pay those pains whose cure he fails to call. 481
Then, great Achilles, honour thou this sacred Seed of Jove,
And yield to them, since other men of greatest minds they move.
If Agamemnon would not give the selfsame gifts he vows,
But offer other afterwards, and in his still-bent brows 485
Entomb his honour and his word, I would not thus exhort,
With wrath appeas'd, thy aid to Greece, though plagu'd in heaviest sort;
But much he presently will give, and after yield the rest.
T' assure which he hath sent to thee the men thou lovest best,
And most renown'd of all the host, that they might soften thee. 490
Then let not both their pains and pray'rs lost and despisèd be,
Before which none could reprehend the tumult of thy heart,
But now to rest inexpiate were much too rude a part.
Of ancient worthies we have heard, when they were more displeas'd,
To their high fames, wth gifts and pray'rs they have been still appeas'd.

⁴⁶⁵ *Thyself*—the second folio has "*myself.*"
⁴⁹³ *Rest inexpiate*—remain implacable.

For instance, I remember well a fact perform'd of old, 490
Which to you all, my friends, I'll tell : The Curets wars did hold
With the well-fought Ætolians, where mutual lives had end
About the city Calydon. Th' Ætolians did defend
Their flourishing country, which to spoil the Curets did contend. 500
Diana with-the-golden-throne, with Oeneus much incens'd,
Since with his plenteous land's first fruits she was not reverenc'd,
(Yet other Gods, with hecatombs, had feasts, and she alone,
Great Jove's bright daughter, left unserv'd, or by oblivion,
Or undue knowledge of her dues) much hurt in heart she swore ; 505
And she, enrag'd, excited much, she sent a sylvan boar
From their green groves, with wounding tusks ; who usually did spoil
King Oeneus' fields, his lofty woods laid prostrate on the soil,
Rent by the roots trees fresh, adorn'd with fragrant apple flow'rs.
Which Meleager (Oeneus' son) slew, with assembled pow'rs 510
Of hunters, and of fiercest hounds, from many cities brought ;
For such he was that with few lives his death could not be bought,
Heaps of dead humans, by his rage, the fun'ral piles applied.
Yet, slain at last, the Goddess stirr'd about his head, and hide,
A wondrous tumult, and a war betwixt the Curets wrought 515
And brave Ætolians. All the while fierce Meleager fought,
Ill-far'd the Curets ; near the walls none durst advance his crest,
Though they were many. But when wrath inflam'd his haughty breast
(Which oft the firm mind of the wise with passion doth infest)
Since 'twixt his mother-queen and him arose a deadly strife, 520
He left the court, and privately liv'd with his lawful wife,
Fair Cleopatra, female birth of bright Marpessa's pain,
And of Ideus ; who of all terrestrial men did reign,
At that time, king of fortitude, and for Marpessa's sake,
'Gainst wanton Phœbus, king of flames, his bow in hand did take, 525
Since he had ravish'd her, his joy ; whom her friends after gave
The surname of Alcyone, because they could not save

[507] *Usually*—as is their wont.

Their daughter from Alcyone's fate. In Cleopatra's arms
Lay Meleager, feeding on his anger, for the harms
His mother pray'd might fall on him ; who, for her brother slain   530
By Meleager, griev'd, and pray'd the Gods to wreak her pain
With all the horror could be pour'd upon her furious birth.
Still knock'd she with her impious hands the many-feeding earth,
To urge stern Pluto and his Queen t' incline their vengeful ears,
Fell on her knees, and all her breast dew'd with her fi'ry tears,   535
To make them massacre her son, whose wrath enrag'd her thus.
Erinnys, wand'ring through the air, heard, out of Erebus,
Pray'rs fit for her unpleaséd mind. Yet Meleager lay
Obscur'd in fury. Then the bruit of the tumultuous fray
Rung through the turrets as they scal'd ; then came th' Ætolian peers
To Meleager with low suits, to rise and free their fears ;   541
Then sent they the chief priests of Gods, with offer'd gifts t' atone
His diff'ring fury, bade him choose, in sweet-soil'd Calydon,
Of the most fat and yieldy soil, what with an hundred steers
Might in a hundred days be plough'd, half that rich vintage bears,   545
And half of naked earth to plough ; yet yielded not his ire.
Then to his lofty chamber-door, ascends his royal sire
With ruthful plaints, shook the strong bars ; then came his sisters' cries ;
His mother then ; and all intreat ;—yet still more stiff he lies ;—
His friends, most rev'rend, most esteem'd ; yet none impression took,
Till the high turrets where he lay, and his strong chamber, shook   551
With the invading enemy, who now forc'd dreadful way
Along the city. Then his wife, in pitiful dismay,
Besought him, weeping ; telling him the miseries sustain'd
By all the citizens, whose town the enemy had gain'd ;   555
Men slaughter'd ; children bondslaves made ; sweet ladies forc'd with
       lust ;
Fires climbing tow'rs, and turning them to heaps of fruitless dust.

⁵³⁸ *Unpleased*—implacable.
⁵⁴³ *Diff'ring*—angry. As we use the word a *difference* in the sense of a quarrel.

These dangers soften'd his steel heart. Up the stout prince arose,
Indu'd his body with rich arms, and freed th' Ætolian's woes,
His smother'd anger giving air; which gifts did not assuage, 560
But his own peril. And because he did not disengage
Their lives for gifts, their gifts he lost. But for my sake, dear friend,
Be not thou bent to see our plights to these extremes descend,
Ere thou assist us; be not so by thy ill angel turn'd
From thine own honour. It were shame to see our navy burn'd, 565
And then come with thy timeless aid. For offer'd presents, come,
And all the Greeks will honour thee, as of celestial room.
But if without these gifts thou fight, forc'd by thy private woe,
Thou wilt be nothing so renown'd, though thou repel the foe."

   Achilles answer'd the last part of this oration thus: 570
"Phœnix, renown'd and reverend, the honours urg'd on us
We need not. Jove doth honour me, and to my safety sees,
And will, whiles I retain a spirit, or can command my knees.
Then do not thou with tears and woes impassion my affects,
Becoming gracious to my foe. Nor fits it the respects 575
Of thy vow'd love to honour him that hath dishonour'd me,
Lest such loose kindness lose his heart that yet is firm to thee.
It were thy praise to hurt with me the hurter of my state,
Since half my honour and my realm thou mayst participate.
Let these lords then return th' event, and do thou here repose, 580
And, when dark sleep breaks with the day, our counsels shall disclose
The course of our return or stay." This said, he with his eye
Made to his friend a covert sign, to hasten instantly
A good soft bed, that the old prince, soon as the peers were gone,
Might take his rest; when, soldier-like, brave Ajax Telamon 585

---

   [567] *As of celestial room*—as one of the family of the Gods.
   [570] The second folio has "*his*," which Dr. Taylor has followed.
   [574] *Impassion my affects*—passionately appeal to my feelings.
   [580] *Return the event*—tell the issue of their embassy. We use the word, to make a parliamentary *return*.

Spake to Ulysses, as with thought Achilles was not worth
The high direction of his speech, that stood so sternly forth
Unmov'd with th' other orators, and spake, not to appease
Pelides' wrath, but to depart. His arguments were these:
    "High-issu'd Laertiades, let us insist no more   590
On his persuasion. I perceive the world would end before
Our speeches end in this affair. We must with utmost haste
Return his answer, though but bad. The peers are elsewhere plac'd,
And will not rise till we return. Great Thetis' son hath stor'd
Proud wrath within him, as his wealth, and will not be implor'd,   595
Rude that he is, nor his friends' love respects, do what they can,
Wherein past all, we honour'd him. O unremorseful man!
Another for his brother slain, another for his son,
Accepts of satisfaction; and he the deed hath done
Lives in belov'd society long after his amends,   600
To which his foe's high heart, for gifts, with patience condescends;
But thee a wild and cruel spirit the Gods for plague have giv'n,
And for one girl, of whose fair sex we come to offer sev'n,
The most exempt for excellence, and many a better prise.
Then put a sweet mind in thy breast, respect thy own allies,   605
Though others make thee not remiss. A multitude we are,
Sprung of thy royal family, and our supremest care
Is to be most familiar, and hold most love with thee
Of all the Greeks, how great an host soever here there be."
    He answer'd: "Noble Telamon, prince of our soldiers here,   610
Out of thy heart I know thou speak'st, and as thou hold'st me dear;
But still as often as I think, how rudely I was us'd,
And, like a stranger, for all rites, fit for our good, refus'd,
My heart doth swell against the man, that durst be so profane
To violate his sacred place; not for my private bane,   615
But since wrack'd virtue's gen'ral laws he shameless did infringe;
For whose sake I will loose the reins, and give mine anger swinge,

    597 *Unremorseful.*—See Bk. VIII. 208.

Without my wisdom's least impeach. He is a fool, and base,
That pities vice-plagu'd minds, when pain, not love of right, gives place.
And therefore tell your king, my lords, my just wrath will not care 620
For all his cares, before my tents and navy chargéd are
By warlike Hector, making way through flocks of Grecian lives,
Enlighten'd by their naval fire ; but when his rage arrives
About my tent, and sable bark, I doubt not but to shield
Them and myself, and make him fly the there strong-bounded field."

 This said, each one but kiss'd the cup, and to the ships retir'd ; 625
Ulysses first. Patroclus then the men and maids requir'd
To make grave Phœnix' bed with speed, and see he nothing lacks.
They straight obey'd, and thereon laid the subtile fruit of flax,
And warm sheep-fells for covering ; and there the old man slept, 630
Attending till the golden Morn her usual station kept.
Achilles lay in th' inner room of his tent richly wrought,
And that fair lady by his side, that he from Lesbos brought,
Bright Diomeda, Phorbas' seed. Patroclus did embrace
The beauteous Iphis, giv'n to him, when his bold friend did race 635
The lofty Scyrus that was kept in Enyeius' hold.

 Now at the tent of Atreus' son, each man with cups of gold
Receiv'd th' ambassadors return'd. All cluster'd near to know
What news they brought ; which first the king would have Ulysses show :
"Say, most praiseworthy Ithacus, the Grecians' great renown, 640
Will he defend us ? Or not yet will his proud stomach down ?"

 Ulysses made reply : "Not yet will he appeaséd be,
But grows more wrathful, prizing light thy offer'd gifts and thee,
And wills thee to consult with us, and take some other course
To save our army and our fleet, and says, ' with all his force, 645
The morn shall light him on his way to Phthia's wishéd soil,
For never shall high-seated Troy be sack'd with all our toil,

---

[629] *Subtile*—Latin *subtilis*, fine. Ben Jonson uses the word in this sense (Catiline, II. 3) when he speaks of " *subtile lips.*" Shakespeare, (Coriolanus, v. 2.)
   " Like to a bowl upon a *subtile* ground,"
where it refers to the smoothness of the bowling ground.

Jove holds his hand 'twixt us and it, the soldiers gather heart.'
Thus he replies, which Ajax here can equally impart,
And both these heralds. Phœnix stays, for so was his desire,   650
To go with him, if he thought good ; if not, he might retire."
All wonder'd he should be so stern ; at last bold Diomed spake :
  "Would God, Atrides, thy request were yet to undertake,
And all thy gifts unoffer'd him ! He's proud enough beside,
But this ambassage thou hast sent will make him burst with pride.   655
But let us suffer him to stay, or go, at his desire,
Fight when his stomach serves him best, or when Jove shall inspire.
Meanwhile, our watch being strongly held, let us a little rest
After our food ; strength lives by both, and virtue is their guest.
Then when the rosy-finger'd Morn holds out her silver light,   660
Bring forth thy host, encourage all, and be thou first in fight."
  The kings admir'd the fortitude, that so divinely mov'd
The skilful horseman Diomed, and his advice approv'd.
Then with their nightly sacrifice each took his sev'ral tent,
Where all receiv'd the sov'reign gifts soft Somnus did present.   665

     659 *Virtue is their guest*—valour accompanies food and rest.

THE END OF THE NINTH BOOK.

THE TENTH BOOK OF HOMER'S ILIADS.

THE ARGUMENT.

Th' Atrides, watching, wake the other peers,
And (in the fort, consulting of their fears)
Two kings they send, most stout, and honour'd most,
For royal scouts, into the Trojan host;
Who meeting Dolon, Hector's bribéd spy,
Take him, and learn how all the quarters lie.
He told them, in the Thracian regiment
Of rich king Rhesus, and his royal tent,
Striving for safety; but they end his strife,
And rid poor Dolon of a dang'rous life.
Then with digressive wiles they use their force
On Rhesus' life, and take his snowy horse.

ANOTHER ARGUMENT.

Kappa the night exploits applies:
Rhesus' and Dolon's tragedies.

THE other princes at their ships soft-finger'd sleep did bind,
But not the Gen'ral; Somnus' silks bound not his labouring mind
That turn'd, and return'd, many thoughts. And as quick lightnings fly,
From well-deck'd Juno's sovereign, out of the thicken'd sky,

[3] " These are the lightnings before snow, &c. that Scaliger's Criticus so unworthily taxeth; citing the place falsely, as in the third book's annotations, &c."—CHAPMAN.

VOL. I.   O

Preparing some exceeding rain, or hail, the fruit of cold, 5
Or down-like snow that suddenly makes all the fields look old,
Or opes the gulfy mouth of war with his ensulphur'd hand,
In dazzling flashes pour'd from clouds, on any punish'd land;
So from Atrides' troubled heart, through his dark sorrows, flew
Redoubled sighs; his entrails shook, as often as his view 10
Admir'd the multitude of fires, that gilt the Phrygian shade,
And heard the sounds of fifes, and shawms, and tumults soldiers made.
But when he saw his fleet and host kneel to his care and love,
He rent his hair up by the roots as sacrifice to Jove,
Burnt in his fi'ry sighs, still breath'd out of his royal heart, 15
And first thought good to Nestor's care his sorrows to impart,
To try if royal diligence, with his approv'd advice,
Might fashion counsels to prevent their threaten'd miseries.
  So up he rose, attir'd himself, and to his strong feet tied
Rich shoes, and cast upon his back a ruddy lion's hide, 20
So ample it his ankles reach'd, then took his royal spear.
  Like him was Menelaus pierc'd with an industrious fear,
Nor sat sweet slumber on his eyes, lest bitter fates should quite
The Greeks' high favours, that for him resolv'd such endless fight.
And first a freckled panther's hide hid his broad back athwart; 25
His head his brazen helm did arm; his able hand his dart;
Then made he all his haste to raise his brother's head as rare,
That he who most excell'd in rule might help t' effect his care.
He found him, at his ship's crook'd stern, adorning him with arms;
Who joy'd to see his brother's spirits awak'd without alarms, 30
Well weighing th' importance of the time. And first the younger spake:
  "Why, brother, are ye arming thus? Is it to undertake
The sending of some vent'rous Greek, t' explore the foe's intent?
Alas! I greatly fear, not one will give that work consent,
Expos'd alone to all the fears that flow in gloomy night. 35
He that doth this must know death well, in which ends ev'ry fright."

[23] *Quite*—requite, put a stop to.

"Brother," said he, "in these affairs we both must use advice,
Jove is against us, and accepts great Hector's sacrifice.
For I have never seen, nor heard, in one day, and by one,
So many high attempts well urg'd, as Hector's pow'r hath done   40
Against the hapless sons of Greece ; being chiefly dear to Jove,
And without cause, being neither fruit of any Goddess' love,
Nor helpful God ; and yet I fear the deepness of his hand,
Ere it be ras'd out of our thoughts, will many years withstand.
But, brother, hie thee to thy ships, and Idomen's dis-ease   45
With warlike Ajax ; I will haste to grave Neleides,
Exhorting him to rise, and give the sacred watch command,
For they will specially embrace incitement at his hand,
And now his son their captain is, and Idomen's good friend,
Bold Merion, to whose discharge we did that charge commend."   50

"Command'st thou then," his brother ask'd, "that I shall tarry here
Attending thy resolv'd approach, or else the message bear,
And quickly make return to thee?" He answer'd : "Rather stay,
Lest otherwise we fail to meet, for many a diff'rent way
Lies through our labyrinthian host. Speak ever as you go,   55
Command strong watch, from sire to son urge all t' observe the foe,
Familiarly, and with their praise, exciting ev'ry eye,
Not with unseason'd violence of proud authority.
We must our patience exercise, and work ourselves with them,
Jove in our births combin'd such care to either's diadem."   60

Thus he dismiss'd him, knowing well his charge before he went.
Himself to Nestor, whom he found in bed within his tent,
By him his damask curets hung, his shield, a pair of darts,
His shining casque, his arming waist ; in these he led the hearts
Of his apt soldiers to sharp war, not yielding to his years.   65
He quickly started from his bed, when to his watchful ears
Untimely feet told some approach ; he took his lance in hand,
And spake to him : "Ho, what art thou that walk'st at midnight? Stand.

⁴⁵ *Dis-ease*—disturb, arouse.   ⁶³ *Damask*—inlaid.

Is any wanting at the guards? Or lack'st thou any peer?
Speak, come not silent towards me; say, what intend'st thou here?" 70
    He answer'd: "O Neleides, grave honour of our host,
'Tis Agamemnon thou mayst know, whom Jove afflicteth most
Of all the wretched men that live, and will, whilst any breath
Gives motion to my toiled limbs, and bears me up from death.
I walk the round thus, since sweet sleep cannot inclose mine eyes, 75
Nor shut those organs care breaks ope for our calamities.
My fear is vehement for the Greeks; my heart, the fount of heat,
With his extreme affects made cold, without my breast doth beat;
And therefore are my sinews strook with trembling; ev'ry part
Of what my friends may feel hath act in my dispersed heart. 80
But, if thou think'st of any course may to our good redound,
(Since neither thou thyself canst sleep) come, walk with me the round;
In way whereof we may confer, and look to ev'ry guard,
Lest watching long, and weariness with labouring so hard,
Drown their oppressed memories of what they have in charge. 85
The liberty we give the foe, alas, is over large,
Their camp is almost mix'd with ours, and we have forth no spies
To learn their drifts; who may perchance this night intend surprise."
    Grave Nestor answer'd: "Worthy king, let good hearts bear
        our ill.
Jove is not bound to perfect all this busy Hector's will; 90
But I am confidently giv'n, his thoughts are much dismay'd
With fear, lest our distress incite Achilles to our aid,
And therefore will not tempt his fate, nor ours, with further pride.
But I will gladly follow thee, and stir up more beside;
Tydides, famous for his lance; Ulysses; Telamon; 95
And bold Phyleus' valiant heir. Or else, if any one
Would haste to call king Idomen, and Ajax, since their sail
Lie so remov'd, with much good speed, it might our haste avail.
But, though he be our honour'd friend, thy brother I will blame,
Not fearing if I anger thee. It is his utter shame 100

He should commit all pains to thee, that should himself employ,
Past all our princes, in the care, and cure, of our annoy,
And be so far from needing spurs to these his due respects,
He should apply our spirits himself, with pray'rs and urg'd affects.
Necessity (a law to laws, and not to be endur'd) 105
Makes proof of all his faculties, not sound if not inur'd."
  "Good father," said the king, "sometimes you know I have desir'd
You would improve his negligence, too oft to ease retir'd.
Nor is it for defect of spirit, or compass of his brain,
But with observing my estate, he thinks, he should abstain 110
Till I commanded, knowing my place; unwilling to assume,
For being my brother, anything might prove he did presume.
But now he rose before me far, and came t' avoid delays,
And I have sent him for the men yourself desir'd to raise.
Come, we shall find them at the guards we plac'd before the fort, 115
For thither my direction was they should with speed resort."
  "Why now," said Nestor, "none will grudge, nor his just rule withstand.
Examples make excitements strong, and sweeten a command."
  Thus put he on his arming truss, fair shoes upon his feet,
About him a mandilion, that did with buttons meet, 120
Of purple, large, and full of folds, curl'd with a warmful nap,
A garment that 'gainst cold in nights did soldiers use to wrap;
Then took he his strong lance in hand, made sharp with provèd steel,
And went along the Grecian fleet. First at Ulysses' keel
He call'd, to break the silken fumes that did his senses bind. 125
The voice through th' organs of his ears straight rung about his mind.

---

   [103] *Improve*—reprove. An unusual signification. NARES quotes two authorities.
   [114] Both the folios read "*man.*" Dr. Taylor has "*men,*" which the context requires.
   [120] *Mandilion*—" A loose cassock such as souldiers use to wear."—BLOUNT, GLOSSOGRAPH. From Ital.

Forth came Ulysses, asking him: "Why stir ye thus so late?
Sustain we such enforcive cause?" He answer'd, "Our estate
Doth force this perturbation; vouchsafe it, worthy friend,
And come, let us excite one more, to counsel of some end   130
To our extremes, by fight, or flight." He back, and took his shield,
And both took course to Diomed. They found him laid in field,
Far from his tent; his armour by; about him was dispread
A ring of soldiers, ev'ry man his shield beneath his head;
His spear fix'd by him as he slept, the great end in the ground,   135
The point, that bristled the dark earth, cast a reflection round
Like pallid lightnings thrown from Jove; thus this heroë lay,
And under him a big ox-hide; his royal head had stay
On arras hangings, rolléd up; whereon he slept so fast,
That Nestor stirr'd him with his foot, and chid to see him cast   140
In such deep sleep in such deep woes, and ask'd him why he spent
All night in sleep, or did not hear the Trojans near his tent,
Their camp drawn close upon their dike, small space 'twixt foes and foes?

He, starting up, said, "Strange old man, that never tak'st repose,
Thou art too patient of our toil. Have we not men more young,   145
To be employ'd from king to king? Thine age hath too much wrong."

"Said like a king," replied the sire, "for I have sons renown'd,
And there are many other men, might go this toilsome round;
But, you must see, imperious Need hath all at her command.
Now on the eager razor's edge, for life or death, we stand   150
Then go (thou art the younger man) and if thou love my ease,
Call swift-foot Ajax up thyself, and young Phyleides."

This said, he on his shoulders cast a yellow lion's hide,
Big, and reach'd earth; then took his spear, and Nestor's will applied,
Rais'd the heroës, brought them both. All met; the round they went,
And found not any captain there asleep or negligent,   155

¹⁴⁸ *And there are, &c.*—The second folio reads, "*As there are;*" and so Dr. Taylor.
¹⁵⁰ "'Ἐπὶ ξυροῦ ἵσταται ἀκμῆς. This went into a proverb, used by Theocritus, in *Dioscuris*, out of Homer."—CHAPMAN.

But waking, and in arms, gave ear to ev'ry lowest sound.
And as keen dogs keep sheep in cotes, or folds of hurdles bound,
And grin at ev'ry breach of air, envious of all that moves, 159
Still list'ning when the rav'nous beast stalks through the hilly groves,
Then men and dogs stand on their guards, and mighty tumults make,
Sleep wanting weight to close one wink ; so did the captains wake,
That kept the watch the whole sad night, all with intentive ear
Converted to the enemies' tents, that they might timely hear
If they were stirring to surprise ; which Nestor joy'd to see. 165
  " Why so, dear sons, maintain your watch, sleep not a wink," said he,
" Rather than make your fames the scorn of Trojan perjury."
  This said, he foremost pass'd the dike, the others seconded,
Ev'n all the kings that had been call'd to council from the bed,
And with them went Meriones, and Nestor's famous son ; 170
For both were call'd by all the kings to consultation.
Beyond the dike they choos'd a place, near as they could from blood,
Where yet appear'd the falls of some, and whence, the crimson flood
Of Grecian lives being pour'd on earth by Hector's furious chace,
He made retreat, when night repour'd grim darkness in his face. 175
There sat they down, and Nestor spake : " O friends, remains not one
That will rely on his bold mind, and view the camp, alone,
Of the proud Trojans, to approve if any straggling mate
He can surprise near th' utmost tents, or learn the brief estate
Of their intentions for the time, and mix like one of them 180
With their outguards, expiscating if the renown'd extreme
They force on us will serve their turns, with glory to retire,
Or still encamp thus far from Troy ? This may he well inquire,
And make a brave retreat untouch'd ; and this would win him fame
Of all men canopied with heav'n, and ev'ry man of name, 185
In all this host shall honour him with an enriching meed,
A black ewe and her sucking lamb (rewards that now exceed

       [157] Dr. Taylor, with the second folio, reads "*give* ear."
       [181] *Expiscating*—inquiring into, fishing out.

THE TENTH BOOK

All other best possessions, in all men's choice requests)
And still be bidden by our kings to kind and royal feasts." 189
    All rev'renc'd one another's worth ; and none would silence break,
Lest worst should take best place of speech ; at last did Diomed speak :
"Nestor, thou ask'st if no man here have heart so well inclin'd
To work this stratagem on Troy ? Yes, I have such a mind.
Yet, if some other prince would join, more probable will be
The strengthen'd hope of our exploit. Two may together see 195
(One going before another still) sly danger ev'ry way ;
One spirit upon another works, and takes with firmer stay
The benefit of all his pow'rs ; for though one knew his course,
Yet might he well distrust himself, which th' other might enforce."
    This offer ev'ry man assum'd ; all would with Diomed go ; 200
The two Ajaces, Merion, and Menelaus too ;
But Nestor's son enforc'd it much ; and hardy Ithacus,
Who had to ev'ry vent'rous deed a mind as venturous.
    Amongst all these thus spake the king : "Tydides, most belov'd,
Choose thy associate worthily ; a man the most approv'd 205
For use and strength in these extremes. Many thou seest stand forth ;
But choose not thou by height of place, but by regard of worth,
Lest with thy nice respect of right to any man's degree,
Thou wrong'st thy venture, choosing one least fit to join with thee,
Although perhaps a greater king." This spake he with suspect 210
That Diomed, for honour's sake, his brother would select.
    Then said Tydides : "Since thou giv'st my judgment leave to
      choose,
How can it so much truth forget Ulysses to refuse,
That bears a mind so most exempt, and vig'rous in th' effect
Of all high labours, and a man Pallas doth most respect ? 215
We shall return through burning fire, if I with him combine,
He sets strength in so true a course, with counsels so divine."
    Ulysses, loth to be esteem'd a lover of his praise,
With such exceptions humbled him as did him higher raise,

And said: "Tydides, praise me not more than free truth will bear, 220
Nor yet impair me; they are Greeks that give judicial ear.
But come, the morning hastes, the stars are forward in their course,
Two parts of night are past, the third is left t'employ our force."
Now borrow'd they for haste some arms. Bold Thrasymedes lent
Advent'rous Diomed his sword (his own was at his tent) 225
His shield, and helm tough and well-tann'd, without or plume or crest,
And call'd a murrion, archers' heads it uséd to invest.
Meriones lent Ithacus his quiver and his bow,
His helmet fashion'd of a hide; the workman did bestow
Much labour in it, quilting it with bow-strings, and without 230
With snowy tusks of white-mouth'd boars 'twas arméd round about
Right cunningly, and in the midst an arming cap was plac'd,
That with the fix'd ends of the tusks his head might not be ras'd.
This, long since, by Autolycus was brought from Eleon,
When he laid waste Amyntor's house, that was Ormenus' son. 235
In Scandia, to Cytherius, surnam'd Amphidamas,
Autolycus did give this helm; he, when he feasted was
By honour'd Molus, gave it him, as present of a guest;
Molus to his son Merion did make it his bequest.
With this Ulysses arm'd his head; and thus they, both address'd, 240
Took leave of all the other kings. To them a glad ostent,
As they were ent'ring on their way, Minerva did present,
A hernshaw consecrate to her, which they could ill discern
Through sable night, but, by her clange, they knew it was a hern.
Ulysses joy'd, and thus invok'd: "Hear me, great Seed of Jove, 245
That ever dost my labours grace with presence of thy love,
And all my motions dost attend! Still love me, sacred Dame,
Especially in this exploit, and so protect our fame
We both may safely make retreat, and thriftily employ
Our boldness in some great affair baneful to them of Troy." 250

[227] *Murrion*—i. e. morion. [244] *Clange*.—See Bk. III. 5.

Then pray'd illustrate Diomed : "Vouchsafe me likewise ear,
O thou unconquer'd Queen of arms ! Be with thy favours near,
As, to my royal father's steps, thou went'st a bounteous guide,
When th' Achives and the peers of Thebes he would have pacified,
Sent as the Greeks' ambassador, and left them at the flood 255
Of great Æsopus ; whose retreat thou mad'st to swim in blood
Of his enambush'd enemies ; and, if thou so protect
My bold endeavours, to thy name an heifer most select,
That never yet was tam'd with yoke, broad-fronted, one year old,
I'll burn in zealous sacrifice, and set the horns in gold." 260

The Goddess heard ; and both the kings their dreadless passage bore
Through slaughter, slaughter'd carcasses, arms, and discolour'd gore.

Nor Hector let his princes sleep, but all to council call'd,
And ask'd, "What one is here will vow, and keep it unappall'd,
To have a gift fit for his deed, a chariot and two horse, 265
That pass for speed the rest of Greece ? What one dares take this
 course,
For his renown, besides his gifts, to mix amongst the foe,
And learn if still they hold their guards, or with this overthrow
Determine flight, as being too weak to hold us longer war ?"

All silent stood ; at last stood forth one Dolon, that did dare 270
This dang'rous work, Eumedes' heir, a herald much renown'd.
This Dolon did in gold and brass exceedingly abound,
But in his form was quite deform'd, yet passing swift to run ;
Amongst five sisters, he was left Eumedes' only son.
And he told Hector, his free heart would undertake t' explore 275
The Greeks' intentions, "but," said he, "thou shalt be sworn before,
By this thy sceptre, that the horse of great Æacides,
And his strong chariot bound with brass, thou wilt (before all these)
Resign me as my valour's prise ; and so I rest unmov'd
To be thy spy, and not return before I have approv'd 280
(By vent'ring to Atrides' ship, where their consults are held)
If they resolve still to resist, or fly as quite expell'd."

He put his sceptre in his hand, and call'd the thunder's God,
Saturnia's husband, to his oath, those horse should not be rode
By any other man than he, but he for ever joy 285
(To his renown) their services, for his good done to Troy.
Thus swore he, and forswore himself, yet made base Dolon bold;
Who on his shoulders hung his bow, and did about him fold
A white wolf's hide, and with a helm of weasels' skins did arm
His weasel's head, then took his dart, and never turn'd to harm 290
The Greeks with their related drifts; but being past the troops
Of horse and foot, he promptly runs, and as he runs he stoops
To undermine Achilles' horse. Ulysses straight did see,
And said to Diomed: "This man makes footing towards thee,
Out of the tents. I know not well, if he be us'd as spy 295
Bent to our fleet, or come to rob the slaughter'd enemy.
But let us suffer him to come a little further on,
And then pursue him. If it chance, that we be overgone
By his more swiftness, urge him still to run upon our fleet,
And (lest he 'scape us to the town) still let thy jav'lin meet 300
With all his offers of retreat." Thus stepp'd they from the plain
Amongst the slaughter'd carcasses. Dolon came on amain,
Suspecting nothing; but once past, as far as mules outdraw
Oxen at plough, being both put on, neither admitted law,
To plough a deep-soil'd furrow forth, so far was Dolan past. 305
Then they pursu'd; which he perceiv'd, and stay'd his speedless haste,
Subtly supposing Hector sent to countermand his spy;
But, in a jav'lin's throw or less, he knew them enemy.
Then laid he on his nimble knees, and they pursu'd like wind.
As when a brace of greyhounds are laid in with hare or hind, 310
Close-mouth'd and skill'd to make the best of their industrious course,
Serve either's turn, and, set on hard, lose neither ground nor force;

---

[291] *Related drifts*—i. e. never returned to harm the Greeks by a relation of their designs. Infrà, line 332.

So constantly did Tydeus' son, and his town-razing peer,
Pursue this spy, still turning him, as he was winding near
Ilis covert, till he almost mix'd with their out-courts of guard. 315

    Then Pallas prompted Diomed, lest his due worth's reward
Should be impair'd if any man did vaunt he first did sheath
His sword in him, and he be call'd but second in his death.
Then spake he, threat'ning with his lance : "Or stay, or this comes on,
And long thou canst not run before thou be by death outgone." 320

    This said, he threw his jav'lin forth ; which missed as Diomed would,
Above his right arm making way, the pile stuck in the mould.
He stay'd and trembled, and his teeth did chatter in his head.
They came in blowing, seiz'd him fast ; he, weeping, offered
A wealthy ransom for his life, and told them he had brass, 325
Much gold, and iron, that fit for use in many labours was,
From whose rich heaps his father would a wondrous portion give,
If, at the great Achaian fleet, he heard his son did live.

    Ulysses bad him cheer his heart. "Think not of death," said he,
"But tell us true, why runn'st thou forth, when others sleeping be ? 330
Is it to spoil the carcasses ? Or art thou choicely sent
T' explore our drifts ? Or of thyself seek'st thou some wish'd event ?"

    He trembling answer'd : "Much reward did Hector's oath propose,
And urg'd me, much against my will, t' endeavour to disclose
If you determin'd still to stay, or bent your course for flight, 335
As all dismay'd with your late foil, and wearied with the fight.
For which exploit, Pelides' horse and chariot he did swear,
I only ever should enjoy." Ulysses smil'd to hear
So base a swain have any hope so high a prise t' aspire,
And said, his labours did affect a great and precious hire, 340
And that the horse Pelides rein'd no mortal hand could use
But he himself, whose matchless life a Goddess did produce.
"But tell us, and report but truth, where left'st thou Hector now ?
Where are his arms ? His famous horse ? On whom doth he bestow

The watch's charge? Where sleep the kings? Intend they still to lie
Thus near encamp'd, or turn suffic'd with their late victory?" 346
  "All this," said he, "I'll tell most true. At Ilus' monument
Hector with all our princes sits, t' advise of this event;
Who choose that place remov'd to shun the rude confuséd sounds
The common soldiers throw about. But, for our watch, and rounds, 350
Whereof, brave lord, thou mak'st demand, none orderly we keep.
The Trojans, that have roofs to save, only abandon sleep,
And privately without command each other they exhort
To make prevention of the worst; and in this slender sort
Is watch and guard maintain'd with us. Th' auxiliary bands 355
Sleep soundly, and commit their cares into the Trojans' hands,
For they have neither wives with them, nor children to protect;
The less they need to care, the more they succour dull neglect."
  "But tell me," said wise Ithacus, "are all these foreign pow'rs
Appointed quarters by themselves, or else commix'd with yours?" 360
  "And this," said Dolon, " too, my lords, I'll seriously unfold.
The Pæons with the crookéd bows, and Cares, quarters hold
Next to the sea, the Leleges, and Caucons, join'd with them,
And brave Pelasgians. Thymber's mead, remov'd more from the
    stream,
Is quarter to the Lycians, the lofty Mysian force, 365
The Phrygians and Meonians, that fight with arméd horse.
But what need these particulars? If ye intend surprise
Of any in our Trojan camps, the Thracian quarter lies
Utmost of all, and uncommix'd with Trojan regiments,
That keep the voluntary watch. New pitch'd are all their tents. 370
King Rhesus, Eioneus' son, commands them, who hath steeds
More white than snow, huge, and well-shap'd, their fi'ry pace exceeds
The winds in swiftness; these I saw; his chariot is with gold
And pallid silver richly fram'd, and wondrous to behold;
His great and golden armour is not fit a man should wear, 375
But for immortal shoulders fram'd. Come then, and quickly bear

Your happy pris'ner to your fleet ; or leave him here fast bound,
Till your well-urg'd and rich return prove my relation sound."
　　Tydides dreadfully replied : " Think not of passage thus,
Though of right acceptable news thou hast advértis'd us, 380
Our hands are holds more strict than so ; and should we set thee free
For offer'd ransom, for this 'scape thou still wouldst scouting be
About our ships, or do us scathe in plain opposéd arms,
But, if I take thy life, no way can we repent thy harms."
　　With this, as Dolon reach'd his hand to use a suppliant's part, 385
And stroke the beard of Diomed, he strook his neck athwart
With his forc'd sword, and both the nerves he did in sunder wound,
And suddenly his head, deceiv'd, fell speaking on the ground.
His weasel's helm they took, his bow, his wolf's skin, and his lance,
Which to Minerva Ithacus did zealously advance, 390
With lifted arm into the air ; and to her thus he spake :
　　"Goddess, triumph in thine own spoils ; to thee we first will make
Our invocations, of all pow'rs thron'd on th' Olympian hill ;
Now to the Thracians, and their horse, and beds, conduct us still."
With this, he hung them up aloft upon a tamrick bough 395
As eyeful trophies, and the sprigs that did about it grow
He proinéd from the leafy arms, to make it easier view'd
When they should hastily retire, and be perhaps pursu'd.
Forth went they through black blood and arms, and presently aspir'd
The guardless Thracian regiment, fast bound with sleep, and tir'd ; 400
Their arms lay by, and triple ranks they, as they slept, did keep,
As they should watch and guard their king, who, in a fatal sleep,
Lay in the midst ; their chariot horse, as they coachfellows were,
Fed by them ; and the famous steeds, that did their gen'ral bear,
Stood next him, to the hinder part of his rich chariot tied. 405
Ulysses saw them first, and said, "Tydides, I have spied
The horse that Dolon, whom we slew, assur'd us we should see.
Now use thy strength ; now idle arms are most unfit for thee ;
Prise thou the horse ; or kill the guard, and leave the horse to me."

　　　　[397] *Proinéd*—plucked off, pruned.

Minerva, with the azure eyes, breath'd strength into her king,   410
Who fill'd the tent with mixéd death. The souls, he set on wing,
Issu'd in groans, and made air swell into her stormy flood.
Horror and slaughter had one pow'r; the earth did blush with blood.
As when a hungry lion flies, with purpose to devour,
On flocks unkept, and on their lives doth freely use his pow'r;   415
So Tydeus' son assail'd the foe; twelve souls before him flew;
Ulysses waited on his sword, and ever as he slew,
He drew them by their strengthless heels out of the horses' sight.
That, when he was to lead them forth, they should not with affright
Boggle, nor snore, in treading on the bloody carcasses;   420
For being new come, they were unus'd to such stern sights as these.
Through four ranks now did Diomed the king himself attain,
Who, snoring in his sweetest sleep, was like his soldiers slain.
An ill dream by Minerva sent that night stood by his head,
Which was Oenides' royal, unconquer'd Diomed.   425
  Meanwhile Ulysses loos'd his horse, took all their reins in hand,
And led them forth; but Tydeus' son did in contention stand
With his great mind to do some deed of more audacity;
If he should take the chariot, where his rich arms did lie,
And draw it by the beam away, or bear it on his back,   430
Or if, of more dull Thracian lives, he should their bosoms sack.
  In this contention with himself, Minerva did suggest
And bade him think of his retreat; lest from their tempted rest
Some other God should stir the foe, and send him back dismay'd.
  He knew the voice, took horse, and fled. The Trojan's heav'nly aid,
Apollo with the silver bow, stood no blind sentinel   435
To their secure and drowsy host, but did discover well
Minerva following Diomed; and, angry with his act,
The mighty host of Ilion he enter'd, and awak'd
The cousin-german of the king, a counsellor of Thrace,   440
Hippocoon; who when he rose, and saw the desert place,

⁴³³ *Tempted*—tried.

Where Rhesus' horse did use to stand, and th' other dismal harms,
Men struggling with the pangs of death, he shriek'd out thick alarms,
Call'd 'Rhesus! Rhesus!' but in vain; then still, 'Arm! Arm!' he cried.
The noise and tumult was extreme on every startled side   445
Of Troy's huge host; from whence in throngs all gather'd, and admir'd
Who could perform such harmful facts, and yet be safe retir'd.

Now, coming where they slew the scout, Ulysses stay'd the steeds,
Tydides lighted, and the spoils, hung on the tamrick reeds,
He took and gave to Ithacus, and up he got again.   450
Then flew they joyful to their fleet. Nestor did first attain
The sounds the horse-hoofs strook through air, and said: "My royal peers!
Do I but dote, or say I true? Methinks about mine ears
The sounds of running horses beat. O would to God they were
Our friends thus soon return'd with spoils! But I have hearty fear,   455
Lest this high tumult of the foe doth their distress intend."
He scarce had spoke, when they were come. Both did from horse descend.
All, with embraces and sweet words, to heav'n their worth did raise.
Then Nestor spake: "Great Ithacus, ev'n heap'd with Grecian praise,
How have you made these horse your prise? Pierc'd you the dang'rous host,   460
Where such gems stand? Or did some God your high attempts accost,
And honour'd you with this reward? Why, they be like the rays
The sun effuseth. I have mix'd with Trojans all my days;
And now, I hope you will not say, I always lie aboard,
Though an old soldier I confess; yet did all Troy afford   465
Never the like to any sense that ever I possess'd.
But some good God, no doubt, hath met, and your high valours bless'd,

---

[464] *Aboard.*—Dr. Taylor has printed "*abord*," and ridiculously says, "*abord, readily;* from the French." Had he consulted the original or given one moment's thought, he would have seen what the true word was. Nestor says, "I have mixed with Trojans all my days, and now, though I confess I am an old man, I hope you will not say I always *lie aboard*, remain on board ship, and avoid the battle."

For He that shadows heav'n with clouds loves both as his delights,
And She that supples earth with blood cannot forbear your sights."
 Ulysses answer'd: "Honour'd sire, the willing Gods can give   470
Horse much more worth than these men yield, since in more pow'r they live.
These horse are of the Thracian breed; their king, Tydides slew,
And twelve of his most trusted guard; and of that meaner crew
A scout for thirteenth man we kill'd, whom Hector sent to spy
The whole estate of our designs, if bent to fight or fly."   475
 Thus, follow'd with whole troops of friends, they with applauses pass'd
The spacious dike, and in the tent of Diomed they plac'd
The horse without contention, as his deserving's meed,
Which, with his other horse set up, on yellow wheat did feed.
Poor Dolon's spoils Ulysses had; who shrin'd them on his stern,   480
As trophies vow'd to her that sent the good-aboding hern.
 Then enter'd they the mere main sea, to cleanse their honour'd sweat
From off their feet, their thighs and necks; and, when their vehement heat
Was calm'd, and their swoln hearts refresh'd, more curious baths they us'd,
Where od'rous and dissolving oils, they through their limbs diffus'd.   485
Then, taking breakfast, a big bowl, fill'd with the purest wine,
They offer'd to the Maiden Queen, that hath the azure eyne.

 [480] *Stern*—hung them up as votive offerings on the stern of his ship.
 [482] *Mere*—pure, unmixed. See Bk. XVII. 420.

THE END OF THE TENTH BOOK.

THE ELEVENTH BOOK OF HOMER'S ILIADS.

THE ARGUMENT.

ATRIDES and his other peers of name
Lead forth their men ; whom Eris doth enflame.
Hector (by Iris' charge) takes deedless breath,
Whiles Agamemnon plies the work of death,
Who with the first bears his imperial head.
Himself, Ulysses, and king Diomed,
Eurypylus, and Æsculapius' son,
(Enforc'd with wounds) the furious skirmish shun.
Which martial sight when great Achilles views,
A little his desire of fight renews ;
And forth he sends his friend, to bring him word
From old Neleides, what wounded lord
He in his chariot from the skirmish brought ;
Which was Machaon. Nestor then besought
He would persuade his friend to wreak their harms,
Or come himself, deck'd in his dreadful arms.

ANOTHER ARGUMENT.

Lambda presents the General,
In fight the worthiest man of all.

AURORA out of restful bed did from bright Tithon rise,
   To bring each deathless Essence light, and use to mortal
      eyes ;
When Jove sent Eris to the Greeks, sustaining in her hand
Stern signs of her designs for war. She took her horrid stand

Upon Ulysses' huge black bark, that did at anchor ride 6
Amidst the fleet, from whence her sounds might ring on ev'ry side,
Both to the tents of Telamon, and th' author of their smarts,
Who held, for fortitude and force, the navy's utmost parts.
    The red-ey'd Goddess, seated there, thunder'd the Orthian song,
High, and with horror, through the ears of all the Grecian throng. 10
Her verse with spirits invincible did all their breasts inspire,
Blew out all darkness from their limbs, and set their hearts on fire ;
And presently was bitter war more sweet a thousand times,
Than any choice in hollow keels to greet their native climes.
    Atrides summon'd all to arms, to arms himself dispos'd. 15
First on his legs he put bright greaves, with silver buttons clos'd ;
Then with rich curace arm'd his breast, which Cinyras bestow'd
To gratify his royal guest ; for ev'n to Cyprus flow'd
Th' unbounded fame of those designs the Greeks propos'd for Troy,
And therefore gave he him those arms, and wish'd his purpose joy. 20
Ten rows of azure mix'd with black, twelve golden like the sun,
Twice-ten of tin, in beaten paths, did through this armour run.
Three serpents to the gorget crept, that like three rainbows shin'd,
Such as by Jove are fix'd in clouds, when wonders are divin'd.
About his shoulders hung his sword, whereof the hollow hilt 25
Was fashion'd all with shining bars, exceeding richly gilt ;
The scabbard was of silver plate, with golden hangers grac'd.
Then he took up his weighty shield, that round about him cast
Defensive shadows ; ten bright zones of gold-affecting brass
Were driv'n about it ; and of tin, as full of gloss as glass, 30
Swell'd twenty bosses out of it ; in centre of them all
One of black metal had engrav'n, full of extreme appall,
An ugly Gorgon, compasséd with Terror and with Fear.
At it a silver bawdrick hung, with which he us'd to bear,
Wound on his arm, his ample shield ; and in it there was wov'n 35
An azure dragon, curl'd in folds, from whose one neck was clov'n

---

[7] *Author*—Achilles. Both folios and Dr. Taylor have erroneously "*authors*."

Three heads contorted in an orb. Then plac'd he on his head
His four-plum'd casque; and in his hands two darts he managéd,
Arm'd with bright steel that blaz'd to heav'n. Then Juno, and the Maid
That conquers empires, trumpets serv'd to summon out their aid   40
In honour of the General, and on a sable cloud,
To bring them furious to the field, sat thund'ring out aloud.
   Then all enjoin'd their charioteers, to rank their chariot horse
Close to the dike. Forth march'd the foot, whose front they did r'enforce
With some horse troops. The battle then was all of charioteers,   45
Lin'd with light horse. But Jupiter disturb'd this form with fears,
And from air's upper region bid bloody vapours rain,
For sad ostent much noble life should ere their times be slain.
The Trojan host at Ilus' tomb was in battalia led
By Hector and Polydamas, and old Anchises' seed   50
Who god-like was esteem'd in Troy, by grave Antenor's race
Divine Agenor, Polybus, unmarried Acamas
Proportion'd like the States of heav'n. In front of all the field,
Troy's great Priamides did bear his all-ways-equal shield,
Still plying th' ord'ring of his pow'r. And as amids the sky   55
We sometimes see an ominous star blaze clear and dreadfully,
Then run his golden head in clouds, and straight appear again;
So Hector otherwhiles did grace the vaunt-guard, shining plain,
Then in the rear-guard hid himself, and labour'd ev'rywhere
To order and encourage all; his armour was so clear,   60
And he applied each place so fast, that, like a lightning thrown
Out of the shield of Jupiter, in ev'ry eye he shone.
And as upon a rich man's crop of barley or of wheat,
Oppos'd for swiftness at their work, a sort of reapers sweat,
Bear down the furrows speedily, and thick their handfuls fall;   65
So at the joining of the hosts ran slaughter through them all,

---

[64] *Opposed*—standing opposite to one another for expedition's sake.
[64] *Sort*—set. See Bk. IV. 460.

None stoop'd to any fainting thought of foul inglorious flight,
But equal bore they up their heads, and far'd like wolves in fight.
Stern Eris, with such weeping sights, rejoic'd to feed her eyes,
Who only show'd herself in field, of all the Deities; 70
The other in Olympus' tops sat silent, and repin'd
That Jove to do the Trojans grace should bear so fix'd a mind.
He car'd not, but, enthron'd apart, triumphant sat in sway
Of his free pow'r, and from his seat took pleasure to display
The city so adorn'd with tow'rs, the sea with vessels fill'd, 75
The splendour of refulgent arms, the killer and the kill'd.
As long as bright Aurora rul'd, and sacred day increas'd,
So long their darts made mutual wounds, and neither had the best;
But when, in hill-environ'd vales, the timber-feller takes
A sharp set stomach to his meat, and dinner ready makes, 80
His sinews fainting, and his spirits become surcharg'd and dull,
Time of accustom'd ease arriv'd, his hands with labour full,
Then by their valours Greeks brake through the Trojan ranks, and cheer'd
Their gen'ral squadrons through the host; then first of all appear'd
The person of the king himself; and then the Trojans lost 85
Bianor by his royal charge, a leader in the host.|
Who being slain, his charioteer, Oïleus, did alight,
And stood in skirmish with the king; the king did deadly smite
His forehead with his eager lance, and through his helm it ran,
Enforcing passage to his brain, quite through the harden'd pan, 90
His brain mix'd with his clotter'd blood, his body strew'd the ground.
There left he them, and presently he other objects found;
Isus and Antiphus, two sons king Priam did beget,
One lawful, th' other wantonly. Both in one chariot met
Their royal foe; the baser born, Isus, was charioteer, 95
And famous Antiphus did fight; both which king Peleus' heir,

[74] *Display*—behold, view. A rare sense. See Bk. XVII. 90.
[90] *Pan*—skull, brain-pan.

Whilome in Ida keeping flocks, did deprehend and bind
With pliant osiers, and, for price, them to their sire resign'd.
Atrides, with his well-aim'd lance, smote Isus on the breast
Above the nipple; and his sword a mortal wound impress'd 100
Beneath the ear of Antiphus; down from their horse they fell.
The king had seen the youths before, and now did know them well,
Rememb'ring them the prisoners of swift Æacides,
Who brought them to the sable fleet from Ida's foody leas.
  And as a lion having found the furrow of a hind, 105
Where she hath calv'd two little twins, at will and ease doth grind
Their joints snatch'd in his solid jaws, and crusheth into mist
Their tender lives; their dam, though near, not able to resist,
But shook with vehement fear herself, flies through the oaken chace
From that fell savage, drown'd in sweat, and seeks some covert place;
So when with most unmatched strength the Grecian Gen'ral bent 111
'Gainst these two princes, none durst aid their native king's descent,
But fled themselves before the Greeks. And where these two were slain,
Pisander and Hippolochus (not able to restrain
Their headstrong horse, the silken reins being from their hands let fall)
Were brought by their unruly guides before the General. 116
Antimachus begat them both, Antimachus that took
Rich gifts, and gold, of Helen's love, and would by no means brook
Just restitution should be made of Menelaus' wealth,
Bereft him, with his ravish'd queen, by Alexander's stealth. 120
Atrides, lion-like, did charge his sons, who on their knees
Fell from their chariot, and besought regard to their degrees,
Who, being Antimachus's sons, their father would afford
A worthy ransom for their lives, who in his house did hoard
Much hidden treasure, brass, and gold, and steel, wrought wondrous
        choice. 125
Thus wept they, using smoothing terms, and heard this rugged voice

[104] *Foody leas*—fertile, fruitful, meads. The word occurs again Bk. xv. 638.
[118] *Helen's love*—Paris.

Breath'd from the unrelenting king : " If you be of the breed
Of stout Antimachus, that stay'd the honourable deed
The other peers of Ilion in council had decreed,
To render Helen and her wealth ; and would have basely slain   130
My brother and wise Ithacus, ambassadors t' attain
The most due motion ; now receive wreak for his shameful part."
This said, in poor Pisander's breast he fix'd his wreakful dart,
Who upward spread th' oppressèd earth ; his brother crouch'd for dread,
And, as he lay, the angry king cut off his arms and head,   135
And let him like a football lie for ev'ry man to spurn.
Then to th' extremest heat of fight he did his valour turn,
And led a multitude of Greeks, where foot did foot subdue,
Horse slaughter'd horse, Need feather'd flight, the batter'd centre flew
In clouds of dust about their ears, rais'd from the horses' hooves,   140
That beat a thunder out of earth as horrible as Jove's.
The king, persuading speedy chace, gave his persuasions way
With his own valour, slaught'ring still. As in a stormy day
In thick-set woods a rav'nous fire wraps in his fierce repair
The shaken trees, and by the roots doth toss them into air ;   145
Ev'n so beneath Atrides' sword flew up Troy's flying heels,
Their horse drew empty chariots, and sought their thund'ring wheels
Some fresh directors.' wough the field his true least the pursuit drives.
Thick fell the Troin iron sleep ; wretched young. as than their wives.
 Then Jove drewly-married wife, in aid of forest, from death and blood,
And from th' pleasure of his love ; yet was to the pursuit stood,   151
Till at olded or mueve he her, and out of all the field,
They reausar the wild fig-keep and long'd to make their town their shield.
Yet th' jay they rested not ; the king still cried, ' Pursue ! Pursue ! '
And all his unreprovèd hands did blood and dust imbrue.   155
But when they came to Scæa's ports, and to the beech of Jove,
There made they stand ; there ev'ry eye, fixed on each other, strove

---

[148] *Directors.*—The second folio erroneously prints "*directions*," which has been adopted by Dr. Taylor.

Who should outlook his mate amaz'd; through all the field they
    fled.
And as a lion, when the night becomes most deaf and dead,
Invades ox-herds, affrighting all, that he of one may wreak   160
His dreadful hunger, and his neck he first of all doth break,
Then laps his blood and entrails up; so Agamemnon plied
The manage of the Trojan chace, and still the last man died,
The other fled, a number fell by his imperial hand,
Some grovelling downwards from their horse, some upwards strew'd
    the sand.   165

  High was the fury of his lance. But, having beat them close
Beneath their walls, the both worlds' Sire did now again repose
On fountain-flowing Ida's tops, being newly slid from heav'n,
And held a lightning in his hand; from thence this charge was giv'n
To Iris with the golden wings: "Thaumantia, fly," said he,   170
" And tell Troy's Hector, that as long as he enrag'd shall see
The soldier-loving Atreus' son amongst the foremost fight,
Depopulating troops of men, so long he must excite
Some other to resist the foe, and he no arms advance;
But when he wounded takes his horse, attain'd with shaft or lance,   175
Then will I fill his arm with death, ev'n till he reach the fleet,
And peaceful night treads busy day beneath her sable feet."
  The wind-foot swift be made of Menelaus' wealth, brings
To famous Ilion, from tish'd queen, by Alexander's steal
And found in his bright care his sons, who on their knees   180
To whom she spake the words of apt regard to their decrees,
  He leapt upon the sounding earth, and woke his lengtht.
And ev'rywhere he breath'd exhorts, and stirr'd up ev'ry heart.
A dreadful fight he set on foot. His soldiers straight turn'd head.
The Greeks stood firm. In both the hosts, the field was perfected.   185

---

¹⁶⁹ *This charge.*—The second folio, followed by Dr. Taylor, reads "*his charge.*"
¹⁷⁵ *Attain'd*—touched, hit. Infrà, line 512, we have "*attainted.*" See note on
Bk. III. 374.

But Agamemnon, foremost still, did all his side exceed,
And would not be the first in name unless the first in deed.

Now sing, fair Presidents of verse, that in the heav'ns embow'r,
Who first encounter'd with the king, of all the adverse pow'r.
Iphidamas, Antenor's son, ample and bigly set, 190
Brought up in pasture-springing Thrace, that sheep beget,
In grave Cisseus' noble house, that was his mother's sire,
Fair Theano; and when his breast was height'n'd with the fire
Of gaysome youth, his grandsire gave his daughter to his love.
Who straight his bridal-chamber left. Love with affection strove, 195
And made him furnish twelve fair ships, and lend fair Troy his hand.
His ships he in Percope left, and came to Troy by land.
And now he tried the fame of Greece, encount'ring with the king,
Who threw his royal lance and miss'd. Iphidamas did fling,
And strook him on the arming waist, beneath his coat of brass, 200
Which forc'd him stay upon his arm, so violent it was,
Yet pierc'd it not his well-wrought zone, but when the lazy head
Tried hardness with the boss at last, he kill'd and again like lead.
He follow'd, caught the lance, and drew't with a lion's wile
That wrests Autonous, Opys, and Clytus caught it by the pile, 205
And pluck'd it from the honour'd hand, whom with his sword he strook
Beneath the ear, and with his wound his timeless death he took.
He fell and slept an iron sleep; wretched young man, he died,
Far from his newly-married wife, in aid of foreign pride,
And saw no pleasure of his love; yet was her jointure great, 210
An hundred oxen gave he her, and vow'd in his retreat
Two thousand head of sheep and goats, of which he store did leave.
Much gave he of his love's first-fruits, and nothing did receive.

When Coon (one that for his form might feast an amorous eye,
And elder brother of the slain) beheld this tragedy, 215

---

[207] *Timeless.*—See Bk. VI. 349.   [215] *This.*—Both folios have "*this*;" the older copies "*his.*"

Deep sorrow sat upon his eyes, and (standing laterally,
And to the Gen'ral undiscern'd) his jav'lin he let fly,
That 'twixt his elbow and his wrist transfix'd his armless arm;
The bright head shin'd on th' other side. The unexpected harm
Impress'd some horror in the king; yet so he ceas'd not fight,
But rush'd on Coon with his lance, who made what haste he might,
Seizing his slaughter'd brother's foot, to draw him from the field,
And call'd the ablest to his aid, when under his round shield
The king's brass jav'lin, as he drew, did strike him helpless dead;
Who made Iphidamas the block, and cut off Coon's head.

  Thus under great Atrides' arm Antenor's issue thriv'd,
And, to suffice precisest fate, to Pluto's mansion div'd.
He with his lance, sword, mighty stones, pour'd his heroic wreak
On other squadrons of the foe, whiles yet warm blood did break
Through his cleft veins; but when the wound was quite exhaust and crude,
The eager anguish did approve his princely fortitude.
As when most sharp and bitter pangs distract a labouring dame,
Which the divine Ilithyæ, that so long he must excite,
Of human child-birth, pour on, and he no arms advance;
The daughters of Saturnia; with horse, attain'd with shaft or
The woman in her travail strives to take till he struck them,
With thought it must be, 'tis love's fruit, the end for which she lives,
The mean to make herself new born, what comforts will redound;
So Agamemnon did sustain the torment of his wound.
Then took he chariot, and to fleet bad haste his charioteer,
But first pour'd out his highest voice to purchase ev'ry ear:
  " Princes and leaders of the Greeks, brave friends, now from our fleet
Do you expel this boist'rous sway. Jove will not let me meet
Illustrate Hector, nor give leave that I shall end the day
In fight against the Ilion pow'r; my wound is in my way."

₂₃₁ *Eager.*—
    " It is a nipping and an *eager* air."—SHAKESPEARE. *Hamlet*, i. 4.
₂₃₁ *Approve*—try.

This said, his ready charioteer did scourge his spriteful horse,
That freely to the sable fleet perform'd their fi'ry course,
To bear their wounded sovereign apart the martial thrust,
Sprinkling their pow'rful breasts with foam, and snowing on the dust.
    When Hector heard of his retreat, thus he fi'ry contends: 250
"Trojans, Dardanians, Lycians, all my close-fought friends,
Think what it is to be renown'd, be soldiers,
Our strongest enemy is gone, Jove vows,
Then in the Grecian faces drive your ominance
And far above their best be best, and glorify your deeds." 255
    Thus as a dog-giv'n hunter sets upon a race of boars
His white-tooth'd hounds, puffs, shouts, breathes terms, and on his
      emprese pours
All his wild art to make them pinch; so Hector urg'd his host
To charge the Greeks, upon the strengthen'f most bold and active most,
He brake into them. Nor. Sty lance when a tempest raves, 260
Stoops from the bankful all on heaps doth cuff the purple waves.
Who then was by bosnd last, he kill'd, when Jove did grace his
      deed?
Assæus, and Autonous, Opys, and Clytus' seed
Prince Dolops, and the honour'd sire of sweet Euryalus
Opheltes, Agelaus next, and strong Hipponous, 265
Orus, Æsymnus, all of name. The common soldiers fell,
As when the hollow flood of air in Zephyr's cheeks doth swell,
And sparseth all the gather'd clouds white Notus' pow'r did draw,
Wraps waves in waves, hurls up the froth beat with a vehement flaw;
So were the common soldiers wrack'd in troops by Hector's hand. 270
Then ruin had enforc'd such works as no Greeks could withstand,
Then in their fleet they had been hous'd, had not Laertes' son
Stirr'd up the spirit of Diomed, with this impression:

[257] *Emprese.*—Thus both the folios, doubtless for *emprise*, the contracted form of *enterprise*.
[258] *Pinch.*—See Bk. v. 462.

"Tydides, what do we sustain, forgetting what we are?
Stand by me, dearest in my love. 'Twere horrible impair   275
For our two valours to endure a customary flight,
To leave our navy still engag'd, and but two fits to fight."
    He answer'd: "I am firm to stay, and anything sustain;
But our delight to prove them will prove but short and vain,
For Jove makes Trojans in their fights, and soon virtually then   280
Wields arms himself. Of aid, less affairs did not 'twixt men and men."
    This said, Thymbrœus when his lance he tumbled from his horse,
Near his left nipple wounding him. Ulysses did enforce
Fair Molion, minion to this king that Diomed subdu'd.
Both sent they thence till they return'd, who now the king pursu'd   285
And furrow'd through the thicken'd troops. As when two chaséd boars
Turn head 'gainst kennels of bold hounds, and race way through their
            gores;   wound was quite
So, turn'd from flight, the forward kingly fortitude. backward death.
Nor fled the Greeks, but by their wills, to get a labouring hector breath.
    Then took they horse and chariot from two excite city foes,   290
Merops Percosius' mighty sons. Their father could disclose,
Beyond all men, hid auguries, and would not give consent
To their egression to these wars, yet wilfully they went,
For Fates, that order sable death, enforc'd their tragedies.
Tydides slew them with his lance, and made their arms his prise.   295
    Hypirochus, and Hippodus, Ulysses reft of light.
But Jove, that out of Ida look'd, then equalis'd the fight,
A Grecian for a Trojan then paid tribute to the Fates.
Yet royal Diomed slew one, ev'n in those even debates,
That was of name more than the rest, Pæon's renownéd son,   300
The prince Agastrophus; his lance into his hip did run;
His squire detain'd his horse apart, that hinder'd him to fly,
Which he repented at his heart, yet did his feet apply

---

283 *Show'd Trojans, &c.*—i. e. as they retreated slew the Trojans.

His 'scape with all the speed they had alongst the foremost bands,
And there his lovéd life dissolv'd. This Hector understands, 305
And rush'd with clamour on the king, right soundly seconded
With troops of Trojans. Which perceiv'd by famous Diomed,
The deep conceit of Jove's high will stiffen'd his royal hair,
Who spake to near-fought Ithacus: "The fiend this affair
Is bent to us. Come let us stand, and brook his violence." 310
Thus threw he his long jav'lin forth, breaks, smote his head's defence
Full on the top, yet pierc'd no skin, roach is took repulse with brass;
His helm (with three fiy brought the harp) the gift of Phœbus was.
The insensible appr put true troop, sunk him upon his hand,
And whom many astard striding pursu'd before the foremost band 315
His appeus, and along Pire stround laid on the purple plain;
By which a torrent from ap'd viv'd, and, taking horse again,
Was far cour'd cals, bupon th strength, and fled his darksome grave.
He follow'd wirht. Nor My lance, and this elusive brave:
"Once more ber byakful to thy heels, proud dog, for thy escape.
Mischief sat near thy bosom now; and now another rape 321
Hath thy Apollo made of thee, to whom thou well mayst pray,
When through the singing of our darts thou find'st such guarded
 way.
But I shall meet with thee at length, and bring thy latest hour,
If with like favour any God be fautour of my pow'r. 325
Meanwhile some other shall repay, what I suspend in thee."
 This said, he set the wretched soul of Pæon's issue free,
Whom his late wound not fully slew. But Priam's amorous birth
Against Tydides bent his bow, hid with a hill of earth,
Part of the ruinated tomb for honour'd Ilus built, 330
And as the curace of the slain, engrav'n and richly gilt,
Tydides from his breast had spoil'd, and from his shoulders raft
His target and his solid helm, he shot, and his keen shaft

---

[325] *Fautour.*—See Bk. I. 441, xv. 399.
[329] *Priam's amorous birth*—Paris.   [332] *Raft*—reft.

(That never flew from him in vain) did nail unto the ground 334
The king's right foot ; the spleenful knight laugh'd sweetly at the wound,
Crept from his covert, and triumph'd : "Now art thou maim'd," said he,
"And would to God my happy hand had so much honour'd me
To have infix'd it in thy breast, as deep as in thy foot,
Ev'n to th' expulsure of thy soul ! Then blest had been my shoot
Of all the Trojans ; who here in breath'd from their long unrests, 340
Who fear thee, as the braying ass after abhor the king of beasts."

Undaunted Diomed replied : "It is language braver with your bow,
You slick-hair'd lover, you that him. Ulysses did excuse so.
Durst thou but stand in arms with me, Diomed subdu'd.
Would give thee little cause to vaunt. I who now the king pursu'd 345
In this same tall exploit of thine, perform ps. As when two chased
As if a woman, or a child that knew not w* and race way thr
Had touch'd my foot. A coward's steel had was qu ge.
But mine, t' assure it sharp, still lays dead carcitude. hedge ;
Touch it, it renders lifeless straight, it strikes the puriers' ends 350
Of hapless widows in their cheeks, and children blind of friends.
The subject of it makes earth red, and air with sighs inflames,
And leaves limbs more embrac'd with birds than with enamour'd
    dames."

Lance-fam'd Ulysses now came in, and stept before the king,
Kneel'd opposite, and drew the shaft. The eager pain did sting 355
Through all his body. Straight he took his royal chariot there,
And with direction to the fleet did charge his charioteer.

Now was Ulysses desolate, fear made no friend remain,
He thus spake to his mighty mind : "What doth my state sustain ?
If I should fly this odds in fear, that thus comes clust'ring on, 360
'Twere high dishonour ; yet 'twere worse, to be surpris'd alone.
'Tis Jove that drives the rest to flight ; but that's a faint excuse.
Why do I tempt my mind so much ? Pale cowards fight refuse.

[234] The second folio, followed as usual by Dr. Taylor, reads, "nail *upon* the ground."

He that affects renown in war must like a rock be fix'd,
Wound, or be wounded. Valour's truth puts no respect betwixt." 365
   In this contention with himself, in flew the shady bands
Of targeteers, who sieg'd him round with misf-fill'd hands.
As when a crew of gallants wat ... a boar,
Their dogs put after ... abh horri eth on before,
Whets, with hi... heart retirlose w... is crooked tusks for blood, 370
And, hear their fleet should brs'd; w... reaks through the deepen'd wood,
These when a dull mill a... the hurt roach be never so abhorr'd;
... om the birds by brough..., the Ilians did accord,
... sensible app... put t... First he hurt, upon his shoulder blade,
... om many ...stard s... rms; then sent to endless shade 375
Thocppcus, anu... long Pir- strook the strong Chersidamas,
As from ... torrent from ap'd down, beneath his targe of brass;
Who fell, and c... ls, b... upon the earth with his sustaining palms,
And left the fight. Nor yet his lance left dealing martial alms,
But Socus' brother by both sides, young Carops, did impress. 380
Then princely Socus to his aid made brotherly access,
And, coming near, spake in his charge: "O great Laertes' son,
Insatiate in sly stratagems, and labours never done,
This hour, or thou shalt boast to kill the two Hippasides
And prise their arms, or fall thyself in my resolv'd access." 385
   This said, he threw quite through his shield his fell and well-driv'n
      lance,
Which held way through his curaces, and on his ribs did glance,
Plowing the flesh alongst his sides; but Pallas did repel
All inward passage to his life. Ulysses, knowing well
The wound undeadly (setting back his foot to form his stand) 390
Thus spake to Socus: "O thou wretch, thy death is in this hand,
That stay'st my victory on Troy, and where thy charge was made
In doubtful terms (or this or that) this shall thy life invade."

---

363 *Muse*—haunt of an animal. The word seems to have been applied more especially to the "run" of a hare.

This frighted Socus to retreat, and, in his faint reverse,   394
The lance betwixt his shoulders fell, and through his breast did perse,
Down fell he sounding, and the king thus play'd with his mis-ease :
" O Socus, you that make by birth the two Hippasides,
Now may your house and you, as deep death can outfly the flyer.
Ah wretch ! thou canst not 'scape !   Then blest had Hippasus thy sire,
Nor thy well-honour'd mother's   breath'd from their long thy worth,
Shall close thy wretched eyes in   bhor the king of beasts."   rth,   401
And hide them with their darksome   braver with your bow,
Divinest Greeks shall tomb my corse   Ulysses
Now from his body and his shield the   med subdu'd.
That princely Socus had infix'd ; which dr   now the king pursu'd   05
Fell from his bosom on the earth ; the woun   As when two chased
And when the furious Trojans saw Ulysses' foil   race way thr
Encouraging themselves in gross, all his destruct   'd.
Then he retir'd, and summon'd aid.   Thrice shouted he aloud,
As did denote a man engag'd.   Thrice Menelaus' ear   410
Observ'd his aid-suggesting voice, and Ajax being near,
He told him of Ulysses' shouts, as if he were enclos'd
From all assistance, and advis'd their aids might be dispos'd
Against the ring that circled him, lest, charg'd with troops alone,
(Though valiant) he might be oppress'd, whom Greece so built upon.
He led, and Ajax seconded.   They found their Jove-lov'd king   416
Circled with foes.   As when a den of bloody lucerns cling
About a goodly-palmèd hart, hurt with a hunter's bow,
Whose 'scape his nimble feet enforce, whilst his warm blood doth
   flow,

[395] *Perse*—pierce ; probably so printed merely to suit the rhyme.
[417] *Lucerns.*—The original is θῶες, *wolves*, or *jackals*. The term "*lucern*" is used by Chapman in his *Bussy d'Ambois*" (Act III.) for a sort of hunting dog. Beaumont and Fletcher apply it to an animal whose fur was much valued, "the rich-skinned *lucerne*," (*Beggar's Bush*, III. 3). Some writers have described it as the *lynx;* others (Minshew and Blount) say it was "a beast almost as big as a wolf, breeding in Muscovia and Russia, of colour between red and brown, mingled with black spots ; its skin is a very rich fur." The etymology seems uncertain.

And his light knees have pow'r to move ; but, master'd of his wound,
Emboss'd within a shady hill, the lucerns charge him round,
And tear his flesh ; when instantly ??? ??? sends in the pow'rs
Of some stern lion, with whose ??? ??? fly, and he devours ;
So charg'd the Ilians ??? ??? ??? and mighty men.
But then ??? ??? ??? abh'd horrid Ajax then,
Bearing ??? ??? heart retir'lose was his violent stand,
And fear their fleet should b's'd ; when, by the royal hand,
K??? when a dull mill a??the hurt Laertes' son,
??? a bl??? ??? ??? m the birds by brought his horse. Victorious Telamon
??? and E??? ??? nsensible app??? put to sword a young Priamides,
Doryclus??? ??? om many ??? astard son ; then did his lance impress
Pandocus, an??? ??? ong Pirasus, Lysander and Palertes.
As when a torrent from the hills, swoln with Saturnian show'rs,
Falls on the fields, bears blasted oaks, and wither'd rosin flow'rs,
Loose weeds, and all dispersed filth, into the ocean's force ;
So matchless Ajax beat the field, and slaughter'd men and horse.
Yet had not Hector heard of this, who fought on the left wing
Of all the host, near those sweet herbs Scamander's flood doth
    spring,
Where many foreheads trod the ground, and where the skirmish
    burn'd
Near Nestor and king Idomen ; where Hector overturn'd
The Grecian squadrons, authoring high service with his lance,
And skilful manage of his horse. Nor yet the discrepance
He made in death betwixt the hosts had made the Greeks retire,
If fair-hair'd Helen's second spouse had not repress'd the fire

---

[421] *Emboss'd.*—See Bk. iv. 258.

[434] *Rosin flow'rs.*—Dr. Taylor has printed "withered *rosy* flow'rs." Had he known the original, he would have found no necessity for altering the reading of both folios. Homer speaks of the river bearing down in its course "many withered oaks and *fir trees ;*" which latter Chapman has fancifully translated "*rosin* flowers."

Of bold Machaon's fortitude, who with a three-fork'd head 445
In his right shoulder wounded him. Then had the Grecians dread,
Lest, in his strength declin'd, the foe should slaughter their hurt
    friend.
Then Crete's king urg'd Neleides his
And getting near him, take him in, and
A surgeon is to be preferr'd, with physic'd from their long 450
Before a multitude; his life gives hurt lives e king of beasts."
With sweet inspersion of fit balms, and perfec with your bow,
    Thus spake the royal Idomen. Neleides obey
And to his chariot presently the wounded Greek bdu'd.
The son of Æsculapius, the great physician.   the king 455
To fleet they flew. Cebriones perceiv'd the slaughter
By Ajax on the other troops, and spake to Hector thus:
    "Whiles we encounter Grecians here, stern Telamonius
Is yonder raging, turning up in heaps our horse and men;
I know him by his spacious shield. Let us turn chariot then, 460
Where, both of horse and foot, the fight most hotly is propos'd,
In mutual slaughters. Hark, their throats from cries are never clos'd."
    This said, with his shrill scourge he strook the horse, that fast ensu'd
Stung with his lashes, tossing shields, and carcasses imbru'd.
The chariot tree was drown'd in blood, and th' arches by the seat 465
Dispurpled from the horses' hoofs, and from the wheelbands beat.
Great Hector long'd to break the ranks, and startle their close fight,
Who horribly amaz'd the Greeks, and plied their sudden fright
With busy weapons, ever wing'd; his lance, sword, weighty stones.
Yet charg'd he other leaders' bands, not dreadful Telamon's; 470
With whom he wisely shunn'd foul blows. But Jove (that weighs above
All human pow'rs) to Ajax' breast divine repressions drove,
And made him shun who shunn'd himself; he ceas'd from fight amaz'd,
Cast on his back his sev'n-fold shield, and round about him gaz'd
Like one turn'd wild, look'd on himself in his distract retreat, 475
Knee before knee did scarcely move. As when from herds of neat,

Whole threaves of boors and mongrels chase a lion skulking near,
Loth he should taint the well-priz'd fat of any stall-fed steer,
Consuming all the night in watch, he, greedy of his prey,
Oft thrusting on is oft thrust off, so thick the jav'lins play 480
On his bold charges, and so hot the burning fire-brands shine,
Which he (though horrible) abhors, about his glowing eyne,
And early his great heart retires ; so Ajax from the foe,
For fear their fleet should be inflam'd, 'gainst his swoln heart did go.
   As when a dull mill ass comes near a goodly field of corn, 485
Kept from the birds by children's cries, the boys are overborne
By his insensible approach, and simply he will eat ;
About whom many wands are broke, and still the children beat,
And still the self-providing ass doth with their weakness bear,
Not stirring till his paunch be full, and scarcely then will steer ; 490
So the huge son of Telamon amongst the Trojans far'd,
Bore show'rs of darts upon his shield, yet scorn'd to fly as scar'd,
And so kept softly on his way ; nor would he mend his pace
For all their violent pursuits, that still did arm the chace
With singing lances. But, at last, when their cur-like presumes 495
More urg'd the more forborne, his spirits did rarify their fumes,
And he revok'd his active strength, turn'd head, and did repell
The horse-troops that were new made in, 'twixt whom the fight grew fell ;
And by degrees he stole retreat, yet with such puissant stay
That none could pass him to the fleet. In both the armies' sway 500
He stood, and from strong hands receiv'd sharp jav'lins on his shield,
Where many stuck, thrown on before, many fell short in field,

---

  477 *Threaves*—properly "a number of sheaves of corn ;" in which sense the word is still in use in the Northern Counties. Metaphorically applied to a collection of any objects. Ben Jonson to people,—
                      "Gallants, men and women,
          And of all sorts, tag, rag, been seen to flock here
            In *threaves*, these ten weeks."—*Alchem.* v. 2.
Bp. Hall (*Satire*, IV. 6.)
        "He sends forth *thraves* of ballads to the sale."
  479 *Taint.*—See suprà, line 175.
  495 *Rarify*—the second folio reads "*ratify ;*" and so Dr. Taylor.

Ere the white body they could reach, and stuck, as telling how
They purpos'd to have pierc'd his flesh. His peril piercéd now
The eyes of prince Eurypylus, Evemon's famous son, 505
Who came close on, and with his dart strook duke Apisaon,
Whose surname was Phausiades, ev'n to the concrete blood
That makes the liver; on the earth, out gush'd his vital flood.
Eurypylus made in, and eas'd his shoulders of his arms;
Which Paris seeing, he drew his bow, and wreak'd in part the harms
Of his good friend Phausiades, his arrow he let fly 511
That smote Eurypylus, and brake in his attainted thigh;
Then took he troop to shun black death, and to the flyers cried:
"Princes, and leaders of the Greeks, stand, and repulse the tide
Of this our honour-wracking chase. Ajax is drown'd in darts, 515
I fear past 'scape; turn, honour'd friends, help out his vent'rous parts."
Thus spake the wounded Greek; the sound cast on their backs their
    shields,
And rais'd their darts; to whose relief Ajax his person wields.
Then stood he firmly with his friends, retiring their retire.
And thus both hosts indiff'rent join'd, the fight grew hot as fire. 520
  Now had Neleides' sweating steeds brought him, and his hurt friend,
Amongst their fleet. Æacides, that wishly did intend,
Standing astern his tall-neck'd ship, how deep the skirmish drew
Amongst the Greeks, and with what ruth the insecution grew,
Saw Nestor bring Machaon hurt, and from within did call 525
His friend Patroclus; who, like Mars in form celestial,

---

⁵⁰⁸ *Vital flood.*—Both the folios have "*blood;*" the older editions however have "*flood.*"
⁵¹² *Attainted.*—See suprà, line 175.
⁵²² *Wishly intend*—anxiously regard, watch. These lines have been adopted by Niccols in his "England's Eliza," (*Mirrour for Magistrates*, Pt. v.)
  "The noble Dev'reux, that undaunted knight,
    Who stood astern his ship, and wishly ey'd
    How deep the skirmish drew on either side."—Stanza 404.
There are frequent plagiarisms from Chapman in the same poem.
⁵²⁴ *Insecution*—pursuit. Latin.

Came forth with first sound of his voice, first spring of his decay,
And ask'd his princely friend's desire. "Dear friend," said he, "this day
I doubt not will enforce the Greeks, to swarm about my knees;
I see unsuffer'd need employ'd in their extremities.   530
Go, sweet Patroclus, and inquire of old Neleides
Whom he brought wounded from the fight; by his back parts I guess
It is Machaon, but his face I could not well descry,
They pass'd me in such earnest speed." Patroclus presently
Obey'd his friend, and ran to know. They now descended were,   535
And Nestor's squire, Eurymedon, the horses did ungear;
Themselves stood near th' extremest shore, to let the gentle air
Dry up their sweat; then to the tent, where Hecamed the fair
Set chairs, and for the wounded prince a potion did prepare.

    This Hecamed, by war's hard fate, fell to old Nestor's share,   540
When Thetis' son sack'd Tenedos; she was the princely seed
Of worthy king Arsinous, and by the Greeks decreed
The prise of Nestor, since all men in counsel he surpass'd.
First, a fair table she appos'd, of which the feet were grac'd
With bluish metal mix'd with black; and on the same she put   545
A brass fruit-dish, in which she serv'd a wholesome onion cut
For pittance to the potion, and honey newly wrought,
And bread, the fruit of sacred meal. Then to the board she brought
A right fair cup with gold studs driv'n, which Nestor did transfer
From Pylos; on whose swelling sides four handles fixéd were,   550
And upon ev'ry handle sat a pair of doves of gold,
Some billing, and some pecking meat; two gilt feet did uphold
The antique body; and withal so weighty was the cup
That, being propos'd brimful of wine, one scarce could lift it up,
Yet Nestor drunk in it with ease, spite of his years' respect.   555
In this the goddess-like fair dame a potion did confect
With good old wine of Pramnius, and scrap'd into the wine
Cheese made of goat's milk, and on it spers'd flour exceeding fine.

    [527] *First spring of his decay*—first dawning of his approaching fate.
    [554] *Propos'd*—held forth, set before (Lat. *proponere*). See Bk. I. 14.

In this sort for the wounded lord the potion she prepar'd,
And bad him drink. For company, with him old Nestor shar'd. 560
    Thus physically quench'd they thirst, and then their spirits reviv'd
With pleasant conference. And now Patroclus, being arriv'd,
Made stay at th' entry of the tent. Old Nestor, seeing it,
Rose, and receiv'd him by the hand, and fain would have him sit.
He set that courtesy aside, excusing it with haste, 565
Since his much-to-be-rev'renced friend sent him to know who past,
Wounded with him in chariot, so swiftly through the shore ;
"Whom now," said he, "I see and know, and now can stay no more ;
You know, good father, our great friend is apt to take offence,
Whose fi'ry temper will inflame sometimes with innocence." 570
    He answer'd : "When will Peleus' son some royal pity show
On his thus wounded countrymen ? Ah ! is he yet to know
How much affliction tires our host ? How our especial aid,
Tainted with lances, at their tents are miserably laid ?
Ulysses, Diomed, our king, Eurypylus, Machaon, 575
All hurt, and all our worthiest friends ; yet no compassion
Can supple thy friend's friendless breast ! Doth he reserve his eye
Till our fleet burn, and we ourselves one after other die ?
Alas, my forces are not now as in my younger life.
Oh would to God I had that strength I uséd in the strife 580
Betwixt us and the Elians, for oxen to be driv'n,
When Itymonius' lofty soul was by my valour giv'n
As sacrifice to destiny, Hypirochus' strong son,
That dwelt in Elis, and fought first in our contention !
We forag'd, as proclaiméd foes, a wondrous wealthy boot, 585
And he, in rescue of his herds, fell breathless at my foot.
All the dorp boors with terror fled. Our prey was rich and great ;
Twice five and twenty flocks of sheep ; as many herds of neat ;
As many goats, and nasty swine ; an hundred fifty mares,
All sorrel, most with sucking foals. And these soon-monied wares 590

587 *Dorp*—village, Anglo-Sax.

We drave into Neleius' town, fair Pylos, all by night.
My father's heart was glad to see so much good fortune quite
The forward mind of his young son, that us'd my youth in deeds,
And would not smother it in moods. Now drew the Sun's bright steeds
Light from the hills; our heralds now accited all that were   595
Endamag'd by the Elians; our princes did appear;
Our boot was parted; many men th' Epeians much did owe,
That, being our neighbours, they did spoil; afflictions did so flow
On us poor Pylians, though but few. In brake great Hercules
To our sad confines of late years, and wholly did suppress   600
Our hapless princes. Twice-six sons renown'd Neleius bred,
Only myself am left of all, the rest subdu'd and dead.
And this was it that made so proud the base Epeian bands,
On their near neighbours, being oppress'd, to lay injurious hands.
A herd of oxen for himself, a mighty flock of sheep,   605
My sire selected, and made choice of shepherds for their keep;
And from the gen'ral spoil he cull'd three hundred of the best.
The Elians ought him infinite, most plagu'd of all the rest.
Four wager-winning horse he lost, and chariots intervented,
Being led to an appointed race; the prize that was presented   610
Was a religious three-foot urn; Augeas was the king
That did detain them, and dismiss'd their keeper sorrowing
For his lov'd charge lost with foul words. Then both for words and deeds
My sire being worthily incens'd, thus justly he proceeds
To satisfaction, in first choice of all our wealthy prise;   615
And, as he shar'd much, much he left his subjects to suffice,
That none might be oppress'd with pow'r, or want his portion due.
Thus for the public good we shar'd. Then we to temples drew
Our complete city, and to heav'n we thankful rites did burn
For our rich conquest. The third day ensuing our return   620
The Elians flew on us in heaps; their gen'ral leaders were
The two Moliones, two boys, untrainéd in the fear

⁵⁹⁵ *Accited*—summoned, roused.　　　　⁶⁰⁸ *Ought*—owed.

Of horrid war, or use of strength. A certain city shines
Upon a lofty prominent, and in th' extreme confines
Of sandy Pylos, seated where Alpheus' flood doth run, 625
And call'd Thryessa; this they sieg'd, and gladly would have won,
But, having pass'd through all our fields, Minerva as our spy
Fell from Olympus in the night, and arm'd us instantly;
Nor muster'd she unwilling men, nor unprepar'd for force.
My sire yet would not let me arm, but hid away my horse, 630
Esteeming me no soldier yet; yet shin'd I nothing less
Amongst our gallants, though on foot; Minerva's mightiness
Led me to fight, and made me bear a soldier's worthy name.
There is a flood falls into sea, and his crook'd course doth frame
Close to Arena, and is call'd bright Minyæus' stream. 635
There made we halt, and there the sun cast many a glorious beam
On our bright armours, horse and foot insea'd together there.
Then march'd we on. By fi'ry noon we saw the sacred clear
Of great Alpheus, where to Jove we did fair sacrifice;
And to the azure God, that rules the under-liquid skies, 640
We offer'd up a solemn bull; a bull t' Alpheus' name;
And to the blue-ey'd Maid we burn'd a heifer never tame.
Now was it night; we supp'd and slept, about the flood, in arms.
The foe laid hard siege to our town, and shook it with alarms,
But, for prevention of their spleens, a mighty work of war 645
Appear'd behind them; for as soon as Phœbus' fi'ry car
Cast night's foul darkness from his wheels (invoking rev'rend Jove,
And the unconquer'd Maid his birth) we did th' event approve,
And gave them battle. First of all, I slew (the army saw)
The mighty soldier Mulius, Augeas' son-in-law, 650
And spoil'd him of his one hoof'd horse; his eldest daughter was
Bright Agamede, that for skill in simples did surpass,
And knew as many kind of drugs, as earth's broad centre bred.
Him charg'd I with my brass-arm'd lance, the dust receiv'd him dead.

₆₃₇ *Insea'd*—enclosed by the sea.
₆₅₁ *Eldest.*—The second folio reads "*elder* daughter."

I, leaping to his chariot, amongst the foremost press'd,
And the great-hearted Elians fled frighted, seeing their best
And loftiest soldier taken down, the gen'ral of their horse.
I follow'd like a black whirlwind, and did for prise enforce
Full fifty chariots, ev'ry one furnish'd with two arm'd men,
Who ate the earth, slain with my lance. And I had slaughter'd then
The two young boys, Moliones, if their world-circling sire,
Great Neptune, had not saft their lives, and cover'd their retire
With unpierc'd clouds. Then Jove bestow'd a haughty victory
Upon us Pylians; for so long we did the chase apply,
Slaught'ring and making spoil of arms, till sweet Buprasius' soil,
Alesius, and Olenia, were fam'd with our recoil;
For there Minerva turn'd our pow'r, and there the last I slew
As, when our battle join'd, the first. The Pylians then withdrew
To Pylos from Buprasius. Of all th' Immortals then,
They most thank'd Jove for victory; Nestor the most of men.
Such was I ever, if I were employ'd with other peers,
And I had honour of my youth, which dies not in my years.
But great Achilles only joys hability of act
In his brave prime, and doth not deign t' impart it where 'tis lack'd.
No doubt he will extremely mourn, long after that black hour
Wherein our ruin shall be brought, and rue his ruthless pow'r.
O friend! my memory revives the charge Menœtius gave
Thy towardness, when thou sett'st forth, to keep out of the grave
Our wounded honour. I myself and wise Ulysses were
Within the room, where ev'ry word then spoken we did hear,
For we were come to Peleus' court, as we did must'ring pass
Through rich Achaia, where thy sire, renown'd Menœtius, was,
Thyself and great Æacides, when Peleüs the king
To thunder-loving Jove did burn an ox for offering,
In his court-yard. A cup of gold, crown'd with red wine, he held
On th' holy incensory pour'd. You, when the ox was fell'd,

⁶⁸⁶ *Incensory*—altar of incense.

Were dressing his divided limbs ; we in the portal stood.
Achilles seeing us come so near, his honourable blood
Was strook with a respective shame, rose, took us by the hands,
Brought us both in, and made us sit, and us'd his kind commands   600
For seemly hospitable rites, which quickly were appos'd.
Then, after needfulness of food, I first of all disclos'd
The royal cause of our repair ; mov'd you and your great friend
To consort our renown'd designs ; both straight did condescend.
Your fathers knew it, gave consent, and grave instruction   605
To both your valours. Peleus charg'd his most unequall'd son
To govern his victorious strength, and shine past all the rest
In honour, as in mere main force. Then were thy partings blest
With dear advices from thy sire ; 'My lovéd son,' said he,
'Achilles, by his grace of birth, superior is to thee,   700
And for his force more excellent, yet thou more ripe in years ;
Then with sound counsels, age's fruits, employ his honour'd years,
Command and overrule his moods ; his nature will obey
In any charge discreetly giv'n, that doth his good assay.'
 "Thus charg'd thy sire, which thou forgett'st. Yet now at last approve,
With forcéd reference of these, th' attraction of his love ;   706
Who knows if sacred influence may bless thy good intent,
And enter with thy gracious words, ev'n to his full consent ?
The admonition of a friend is sweet and vehement.
If any oracle he shun, or if his mother-queen   710
Hath brought him some instinct from Jove, that fortifies his spleen,
Let him resign command to thee of all his Myrmidons,
And yield by that means some repulse to our confusions,
Adorning thee in his bright arms, that his resembled form
May haply make thee thought himself, and calm this hostile storm ;   715

---

[639] *Respective*—respectful.

"For new-made honour doth forget men's names ;
'Tis too *respective*, and too sociable."
    SHAKESPEARE. *K. John*, I. 1.

That so a little we may ease our overchargéd hands,
Draw some breath, not expire it all. The foe but faintly stands
Beneath his labours; and your charge being fierce, and freshly giv'n,
They eas'ly from our tents and fleet may to their walls be driv'n."
 This mov'd the good Patroclus' mind; who made his utmost haste
T' inform his friend; and as the fleet of Ithacus he past, 721
(At which their markets were dispos'd, councils, and martial courts,
And where to th' altars of the Gods they made divine resorts)
He met renown'd Eurypylus, Evemon's noble son,
Halting, his thigh hurt with a shaft, the liquid sweat did run 725
Down from his shoulders and his brows, and from his raging wound
Forth flow'd his melancholy blood, yet still his mind was sound.
His sight in kind Patroclus' breast to sacred pity turn'd,
And (nothing more immartial for true ruth) thus he mourn'd:
"Ah wretched progeny of Greece, princes, dejected kings, 730
Was it your fates to nourish beasts, and serve the outcast wings
Of savage vultures here in Troy? Tell me, Evemon's fame,
Do yet the Greeks withstand his force, whom yet no force can tame?
Or are they hopeless thrown to death by his resistless lance?"
"Divine Patroclus," he replied, "no more can Greece advance 735
Defensive weapons, but to fleet they headlong must retire,
For those that to this hour have held our fleet from hostile fire,
And are the bulwarks of our host, lie wounded at their tents,
And Troy's unvanquishable pow'r, still as it toils, augments.
But take me to thy black-stern'd ship, save me, and from my thigh 740
Cut out this arrow, and the blood, that is ingor'd and dry,
Wash with warm water from the wound; then gentle salves apply,
Which thou know'st best, thy princely friend hath taught thee surgery,
Whom, of all Centaurs the most just, Chiron did institute.
Thus to thy honourable hands my ease I prosecute, 745

---

 [721] *As.*—Both folios have "*at.*"
 [729] *Nothing more immartial for true ruth*—not the worse soldier for feeling true pity.

Since our physicians cannot help.   Machaon at his tent
Needs a physician himself, being leech and patient ;
And Podalirius, in the field, the sharp conflict sustains."
Strong Menœtiades replied : " How shall I ease thy pains?
What shall we do, Eurypylus?   I am to use all haste,　　　　　750
To signify to Thetis' son occurrents that have past,
At Nestor's honourable suit.   But be that work achiev'd
When this is done, I will not leave thy torments unreliev'd."

　　This said, athwart his back he cast, beneath his breast, his arm,
And nobly help'd him to his tent.   His servants, seeing his harm,　　755
Dispread ox-hides upon the earth, whereon Machaon lay.
Patroclus cut out the sharp shaft, and clearly wash'd away
With lukewarm water the black blood ; then 'twixt his hands he bruis'd
A sharp and mitigatory root ; which when he had infus'd
Into the green, well-cleansèd, wound, the pains he felt before　　　760
Were well, and instantly allay'd ; the wound did bleed no more.

　　　　　　　　THE END OF THE ELEVENTH BOOK.

THE TWELFTH BOOK OF HOMER'S ILIADS.

THE ARGUMENT.

THE Trojans at the trench their pow'rs engage,
Though greeted by a bird of bad presage.
In five parts they divide their pow'r to scale,
And Prince Sarpedon forceth down the pale.
Great Hector from the ports tears out a stone,
And with so dead a strength he sets it gone
At those broad gates the Grecians made to guard
Their tents and ships, that, broken, and unbarr'd,
They yield way to his pow'r; when all contend
To reach the ships; which all at last ascend.

ANOTHER ARGUMENT.

MY works the Trojans all the grace,
And doth the Grecian fort deface.

PATROCLUS thus employ'd in cure of hurt Eurypylus,
Both hosts are all for other wounds doubly contentious,
One always labouring to expel, the other to invade.
Nor could the broad dike of the Greeks, nor that strong wall they made
To guard their fleet, be long unrac't; because it was not rais'd
By grave direction of the Gods, nor were their Deities prais'd
(When they begun) with hecatombs, that then they might be sure
(Their strength being season'd well with heav'n's) it should have force t' endure,

And so, the safeguard of their fleet, and all their treasure there,
Infallibly had been confirm'd ; when, now, their bulwarks were   10
Not only without pow'r of check to their assaulting foe
(Ev'n now, as soon as they were built) but apt to overthrow ;
Such as, in very little time, shall bury all their sight
And thought that ever they were made. As long as the despite
Of great Æacides held up, and Hector went not down,   15
And that by those two means stood safe king Priam's sacred town,
So long their rampire had some use, though now it gave some way ;
But when Troy's best men suffer'd fate, and many Greeks did pay
Dear for their suffrance, then the rest home to their country turn'd,
The tenth year of their wars at Troy, and Troy was sack'd and burn'd.
And then the Gods fell to their fort ; then they their pow'rs employ 21
To ruin their work, and left less of that than they of Troy.
Neptune and Phœbus tumbled down, from the Idalian hills,
An inundation of all floods, that thence the broad sea fills
On their huge rampire ; in one glut, all these together roar'd,   25
Rhesus, Heptaporus, Rhodius, Scamander the ador'd,
Caresus, Simois, Grenicus, Æsepus ; of them all
Apollo open'd the rough mouths, and made their lusty fall
Ravish the dusty champian, where many a helm and shield,
And half-god race of men, were strew'd. And, that all these might yield
Full tribute to the heav'nly work, Neptune and Phœbus won   31
Jove to unburthen the black wombs of clouds, fill'd by the sun,
And pour them into all their streams, that quickly they might send
The huge wall swimming to the sea. Nine days their lights did spend
To nights in tempests ; and when all their utmost depth had made, 35
Jove, Phœbus, Neptune, all came down, and all in state did wade
To ruin of that impious fort. Great Neptune went before,
Wrought with his trident, and the stones, trunks, roots of trees, he tore
Out of the rampire, toss'd them all into the Hellespont,
Ev'n all the proud toil of the Greeks, with which they durst confront 40

²⁹ *Champian*—champain, level country.

The to-be shunnéd Deities, and not a stone remain'd
Of all their huge foundations, all with the earth were plain'd.
Which done, again the Gods turn'd back the silver-flowing floods
By that vast channel, through whose vaults they pour'd abroad their
    broods,
And cover'd all the ample shore again with dusty sand.   45
And this the end was of that wall, where now so many a hand
Was emptiéd of stones and darts, contending to invade;
Where Clamour spent so high a throat; and where the fell blows made
The new-built wooden turrets groan. And here the Greeks were pent,
Tam'd with the iron whip of Jove, that terrors vehement   50
Shook over them by Hector's hand, who was in ev'ry thought
The terror-master of the field, and like a whirlwind fought,
As fresh as in his morn's first charge. And as a savage boar,
Or lion, hunted long, at last, with hounds' and hunters' store
Is compass'd round; they charge him close, and stand (as in a tow'r   55
They had inchas'd him) pouring on of darts an iron show'r;
His glorious heart yet nought appall'd, and forcing forth his way,
Here overthrows a troop, and there a running ring doth stay
His utter passage; when, again, that stay he overthrows,
And then the whole field frees his rage; so Hector wearies blows,   60
Runs out his charge upon the fort, and all his force would force
To pass the dike; which, being so deep, they could not get their horse
To venture on, but trample, snore, and on the very brink
To neigh with spirit, yet still stand off. Nor would a human think
The passage safe; or, if it were, 'twas less safe for retreat;   65
The dike being ev'rywhere so deep, and, where 'twas least deep, set
With stakes exceeding thick, sharp, strong, that horse could never pass,
Much less their chariots after them; yet for the foot there was
Some hopeful service, which they wish'd. Polydamas then spake:
    "Hector, and all our friends of Troy, we indiscreetly make   70
Offer of passage with our horse; ye see the stakes, the wall,
Impossible for horse to take; nor can men fight at all,

     42 *Plain'd*—levelled.   59 *Utter passage*—egress.

The place being strait, and much more apt to let us take our bane
Than give the enemy. And yet, if Jove decree the wane
Of Grecian glory utterly, and so bereave their hearts 75
That we may freely charge them thus, and then will take our parts,
I would with all speed wish th' assault, that ugly shame might shed
(Thus far from home) these Grecians' bloods. But, if they once turn head
And sally on us from their fleet, when in so deep a dike
We shall lie struggling, not a man of all our host is like 80
To live and carry back the news. And therefore be it thus :
Here leave we horse kept by our men, and all on foot let us
Hold close together, and attend the grace of Hector's guide,
And then they shall not bear our charge, our conquest shall be dyed
In their lives' purples." This advice pleas'd Hector, for 'twas sound ;
Who first obey'd it, and full-arm'd betook him to the ground. 86
And then all left their chariots when he was seen to lead,
Rushing about him, and gave up each chariot and steed
To their directors to be kept, in all procinct of war,
There, and on that side of the dike. And thus the rest prepare 90
Their onset: In five regiments they all their pow'r divide,
Each regiment allow'd three chiefs. Of all which ev'n the pride
Serv'd in great Hector's regiment ; for all were set on fire
(Their passage beaten through the wall) with hazardous desire
That they might once but fight at fleet. With Hector captains were
Polydamas, and Cebriones, who was his charioteer ; 96
But Hector found that place a worse. Chiefs of the second band
Were Paris, Alcathous, Agenor. The command
The third strong phalanx had, was giv'n to th' augur Helenus,
Deiphobus, that god-like man, and mighty Asius, 100
Ev'n Asius Hyrtacides, that from Arisba rode
The huge bay horse, and had his house where river Selleës flow'd.

[89] *Procinct*—preparation, girding for war. Lat. *procinctus*. Blunt preserves it as a technical word in his Glossographia. Todd observes that he was unable to meet with an example besides the one quoted by Johnson from Milton.

The fourth charge good Æneas led, and with him were combin'd
Archelochus, and Acamas, Antenor's dearest kind,
And excellent at ev'ry fight. The fifth brave company   105
Sarpedon had to charge, who choos'd, for his command's supply,
Asteropæus great in arms, and Glaucus; for both these
Were best of all men but himself, but he was fellowless.
    Thus fitted with their well-wrought shields, down the steep dike
       they go,
And (thirsty of the wall's assault) believe in overthrow,   110
Not doubting but with headlong falls to tumble down the Greeks
From their black navy. In which trust, all on; and no man seeks
To cross Polydamas' advice with any other course,
But Asius Hyrtacides, who (proud of his bay horse)
Would not forsake them, nor his man, that was their manager,   115
(Fool that he was) but all to fleet, and little knew how near
An ill death sat him, and a sure, and that he never more
Must look on lofty Ilion; but looks, and all, before,
Put on th' all-cov'ring mist of fate, that then did hang upon
The lance of great Deucalides; he fatally rush'd on   120
The left hand way, by which the Greeks, with horse and chariot,
Came usually from field to fleet; close to the gates he got,
Which both unbarr'd and ope he found, that so the easier might
An entry be for any friend that was behind in flight;
Yet not much easier for a foe, because there was a guard   125
Maintain'd upon it, past his thought; who still put for it hard,
Eagerly shouting; and with him were five more friends of name,
That would not leave him, though none else would hunt that way for
    fame
(In their free choice) but he himself. Orestes, Iamenus,
And Acamas Asiades, Thoon, Oenomaus,   130
Were those that follow'd Asius. Within the gates they found
Two eminently valorous, that from the race renown'd

    [112] *All on*—go onwards.   [120] Idomeneus.

Of the right valiant Lapithes deriv'd their high descent ;
Fierce Leontëus was the one, like Mars in detriment,
The other mighty Polypæt, the great Pirithous' son.   135
These stood within the lofty gates, and nothing more did shun
The charge of Asius and his friends, than two high hill-bred oaks,
Well-rooted in the binding earth, obey the airy strokes
Of wind and weather, standing firm 'gainst ev'ry season's spite.
Yet they pour on continu'd shouts, and bear their shields upright ;   140
When in the mean space Polypæt and Leontëus cheer'd
Their soldiers to the fleet's defence. But when the rest had heard
The Trojans in attempt to scale, clamour and flight did flow
Amongst the Grecians ; and then, the rest dismay'd, these two
Met Asius ent'ring, thrust him back, and fought before their doors.   145
Nor far'd they then like oaks that stood, but as a brace of boars,
Couch'd in their own bred hill, that hear a sort of hunters shout,
And hounds in hot trail coming on, then from their dens break out,
Traverse their force, and suffer not, in wildness of their way,
About them any plant to stand, but thickets off'ring stay   150
Break through, and rend up by the roots, whet gnashes into air,
Which Tumult fills with shouts, hounds, horns, and all the hot affair
Beats at their bosoms ; so their arms rung with assailing blows,
And so they stirr'd them in repulse, right well assur'd that those   154
Who were within, and on the wall, would add their parts, who knew
They now fought for their tents, fleet, lives, and fame, and therefore threw
Stones from the walls and tow'rs, as thick as when a drift wind shakes
Black clouds in pieces, and plucks snow, in great and plumy flakes,
From their soft bosoms, till the ground be wholly cloth'd in white ;
So earth was hid with stones and darts, darts from the Trojan fight,   160
Stones from the Greeks, that on the helms and bossy Trojan shields
Kept such a rapping, it amaz'd great Asius, who now yields

₁₃₄ "Such maketh Virgil Pandarus and Bitias."—CHAPMAN.
₁₅₆ *Fame.*—The second folio has "*fames.*"

Sighs, beats his thighs, and in a rage his fault to Jove applies:
"O Jove," said he, "now clear thou show'st thou art a friend to lies,
Pretending, in the flight of Greece, the making of it good, 165
To all their ruins, which I thought could never be withstood;
Yet they, as yellow wasps, or bees (that having made their nest
The gasping cranny of a hill) when for a hunter's feast
Hunters come hot and hungry in, and dig for honeycombs,
Then fly upon them, strike and sting, and from their hollow homes 170
Will not be beaten, but defend their labour's fruit, and brood;
No more will these be from their port, but either lose their blood
(Although but two against all us) or be our pris'ners made."
All this, to do his action grace, could not firm Jove persuade,
Who for the gen'ral counsel stood, and, 'gainst his singular brave, 175
Bestow'd on Hector that day's fame. Yet he and these behave
Themselves thus nobly at this port; but how at other ports,
And all alongst the stony wall, sole force, 'gainst force and forts,
Rag'd in contention 'twixt both hosts, it were no easy thing,
Had I the bosom of a God, to tune to life and sing. 180
The Trojans fought not of themselves, a fire from heav'n was thrown
That ran amongst them, through the wall, mere added to their own.
The Greeks held not their own; weak Grief went with her wither'd hand,
And dipp'd it deeply in their spirits, since they could not command
Their forces to abide the field, whom harsh Necessity, 185
To save those ships should bring them home, and their good fort's supply,
Drave to th' expulsive fight they made; and this might stoop them more
Than Need itself could elevate, for ev'n Gods did deplore
Their dire estates, and all the Gods that were their aids in war,
Who, though they could not clear their plights, yet were their friends thus far, 190

[167] "Apta ad rem comparatio."—CHAPMAN.
[175] *'Gainst his singular brave*—in opposition to his individual boasting.
[187] *Expulsive*—fight made for expelling their foes.

Still to uphold the better sort; for then did Polypæt pass
A lance at Damasus, whose helm was made with cheeks of brass,
Yet had not proof enough, the pile drave through it and his skull,
His brain in blood drown'd, and the man, so late so spiritfull,
Fell now quite spiritless to earth. So emptied he the veins 195
Of Pylon, and Ormenus' lives. And then Leonteüs gains
The life's end of Hippomachus, Antimachus's son;
His lance fell at his girdle-stead, and with his end begun
Another end. Leonteüs left him, and through the prease
(His keen sword drawn) ran desp'rately upon Antiphates, 200
And lifeless tumbled him to earth. Nor could all these lives quench
His fi'ry spirit, that his flame in Menon's blood did drench,
And rag'd up ev'n to Iamen's, and young Orestes' life;
All heap'd together made their peace in that red field of strife.
Whose fair arms while the victors spoil'd, the youth of Ilion 205
(Of which there serv'd the most and best) still boldly built upon
The wisdom of Polydamas, and Hector's matchless strength,
And follow'd, fill'd with wondrous spirit, with wish and hope at length,
The Greeks' wall won, to fire their fleet. But, having pass'd the dike,
And willing now to pass the wall, this prodigy did strike 210
Their hearts with some delib'rate stay: A high-flown eagle soar'd
On their troops' left hand, and sustain'd a dragon, all engor'd,
In her strong seres, of wondrous size, and yet had no such check
In life and spirit but still she fought, and turning back her neck
So stung the eagle's gorge, that down she cast her fervent prey 215
Amongst the multitude, and took upon the winds her way,
Crying with anguish. When they saw a branded serpent sprawl
So full amongst them from above, and from Jove's fowl let fall,
They took it an ostent from him, stood frighted, and their cause
Polydamas thought just, and spake: "Hector, you know, applause 220
Of humour hath been far from me; nor fits it, or in war,
Or in affairs of court, a man employ'd in public care

[217] *Branded*—Halliwell tell us is "a mixture of red and black."

To blanch things further than their truth, or flatter any pow'r;
And therefore for that simple course your strength hath oft been
    sour
To me in councils; yet again, what shows in my thoughts best,   225
I must discover. Let us cease, and make their flight our rest
For this day's honour, and not now attempt the Grecian fleet,
For this, I fear, will be th' event, the prodigy doth meet
So full with our affair in hand. As this high-flying fowl
Upon the left wing of our host, implying our control,   230
Hover'd above us, and did truss within her golden seres
A serpent so embru'd and big, which yet, in all her fears,
Kept life and fervent spirit to fight, and wrought her own release,
Nor did the eagle's eyry feed; so though we thus far prease
Upon the Grecians, and perhaps may overrun their wall,   235
Our high minds aiming at their fleet, and that we much appall
Their trussèd spirits; yet are they so serpent-like dispos'd
That they will fight, though in our seres, and will at length be los'd
With all our outcries, and the life of many a Trojan breast
Shall with the eagle fly, before we carry to our nest   240
Them, or their navy." Thus expounds the augur this ostent,
Whose depth he knows, and these should fear. Hector, with count'nance
    bent,
Thus answer'd him: "Polydamas, your depth in augury
I like not, and know passing well thou dost not satisfy
Thyself in this opinion; or if thou think'st it true,   245
Thy thoughts the Gods blind, to advise, and urge that as our due,
That breaks our duties, and to Jove, whose vow and sign to me
Is pass'd directly for our speed; yet light-wing'd birds must be,
By thy advice, our oracles, whose feathers little stay
My serious actions. What care I, if this, or th' other, way   250

---

²²³ *Blanch*—give a fair appearance to a thing, disguise. Lord Bacon says, "And commonly by amusing men with a subtlety *blanch* the matter," (Essay XXVI.) The word is not uncommon, yet it seems to have puzzled Nares.

Their wild wings sway them ; if the right, on which the sun doth rise,
Or, to the left hand, where he sets ? 'Tis Jove's high counsel flys
With those wings that shall bear up us; Jove's, that both earth and heav'n,
Both men and Gods, sustains and rules. One augury is giv'n
To order all men, best of all : Fight for thy country's right.   255
But why fear'st thou our further charge ? For though the dang'rous fight
Strew all men here about the fleet, yet thou need'st never fear
To bear their fates ; thy wary heart will never trust thee where
An enemy's look is ; and yet fight, for, if thou dar'st abstain,
Or whisper into any ear an abstinence so vain   260
As thou advisest, never fear that any foe shall take
Thy life from thee, for 'tis this lance." This said, all forwards make,
Himself the first ; yet before him exulting Clamour flew,
And thunder-loving Jupiter from lofty Ida blew
A storm that usher'd their assault, and made them charge like him.
It drave directly on the fleet a dust so fierce and dim   266
That it amaz'd the Grecians, but was a grace divine
To Hector and his following troops, who wholly did incline
To him, being now in grace with Jove, and so put boldly on
To raze the rampire ; in whose height they fiercely set upon   270
The parapets, and pull'd them down, raz'd ev'ry foremost fight,
And all the buttresses of stone, that held their tow'rs upright,
They tore away with crows of iron, and hop'd to ruin all.
  The Greeks yet stood, and still repair'd the fore-fights of their wall
With hides of oxen, and from thence, they pour'd down stones in show'rs
Upon the underminers' heads. Within the foremost tow'rs   270
Both the Ajaces had command, who answer'd ev'ry part,
Th' assaulters, and their soldiers, repress'd, and put in heart ;
Repairing valour as their wall ; spake some fair, some reprov'd,
Whoever made not good his place ; and thus they all sorts mov'd :   280
  "O countrymen, now need in aid would have excess be spent,
The excellent must be admir'd, the meanest excellent,

[271] *Fight.*—Here, and in v. 274, defence, bulwark.

The worst do well. In changing war all should not be alike,
Nor any idle; which to know fits all, lest Hector strike
Your minds with frights, as ears with threats. Forward be all your hands,
Urge one another. This doubt down, that now betwixt us stands,   286
Jove will go with us to their walls." To this effect aloud
Spake both the princes; and as high, with this, th' expulsion flow'd.
And as in winter time, when Jove his cold sharp jav'lins throws
Amongst us mortals, and is mov'd to white earth with his snows,   290
The winds asleep, he freely pours, till highest prominents,
Hill tops, low meadows, and the fields that crown with most contents
The toils of men, seaports, and shores, are hid, and ev'ry place,
But floods, that snow's fair tender flakes, as their own brood, embrace;
So both sides cover'd earth with stones, so both for life contend,   295
To show their sharpness; through the wall uproar stood up an end.
Nor had great Hector and his friends the rampire overrun,
If heav'n's great Counsellor, high Jove, had not inflam'd his son
Sarpedon (like the forest's king when he on oxen flies)
Against the Grecians; his round targe he to his arm applies,   300
Brass-leav'd without, and all within thick ox-hides quilted hard,
The verge nail'd round with rods of gold; and, with two darts prepar'd,
He leads his people. As ye see a mountain-lion fare,
Long kept from prey, in forcing which, his high mind makes him dare
Assault upon the whole full fold, though guarded never so   305
With well-arm'd men, and eager dogs; away he will not go,
But venture on, and either snatch a prey, or be a prey;
So far'd divine Sarpedon's mind, resolv'd to force his way
Through all the fore-fights, and the wall; yet since he did not see
Others as great as he in name, as great in mind as he,   310
He spake to Glaucus: "Glaucus, say, why are we honour'd more
Than other men of Lycia, in place; with greater store

    [286] *Doubt*—redoubt.
    [296] *Wall.*—The second folio incorrectly prints "*war*," followed by Dr. Taylor.
    [311] "Sarpedon's speech to Glaucus, neither equalled by any (in this kind) of all that have written."—CHAPMAN.

Of meats and cups ; with goodlier roofs ; delightsome gardens ; walks ;
More lands and better ; so much wealth, that court and country talks
Of us and our possessions, and ev'ry way we go, 315
Gaze on us as we were their Gods ? This where we dwell is so ;
The shores of Xanthus ring of this ; and shall we not exceed
As much in merit as in noise ? Come, be we great in deed
As well as look ; shine not in gold, but in the flames of fight ;
That so our neat-arm'd Lycians may say : ' See, these are right 320
Our kings, our rulers ; these deserve to eat and drink the best ;
These govern not ingloriously ; these, thus exceed the rest,
Do more than they command to do.' O friend, if keeping back
Would keep back age from us, and death, and that we might not wrack
In this life's human sea at all, but that deferring now 325
We shunn'd death ever, nor would I half this vain valour show,
Nor glorify a folly so, to wish thee to advance ;
But since we must go, though not here, and that, besides the chance
Propos'd now, there are infinite fates of other sort in death,
Which, neither to be fled nor 'scap'd, a man must sink beneath, 330
Come, try we, if this sort be ours, and either render thus
Glory to others, or make them resign the like to us."

   This motion Glaucus shifted not, but without words obey'd.
Foreright went both, a mighty troop of Lycians followéd.
Which by Menestheus observ'd, his hair stood up on end, 335
For, at the tow'r where he had charge, he saw Calamity bend
Her horrid brows in their approach. He threw his looks about
The whole fights near, to see what chief might help the mis'ry out
Of his poor soldiers, and beheld where both th' Ajaces fought,
And Teucer newly come from fleet ; whom it would profit nought 340
To call, since tumult on their helms, shields, and upon the ports,
Laid such loud claps ; for ev'ry way, defences of all sorts
Were adding, as Troy took away ; and Clamour flew so high
Her wings strook heav'n, and drown'd all voice. The two dukes yet so nigh

               ³³¹ *Sort*—fate, lot.

And at the offer of assault, he to th' Ajaces sent 345
Thoos the herald with this charge : " Run to the regiment
Of both th' Ajaces, and call both, for both were better here,
Since here will slaughter, instantly, be more enforc'd than there.
The Lycian captains this way make, who in the fights of stand
Have often show'd much excellence. Yet if laborious hand 350
Be there more needful than I hope, at least afford us some,
Let Ajax Telamonius and th' archer Teucer come."

    The herald hasted, and arriv'd ; and both th' Ajaces told,
That Peteus' noble son desir'd their little labour would
Employ himself in succouring him. Both their supplies were best, 355
Since death assail'd his quarter most ; for on it fiercely press'd
The well-prov'd mighty Lycian chiefs. Yet if the service there
Allow'd not both, he pray'd that one part of his charge would bear,
And that was Ajax Telamon, with whom he wish'd would come
The archer Teucer. Telamon left instantly his room 360
To strong Lycomedes, and will'd Ajax Oiliades
With him to make up his supply, and fill with courages
The Grecian hearts till his return ; which should he instantly
When he had well reliev'd his friend. With this the company
Of Teucer he took to his aid ; Teucer, that did descend 365
(As Ajax did) from Telamon. With these two did attend
Pandion, that bore Teucer's bow. When to Menestheus' tow'r
They came, alongst the wall, they found him, and his hearten'd pow'r,
Toiling in making strong their fort. The Lycian princes set
Black whirlwind-like, with both their pow'rs, upon the parapet. 370
Ajax, and all, resisted them. Clamour amongst them rose.
The slaughter Ajax led ; who first the last dear sight did close
Of strong Epicles, that was friend to Jove's great Lycian son.
Amongst the high munition heap, a mighty marble stone

---

    [373] Dr. Taylor has followed the error of the second folio, in printing "*that war-friend* to Jove's," &c.

Lay highest, near the pinnacle, a stone of such a paise 375
That one of this time's strongest men with both hands could not raise,
Yet this did Ajax rouse and throw, and all in sherds did drive
Epicles' four-topp'd casque and skull; who (as ye see one dive
In some deep river) left his height; life left his bones withall.

    Teucer shot Glaucus, rushing up yet higher on the wall, 380
Where naked he discern'd his arm, and made him steal retreat
From that hot service, lest some Greek, with an insulting threat,
Beholding it, might fright the rest. Sarpedon much was griev'd
At Glaucus' parting, yet fought on, and his great heart reliev'd
A little with Alcmaon's blood, surnam'd Thestorides, 385
Whose life he hurl'd out with his lance; which following through the prease
He drew from him. Down from the tow'r Alcmaon dead it strook;
His fair arms ringing out his death. Then fierce Sarpedon took
In his strong hand the battlement, and down he tore it quite,
The wall stripp'd naked, and broad way for entry and full fight 390
He made the many. Against him Ajax and Teucer made;
Teucer the rich belt on his breast did with a shaft invade;
But Jupiter averted death, who would not see his son
Die at the tails of th' Achive ships. Ajax did fetch his run,
And, with his lance, strook through the targe of that brave Lycian king;
Yet kept he it from further pass, nor did it anything 396
Dismay his mind, although his men stood off from that high way
His valour made them, which he kept, and hop'd that stormy day
Should ever make his glory clear. His men's fault thus he blam'd:
"O Lycians, why are your hot spirits so quickly disinflam'd? 400
Suppose me ablest of you all, 'tis hard for me alone
To ruin such a wall as this, and make confusion
Way to their navy. Lend your hands. What many can dispatch,
One cannot think. The noble work of many hath no match."

    The wise king's just rebuke did strike a rev'rence to his will 405
Through all his soldiers; all stood in, and 'gainst all th' Achives still

---

[375] *Paise*—weight. In v. 430, balance.

Made strong their squadrons, insomuch, that to the adverse side,
The work show'd mighty, and the wall, when 'twas within descried,
No easy service; yet the Greeks could neither free their wall   409
Of these brave Lycians, that held firm the place they first did scale;
Nor could the Lycians from their fort the sturdy Grecians drive,
Nor reach their fleet. But as two men about the limits strive
Of land that toucheth in a field, their measures in their hands,
They mete their parts out curiously, and either stiffly stands
That so far is his right in law, both hugely set on fire   415
About a passing-little ground; so, greedily aspire
Both these foes to their sev'ral ends, and all exhaust their most
About the very battlements (for yet no more was lost).

With sword and fire they vex'd for them their targes hugely round,
With ox-hides lin'd, and bucklers light; and many a ghastly wound
The stern steel gave for that one prise; whereof though some receiv'd
Their portions on their naked backs, yet others were bereav'd
Of brave lives, face-turn'd, through their shields; tow'rs, bulwarks, ev'rywhere
Were freckled with the blood of men. Nor yet the Greeks did bear
Base back-turn'd faces; nor their foes would therefore be out-fac'd.   425
But as a spinster poor and just, ye sometimes see, straight-lac'd
About the weighing of her web, who, careful, having charge
For which she would provide some means, is loth to be too large
In giving or in taking weight, but ever with her hand
Is doing with the weights and wool, till both in just paise stand;   430

[408] *When.*—The second folio has incorrectly "*then;*" and so Dr. Taylor.
[413] *A field.*—The second folio, and Taylor, "*the field.*"
[418] "*Admiranda et penè inimitabilis comparatio* (saith Spond.); and yet in the explication of it, he thinks all superfluous but three words, ὀλίγῳ ἐνὶ χώρῳ, *exiguo in loco*, leaving out other words more expressive, with his old rule, *uno pede, &c.*"
CHAPMAN.
[430] *Paise.*—The second folio, and Taylor, "*poise.*"
[430] "A simile superior to the other, in which, comparing mightiest things with meanest, and the meanest illustrating the mightiest, both meeting in one end of this life's preservation and credit, our Homer is beyond comparison and admiration.—" CHAPMAN.

So ev'nly stood it with these foes, till Jove to Hector gave
The turning of the scales; who first against the rampire drave,
And spake so loud that all might hear: "O stand not at the pale,
Brave Trojan friends, but mend your hands; up, and break through the wall,
And make a bonfire of their fleet." All heard, and all in heaps   435
Got scaling-ladders, and aloft. In mean space, Hector leaps
Upon the port, from whose out-part he tore a massy stone,
Thick downwards, upward edg'd; it was so huge an one
That two vast yeomen of most strength, such as these times beget,
Could not from earth lift to a cart, yet he did brandish it   440
Alone, Saturnius made it light; and swinging it as nought,
He came before the planky gates, that all for strength were wrought,
And kept the port; two-fold they were, and with two rafters barr'd,
High, and strong-lock'd; he rais'd the stone, bent to the hurl so hard,[1]
And made it with so main a strength, that all the gates did crack,   445
The rafters left them, and the folds one from another brake,
The hinges piecemeal flew, and through the fervent little rock
Thunder'd a passage; with his weight th' inwall his breast did knock,
And in rush'd Hector, fierce and grim as any stormy night;
His brass arms round about his breast reflected terrible light;   450
Each arm held-up held each a dart; his presence call'd up all
The dreadful spirits his being held, that to the threaten'd wall
None but the Gods might check his way; his eyes were furnaces;
And thus he look'd back, call'd in all. All fir'd their courages,   454
And in they flow'd. The Grecians fled, their fleet now and their freight
Ask'd all their rescue. Greece went down; Tumult was at his height.

[439] "Δύ' ἀνέρε δήμου. Duo viri plebei."—CHAPMAN.

THE END OF THE TWELFTH BOOK.

PRINTED BY BALLANTYNE, HANSON AND CO.,
EDINBURGH AND LONDON.

www.ingramcontent.com/pod-product-compliance
Lightning Source LLC
Chambersburg PA
CBHW020235240426
43672CB00006B/535